GW00725384

HISTORICAL PHONOLOGY OF ASIAN LANGUAGES

AMSTERDAM STUDIES IN THE THEORY AND HISTORY OF LINGUISTIC SCIENCE

General Editor
E.F. KONRAD KOERNER
(University of Ottawa)

Series IV - CURRENT ISSUES IN LINGUISTIC THEORY

Volume 77

William G. Boltz and Michael C. Shapiro (eds)

Studies in the Historical Phonology of Asian Languages

STUDIES IN THE HISTORICAL PHONOLOGY OF ASIAN LANGUAGES

Edited by

WILLIAM G. BOLTZ and MICHAEL C. SHAPIRO
University of Washington, Seattle

JOHN BENJAMINS PUBLISHING COMPANY
AMSTERDAM/PHILADELPHIA

1991

Library of Congress Cataloging-in-Publication Data

Studies in the historical phonology of Asian languages / edited by William G. Boltz and Michael C. Shapiro.
p. cm. -- (Amsterdam studies in the theory and history of linguistic science. Series IV, Current issues in linguistic theory, ISSN 0304-0763; v. 77)
Chiefly revised papers based on a series of lectures, 1985-1986, sponsored by the Asian Linguistics Consortium of the Dept. of Asian Languages and Literature, University of Washington, Seattle.
Includes bibliographical references and indexes.
1. Asia -- Languages -- Phonology, Historical. I. Boltz, William G. II. Shapiro, Michael C. III. Series.
P381.A75S78 1991
495--dc20 91-34227
ISBN 90 272 3574 0 (Eur.)/1-55619-132-4 (US)(alk. paper) CIP

CONTENTS

Preface and Acknowledgements vi

William H. Baxter III: Zhōu and Hàn Phonology in the Shījīng 1

Robert I. Binnick: Vowel Harmony Loss in Uralic and Altaic 35

William G. Boltz: The Old Chinese Terrestrial Rames in Saek 53

Reinhard F. Hahn: Diachronic Aspects of Regular Disharmony in Modern Uyghur 68

Ian Hancock: Vlax Phonological Divergence From Common Romani: Implications for Standardization and Orthography 102

Hans Henrich Hock: Dialects, Diglossia, and Diachronic Phonology in Early Indo-Aryan 119

Bh. Krishnamurti: The Emergence of the Syllable Types of Stems (C)VCC(V) and (C)V̄C(V) in Indo-Aryan and Dravidian: Conspiracy or Convergence? 160

Roy Andrew Miller: How Many Verner's Laws Does an Altaicist Need? 176

Jerry Norman: Nasals in Old Southern Chinese 205

S. Robert Ramsey: Proto-Korean and the Origin of Korean Accent .. 215

Index of Languages 239

Index of Names 245

PREFACE AND ACKNOWLEDGEMENTS

This collection of papers owes its genesis to a series of lectures on various aspects of the historical phonology of Asian languages, sponsored by the Asian Linguistics Colloquium of the Department of Asian Languages and Literature of the University of Washington, in Seattle. These lectures were given during the 1985–86 academic year and subsequently revised for publication. Two papers, namely those by Reinhard F. Hahn and Bh. Krishnamurti, although not originally presented in the lecture series, were solicited for inclusion in this volume because the editors believed them to be pertinent to the topics, approaches, and language families treated in the book.

It will be evident to the reader that the papers included in this book do not represent any single theory of historical phonology or linguistics in general. Nor can it be claimed that the papers present a single thesis or point of view. What the editors have aimed for in this book is a set of papers that provide coverage of topics, all subsumed under the rubric of historical phonology, that range from the applied to the highly theoretical. The collection includes papers that deal with such diverse matters as language standardization and orthography (Hancock), vowel harmony (Binnick, Hahn), dialect variation and 'inherent variability' (Hock), historical reconstruction based on written records (Baxter), historical reconstruction based on the comparative method (Miller), and accentology (Ramsey). Several of the papers are clearly comparative in nature (Binnick, Hahn, Krishnamurti, Miller, Ramsey), while others examine effects of language contact (Boltz, Krishnamurti). Although it was obviously impossible to include here papers dealing with all language families represented in Asia, an attempt was made to be as representative as possible. Converage includes Indo-Aryan (Hancock—allowing Romani to be included as 'Asian' on grounds of genealogy, if not geography—, Hock, Krishnamurti), Dravidian (Krishnamurti), Altaic (Binnick, Hahn, Miller), Chinese (Baxter, Boltz, Norman), Uralic (Binnick), Korean (Ramsey), and Tai (Boltz).

The production of this volume has involved the use of computer technologies in which the editors can scarcely called expert. Left to their own devices, the editors would have been unable to solve many of the technical problems involved in producing the final copy. There are many people and institutions who in one way or another aided in bringing out this book. Manuscripts were submitted to the editors in a variety of forms, both computerized and not, which had to be either transferred or reentered. Phonetic type and diacritics had to be provided, including some that would tax the abilities of even the most skilled typesetter. Ms. Laura Hess and Ms. Carrie Reed provided invaluable service in getting the manuscripts into a standardized machine-readable format. Professors Richard Salomon, Harold F. Schiffman, and David R. Knechtges provided counsel and assistance in several editorial matters. Mr. Stuart Aque frequently bailed out the editors when they got over their heads in computer matters, especially in the generation of Chinese characters. Ms. Vicki Shinneman helped the editors greatly in the compilation of the language and name indices. To all of these individuals we are extremely grateful.

Financial support for this volume has been received from two University of Washington sources, which we would like to acknowledge, namely the Graduate School and the China Program of the Henry M. Jackson School of International Studies. We are particularly indebted to Professor Jack L. Dull, Acting Director of the Jackson School, for his support and encouragement.

One of the advantages of being at the University of Washington is having access to the services available at its Humanities and Arts Computing Center. This Center provides assistance in custom typographic design that is rarely available elsewhere. The entire visual layout of this book, with its complexity of typographic format and font design, is a product of and tribute to the Center and to its extraordinarily resourceful and talented director, Thomas B. Ridgeway. To Dr. Ridgeway, as well as to Ms. Ann Shilling, who designed many of the phonetic characters as well as entered the special code necessary to generate them in print, we are deeply endebted.

A word of thanks must also be extended to the John Benjamins Publishing Company, particularly Paul M. Peranteau and Ms. Brenda McNally, for their support and willingness to carry out this project. A special word of thanks is due to the General Editor, E. F. Konrad Koerner, for his patience, encouragement, and assistance. Without his oversight it is doubtful that this book would have come into existence.

The fact that the publication of these papers has taken much longer than originally anticipated has no doubt tested the patience of our contributors, the General Editor, and the publisher as much as it has our own. The difference was, of course, that for most of the time production was out of their hands, and in ours, and we therefore must assume the responsibility for, and offer the apologies for, that delay. We are sincerely grateful to our contributors not only for their fine scholarly efforts, but also for their unhesitant cooperation and good-natured forbearance.

William G. Boltz & Michael C. Shapiro
Seattle, 1 November, 1990

ZHŌU AND HÀN PHONOLOGY IN THE SHĪJĪNG

WILLIAM H. BAXTER III
University of Michigan

1. Introduction.[1] We have three main sources of information about Old Chinese phonology: (1) the rhymes of Zhōu 周 dynasty poetry, principally the *Shījīng* 詩經; the phonetic compounds (*xiéshēng* 諧聲) and phonetic loans (*jiǎjiè* 假借) of the Chinese script; and (3) the phonological system of Middle Chinese.[2] However, much past research in Old Chinese has suffered from a curious anachronism: while the rhyme evidence used comes from texts apparently composed in mid and early Zhōu, the script analyzed is usually that of the classical texts as we now see them—even though both the script and the texts were basically fixed in the Hàn 漢 dynasty, several centuries after the texts were originally composed.[3]

---

[1] The research for this paper was supported by a grant from the American Council of Learned Societies and by further assistance from the Center for Chinese Studies and the College of Literature, Science, and the Arts of the University of Michigan.

[2] The importance of this third kind of evidence is sometimes overlooked, but since we generally assume Middle Chinese to be descended from Old Chinese, the phonological structure of Middle Chinese is probably the strongest single constraint on how Old Chinese may be reconstructed.

[3] The dangers of such anachronistic use of evidence have been pointed out by Noel Barnard:

> If...it should be discovered that any considerable number of characters in pre-Ch'in archaeological "documents" contain phonetic elements (or that these elements existed as characters without additional radicals) which have no relationship to the phonetic elements employed since Ch'in and Han times for the same written words, then linguistic research conducted on the written language in general should take into account more fully the obvious implications of such visually unrelated phenomena. (1978: 185)

There are several possible reasons for this apparently anachronistic approach. The Qīng 清 scholars who pioneered in the reconstruction of Old Chinese lacked access to the paleographic materials now available, and necessarily had a limited understanding of the nature of the early development of Chinese writing, and of the script reform of Qín 秦 and Hàn. The *Shuōwén jiězì* 說文解字 enjoyed great prestige, and it was generally taken as a reliable guide to the structure of the early script, even though composed in Eastern Hàn. And although the Qīng phonologists recognized that Chinese pronunciation had changed since ancient times, they may have thought of sound change as a relatively recent phenomenon, not much affecting the pre-Hàn period. In the twentieth century, great progress has been made in Chinese paleography, but paleography and phonology have tended to remain separate, and phonological research (e.g., that of Karlgren and Dǒng Tónghé) has still largely relied on the script of the received classical texts, or on the *Shuōwén jiězì*. Karlgren did include some graphs from oracle bones and bronze inscriptions in *Grammata Serica* (1940) and *Grammata Serica Recensa* (1957), but they do not affect his reconstruction in any major way.[4]

It is the thesis of this paper that both the script and the text of the *Shījīng* have been influenced by post-*Shījīng* phonology. Since past reconstructions of Old Chinese have been based on this script and text, these reconstructions tend to be a conflation of Zhōu and Hàn phonology. In general, the script of the classical texts as we have them is not a reliable guide to Old Chinese phonology; reconstructions should be based on genuine Zhōu texts (e.g. bronze inscriptions) as much as possible.

Below I will show some specific examples of the influence of late phonological changes on the received text of the *Shījīng*. Such influences take two main forms: changes in the Chinese script, and changes in the text of the *Shījīng* itself. In the first case, characters in general use during Zhōu times have been replaced by newer characters. Not all such replacements have phonological significance, of course. In some cases, the new character is just a graphic simplification of the older one, and various parts of the character still retain their identity. Or often the new character has the same phonetic element as the old, but a radical is added, or the original radical is changed or removed. However, in cases where a new phonetic compound is created, the new compound may be appropriate for some post-*Shījīng* phonological system, but inappropriate for Old Chinese phonology. Using

[4] In fact, Karlgren specifically excluded from these works pre-Qín characters which differ significantly from their modern counterparts (1940: 2).

such characters as evidence in reconstructing Old Chinese may distort our reconstructions, making them look more like Hàn phonology than Zhōu phonology.

In addition to changes affecting only the script, a second problem is that our present classical texts contain corruptions of the original text which are influenced by post-*Shījīng* phonology. Since the text was transmitted orally at least in part, and sometimes incompletely understood by those who transmitted it (otherwise why were the Hàn-time glosses necessary?), some of the original words may have been replaced by others which were homonyms or near-homonyms according to post-*Shījīng* phonology. A good reconstruction of Old Chinese phonology, based on Zhōu script, should help us solve such textual problems.

The idea for this paper arose when I was testing several hypotheses about *Shījīng* rhyming, and discovered cases where the xiéshēng connections of the characters in the received text seemed to conflict with the general pattern of *Shījīng* rhyming. In many of these cases, the conflicts can be attributed to post-*Shījīng* changes in the script, and disappear when one examines the script of Zhōu bronze inscriptions. In other cases, the conflict can plausibly be attributed to textual corruptions which reflect post-*Shījīng* phonology.

In section 2 of this paper I will discuss several post-*Shījīng* sound changes and show how they may have affected either the script or the text of the *Shījīng*. Some of these sound changes have long been recognized; others are assumed in the Bodman/Baxter reconstruction system for Old Chinese (though some were originally proposed by others).[5] Before presenting the examples themselves, I will summarize five of the major hypotheses of this system which will be referred to in what follows. I call these hypotheses (1) the ROUNDED- VOWEL HYPOTHESIS, (2) the FRONT-VOWEL HYPOTHESIS, (3) the FINAL-**S* HYPOTHESIS, (4) the **R*-HYPOTHESIS, and (5) the **RJ*-HYPOTHESIS.

1.1. The rounded-vowel hypothesis. The rounded-vowel hypothesis, due to S. E. Jaxontov (1960a), assumes that Old Chinese had no freely-occurring medial **-w-* between the initial consonant and the main vowel of a syllable, although it did have labiovelar and labiolaryngeal initials of the form $*K^{w}$-. The hypothesis is suggested by the restricted distribution

[5] The Bodman/Baxter system has been developed by Professor Nicholas C. Bodman and myself over the last several years; I am currently working on a full presentation of it, tentatively entitled *A Handbook of Old Chinese Phonology*.

of *-w-* in Middle Chinese; Middle Chinese *-w-* occurs in syllables like *twan* (*tuân*),[6] but there are significant gaps in its distribution; for example, there is no syllable '*twen*' (*tiwen*). Under the rounded-vowel hypothesis, Middle Chinese *-w-*, unless it can be traced to a labialized initial like *K^w-, is assumed to arise from the diphthongization of an earlier rounded vowel: in our system, **o* > **wa* and **u* > **wi*. For example, a word like 端 *duān* < *twan* (*tuân*) 'tip, end' must be reconstructed as **ton*; a reconstruction like Karlgren's **twân*, with medial **-w-*, is ruled out, as is Li Fang-kuei's **tuan* with a "vocalic cluster" **ua*. If this hypothesis is correct, then certain traditional Old Chinese rhyme categories must be split: for example,

單 *dān* < *tan* (*tân*) < **tan* 'single'

and

端 *duān* < *twan* (*tuân*) < **ton* 'tip, end',

both traditionally assigned to the Yuán 元 rhyme category, are now reconstructed with different main vowels, and must be assigned to different categories, which I label simply as **-AN* and **-ON*, respectively.[7] To verify the hypothesis, one must show that the rhyme distinctions predicted by it are actually made regularly in the *Shījīng*.

1.2. The front-vowel hypothesis. The front-vowel hypothesis is, as far as I know, original with the Bodman/Baxter system.[8] It rejects, for both Old and Middle Chinese, the "strong vocalic medial *-i-*" reconstructed

---

[6] I cite Middle Chinese forms in a typeable transcription described in Baxter 1985 and 1986; Karlgren's Ancient Chinese reconstruction is given in parentheses for comparison. In this sytem, some single sounds are represented by groups of letters; e.g., the vowels of division-II finals are written *-ae-* (Karlgren's *-a-* and *-ɐ-*) and *-ea-* (Karlgren's *-ă-* and *-ɛ-*), but are assumed to be monophthongs. The letter *-o-* may be interpreted as a mid back unrounded vowel [ʌ]. The letters *-x* and *-h* are added at the end of a syllable to indicate shǎngshēng 上聲 and qùshēng 去聲 respectively.

[7] There are several sets of traditional labels for Old Chinese rhyme categories; I use those of Zhōu Zǔmó 1966. To say that **-an* and **-on* must be in different rhyme groups assumes, of course, that Old Chinese syllables must have the same main vowel to rhyme regularly. Most recent work adopts this assumption in some form, though Karlgren did not. Baxter 1986 sketches a new set of rhyme categories consistent with the Bodman/Baxter system, in which each rhyme category is identified by giving, in capital letters, the reconstruction of the rhyming portion of the syllable.

[8] It was to some extent anticipated by Huáng Kǎn 黃侃 (1886-1934), however.

by Karlgren in the so-called pure division-IV (sìděng 四等) rhymes of Middle Chinese. Karlgren reconstructed the finals of these rhymes with the vocalism *-ie-* in Middle Chinese, where the "strong vocalic medial *-i-*" is distinguished from the "weak consonantal medial *-i̯-*" reconstructed in so-called division-III finals. Karlgren's *-i-* is not contrastive in Middle Chinese (the vowel *-e-* never occurs without it in his system), and the distribution of initial consonants in Middle Chinese suggests that the pure division-IV finals actually had no high front medial at all, but simply a front vowel, which I write as *-e-* in my transcription system (see note 6).[9] The front-vowel hypothesis assumes that these division-IV finals reflect earlier front vowels with no preceding medial. I also assume that certain other finals (including the so-called division-IV chóngniŭ 重紐 finals[10]) likewise reflect earlier front vowels. Like the rounded-vowel hypothesis, the front-vowel hypothesis requires us to reconstruct different main vowels in words traditionally assigned to the same Old Chinese rhyme category. Thus the words

干 *gān* < *kan* (*kân*) 'shield'

and

肩 *jiān* < *ken* (*kien*) 'shoulder'

are reconstructed **kan* and **ken* respectively, even though they are both traditionally assigned to the Yuán 元 rhyme category. I assign them to the rhyme categories **-AN* and **-EN* respectively.[11]

---

[9] The pure division-IV finals occur with exactly the same set of initial consonants as the division-I finals, while finals reconstructed with medials *r* or *j* occur with a different set of Middle Chinese initial consonants.

[10] The term *chóngniŭ* or 'repeated initials' refers to pairs of syllables which are included in a single *Qièyùn* rhyme, but are distinguished from each other by being listed in different homonym groups. In such cases, one of the syllables is placed in division III of the rhyme tables, and the other in division IV. The distinction has been almost entirely lost in modern dialects, and was overlooked by Karlgren. In the Middle Chinese notation used here, syllables containing both *-j-* and *-i-* are division-IV chóngniŭ syllables; division-III chóngniŭ (and ordinary division-III words) have *-j-* or *-i-*, but not both. In quoting Karlgren's Ancient Chinese reconstruction (corresponding to what I call Middle Chinese), I add a subscript 3 or 4 to indicate division-III or division-IV chóngniŭ words. An example is 密 *mì* < *mit* (*mi̯ĕt*$_3$), **mrjit* 'dense' versus 蜜 *mì* < *mjit* (*mi̯ĕt*$_4$), **mjit* 'honey'.

[11] In Karlgren's reconstruction, they are **kân* and **kian*; in Li Fang-kuei's, **kan* and *kian*.

1.3. The final-*s hypothesis. This hypothesis, which has by now a long history[12], states that the departing tone (qùshēng 去聲) of Middle Chinese reflects an earlier final **-s*, which was later lost, leaving a distinctive tone contour behind. In many cases, the final **-s* was a derivational suffix. The result is often that a single character has two readings: one in qùshēng and one (with a different meaning) in some other tone. A final **-s* added to a rùshēng 入聲 word (one ending in a final *-p*, *-t*, or *-k*) causes the stop to be lost. For example:

結 *jié* < *ket* (*kiet*) < **kit* 'to tie'

髻 *jì* < *kejh* (*kiei-*) < **kits* 'hair-knot, chignon'.

Other reconstructions (e.g., those of Karlgren, Dǒng Tónghé, and Li Fang-kuei) generally have final voiced stops **-b*, **-d*, and **-g* where we have **-ps*, **-ts*, and **-ks*.[13]

As we will see below (section 2.1), original **-ps* changed to **-ts*, apparently at an early enough period to affect *Shījīng* rhyming. (The final-**s* hypothesis makes it possible to regard this change as an assimilation of **p* to the following **s*; in other reconstructions it is an unconditioned merger of final **-b* with **-d*.) The next step was probably a simplification of the consonant clusters: **-ts* changed to **-js*, and **-ks* to **-s*. The final step (which may have been quite late in some dialects; see Pulleyblank 1973b) was the loss of final **-s*.

1.4. The *r-hypothesis. The **r*-hypothesis derives from a proposal by Jaxontov (1960b) to account for the contrast between Middle Chinese division-I and division-II finals by reconstructing a medial **-l-* in words of division-II. An example of such a contrast is

Division I: 甘 *gān* < *kam* (*kâm*) 'sweet'

Division II: 監 *jiān* < *kaem* (*kam*) 'inspect'.[14]

---

[12] See Haudricourt 1954a, 1954b, Downer 1959, Pulleyblank 1961-1962, Jaxontov 1965, Bodman 1969, Pulleyblank 1973a, 1973b.

[13] However, not all voiced stops in these reconstructions correspond to our **-s* clusters; e.g., in Karlgren's system, although **-b* and **-d* occur only in qùshēng words (and thus correspond to our **-ps* and **-ts*), **-g* occurs in all tones.

[14] In my notation for Middle Chinese, division-II words are written with one of the digraphs *-ae-* or *-ea-* as the main vowel (see note 6). These may be interpeted phonetically as [æ] and [ɛ] respectively. The phonetic nature of these vowels is not certain, of course; Pulleyblank, for example,

In Middle Chinese, division-I and division-II words had different main vowels; but in Old Chinese they typically interrhymed. Jaxontov reconstructed division- I 甘 as **kâm* and division-II 監 as **klâm*, proposing that the medial **-l-* caused a change in the following vowel in division-II words which became distinctive when the **-l-* was lost. Simultaneously, the reconstruction of **l-* clusters helped to account for the many cases where division-II words had xiéshēng connections with words in Middle Chinese initial *l-*, e.g.,

監 *jiān* < *kaem* (*kam*) < **klâm* (Jaxontov) 'inspect'
藍 *lán* < *lam* (*lâm*) 'indigo'.

Jaxontov's proposal was a significant advance over Karlgren's reconstruction; although Karlgren, too, reconstructed **l-* clusters to account for xiéshēng connections with initial *l-*, he also reconstructed different vowels in divisions I and II, not recognizing the connection between **l-* clusters and division-II vocalism. Jaxontov's proposal makes it possible to reconstruct a simpler vowel system for Old Chinese, and to account for Old Chinese rhyming in a more satisfactory way than Karlgren's.

Jaxontov's proposal was adopted by Pulleyblank, who reports having earlier reached the same conclusion independently (1961-62: 110), and in modified form by Li (1971). Pulleyblank (1973a) later substituted **r* for Jaxontov's **l*, influenced partly by the fact that Jaxontov's **l* often seems to correspond to Tibeto-Burman **r*; it is assumed that original **r* changed to *l-* at some point. It is this form of the hypothesis that we adopt in our system.[15] To account for the effect of medial **r* on following vowels, I

---

reconstructs them as vowels followed by a retroflex glide: [a^{r}] and [ɛ^{r}] (see Pulleyblank 1984: 191-4).

[15] More precisely, in the Bodman/Baxter system, we assume that Middle Chinese initial *l-* normally reflects Old Chinese initial clusters which we write **b-r-*, **d-r-*, or **g-r-*. For example, initial **b-r-* is used for syllables in Middle Chinese *l-* which show xiéshēng connections with labial initials (Bodman 1980: 83-4). I use the notation **C-r-* in cases where xiéshēng connections give no information about the nature of the initial consonant. The hyphen between the voiced stop and **r* is a notational device for distinguishing these clusters from **br-*, **dr-*, and **gr-*, where the initial stop is not lost; I leave open for now the question of the actual phonetic distinction involved. Note that Li (1971) reconstructs **r* in division II, but retains initial **l-* for Middle Chinese initial *l-*. This weakens one of the original motivations for the hypothesis; the relationship between division-II and xiéshēng connections with MC *l-*.

assume a sound change called *R-COLOR which caused a following vowel to become front ([−back]) and lax ([−tense]). This change is further described in section 2.4 below.

1.5. The *rj-hypothesis. By the *rj-hypothesis I mean the proposal to reconstruct medial *r in certain division-III words, to account for the so-called division-III chóngniŭ finals. It was first stated, in somewhat different form, by Pulleyblank (1961-62: 111-114) as an extension of the *r-hypothesis.[16] Like the words of division II, many of the division-III chóngniŭ words also show xiéshēng contacts with words in Middle Chinese initial *l-*; the reconstruction of *r accounts simultaneously for the chóngniŭ distinctions and for the xiéshēng evidence. This is illustrated by the contrasts like the following:

弗 *fú* < *pjut* (*pi̯uət*) < **pjut* 'not'

versus

筆 *bǐ* < *pit* (*pi̯ĕt*$_3$) < **prjut* 'writing tool'.

Compare, in the same phonetic series as the latter,

律 *lǜ* < *lwit* (*li̯uĕt*) < **b-rjut* 'law, rule'.

The fronting of the following vowel in such words as 筆 *bǐ* < *pit* (*pi̯ĕt*$_3$) (< **pr(w)jit*) < **prjut* can be attributed to the same change *R-COLOR which produced the distinctive vocalism of the division-II finals.[17]

2. Some post-*Shījīng* sound changes and their consequences. In this section I briefly describe some of the sound changes which had transformed the Old Chinese phonological system by Hàn times, when the *Shījīng* took more or less its present form, giving examples of how both the Chinese script and the text of the *Shījīng* have been affected by these changes. It should be noted that some of the examples illustrate more than one sound change.

2.1. **-ps* > **-ts*. As mentioned above, the final **-ps* clusters which are assumed under the final-*s hypothesis changed to **-ts* at a rather early

[16] Pulleyblank's original proposal was to reconstruct *l in these words, as in division II; he later substituted *r in division III as in division II. Note that my *-j- is not found in Pulleyblank's reconstruction, as he reconstructs an Old Chinese prosodic feature in Middle Chinese division-III words: long vowels in Pulleyblank 1961-62, a distinctive type of mora accent ("type-B syllable") in subsequent work.

[17] The fronting due to *R-COLOR was also responsible for the failure of labial initials in words like 筆 *bǐ* < *pit* < **prjut* to change to labiodentals, while the initials of words like 弗 *fú* < *pjut* < **pjut* did change.

date—apparently early enough, in fact, to affect *Shījīng* rhyming.[18] This change led to a change in phonetic element in example (1):

(1) 廢 *fèi* < *pjojh* (*pi̯wɐi-*) < **pjats* < **pjaps* 'to abandon'.

In its present form, this character has the following character as phonetic:

發 *fā* < *pjot* (*pi̯wɐt*) < **pjat* 'go forth, send forth'.[19]

For this reason, 廢 *fèi* has generally been reconstructed with a final *-*d*, corresponding to our *-*ts*, e.g.,

Karlgren **pi̯wăd* (GSR 275f)

Dǒng Tónghé **pi̯wăd* (1948: 192)

Li Fang-kuei **pjadh* (1982: 53).

The corresponding reconstruction in our system would be **pjats*.

However, the word *fèi* 'to abandon' is written in Zhōu dynasty bronze inscriptions with the graph 灋, which is an early form of

法 *fǎ* < *pjop* (*pi̯wɐp*) < **pjap* 'law'.[20]

For example, the phrase 無廢朕命 *wú fèi zhèn mìng* ('do not reject my charge') occurs in the *Shījīng* (Ode 261.1), with the modern character for *fèi*.[21] Almost the identical phrase occurs in at least six different bronze inscriptions, with 灋 instead of 廢:[22] 勿灋朕令. This use of 灋 as a loan graph for *fèi* suggests that we should reconstruct *fèi* as **pjaps*, not **pjats*, for Old Chinese times. If Karlgren, Dǒng Tónghé, and Li Fang-kuei had worked from the Chinese script of bronze inscriptions instead of from the characters as found in received classical texts, they would have reconstructed a final *-*b* instead of a *-*d*. The character 發 *fā* < **pjat*

---

[18] For example, 對 *duì* < *twojh* (*tuâi-*) < **tups* 'respond' rhymes with 醉 *zuì* < *tswijh* (*tswi-*) < **tsjuts* 'drunk' in Ode 257.13 (i.e., Ode 257, stanza 13; this notation is used throughout this paper). Karlgren mentions this change in 1940: 28-9.

[19] Other reconstructions for 發 *fā*: Karlgren **pi̯wăt* (*Grammata Serica Recensa*—hereafter "*GSR*"—275c), Dǒng Tónghé *pi̯wăt* (1948: 195), Li Fang-kuei *pjat* (1982: 51).

[20] Other reconstructions for 法 *fǎ*: Karlgren **pi̯wăp* (*GSR* 645k), Dǒng Tónghé **pi̯wăp* (1948: 235), Li Fang-kuei **pjap* (1982: 56).

[21] Translations from the *Shījīng* are from Karlgren 1950 unless otherwise specified.

[22] See citations in *Jīnwén Gǔlín* #1297 (Chou Fa-kao, *et. al.* 1974); hereafter "*JWGL*."

became a suitable phonetic for 廢 *fèi* only after the change of **-ps* > **-ts* (or **-b* > **-d*).

In this case, the character 廢 probably does not misrepresent the phonology of the *Shījīng* itself, since the change **-ps* > **-ts* appears to be reflected already in *Shījīng* rhyming;[23] but this example shows how a late graph can obscure earlier phonology.[24]

Summary: The use of 發 *fā* < **pjat* as phonetic in 廢 *fèi* < **pjaps* 'to abandon' reflects the sound change **-ps* > **-ts*; the earlier use of 灋 *fǎ* < **pjap* as a loan character for 廢 *fèi* < **pjaps* better represents early Old Chinese phonology.

2.2. Diphthongization of rounded vowels before acute codas (-n*, **-t*, **-ts*, **-j*).** As noted above, the rounded-vowel hypothesis assumes that Middle Chinese *-w-*, unless it is attributable to a labialized initial, originates with the diphthongization of rounded vowels. This process of diphthongization affected syllables with acute codas (i.e., codas that are [+ coronal] in the system of Chomsky and Halle 1968). Suppose we use capital letters as cover symbols for classes of consonants as follows:

T for acute ([+coronal]) consonants;
P for labial consonants;
K for velar and laryngeal consonants;
K^w for labiovelar and labiolaryngeal consonants.

Then we can summarize DIPHTHONGIZATION as follows:

**TuT* > **TwiT*;
KuT* > **KwiT* (merging with original *K^w*ɨT*);
**PuT* > **PwiT* (merging with original **PɨT*);
**ToT* > **TwaT*;
KoT* > **KwaT* (merging with original *K^w*aT*);
**PoT* > **PwaT* (merging with original **PaT*).

Note that Middle Chinese *-w-* is not contrastive after labial initials, so that syllables like **PwɨT* and **PɨT* must be assumed to merge, either as **PɨT* or as **PwɨT*; and similarly with **PwaT* and **PaT*. These mergers, and the similar mergers of syllables like **Kut* with ***K^w*ɨT*, are reflected in the writing system and in the text of the *Shījīng* in a number of cases, though

---

23 See note 18 above for an example.

24 Of course, some words in **-ps* retained their original graphic connections with words in final **-p*; such characters were the original basis for Karlgren's reconstruction of **-b* (our **-ps*). This shows that the script sometimes reflects sound changes only after a certain time delay, if at all.

Shījīng rhyming generally reflects the earlier stage. Example (2) illustrates this:

(2) 願 *yuàn* < *ngjwonh* (*ngi̯wɐn-*) < **ngjons* 'wish'.

According to the rounded vowel hypothesis, this word must be reconstructed with *-*on* in order to account for its rhyming behavior. In the *Shījīng*, it rhymes in Ode 94.1 with 漙 *tuán* < *dwan* (*d'uân*) 'plentiful (dew)', which can only represent **don* in our system; Zhū Jùnshēng 朱駿聲 (quoted in the *Shuōwén jiězì gǔlín*, Dīng Fúbǎo 1959: 3926, hereafter referenced as "*SWGL*") also lists two cases in the *Yìjīng* 易經 where it rhymes with 亂 *luàn* < *lwanh* (*luân-*) 'disorder', which also must have a rounded vowel (I reconstruct it as **C-rons*).

But *yuán* 原, the phonetic element of 願, rhymes consistently as *-*an*, and must be reconstructed as

原 *yuán* < *ngjwon* (*ngi̯wɐn*) < **ng*^{w}*jan* 'spring, source'.

The reconstruction with *-*an* is necessary because 原 *yuán* rhymes with *-*an* words in Odes 164.3, 177.5, 250.2, 250.5, and probably in 137.2; in its other rhymes, 241.6 and 250.3 it rhymes with

泉 *quán* < *dzjwen* (*dz'i̯wän*) < **sg*^{w}*jan*? 'spring, source'.

We would normally interpret Middle Chinese *dzjwen* (*dz'i̯wän*) as reflecting OC **dzjon*, but 泉 *quán* rhymes consistently as *-*an*, as Jaxontov pointed out (1960a: 106);[25] possibly the -*w*- derives from a cluster containing a labialized initial like **g*^{w}-. (If so, then 原 *yuán* and 泉 *quán* are probably etymologically related.)

Thus, the rhyme evidence indicates that 願 *yuàn* should be reconstructed as **ngjons*, while 原 *yuán* should be reconstructed as **ng*^{w}*jan*. But to use **ng*^{w}*jan* as phonetic to write **ngjons* fits poorly with Old Chinese phonology. However, there is evidence that the character 願 is of late origin. Neither this character nor its alternate form 愿 is found in oracle bones or bronze inscriptions; while in the lengthy inscription on the vessel 中山王方壺 (Zhōngshān Wáng Fāng Hú), dated at 310 B.C., 願 *yuàn* is written as 忨 (see Luó Fúyí 1979), in which the radical is 'heart' and the phonetic is

元 *yuán* < *ngjwon* < **ngjon* 'head; great'.

Though this word itself does not rhyme in the *Shījīng*, it is clearly to be reconstructed with *-*on*; it has xiéshēng contacts with several words which rhyme as *-*on* rather than *-*an*:

---

[25] In addition to Odes 241.6 and 250.3, where it rhymes with 原 *yuán* < **ng*^{w}*jan*, it rhymes with *-*an* words in Odes 39.4, 153.1-3, 197.8, 203.3, and 250.5.

冠 *guān* < *kwan* (*kuân*) < **kon* 'hat'

(rhymes in Ode 174.1 with 欒 *luán* < *lwan* (*luân*) 'emaciated' and 慱 *tuán* < *dwan* (*d'uân*) 'grieved', both of which must be reconstructed with **-on*);

完 *wán* < *hwan* (*ɣuân*) < **gon* 'complete'

(rhymes in Ode 261.6 with 蠻 *mán* < *maen* (*mwan*) < **mron* 'Southern barbarians', reconstructed with **-on* because of its phonetic 䜌 *luán* < *lwan* (*luân*) < **b-ron* 'harness bells').

As Jaxontov suggested (1960a:110), 完 *wán* may also be phonetic in the following, although the *Shuōwén* does not say so:[26]

寇 *kòu* < *khuwh* (*k'ə̯u-*) < **khos* 'rob; robber'.

The presence of 完 *wán* in this character is well-attested in bronze inscriptions.

Summary: The use of 原 *yuán* < **ngʷjan* 'source; spring' as phonetic in 願 *yuàn* < **ngjons* 'wish' reflects the post-*Shījīng* diphthongization **-on* > **-wan*. The earlier graph 忨, with 元 *yuán* < **ngjon* 'great; head' as phonetic, is more representative of Old Chinese phonology.[27]

2.3. **hm- > x-*. There are a number of cases where words in MC *x-* (χ-) show xiéshēng connections with words in MC *m-*. Karlgren reconstructed some of these words with clusters **χm-*; nowadays it is common to reconstruct a whole series of voiceless nasals **hm-*, **hn-*, and **hng-* (Li 1971), or (perhaps representing an earlier stage) clusters of **s-* plus nasal (Jaxontov 1960b). I adopt the voiceless nasal reconstruction here. At some point prior to Middle Chinese, **hm-* merged with original **x-*, becoming Middle Chinese *x-*. According to Coblin, this change had probably already taken place in the language of Xŭ Shèn 許慎, although Gāo Yòu 高誘

---

[26] Aso, *guăn* < *kwanx* (*kuân:*) < **kon* 'tube; pipe', now written 管, has an alternate form 筦 (Morohashi #26057), with 完 *wán* as phonetic, which I suspect may be of earlier origin. The word 管 *guăn* 'tube' rhymes as **-on* in Ode 42.2 (with 孌 *luán* < *ljwenx* (*li̯wän:*) < **b-rjon:*), but the 官 *guān* phonetic otherwise generally seems to indicate **-an* rather than **-on*. On the other hand, 管 *guăn* in Ode 254.1 rhymes as **-an*, and is probably unrelated to the word for 'tube'; the *Guăngyùn* 廣韻 quotes a version of the text which writes this character as 願 (see Karlgren, Gloss 923).

[27] Another early form for 惌 *yuàn* 'wish' is 顯, found in bamboo strips from the Qín tomb in Yúnmèng county, Húběi (see Shuìhŭdì Qín Mù Zhújiăn Zhĕnglĭ Xiăozŭ 1978: 281). I do not know what phonological significance this form might have.

sometimes uses words in **m-* as sound glosses for words in **hm-* (see Coblin 1978: 43, 1983: 66). This change may be reflected in example (3), which also involves the diphthongization described in the previous section:

(3) 聞 *wén* < *mjun* (*mi̯uən*) < **mjun* 'hear' and
問 *wèn* < *mjunh* (*mi̯uən-*) < **mjuns* 'ask'.

The first character also has a qùshēng reading, where the suffix **-s* appears to have a nominalizing effect:

聞 *wèn* < *mjunh* (*mi̯uən-*) < **mjuns* 'fame'.

According to the *Shuōwén*, both these characters have as phonetic

門 *mén* < *mwon* (*muən*) < **mɨn* 'door'.

However, according to the rounded-vowel hypothesis, both 聞 *wén* and 問 *wèn* must be reconstructed with **-un*, while 門 *mén* must be reconstructed with **-ɨn* and should not be a good phonetic for them. In fact, the modern graphs for 聞 *wén* and 問 *wèn* are probably rather late, and reflect post-*Shījīng* sound changes, including DIPHTHONGIZATION and **HM- > X-*.

The reconstruction of 聞 *wén* and 問 *wèn* with **-un* is required by their *Shījīng* rhymes. According to the rounded-vowel hypothesis, Middle Chinese acute-initial words with medial *-w-* must normally be reconstructed with rounded vowels.[28] 聞 *wén* 'hear' rhymes with such words in Odes 71.3 and 258.3; 問 *wèn* 'ask' rhymes with such words in 82.3.[29] The rhymes in Ode 237.8 (where 問 is a loan for 'fame') may also be reconstructed with **-un*. On the other hand, Middle Chinese velar- or laryngeal-initial words without medial *-w-* must be reconstructed with non-rounded vowels; 門 *mén* rhymes with such words in Odes 40.1, 93.1, and 199.1.[30]

---

[28] Grave initials include labials, velars, and laryngeals; all others are acute (see section 2.2). The Middle Chinese initial which I write as *y-* (Karlgren's *i̯-*, traditionally labelled 喻四) is also acute, although traditionally listed among the laryngeals.

[29] For example, in Ode 71.3, 聞 *wén* rhymes with 漘 *chún* < *zywin* (*dź'i̯uĕn*) < **(s)djun* 'lips (= banks of a river)'; in 258.3 it rhymes with 川 *chuān* < *tsyhwen* (*tś'i̯wän*) and 遯 *dùn* < *dwonh* (*d'uən-*) < **duns*. 川 *chuān* is irregular, as Karlgren points out (*GSR* 462a); based on Old Chinese rhymes, we would expect MC *tsyhwin* (*tś'i̯uĕn*).

[30] For example, 門 *mén* rhymes in 40.1 and 199.1 with 艱 *jiān* < *kean* (*kăn*) < **krɨn* 'difficulty', and in 93.1 with 巾 *jīn* < *kin* (*ki̯ĕn*$_3$) < **krjɨn* 'kerchief'. The word 存 *cún* < *dzwon* (*dz'uən*) 'exist, remain', which also rhymes with 門 *mén* in Ode 93.1, looks as if it should be **dzun*, but it is an irregular development from **dzɨn*, which would regularly give MC

In oracle bones and bronze inscriptions, 聞 *wén* is not written with 門 *mén* as phonetic. The oracle bone forms appear to show a kneeling person with one hand raised beside the head and a large 'ear':

~

Many bronze forms appear to be simplifications or corruptions of this basic form. This same character (sometimes with 'female' added) is also used for 婚 *hūn* < *xwon* < **hmun* 'marriage'. Later we also find 'hear' written 聒, with 'ear' as signific and 昏 *hūn* < *xwon* < **hmun* 'dusk' as phonetic; this form is given in the *Shuōwén* as the gǔwén of 聞.[31] Thus these graphs connect 聞 *wén* < **mjun* with the phonetic series of 昏 *hūn* < **hmun*, but not with 門 *mén* < **min*.

The bronze inscription form of 問 *wèn* is similar to the bronze form of 聞 *wén*; the former being and the latter . Both oracle bone and bronze characters consisting of 'door' plus 'mouth' are also attested, but as far as I know there is no reason to believe that they represent the word 'ask'. I know of two such cases of such a character in oracle bone inscriptions. One is found on a fragment containing only two characters; Lǐ Xiàodìng (1965: 363) says that the meaning of the graph is unclear.[32] The other oracle bone inscription, listed by Menzies (1917, #813), is likewise fragmentary and of unclear meaning.[33] Xú Zhōngshū lists such a character from a bronze bell (1980: 42), but here it is a personal name.[34] Finally, Gāo Míng (1980: 409) lists two forms from seals of the Warring States period. It remains to be seen whether the meaning 'ask' can be justified in any of these cases.

---

dzen > *qián*. (This word is discussed in Jaxontov 1960a: 106.) In the same phonetic series, compare 荐 *jiàn* with the regular MC reading *dzenh* (*dz'ien-*), and also irregular *dzwonh* (*dz'uən-*), according to the *Jīngdiǎn Shìwén*; see *GSR* 632b. 存 *cún* < **dzin* 'exist' is probably cognate to 在 *zài* < *dzojx* (*dz'ậi:*) < **dzi*: 'be at', which is also its phonetic, according to the *Shuōwén* (*SWGL* 6607).

[31] See *JWGL* #0881 and #1534, Gāo Míng 1980: 136, Xú Zhōngshū 1980: 454-55 and 464, *SWGL* 5356.

[32] This is also the conclusion of Ikeda Suetoshi (1964, vol. 2, p. 37). A rubbing of the fragment may be found in Luó Zhènyù 1916, vol. 2, 9/10. The other character on the fragment appears to be 若 *ruò*.

[33] Shima Kunio lists only two characters from this inscription: 貞問 (i.e.,); see Shima 1967:285.

[34] The name of the bell is 史問鍾 Shǐ 'Wèn' Zhōng. I have not been able to locate the full inscription.

The main sound change which made 門 *mén* a suitable phonetic for 聞 *wén* and 問 *wèn* was the diphthongization of original **-un* to **-win*; after labial initials, the resulting **w* was probably non-contrastive, so that **-un* and **-in* simply merged in this environment. At about the same time, the change of **hm-* to *x-* may have made 昏 *hūn* < *xwon* < **hmun* seem less appropriate as a phonetic for words beginning with *m-*.

Summary: The use of 門 *mén* < **min* 'door' as phonetic in 聞 *wén* < **mjun* 'hear' and 問 *wèn* < **mjuns* 'ask' reflects the post-*Shījīng* merger of **-in* and **-un* after labials which resulted from the diphthongization **-un* > **-win*. The earlier graphs which connect 聞 *wén* and 問 *wèn* instead with 婚 *hūn* < **hmun* 'marriage' or 昏 *hūn* < **hmun* 'dusk' are more representative of Old Chinese phonology, but may have been felt to be less appropriate after the change **HM-* > *X-*.

2.4 *r-color. The change which I call **R*-COLOR was mentioned above in connection with the **r*-hypothesis and the **rj*-hypothesis. It can be formulated as a change adding frontness and laxness ([−back] and [−tense], in the features of Chomsky and Halle 1968) to a main vowel after medial **-r-* or **-rj-*:

V -> [−back], [−tense] / *r(j)*______

The feature of frontness accounts for the fact that division-II finals have fronter vowels than their division-I counterparts; and it also accounts for the failure of labial initials to become labiodental in division-III chóngniŭ words (see the examples cited in section 1.5 above). Laxness or some other additional feature is necessary to account for (among other things) the fact that original **-re-* failed to merge with **-e-* after medial **r* was lost. The following words illustrate this contrast:

耕 *gēng* < *keang* (*kɛng*) < **kreng* 'to plough'

經 *jīng* < *keng* (*kieng*) < **keng* 'warp; norm'.

Laxness is also one possible candidate for the feature distinguishing division-III and division-IV chóngniŭ syllables in Middle Chinese. Laxness probably remained non-distinctive until the loss of medial **r*.[35]

[35] Another possible candidate for the distinction left behind by medial **r* is, of course, retroflexion, as suggested by Bodman (1971). Pulleyblank (1984) reconstructs a retroflex offglide in division-II finals for the Early Middle Chinese stage, and suggests that retroflexion may have been present in division-III chóngniŭ as well. The difficulty with reconstructing retroflexion in Middle Chinese is that by Early Middle Chinese, some chóngniŭ syllables had already merged with syllables where there appears to be no reason to

The effects of **R*-COLOR can be seen as early as the Hàn dynasty. According to Luó and Zhōu (1958: 13-14), the division-II portion of the Yú 魚 rhyme group—those words with the Middle Chinese final *-ae* (*-a*)—had shifted by Eastern Hàn to the Gē 歌 rhyme group. In my system, this means that original **-ra* no longer rhymed with **-a*, but rather with **-aj* and **-raj*. One way to account for this is to assume that **-aj* had monophthongized by this time to [æ], and that **R*-COLOR caused **-ra* to change to [ræ], merging with original **-raj*. Hàn-time [æ] < **-aj* developed into Middle Chinese division-I *-a* (*-â*), while [ræ] developed into division-II *-ae* (*-a*). Confusion of **-ra* and **-raj*, probably dating from Hàn times or shortly before, is found in example (4), contained in Ode 249.1:

(4) 假樂君子 *jiǎ lè jūn zǐ*
'Greatly happy be the lord'.

The *Zhōng yōng* 中庸 quotes this line with 嘉 *jiā* substituted for 假 *jiǎ*. 假 *jiǎ* is from the Old Chinese Yú 魚 rhyme group:

假 *jiǎ* < *kaex* (*ka:*) < **kraʔ* '(loan for) great'.

嘉 *jiā*, on the other hand, is from the Old Chinese Gē 歌 rhyme group:

嘉 *jiā* < *kae* (*ka*) < **kraj* 'good, excellent'.

It is difficult to decide whether 假 *jiǎ* or 嘉 *jiā* is the better reading here, but whichever it is, either the version in the Máo *Shī* or the version in the *Zhōng yōng* was influenced by the Hàn-time merger of **-ra* and **-raj*, which resulted in part from **R*-COLOR.

Both **R*-COLOR and DIPTHONGIZATION can be seen to be operative in the following example:

(5) 緡 *mín* < *min* (*mi̯ĕn*$_3$) < **mrjun* 'cord; to wrap around'.

First let me support my reconstruction **mrjun*. This word occurs in two passages in the *Shījīng*:

1. In Ode 24.3, it occurs in the following line:

維絲伊緡 *wéi sī yī mín*
'Of silk is the line'.

Here it rhymes with

孫 *sūn* < *swon* (*suən*) < **sun* 'grandson',

which must be reconstructed with **-u-* according to the rounded-vowel hypothesis.

---

reconstruct **r*, and where it would thus be surprising to find retroflexion. See Pulleyblank 1984: 173.

2. In Ode 256.9 it occurs in the line:

言緡之絲 *yán mín zhī sī*
'one strings it with silk'.

Medial **-rj-* is reconstructed according to the **rj*-hypothesis in order to account for the fact that the word has the division-III chóngniǔ final *-in* (*-i̯ĕn*$_3$) (plain **mjun* would give MC *mjun* > *wén*). Note that both the *Ěryǎ* 爾雅 and the Máo commentary to the *Shījīng* gloss this word as

綸 *lún* < *lwin* (*li̯uĕn*) < **C-rjun* 'twist a cord',

which is probably from the same root. In fact, this word occurs in Ode 226.3, in the line

言綸之繩 *yán lún zhī shéng*
'I twisted the line for him',

which is strikingly similar to the line in Ode 256.9 just quoted, except that 綸 *lún* < **C-rjun* is used instead of 緡 *mín* < **mrjun*. (The word 綸 *lún* must also be reconstructed with **-u-* according to the rounded-vowel hypothesis.)[36]

In its modern form, this character contains the character

民 *mín* < *mjin* (*mi̯ĕn*$_4$) < **mjin* 'people'.

Karlgren takes this as phonetic (GSR 457a). But 民 *mín* 'people' rhymes in the Zhēn 真 rhyme category,[37] while 緡 *mín* 'cord', in its only *Shījīng* rhyme, rhymes with 孫 *sūn* < **sun*, which is in the traditional Wén 文 category.[38] Thus the rhyming behavior of this word conflicts with its modern graph. Actually, the *Shuōwén* says that the phonetic is

昏 *hūn* < *xwon* (*χwən*) < **hmun* 'dusk'.

In this case I believe the *Shuōwén* is correct. The confusion of the 民 *mín* series with the 昏 *hūn* series was partly a matter of graphic confusion due to the similarity of 民 *mín* to the top element in 昏 *hūn*; but it may also reflect several post-*Shījīng* sound changes:

— **HM-* > *X-*, which would have made 昏 *hūn* seem less suitable as a phonetic for 緡 *mín*;
— DIPHTHONGIZATION, which changed **mrjun* > **mrj(w)in* > **mrjin*;

---

36 The character 綸 also has a reading *guān* < *kwean* (*kwăn*) < **krun* 'scarf or sash'. The root meaning seems to be 'twist' or 'wrap'.

37 See Odes 234.2, 257.1.

38 In my revised rhyme categories, 民 *mín* 'people' belongs to the **-IN* group, while 緡 *mín* 'cord, twist' belongs to the **-UN* group.

— *R-COLOR, which fronted vowels after medial *-r-, ultimately causing *mrjun to become Middle Chinese min.

By the end of the Hàn dynasty, as a result of these changes, 緡 *mrjun had probably already become *mrin, so that 民 mín < *mjin would have seemed a more suitable phonetic for it than 昏 hūn.

Summary: The use of 民 mín < *mjin 'people' as phonetic in 緡 mín < *mrjun 'twine' reflects several post-*Shījīng* sound changes (see above). The *Shuōwén*'s form, with 昏 hūn < *hmun 'dusk' as phonetic, is more representative of Old Chinese phonology.

*R-COLOR and DIPHTHONGIZATION can also be seen in the following example (6):

(6) 卷/婘/鬈 *quán* < *gjwen* (*gi̯wän*$_3$) < *g^{w}rjen 'handsome'.

The usual use of the character 卷 is to write the word

juǎn < *kjwenx* (*ki̯wän:*$_3$) < *krjonʔ 'roll'.

The Middle Chinese reading *kjwenx* (*ki̯wän:*$_3$) could reflect any one of *krjonʔ, *k^{w}rjanʔ, or *k^{w}rjenʔ, but this word, in the meaning 'roll', rhymes as *-on in Ode 26.3, so the reconstruction *krjonʔ is to be preferred.[39] However, the same character, sometimes with 'woman' or 'hair' added, is also used for a word glossed by Máo as '好貌 *hǎo mào*' ('handsome'), and in this case it rhymes as *-en.

For example, in Ode 145.2, we have the line

碩大且卷 *shuò dà qiě quán*
'grandly large and handsome';

here 卷 *quán* rhymes with

悁 *yuān* < *'jiwen* (*·i̯wän*$_4$) < *ʔ^{w}jen 'grieved',

which must be reconstructed with *-en according to the front vowel hypothesis.[40] The *Jīngdiǎn Shìwén* 經典釋文 gives 婘 as an alternate form in this line. In Ode 103.2, we have the character with 'hair' added:

其人美且鬈 *qí rén měi qiě quán*
'that man is beautiful and handsome'.

Here 鬈 *quán* rhymes with

[39] The other rhyme words in 26.3 are 轉 *zhuǎn* < *trjwenx* (*t̂i̯wän:*) < *trjonʔ and 選 *xuǎn* < *sjwenx* (*si̯wän:*) < *s(k)jonʔ, both of which must be reconstructed with *-on.

[40] The other rhyme word of this sequence, 蕑 *jiān*, is discussed below; it also shoud be reconstructed with *-en here.

環 *huán* < *hwaen* (*ɣwan*) < **gʷren* 'ring',

also to be reconstructed with **-en*, as are other words with the phonetic 睘.[41]

Finally, in Ode 97.1, we have the line

揖我謂我儇兮 *yī wǒ wèi wǒ xuān xī,*

which Karlgren translates 'You bowed to me and said I was smart'. Máo glosses 儇 *xuān* here as 'sharp, quick, smart'. But according to the *Jīngdiǎn Shìwén*, the Hán *Shī* 韓詩 version has 婘 *quán* < *gjwen* (*gi̯wän*$_3$) here, with the gloss '好貌 *hǎo mào*' ('handsome'). For Máo's 儇 *xuān*, the *Jīngdiǎn Shìwén* gives the pronunciation

xuān < *xjwien* (*χi̯wän*$_4$),

which must be reconstructed with **-en* because of its division-IV chóngniǔ final. The other rhyme words of the stanza must be reconstructed with **-en* in this case also.[42]

I conjecture that the word 'handsome' written with 卷, 婘, or 鬈 was originally **gʷrjen*, and came to be written with the 卷 *juǎn* < **krjonʔ* 'roll' as loan character or phonetic only after certain post-*Shījīng* sound changes, including DIPHTHONGIZATION (changing **-on* to **-wan*) and **R*-COLOR (fronting vowels after **-r-*). These changes caused syllables of the form **Krjon* and **Kʷrjen* to merge, and made 卷 **krjonʔ* 'roll' a suitable phonetic for **gʷrjen* 'handsome'. I do not know what the earlier graph for **gʷrjen* 'handsome' may have been, although it may have been the 儇 we find in Máo's version of Ode 97.1, or something similar. In other words, the Máo version may have made substitutions in Odes 103.2 and 145.2 similar to that found in the Hán *Shī* in Ode 97.1.

Summary: The use of 卷 **krjonʔ* 'roll' as loan character or phonetic for **gʷrjen* 'handsome' is influenced by the post-*Shījīng* sound changes DIPHTHONGIZATION and **R*-COLOR, which caused syllables like **Krjon* and **Kʷrjen* to merge. A character with the phonetic 中心悁悁, like the 儇 *xuān* < **hwjen* 'smart' found in Máo's version of Ode 97.1, would be more representative of Old Chinese phonology.

---

[41] We might expect syllables like **Kʷren* to give MC *Kwean* (*Kwǎn*), by analogy to **Kren* > *Kean* (*Kǎn*), but the regular reflex of **Kʷren* appears to be *Kwaen* (*Kwan*).

[42] They are 還 *xuán* < *zjwen* (*zi̯wän*) < **sgʷjen* 'agile', 閒 *jiān* < *kean* (*kǎn*) < **kren* 'among, around', and 肩 *jiān* < *ken* (*kien*) < **ken* '(loan for) boar'. 還 *xuán* has the phonetic 睘, which normally indicates **-en*, and it also rhymes as **-en* in Ode 111.1. 閒 *jiān* and 肩 *jiān* must be reconstructed with **-en* because of their Middle Chinese finals.

In the following example, too, **R*-COLOR has caused two originally distinct words to be written the same way in the *Shījīng*.

(7) The character 蕳 *jiān* occurs in Odes 95.1 and 145.2. In both cases it is a rhyme word, but it rhymes in one case as **-an*, in the other case as **-en*. Consider first 95.1 (the rhyme words are capitalized):

> 溱與洧 *Zhēn yǔ Wěi*
> 'The Chen and the Wei (streams)
>
> 方渙渙兮 *fāng huàn HUÀN xī*
> 'are just now amply-flowing;
>
> 士與女 *shì yǔ nǚ*
> 'knights and girls
>
> 方秉蕳兮 *fāng bǐng JIĀN xī*
> 'are just holding k i e n plants in their hands'.

The *Jīngdiǎn Shìwén* here assigns 蕳 *jiān* the fǎnqiè spelling 古顏反, i.e., *kux* + *ngaen* (*kuo:* + *ngan*) = *kaen* (*kan*), which would reflect Old Chinese **kran*.[43] As for the meaning of *jiān*, the Máo commentary glosses it with the word

> 蘭 *lán* < *lan* (*lân*) < **g-ran* 'orchid'.

This is certainly a sound gloss for 蕳 *jiān* < **kran*. Probably 蕳 *jiān* and 蘭 *lán* are simply different forms of the same word; 蕳 *jiān* could even be a graphic error for 蘭 *lán*, since the characters are graphically as well as phonetically similar.[44]

Now let us turn to Ode 145.2:

> 彼澤之陂 *bǐ zé zhī bēi*
> 'By the shores of that marsh
>
> 有蒲與蕳 *yǒu pú yǔ JIĀN*

[43] The other rhyme word 渙 *huàn* < *xwanh* (*χuân-*) could reflect either **hwans* or **xons*, but the same character rhymes as **-an* in Ode 287 (although with a different meaning), and in any case 蕳 *jiān* < *kaen* < **kran* cannot be reconstructed with **-on* because it has no medial *-w-* in Middle Chinese. According to the *Jīngdiǎn Shìwén*, the Hán *Shī* 韓詩 has 洹 *huán* < *hwan* (*ɣuân*) for 渙 *huàn*; this is also to be reconstructed with **-an*. Karlgren (Gloss 243) lists other variant graphs as well.

[44] According tohe *Jīngdiǎn Shìwén*, the Hán *Shī* glossed 蕳 *jiān* as 蓮 *lián* < **g-ren* 'lotus seed'; this probably shows a confusion of **-ran* with **-ren*, or else influence from Ode 145.2; see below.

'there are sedges and lotus fruits;

有美一人 *yǒu měi yī rén*

'there is a certain beautiful person,

碩大且卷 *shuò dà qiě QUÁN*

'grandly large and handsome;

寤寐無爲 *wù mèi wú wéi*

'waking and sleeping, I know not what to do,

中心悁悁 *zhōng xīn yuān YUĀN*,

'in the core of my heart I am grieved.'

The Máo commentary glosses this 蕑 *jiān* as 蘭 *lán* 'orchid', as in Ode 95.1 above; but Zhèng Xuán 鄭玄 says '蕑當作蓮 *jiān dāng zuò lián*' ('蕑 should be 蓮 *lián* "lotus seed"'). This is said to be the reading of the Lǔ *Shī* 魯詩. Most commentators have agreed with Zhèng Xuán here, because of the parallelism with the other stanzas: the corresponding lines in the other two stanzas of the ode both mention some part of the lotus plant (荷 *hé* 'lotus plant' in stanza 1, 菡萏 *hàndàn* 'lotus flower' in stanza 3).[45]

The front-vowel hypothesis allows us to add phonological support for the reading 蓮 *lián* 'lotus seed' here. Because of the front-vowel hypothesis, the division-IV word 蓮 *lián* < *len* (*lien*) must be reconstructed with **-en* (see example (10) in section 2.6 below). This fits well with the other two rhyme words of the stanza, which are also to be reconstructed with **-en*.[46] Also the graph 蕑 appears to have as phonetic

閒 *jiān* < *kean* (*kăn*) < **kren* 'between, among',

a character which could easily be used for **g-ren* 'lotus seed', under the **r*-hypothesis.

How did *lán* < **g-ran* 'orchid' and *lián* < **g-ren* 'lotus seed' come to be written with the same character 蕑 in our text? Possibly the confusion was originally graphic, 蕑 being substituted for 蘭. But **R-COLOR* may have had a role as well. In some Hàn dialects, **R*-COLOR may have caused the

[45] See Karlgren, Gloss 352, and the commentary by Kǒng Yǐngdá 孔穎達 in *Máo Shī zhù shū* 631–32.

[46] The other two rhyme words are to be reconstructed 卷 *quán* < *gjwen* (*gi̯wän$_3$*) < **gʷrjen* 'handsome' and 悁 *yuān* < *'jwien* < **ʔʷjen* 'grieved'. The first is discussed in example (9) above; as mentioned there, 悁 *yuān* must be reconstructed with **-en* because of its division-IV chóngniǔ final.

finals **-ran* and **-ren* to merge completely, as they eventually merged in the Middle Chinese period (*-aen* < **-ran* and *-ean* < **-ren* are often confused in Middle Chinese sources, and merge in Late Middle Chinese). It is also possible that the merger of **-jan* with **-jen* in some environments (see section 2.6 below) may have disrupted the rhyming pattern of the *Shījīng* to the extent that Hàn readers would not realize that, by Old Chinese standards, the same word could not make a good rhyme in both Odes 95.1 and 145.2.

Summary: The character 蕳 probably represents **g-ran* 'orchid' in Ode 95.1, but **g-ren* 'lotus fruit' in Ode 145.2, as the rhymes (and, in Ode 145.2, the context) imply. The confusion of the two words may in part be graphic, but may also be influenced by **R*-COLOR or other post-*Shījīng* sound changes.

Example (8) is another case where post-*Shījīng* sound changes appear to have influenced the text of the Máo *Shī*:

(8) Ode 106.3 in the Máo *Shī* reads as follows:

猗嗟孌兮 *yī jiē LUÁN xī*
'Lo! How handsome,

清揚婉兮 *qīng yáng WǍN xī*
'the clear forehead how beautiful;

舞則選兮 *wǔ zé XUǍN xī*
'when dancing he is in counting;

射則貫兮 *shè zé GUÀN xī*
'when shooting he pierces (the target);

四矢反兮 *sì shǐ FǍN xī*
'his four arrows succeed one another in a regular sequence,

以禦亂兮 *yǐ yù LUÀN xī*
'so as to prevent (disorder:) violation of the rules'.

Karlgren notes that the Hán *Shī* has 變 *biàn* 'change' for 反 *fǎn* 'revert' in the next to the last line. If we follow Máo and Zhèng Xuán, we get an interpretation like 'The four arrows (revert=) come (one after the other) to the same place'; if we follow the Hán *Shī*, we get 'The four arrows (change=) succeed one another'. Karlgren's conclusion is that it is... "[u]ndecidable which version best repr[esents] the orig[inal] Shi" (see Gloss 268).

However, the rounded-vowel hypothesis allows us to choose the Hán version's 變 *biàn* over the Máo version's 反 *fǎn* on phonological grounds, for only the former makes a good rhyme. All the other rhyme words in the stanza are to be reconstructed with **-on*.[47] 變 *biàn* is also to be reconstructed with **-on*:

變 *biàn* < *pjenh* (*pi̯än-*$_3$) < **prjons* 'to change'.

The reconstruction with **-on* is based on the phonetic, which must be reconstructed with **-on* according to the rounded-vowel hypothesis:

䜌 *luán* < *lwan* (*luân*) < **b-ron* 'harness bells'[48]

Though the phonetic compound 變 does not occur in bronze inscriptions, as far as I know, it does occur in the Zhànguó 戰國 inscription Zŭ Chŭ Wén 詛楚文, dating from the late 4th century B. C. (see Xú Zhōngshū 1980: 123, Gāo Míng 1980: 82). I conjecture that 變 *biàn* < **prjons* 'change' may be cognate to

亂 *luàn* < *lwanh* (*luân-*) < **C-rons* 'disorder'.

The word 反 *făn*, on the other hand, rhymes elsewhere as **-an*,[49] and is to be reconstructed

反 *făn* < *pjonx* (*pi̯wɐn:*) < **pjanˀ* 'reverse; revert'.

Summary: The rounded-vowel hypothesis leads us to prefer the reading of the Hán *Shī* as more representative of Old Chinese phonology. The confu-

---

[47] 孌 [*luán*] < *ljwenx* (*li̯wän:*) < **b-rjonˀ* and 亂 *luàn* < *lwanh* (*luân-*) < **C-rons* must be reconstructed with **-on* because of their Middle Chinese readings. 婉 [*wǎn*] < *'jwonx* (*·iwɐn:*) < **ʔjonˀ* rhymes as **-on* also in 94.1, and internally in 102.3 and 151.4. 選 *xuǎn* < *sjwenx* (*si̯wän:*) < **s(k)jonˀ* rhymes as **-on* in 26.3. 貫 *guàn* < *kwanh* (*kuân-*) < **kons* may rhyme as **-on* in 199.7. (Square brackets in the above examples indicate that the modern readings are irregular.) It is possible that the sequence should be split into a three-word shăngshēng sequence and a three-word qùshēng sequence.

[48] Words written with this phonetic rhyme consistently as **-on* in the *Shījīng*: 孌 *luán* < *ljwenx* (*li̯wän:*) < **b-rjonˀ* 'beautiful' in Odes 42.2, 102.3, 106.3, and the first line of this ode; 欒 *luán* < *lwan* (*luân*) < **b-ron* 'emaciated' in Ode 147.1; and 蠻 *mán* < *maen* (*mwan*) < **mron* 'Southern barbarian' in Ode 261.6.

[49] See Odes 54.2, 58.6, 220.3, 223.1, 253.5, and 274.1. Ode 58.6 appears to include one **-on* word, but is otherwise **-an*; it seems to be a genuine exception to the principle that **-on* and **-an* rhyme separately. In Ode 274.1, 反 *făn* rhymes with 簡, normally *jiăn* < *keanx* (*kăn:*) < **krenˀ* 'bamboo strip', but here 簡簡 means 'great', and I suspect that the apparent irregular rhyming of **an* and **-en* is a result of textual corruption.

sion between 變 biàn < *prjons 'change' and 反 fǎn < *pjanʔ 'revert' in the Máo text probably reflects the change DIPHTHONGIZATION, which would have made 反 *pjanʔ a good rhyme with original *-on, and also *R-COLOR, which fronted the vowel of 變 *prjons > *pr(w)jans > *prjens and may have made it seem less good as a rhyme.

2.5. *Pja > *Pjo. Middle Chinese syllables of the form Pju (i.e., labial-initial words in the Yú 虞 rhyme) have two possible Old Chinese sources: one in the Yú 魚 rhyme group, which I reconstruct *Pja, and one in the Hóu 侯 rhyme group, which I reconstruct as *Pjo. An example of this contrast is

釜 fǔ < pjux (pi̯u:) < *pjaʔ 'axe'

versus

俯 fǔ < pjux (pi̯u:) < *pjoʔ 'to bend down'.

(Karlgren reconstructs these words as *pi̯o and *pi̯u respectively; in Li's system they are *pjagx and *pjugx.)

It is difficult to date the merger of such syllables precisely, but it probably had begun in Hàn times. Luó and Zhōu argue that the Yú 魚 and Hóu 侯 rhyme groups had simply merged by Western Hàn (1958: 49). This view is questioned by Shào Róngfēn (1983), but it is clear even from Shào Róngfēn's data that much interrhyming took place between *-ja and *-jo in Hàn. In the Qièyùn system, *-ja and *-jo are generally kept apart as -jo (-i̯wo) and -ju (-i̯u) respectively, but the two finals merge as -ju (-i̯u) after labial or labialized initials. In fact, in most dialects *-ja and *-jo merged completely; according to Luó Chángpéi, the distinction between -jo (-i̯wo) and -ju (-i̯u) was maintained only in a small area (Luó Chángpéi 1931). Example (9) shows how the merger of *Pja and *Pjo may have affected the text of the *Shījīng*.

In our classical texts the two characters given below in example (9) are sometimes used interchangeably:

(9) 毋 wú < mju (mi̯u) < *mjo 'do not'
無 wú < mju (mi̯u) < *mja 'have not; do not'.

For example, consider Ode 23.3:

無感我帨兮 wú gǎn wǒ shuì xī
'Do not move my kerchief;
無使尨也吠 wú shǐ máng yě fèi
'do not make the dog bark!'

This usage reflects the merger of the syllables *mja and *mjo in Hàn times. Let me first justify these reconstructions.

As mentioned above, the Middle Chinese syllable *mju* can reflect either **mja* or **mjo*; that is, it can come from either the Yú 魚 rhyme group (**mja*) or the Hóu 侯 rhyme group (**mjo*). I reconstruct 毋 *wú* as **mjo* for the following reasons:

1. The word 侮 *wǔ* < *mjux* (*mi̯u:*) < **mjoʔ* 'insult' in the same phonetic series must be reconstructed with **-jo* to account for its *Shījīng* rhymes;[50] and

2. In bronze inscriptions, 毋 *wú* is written the same as 母 *mǔ* < *muwx* (*mə̯u:*) < **moʔ* 'mother'.

In a previous paper (Baxter 1980: 24–25), I proposed reconstructing 母 *mǔ* 'mother' as **moʔ*. This reconstruction accounts easily for the Middle Chinese reading *muwx* (*mə̯u:*), since **-o* regularly gives MC *-uw* (*-ə̯u*). It also explains why 毋 *wú* < **mjo* 'do not' and 母 *mǔ* < **moʔ* 'mother' could be written with the same character in bronze inscriptions.

A complication arises because 母 *mǔ* undeniably rhymes in the *Shījīng* as **-ɨ* (the Zhī 之 rhyme group), not **-o*.[51] This creates a difficulty in reconstruction, since the Zhī 之 group also contains words like

每 *měi* < *mwojx* (*muặi*) < **mɨʔ* 'every',

which contrasts with 母 *mǔ* < *muwx* (*mə̯u:*). How can this contrast be accounted for? Karlgren reconstructed 母 *mǔ* < **məg* and 每 *měi* < **mwəg* (*GSR* 947a, i); but this makes **-w-* contrastive after labials, which is otherwise unnecessary.[52] Dǒng Tónghé appeals to a contrast of length, reconstructing 母 *mǔ* < **mwə̣̂g* versus 每 *měi* < **mwə̂g* (Dǒng Tónghé 1948: 126). Li Fang-kuei (1982: 37-38) leaves the problem unresolved.

We can solve this problem by reconstructing 母 *mǔ* < **moʔ*, providing that we assume that the *Shījīng* rhymes reflect a dialect in which labial-initial syllables of the form **Po* dissimilated to **Pɨ*. This reconstruction fills a systematic gap in the Hóu 侯 rhyme group, which otherwise has no

---

50 See Odes 192.2, 237.9, 241.8, and 246.3.

51 Except possibly in Ode 101.2, where it rhymes with its homonym 畝 *mǔ* 'acre', which I believe should also be reconstructed as **moʔ*. both words are traditionally assigned to the Zhī 之 group. In Ode 51.2, 母 *mǔ* appears to rhyme with 雨 *yǔ* < *hjux* (*ji̯u:*) < **wjaʔ* 'rain'. It is possible that here 父母 *fù mǔ* 'father and mother' is a reversal of original 母父 *mǔ fù* 'mother and father'; 父 *fù* < **bjaʔ* 'father' would make a good rhyme with 雨 *yǔ* < **wjaʔ*.

52 If one follows the rounded-vowel hypothesis, **-w-* is not available at all.

labial-initial syllables of the form *Po.[53] This dialect also appears to be reflected in xiéshēng characters, which sometimes mix *P(j)ɨ with *P(j)o. Middle Chinese is not directly descended from this dialect, however, since it shows instead the expected development of *Po to Puw (Pə̯u).

If 毋 *wú* 'do not' should be reconstructed as **mjo*, it is equally clear that 無 *wú* should be reconstructed as **mja*. Although it is not used as a rhyme word in the *Shījīng*, in oracle bones and bronze inscriptions it is regularly written with the same character as

舞 *wǔ* < *mjux* (*mi̯u:*) 'dance',

which rhymes consistently as **-a* in the *Shījīng*.[54] Because 無 *wú* < **mja* 'have not' is also used with the meaning 'do not', 毋 *wú* 'do not' has also generally been reconstructed as if it, too, is from the Yú 魚 group; Karlgren reconstructed it as **mi̯wo*, Dǒng Tónghé as **mi̯wag*;[55] the corresponding reconstruction in my system would be **mja*. But the confusion of 毋 *wú* < **mjo* 'do not' with 無 *wú* < **mja* 'have not' probably reflects the sound change **PJA* > **PJO* by which OC **-ja* merged with **-jo* under the influence of a labial or labialized initial, becoming MC *-ju* (*-iu*).

Summary: The use of 無 *wú* < **mja* 'have not' for 毋 *wú* < **mjo* 'do not' reflects the post-*Shījīng* merger of **-ja* with **-jo* after labials and labialized initials. The earlier use of 母 *mǔ* < **moʔ* 'mother' (dialect form **mɨʔ*?) to write 毋 *wú* < **mjo* 'do not' is more representative of Old Chinese phonology.

2.6. Acute fronting. The change which I refer to as ACUTE FRONTING changed **-jaT* to **-jeT*; that is, it changed **a* to a front mid vowel [e] in syllables with medial **-j-*, when both the initial consonant and the coda were acute ([+coronal]).[56] An example is

---

[53] See the table in Dǒng Tónghé 1948: 149. Dǒng lists a word 仆 *phuwh* (*p'əu-*), but this is to be reconstructed **phoks*, not **phos*, as its phonetic 卜 *bǔ* < *puwk* (*puk*) < **pok* shows. The words in Dǒng's table with the Middle Chinese reading *muwh* (*mə̯u-*) probably come from earlier *mjuwh* (*mi̯ə̯u-*); a sound change *mjuw-* > *muw-* was in progress about the time of the *Qièyùn*. These words can be reconstructed as *mjuws* or **mjuks*, from the Yōu 幽 rhyme group.

[54] See Gāo Míng 1980: 94, Xú Zhōngshū 1980: 229. For the rhymes of 舞 *wǔ*, see Odes 38.1, 38.2, 78.1, 218.3, and 298.1.

[55] See *GSR* 107a, Dǒng Tónghé 1948: 161. Li Fang-kuei does not list 毋 *wú* among his examples in Li 1982.

[56] Karlgren recognized this change, describing it as an "Umlaut" (1940:

然 *rán* < *nyen* (*nźi̯än*) < **njan* 'burn'.

This word rhymed as **-an* in Old Chinese, and was earlier written with

難 *nán* < *nan* (*nân*) < **nan* 'difficult'

as phonetic (see GSR 152i-j). But by Wèi-Jìn times 然 *rán* and similar words had split off from **-an* and were in a separate rhyme (See Dīng Bāngxīn 1975: 154, 163). Example (10) shows how this change has affected the script in a way which tends to obscure the underlying Old Chinese phonology of the *Shījīng*.

In the modern script, character (a) of example (10) is phonetic in character (b):

(10a) 連 *lián* < *ljen* (*li̯än*) < **C-rjan* 'connect';
(10b) 蓮 *lián* < *len* (*lien*) < **g-ren* 'lotus (seed)'.[57]

According to the front-vowel hypothesis, 蓮 *lián* 'lotus seed' must be reconstructed with a front vowel in Old Chinese, since it has the division-IV final *-en* (*-ien*); 連 *lián* 'connect', however, rhymes as **-an* in the *Shījīng*.[58] According to Old Chinese phonology, then, 連 *lián* < **C-rjan* 'connect' should not be a good phonetic for 蓮 *lián* < **g-ren* 'lotus seed'. But the character 連 *lián* seems to be of late origin, at least in the meaning 'connect'. According to Duàn Yùcái 段玉裁, the character 連 is the gǔwén form for

輦 *niǎn*[59] < *ljenx* (*li̯än:*) < **C-rjenʔ* or **C-rjanʔ* 'handcart',

the earlier character for 'connect' being

---

19). This change is similar in some ways to **R*-COLOR, and it might be possible to unify the two changes; but note that **R*-COLOR affects also syllables without medial **-j-*, while ACUTE FRONTING does not.

[57] I reconstruct the velar cluster **g-r-* here because of the use of 蕑, with phonetic 間 *jiān* < *kean* < **kren* 'between', to write this word; see example (7) above.

[58] See Ode 241.8. The other rhyme words are all clearly to be reconstructed with **-an*, except possibly for 閑 *xián* < *hean* (*ɣăn*) 'large', which would appear from its Middle Chinese reading to be **gren*. But 閑 *xián* also rhymes as **-an* in Ode 305.6 (where it also means 'large'), and in Odes 127.3 and 177.5 (where it means 'well-trained'). It rhymes as **-en* in Ode 111.1, where it means 'leisurely'. I suspect that two or more unrelated words have been confused here through the operation of **R*-COLOR, as in example (7). Note that Middle Chinese sources often confuse the finals *-ean* (*-ăn*) < **-ren* and *-aen* (*-an*) < **-ran*.

[59] The modern form irregularly substitutes *n-* for *l-*.

聯 _lián_ < _ljen_ (_li̯än_) < _*C-rjan_.[60]

Unfortunately, 輦 _niăn_ 'handcart' does not rhyme in the _Shījīng_, and there is insufficient evidence to decide whether it should be reconstructed as _*C-rjenʔ_ or as _*C-rjanʔ_. If it is _*C-rjenʔ_, then this would explain why it could be phonetic in 蓮 _lián_ < _*g-ren_ 'lotus seed'; the use of the character 連 beside the older 聯 to write the word 'connect' _*C-rjan_ would reflect the partial merger of _*-jan_ with _*-jen_ discussed above. But the character 蓮 for 'lotus seed' may be rather recent; it is also possible that 'handcart' was _*C-rjanʔ_, and that it came to be used for _*g-ren_ 'lotus seed' only after _*C-rjanʔ_ had become _*C-rjenʔ_. (Perhaps the earlier graph for 'lotus seed' was the 蕑 found in example (7).) In either case, the modern characters 連 'connect' and 蓮 'lotus seed' probably reflect the change of _*-jan_ to _*-jen_ after acute initials.

Summary: The presence of 連 _lián_ < _*C-rjan_ and 蓮 _lián_ < _*g-ren_ in the same phonetic series is probably influenced by the late change of _*-jan_ to _*-jen_ after acute initials.

2.7. _*sk-_ > _s-_. In a number of cases, words in Middle Chinese initial _s-_ show xiéshēng connections with velar-initial words. In these cases we can reconstruct _s-_ < _*sk-_ (Li 1971); for example,

楔 _xiē_ < _set_ (_siet_) < _*sket_ 'wedge'

whose phonetic is the possibly cognate

契 _qì_ < _khejh_ (_k'iei-_) < _*khets_ 'script notches; contract'

which has the additional reading _qiè_ < _khet_ (_k'iet_) < _*khet_ 'separated' (_GSR_ 279b). It is not clear when _*sk-_ changed to _s-_; there is some evidence for such clusters in the glosses of Xŭ Shèn in Eastern Hàn (Coblin 1983: 52). At any rate, example (11) appears to reflect both the change _*SK-_ > _S-_ and the change of ACUTE FRONTING.

In its present form, the character (a) of example (11) appears to have character (b) as phonetic:

(11a) 霰 _xiàn_ < _senh_ (_sien-_) < _*skens_ 'sleet';
(11b) 散 _sàn_ < _sanh_ (_sân-_) < _*sans_ 'loose; to scatter'.[61]

---

[60] "Zhōu rén yòng 聯 zì, Hàn rén yòng 連 zì, gŭ jīn zì yě 周人用聯字漢人用連字 古今字也" ('The men of Zhōu used the character 聯 [for 'connect']; the men of Hàn used the character 連; it is a case of ancient and modern characters.' Quoted in _SWGL_ 5351; see also _SWGL_ 777.

[61] This character is also read _săn_ < _sanx_ (_sân:_) < _*san:_.

However, according to the front-vowel hypothesis, 霰 _xiàn_ < _senh_ and 散 _sàn_ < _sanh_ cannot be reconstructed with the same main vowel. 散 _sàn_ < _sanh_ is reconstructed with _*-an_, while a Middle Chinese front-vowel syllable like _senh_ (_sien-_) must be reconstructed with a front vowel in Old Chinese as well. 霰 _xiàn_ rhymes once in the _Shījīng_ (Ode 217.3), and the rhyme sequence confirms this reconstruction; the other rhyme words must also be reconstructed with _*-en_, for the same reason:

霰 _xiàn_ < _senh_ (_sien-_) < _*skens_ 'sleet';
見 _jiàn_ < _kenh_ (_kien-_) < _*kens_ 'see';
宴 _yàn_ < _'enh_ (_·ien-_) < _*ʔens_ 'feast'.

Since words in the same phonetic series normally have the same main vowel, 散 _sàn_ < _*sans_ seems an inappropriate phonetic for 霰 _xiàn_ < _*skens_ according to Old Chinese phonology. The _Shuōwén_, however, says that an alternative form for 霰 _xiàn_ is 䨘, in which 見 _jiàn_ < _*kens_ appears to be used as phonetic (see _SWGL_ 5184). It is for this reason also that I reconstruct an _*sk-_ cluster in 霰 _xiàn_.

If 散 _sàn_ < _*sans_ was inappropriate as a phonetic for 霰 _xiàn_ < _*skens_ in Old Chinese, what made it become appropriate later? The change of _*sk-_ to _*s-_ may have been a factor. Another factor may have been the change ACUTE FRONTING. This change created cases where both _*-an_ and _*-jen_ (< _*-jan_) were to be found in the same phonetic series; and if _*-an_ and _*-jen_ could appear in the same phonetic series, why not _*-an_ and _*-en_? Thus ACUTE FRONTING probably had the effect of loosening the requirements for how similar words had to be in order to be written with the same phonetic element.[62]

As further evidence of the front vowel in 霰 _xiàn_, note that the _Shìmíng_ 釋名 uses

星 _xīng_ < _seng_ (_sieng_) < _*seng_ 'star'

as a sound gloss for 霰 _xiàn_ < _*skens_ 'sleet'.[63] (Probably _*-en_ and _*- eng_

---

[62] It is possible that in some dialects this change may have taken a more general form, in which not just the finals _*-jan_ and _*-jen_, but also the finals _*-an_ and _*-en_, merged in this environment. In such dialects, 散 _sàn_ < _*sans_ and 霰 _xiàn_ < _*skens_ might actually have become homonyms, and it would not be surprising to find 散 _sàn_ used as a phonetic to write 霰 _xiàn_.

[63] In other reconstructions, the similarity between 霰 _xiàn_ < _*sens_ < _*skens_ and 星 _xīng_ < _*seng_ is less apparent. Karlgren reconstructs these words as _*sian_ (_GSR_ 156d) and _*sieng_ (_GSR_ 812xy) respectively; in Li Fang-kuei's system they would be _*sianh_ and _*sing_ (1982: 56, 70).

had merged in some Hàn dialects; see Coblin 1983: 88-89.) The *Shìmíng*'s entry for 霰 *xiàn* continues: "Ice and snow roll up with each other like stars (**seng*) and scatter (**sans*)."[64] The use of *sàn* 散 in the definition may reflect the graphic similarity of *sàn* 散 and *xiàn* 霰, not necessarily any phonetic similarity (but see note 58).

Summary: The use of 散 *sàn* < *sanh* (*sân-*) < **sans* 'scatter' as phonetic in 霰 *xiàn* < *senh* (*sien-*) < **skens* 'sleet' is probably of late origin, the mixing of **-an* and **-en* in a single phonetic series being influenced by the post-*Shījīng* merger of **-jan* and **-jen* after acute initials. The alternate form 霓, with 見 *jiàn* < **kens* as phonetic, is more representative of Old Chinese phonology, and is probably of earlier origin, but became less suitable after the change **SK-* > *S-*.

3. Conclusion. I stated at the beginning of this paper that we have three main kinds of evidence about Old Chinese phonology: (1) the rhymes of Old Chinese poetry, (2) the phonetic compounds and loan characters of the Chinese script, and (3) the phonological system of Middle Chinese. It is common knowledge that the Chinese script underwent major changes in Qín and Hàn; the example cited in this paper indicate that these changes often reflect phonological changes. Past reconstructions of Old Chinese have largely ignored these changes; the script of Hàn has been taken as evidence for the phonology of Zhōu, and the resulting reconstructions are like a least common denominator of Zhōu and Hàn phonology. The corrective for this situation is to make more use of the other two kinds of evidence (Old Chinese rhymes and Middle Chinese phonology), along with genuine Zhōu inscriptions when they are available. In this way we can begin to sketch a more accurate picture of early Chinese phonological history.

The *Shījīng* as we now have it is a Zhōu text in Hàn clothing: both its script and, to some extent, its text have been influenced by post-*Shījīng* phonology, and are not always reliable guides to the phonology of Old Chinese. Of course, the *Shījīng* text and its script are still indispensable in Old Chinese reconstruction; but they must be used critically and with caution, and checked whenever possible against other evidence. In turn, hypotheses suggested by other kinds of evidence (such as the rounded-vowel hypothesis and the front-vowel hypothesis) may help us to better understand the text of the *Shījīng* and its history.

---

[64] "冰雪相慱 如星而散也 *bīng xuě xiāng tuán, rú xīng ér sàn yě.*" Quoted in Morohashi #42458; my translation.

References

Barnard, Noel. 1978. "The nature of the Ch'in 'Reform of the Script' as reflected in archaeological documents excavated under conditions of control." In *Ancient China: Studies in Early Civilization*, ed. by David T. Roy and Tsuen-hsuin Tsien (Hong Kong: The Chinese University Press), pp. 181–213.

Baxter, William H. III. 1980. "Some proposals on Old Chinese phonology." In *Contributions in Historical Linguistics: Issues and Materials* (*Cornell Linguistic Contributions*, vol. 3), ed. by Frans van Coetsem and Linda R. Waugh (Leiden: E. J. Brill), pp. 1–33.

——. 1985. "Zhōnggŭ Hànyŭ de yìzhŏng shíyòng pīnxiĕfă 中古漢語的一種實用拼寫法." Paper presented at the 1st International Symposium on Teaching Chinese as a Foreign Language, Beijing, August 12–17, 1985.

——. 1986. "New rhyme categories for Old Chinese." Paper presented at the XIXth International Conference on Sino-Tibetan Languages and Linguistics, Columbus, Ohio, September 11–14, 1986.

Bodman, Nicholas C. 1969. "Tibetan *sdud* 'folds of a garment', the character 卒, and the **st-* hypothesis." *Bulletin of the Institute of History and Philology, Academia Sinica* 39: 327–45.

——. 1971. "A phonological interpretation for Old Chinese." Paper read for the Chinese Linguistics Project, Princeton University.

——. 1980. "Proto-Chinese and Sino-Tibetan: data towards establishing the nature of the relationship." In *Contributions in Historical Linguistics: Issues and Materials* (*Cornell Linguistic Contributions*, vol. 3), ed. by Frans van Coetsem and Linda R. Waugh (Leiden: E. J. Brill), pp. 34–199.

Chomsky, Noam, and Morris Halle. 1968. *The Sound Pattern of English*. New York: Harper & Row.

Chou Fa-kao (Zhōu Făgāo) 周法高 *et. al.* 1974. Jīnwén Gŭlín 金文诂林. Hong Kong: Chinese University.

Coblin, W. South. 1978. "The initials of Xu Shen's language as reflected in the *Shuowen* duruo glosses." *Journal of Chinese Linguistics* 6: 27–75.

——. 1983. *A Handbook of Eastern Han Sound Glosses*. Hong Kong: The Chinese University Press.

Dīng Bāngxīn 丁邦新. 1975. *Chinese Phonology of the Wei-Chin Period: Reconstruction of the Finals as Reflected in Poetry*. (IHP Special Publications, 65.) Taipei: Academia Sinica, Institute of History and Philology.

Dīng Fúbǎo 丁福保, ed. 1959. *Shuōwén jiězì gǔlín* 説文解字詁林. Taipei: Shāngwù. [Rpt. of 1928 ed.]

Dǒng Tónghé 董同龢. 1948. "Shànggǔ yīnyùn biǎogǎo 上古音韻表稿." *BIHP* 18: 1–249.

Downer, Gordon B. 1959. "Derivation by tone change in Classical Chinese." *Bulletin of the School of Oriental and African Studies* (University of London) 22: 258–90.

Gāo Míng 高明. 1980. *Gǔ wénzì lèibiān* 古文字類編. Běijīng: Zhōnghuá.

Haudricourt, André-Georges. 1954a. "De l'origine des tons en vietnamien." *Journal Asiatique* 242: 68–82.

——. 1954b. "Comment reconstruire le chinois archaïque." *Word* 10: 351–64.

Ikeda Suetoshi 池天末利. 1964. *Inkyo shokei kōhen shakubun kō* 殷墟書契後編釋文稿. Hiroshima: Literature Department, Hiroshima University.

Jaxontov, Sergej Evgenevič. 1960a. "Fonetika kitajskogo jazyka 1 tysjačeletija do n. e. (labializovannye glasnye)." *Problemy Vostokovedenija* 1960 (6).102–115. [Translation by Jerry Norman: "The phonology of Chinese of the first millenium B.C. (rounded vowels)." *Chi-lin* 6: 52–75 (1970).]

——. 1960b. "Sočetanija soglasnyx v drevnekitajskom jazyke." In *Trudy dvadcat' pjatogo meždunarodnogo kongressa vostokovedov, Moskva, 9–16 Avgusta 1960 g.*, v. 5, pp. 89–95. Moskva: Izdatel'stvo Vostočnoj Literatury, 1963. [Translated as "Consonant combinations in Archaic Chinese" (Moscow: Oriental Literature Publishing House, 1960).]

——. 1965. *Drevnekitajskij jazyk.* (Jazyki narodov Azii i Afriki.) Moscow: Izdatel'stvo 'Nauka'.

Karlgren, Bernhard. 1940. "Grammata Serica: script and phonetic in Chinese and Sino-Japanese." *Bulletin of the Museum of Far Eastern Antiquities* 12: 1–471.

——. 1942–46. "Glosses to the Book of Odes." *Bulletin of the Museum of Far Eastern Antiquities* 14: 71–247 (1942); 16: 25–169 (1944); 18: 11–198 (1946).

——. 1950. *The Book of Odes: Chinese Text, Transcription and Translation.* Stockholm: Museum of Far Eastern Antiquities.

——. 1957. Grammata Serica Recensa. *Bulletin of the Museum of Far Eastern Antiquities* 29: 1–332.

Li Fang-kuei (Lǐ Fānggui) 李方桂. 1971. "Shànggǔ yīn yánjiū 上古音究羅振玉." *Tsinghua Journal of Chinese Studies*, n.s., 9: 1–61.

——. 1982. *Shànggǔ yīn yánjiū* 上古音研究. Běijīng: Shāngwù. [Includes reprint of Li Fang-kuei 1971.]

Lǐ Xiàodìng 李孝定. 1964. *Jiǎgǔ wénzì jí shì* 甲骨文字集釋. 14 vols. Taipei: Academia Sinica.

Lù Démíng 陸德明. 1975. *Jīngdiǎn shìwén* 經典釋文. Taipei: Dǐngwén.

Luó Chángpéi 羅常培. 1931. "*Qièyùn* yú 魚 yú 虞 zhī yīnzhí jí qí suǒ jù fāngyīn kǎo 切韻魚虞之音值及其所據方音考." *Bulletin of the Institute of History and Philology, Academia Sinica* 2: 258–385.

——, and Zhōu Zǔmó 周祖謨. 1958. *Hàn Wèi Jìn Nán-běi cháo yùnbù yǎnbiàn yánjiū* 漢魏晉南北朝韻部演變研究 (vol. 1). Běijīng: Kēxué.

Luó Fúyí 罗福颐. 1979. "Zhōngshān wáng mù dǐng hú míngwén xiǎo kǎo 中山王墓鼎壶铭文小考." *Gùgōng Bówùyuàn Yuànkān* 1979.2: 81–85. [Reprinted in *Jīn shí wén zīliào jí* 金石文资料集 (Collected Articles, E10), Hong Kong: The Sinological Bibliocenter, 1983).]

Luó Zhènyù 羅振玉. 1916. *Yīnxū shūqì hòu biān* 殷墟書契後編. n.p.

Máo Shī zhù shū 毛詩注疏. 1936. Shànghǎi: Shāngwù.

Menzies, James Mellon (Míng Yìshì 明義士). 1917. *Oracle Records from the Waste of Yin (殷墟卜辭 Yīnxū bǔcí)*. [Reprint: Taipei: Yee Wen Publishing Co., 1972.]

Morohashi Tetsuji 諸橋轍次. 1955–1960. *Dai Kan-Wa jiten* 大漢和字典. 13 vols. Tokyo: Taishūkan.

Pulleyblank, Edwin G. 1961–1962. "The consonantal system of Old Chinese." *Asia Major* 9: 58–144, 206–65.

——. 1973a. "Some new hypotheses concerning word families in Chinese." *Journal of Chinese Linguistics* 1: 111–25.

——. 1973b. "Some further evidence regarding Old Chinese *-s* and the time of its disappearance." *Bulletin of the School of Oriental and African Studies* (University of London) 36: 368–73.

——. 1984. *Middle Chinese: a Study in Historical Phonology.* Vancouver: University of British Columbia Press.

Shào Róngfēn 邵荣芬. 1983. "Gǔ yùn Yú 鱼 Hóu 侯 liǎng bù zài qián Hàn shíqī de fēnhé 古韵鱼侯两部在前汉时期的分合." *Zhōngguó Yǔyán Xuébào* 中国语言学报 1: 127–38.

Shima Kunio 島邦男. 1967. *Inkyo bokuji sōrui* 殷墟卜辭綜類. Tokyo: Daian.

Shirakawa Shizuka 白川靜. 1962- . *Kimbun tsūshaku* 金文通釋. Hakutsuru Bijutsukan shi 白鶴美術舘誌.

Shuìhǔdì Qín Mù Zhújiǎn Zhěnglǐ Xiǎozǔ 睡虎地秦墓竹簡整理小组. 1978. *Shuìhǔdì Qín mù zhújiǎn* 睡虎地秦墓竹简. Běijīng: Wénwù.

Xú Zhōngshū 徐中舒, ed. 1980. *Hànyǔ gǔ wénzì zìxíng biǎo* 汉语古文字字形表. Sìchuān Rénmín. [Rpt. Hong Kong: Zhōnghuá, 1981.]

Zhōu Zǔmó 周祖謨. 1966. "Shījīng yùn zì biǎo 詩經韻字表." *Wèn xué jí* 問學集, 218–269. Běijīng: Zhōnghuá.

VOWEL HARMONY LOSS IN URALIC AND ALTAIC

ROBERT I. BINNICK
Scarborough College, The University of Toronto

The Problem of Vowel Harmony Loss. Most Uralic and Altaic languages, including Finnish, Hungarian, Mongolian, and Turkish exhibit what is called palatal vowel harmony.* In palatal vowel harmony vowels are classified into separate sets. Within a given word members of different sets may not co-occur (see Vago 1980b: xi). The harmonic sets consist of front vowels (vowels articulated in the palatal region) such as /i, e, ö, ü/ and back vowels (those in the velar region) such as /ɨ, a, o, u/.[1] Root morphemes generally govern which vowels occur in suffixes. Palatal vowel harmony is a process of assimilation or agreement, and has been called (for example by Anderson (1980: 44)) a type of metaphony.

		Round			
		−		+	
		High		High	
		−	+	−	+
Back	−	e	i	ö	ü
	+	a	ɨ	o	u

It may be useful here to sketch briefly the classical form of palatal vowel harmony as exemplified in Turkish. Standard Turkish has an eight-vowel system, comprising /a, ɨ, o, u, e, i, ö, ü/. This system is totally

* This article was largely written while I was on leave, 1985-86, at the Department of Oriental Languages, University of California at Berkeley. An earlier version was discussed at the Asian Linguistics Colloquium of the Department of Asian Languages and Literature of the University of Washington on April 9, 1986. I would like to thank R. Hahn, J. Norman, H. Schiffman, M. Shapiro, and N. Poppe for their comments and questions.

[1] The feature of backness will further pertain to such consonants as the oral velar stops and the lateral liquids, which also have front and back variants. There is considerable debate as to whether the consonant harmony is the same phenomenon, and can be handled by the same rule, as vowel harmony. See for example Anderson 1974: 210f.

symmetrical, and it may be characterized phonologically in terms of three distinctive features, namely those of height, backness, and rounding.[2]

[2] See Anderson 1974: 210, 1980: 7. Lightner (1965) used the term "gravity" for the phonological feature of backness. Gravity is a feature of both consonants and vowels and in consonants covers segments further forward in the oral cavity than the palatal region as well as those further back. Aoki 1968: 143 gives "gravity harmony" as an alternative name for "palatal harmony." Crothers and Shibatani (1980) use the feature "palatal" (i.e., essentially "front") rather than "back."

There is reason to regard as the marked values in the system the high, back, and round(ed) vowels, and thus as unmarked the non-high (phonetically low), non-back (phonetically front), and non-round (phonetically "flat") vowels.

Greenberg (1966: 13f., 21f.) cites several criteria for markedness of phonological segments, including these: (1) the unmarked segment occurs as the "otherwise," "elsewhere," or unconditioned alternant; (2) in neutralization it is the unmarked member which tends to occur; (3) unmarked segments are of higher frequency than marked ones; (4) the number of segments in a languages which have a marked characteristic (feature) is never greater than the number having the corresponding unmarked characteristic; (5) languages do not have segments (or sequences containing segments) of a marked type unless they also have segments (or sequences containing segments) of the corresponding unmarked type.

In line with his not uncontroversial proposals, evidence for front vowels being unmarked and back ones marked would include: (a) the tendency of /i, e/ to neutrality; (b) the frontness of neutral /i/ in Mongolian, Finnish, Hungarian, etc.; and (c) the preference for back vocalism in prestigious loans in Finnish containing /ü/ (Campbell 1980: 250f.). One indication low (non-high) vowels are unmarked and high vowels marked is that under general conditions /e, a, o/, i.e., low vowels, tend to appear as opposed to high vowels.

Evidence that non-round (flat, unrounded) vowels are unmarked and round vowels marked include the facts that: (a) under general conditions, /e, a, i, ɨ/ tend to appear rather than round vowels, which have more highly restricted environments; (b) there is unconditioned loss of front rounded and back flat vowels, but not unconditioned loss of front flat or back rounded vowels; and (c) /o, ö/ only occur in the first syllable or under assimilation, and occur in highly restricted environments.

This is supported by the figures I have seen for the relative frequency of

The precise formulation of Uralic-Altaic palatal vowel harmony is controversial, as it challenges particular proposals in general theoretical phonology. There have been many different approaches to stating the rule.[3]

However formulated, the palatal vowel harmony rule for Turkish predicts the occurrence of words like *asla* 'never' and *sonlar* 'ends' which contain only [+back] vowels, and words like *nispeten* 'relatively' and *üzüm* 'grapes', which contain only [-back] (front) vowels. It excludes potential words which mix the two, for example **aslen*, **sönlar*, and **uzüm*. This Turkish system is highly ideal, given that in no Uralic or Altaic spoken dialect or written standard language does such a system occur without exception.

In some synharmonic (harmonizing) languages there exist neutral vowels, neutral velar stops or both, which under given circumstances, can occur in both back-vocalic and front-vocalic words. There also occur invariable suffixes which do not obey vowel harmony. This is the situation in standard modern Turkish. In other languages palatal vowel harmony is entirely or for the most part lost, or at least fossilized and non-productive. For those languages it is impossible to identify harmonic sets of vowels. In a sense, all vowels are neutral with respect to vowel harmony. Affixes either do not alternate, or do so only sporadically. Very few Altaic dialects have reached this stage.[4] Many more Uralic ones (e.g., northern and standard Estonian, and Lapp) have.

Scholars have often attributed this weakening or loss to foreign influence. Thus Räsänen, in discussing exceptions in Turkic, writes (1949:104f.) that the stronger the foreign influence to which Turkic languages have been subjected, the more they violate vowel harmony, to the point where in Iranized Uzbek dialects (quoting S. Wurm) "the vowel-harmony is almost entirely destroyed." At the same time he notes that without having to assume foreign influence, we encounter in many Turkic languages unvocalharmonic forms. Similarly, Gabain (1952: 107) is critical of the assumption of Slavic and Iranian influence in the loss of vowel harmony in Turkic, ar-

---

various vowels in Finnish (Hakulainen 1961: 5): o—10%, u—10%, ö—1%, ü—3%; and as percentages of all sounds in Hungarian (Kálmán 1972: 77): o—4.19%, ö—1.14%, u—0.85%, ü—0.42%, ó—1.12%, ő—0.75%, ú—0.45%, ű—0.07%. Greenberg (1966: 18f.) gives roughly comparable figures.

[3] Vago (1973, 1976, 1980b) has set out the major issues well.

[4] Examples are the Mongolian language Monguor, certain dialects of the Turkic language Uzbek, and the Tungusic language Sibe (which is closely related to classical Manchu).

guing that substratal influence remains to be proved, and does not explain similar effects in cases where no foreign influence is apparent.

Even if one accepts the proposition that vowel harmony loss can be explained by foreign influence, one would still wish to know what the mechanisms of such a massive, systematic change might be. Knowledge of those factors that initiate these phonological changes does not in and of itself provide an understanding of the diachronic processes involved. Nor does it explain the difference between dialects which under foreign influence have substantially or totally lost harmony and those which under similar influences have not. It remains an interesting question to what extent this historical process can be attributed to factors external to the languages in question, as opposed to those within the system of harmonization itself. This is particularly true where foreign influence is weak or non-existent.

It would be possible to describe the historical process of vowel harmony weakening and loss as consisting of the proliferation of exceptions—disharmonic stems (such as Turkish *elma* 'apple'), invariable affixes (like Khalkha *-güj* 'without, not'), and neutral vowels (/i, e/ in many languages)—and certainly this process is associated with such a proliferation. At the same time such an approach assumes that harmony is inherently stable and that it changes only under specific, contingent conditions that induce such developments.

Alternatively, it may be the case that vowel harmony is inherently unstable and that vowel harmony loss is an example of the tendency of related, structurally similar languages to undergo similar changes over time in a relatively fixed sequence. While foreign influence may accelerate or even trigger certain changes, it does not dictate the nature or sequence of such changes. This is the view that will be explored and supported here. Language-internal developments of a relatively predictable, non-contingent sort play the dominant role in the weakening and ultimate loss of vowel harmony.

Exceptionality and Disharmony in Palatal Vowel Harmony Systems

1. Disharmonic Loan Words. In many Uralic and Altaic languages numerous foreign borrowings violate vowel harmony by mixing front and back vowels. Examples of this include: Turkish *mikrop* 'microbe' (< French) and *beyan* 'declaration' (< Arabic) (Lewis 1975: 17); Mongolian *farmačevt* 'pharmacist' and *professor* 'professor' (both < Russian) (Lessing 1973: 338, 649); Hungarian *sofőr* 'chauffeur' and *amőbá* 'amoeba' (Ringen 1980: 138); Finnish *akronyymi* 'acronym', *etymologia* 'etymology', *flygata* 'to fly' (<

Swedish *flyga*), *hieroglyfi* 'hieroglyph' and *jonglööri* 'juggler' (< French *jongleur*).

The vocalism of totally unassimilated recent loans, such as *baby* [beibi], *copyright* [kopirait], and *design* [disain] in Finnish (Campbell 1980: 249, 253), vacillate, taking indifferently a front or back form, without regard to the vowels in the stems. Vacillation of vowels is also found in Hungarian. Vago (1980a: 157) refers to vacillating stems such as *Ágnes*: cf. *Ágnes-nak/Ágnes-nek* 'to Agnes'. Other Hungarian examples, from Ringen (1980: 140), include *dzsungel* 'jungle' (*dzsungelben/dzsungelban* 'in the jungle'), and *analízis* 'analysis' (*analízisnek/analízisnak*).

Most borrowed forms, by contrast, take perfectly normal suffixation, as determined by the last vowel of the stem.[5] Thus there is little, if any, systematic impact of such irregularities. Moreover, foreign borrowings in Turkish, as well as in other languages, do not invariably remain in conflict with vowel harmony. There is a tendency for such forms to change in order to come into conformity with it, e.g., Turkish *madalya* 'medal' < Italian *medaglia* (Lewis 1975: 17); Finnish *olympialaiset* 'Olympic games' has the variants *olump(p)ialaiset* and *ölympiäläiset* (Campbell 1980: 246).

2. Disharmony in Native Morphemes. Loan words complicate vowel harmony by introducing disharmonic stems and, as in prestigious borrowings in Finnish, by introducing new neutral vowels (/ü/ in this case). However, very similar disharmonic effects are already to be found in compound native forms in many Uralic and Altaic languages, e.g., Turkish *bugün* 'today' (= *bu* 'this' + *gün* 'day'). Such forms generally conform to vowel harmony constraints in suffixation. Compare the compound names of Tibetan origin in Mongolian; e.g., *Tserendulmaa* (Street 1963: 68).

In many languages there are invariable suffixes, such as the Turkish present-tense marker *-yor* (Lewis 1975: 17, 107), the Hungarian suffix *-kor*

[5] Lewis (1975: 19-20) points out numerous exception to this in Turkish, in which foreign borrowings, even some of which obey palatal harmony within the root or stem, take exceptional suffixation. Such examples are generally predictable. For example, words of Arabic or French origin ending in *l* are treated as front-vocalic (e.g., *rol* 'role': accusative *rolü*, not **rolu*). In many cases such irregular forms are being regularized. Lewis predicts (20) that while "some elderly people still give *sanat* ['art', < Arabic]...front-vocalic suffixes[,] for a young person to do so would be regarded as affectation, and it is a fairly safe prediction that *rolü*, *idraki*, *harbi*, and so on will one day yield to *rolu*, *idrakı*, *harbı*, first in vulgar speech, then in educated speech, and finally in writing."

(*hatkor* 'at six', *ötkor* 'at five') (Vago 1980a: 172), and the Khalkha negator *-güj* 'not, without' (*javsangüj* 'didn't go, without going', *ögsöngüj* 'didn't give, without giving') (Street 1963: 10). However we might wish to treat these in phonology, they pose no systematic challenge to harmony, since they do not function to block or modify the operation of the rule outside of their own syllable(s). For example, the instrumental suffix of Khalkha would be the expected *-gaar* with *javsangüj* (*javsangüjgaar* 'by not going') and the expected *-göör* with *ögsöngüj* (*ögsöngüjgöör* 'by not giving').

The system as a whole remains productive, these exceptions do not significantly weaken it, and in most Turkic languages vowel harmony is in no apparent danger of disappearing.[6]

3. The Proliferation of Neutral Vowels. The decay of vowel harmony has been closely associated with the proliferation of neutral vowels in many languages in which palatal vowel harmony is essentially productive and generally regular, for example Turkish. In many languages /i/ and /e/ are such neutral vowels, and appear so often and under so many conditions in back-vocalic stems that scholars have simply been forced to treat them as exceptional.

In languages in which palatal vowel harmony has been rendered partially non-productive, such neutral segments abound. These are typically engendered by the coalescence of corresponding front and back vocalic phonemes, e.g., /i/ with /ɨ/, /ü/ with /u/, /ö/ with /o/, and the like. This is a phenomenon of markedness, the neutral vowels *par excellence* being /i/ and /e/, which are, from the point of view of the Turkish system set out above, relatively unmarked; indeed, /e/ is the most highly unmarked vowel, being non-high, non-back, and non-round. It is generally accepted that "historical changes are from the marked to the unmarked"; consequently "it is easy to see why the neutral vowels are among the least marked" (Aoki 1968: 145).

A number of changes in synharmonic languages resulting in the neutralization of segments can be seen as markedness effects, for it is a universal phenomenon that front vowels tend to be unrounded while rounded vowels tend to be back. Thus /i/ is less marked than /ɨ/ and/o/ and /u/ are

[6] In Turkish, as in most vowel-harmonizing (synharmonic) languages there exist some exceptions to vowel harmony, of native origin or older loans, such as Turkish *dahi* 'also' or *elma* 'apple'. Many of these represent unassimilated loans or the remnants of no longer productive phonological processes. This is evidently the case of *elma* 'apple', which < **alima*. See Sevortjan 1974: 138.

less marked than /ö/ and /ü/. (See fn. 2.) This universal tendency to reduce such characteristically marked vowels to the respective unmarked ones clearly applies within the Uralic and Altaic languages. But the consequence of this is a tendency for certain vowels to be rendered neutral.

3.1. Fronting of /ɨ/ to /i/. A pervasive change in Altaic is the fronting of the [+back] segment /ɨ/ (that is, a high back unrounded vowel) to /i/. This vowel is generally preserved in Altaic only in the Turkic sub-family, but even there, in East Turki, no /ɨ/ has survived, and /i/ from older /ɨ/ has secondarily fronted a preceding **a* to *e*, e.g., East Turki *eliš* 'the taking' from *al-* 'to take' (Poppe 1965: 182).

The same change of /ɨ/ to /i/ is quite general in Mongolian and Tungusic. No attested Mongolian language shows any residue of the old phoneme /ɨ/ outside of the collocations /qɨ/ and /ɣɨ/: Moghol, Middle Mongolian *qɨlɣasun* 'hair, horsehair' = Middle Mongolian (*Secret History*) and Classical *kilɣasun* (Poppe 1955: 33, 133).

In the vast majority of Mongolian languages /ɨ/ has been lost and /i/ is a neutral vowel, cf. written Khalkha *morior* 'by horse', *amžilttajgaar* 'successfully' (Street 1963: 218f.).[7] Thus in Classical Mongolian we find both forms like *dakin* 'again' and those like *tegši* 'level'. In Tungusic, according to Poppe (1965: 203), the same development has taken place; Mongol *čiqul* 'anger' corresponds to Evenki *tikul-* 'to become angry'. It was these facts that prompted Lightner (1965) and others in their synchronic analyses of Classical Mongolian to posit an underlying eight vowel system identical to that of Turkish, with the opposition of /ɨ/ and /i/ being neutralized by a transformational rule. This abstract solution considerably simplified the statement of the vowel harmony rule by eliminating the need to posit neutral vowels in Mongolian palatal vowel harmony. Similarly, Vago (1973: 583ff.) and Odden (1978: 62) assumed an underlying seven vowel system for Manchu with absolute neutralization of back /ɨ/ → /i/ and front /ü/ → /u/.[8]

Ringen (1980: 173f.) discusses, and rejects, arguments by Vago (1973, 1980d) and Jensen (1972, 1978) for a similar abstract treatment of Hungarian /i/ in *híd* 'bridge' and such examples of neutral stems which nonetheless

[7] /i/ in the first syllable is generally front-vocalic.

[8] Ard (1981, 1984) argues that harmony in Proto-Tungusic and Manchu was not one of backness but rather of tenseness or tongue-root retraction (height harmony). Consequently, many of the details of the development of Tungusic vowel harmony are regarded as controversial.

take back vocalic affixation. Vago (1980a: 176, 1980d: 10) offers historical support for his synchronic analysis, reporting that such vowels historically come from back /ɨ/.[9] Presumably one could argue for an abstract solution to the neutral vowel problem in Finnish as well. Campbell (1980: 255) similarly reports that some, although perhaps not most, scholars believe that Proto-Finnic had no neutral vowels, present-day /i/ and /e/ partly reflecting earlier back /i̯/ and /e̯/. (See 254f., and Hakulainen 1961: 20f., for a contradictory view.)

The problem here is that some scholars attempt to explain apparent anomolies in the synchronic analysis of vowel harmony by making recourse to historical phenomena. This practice can lead to a circularity in that in some cases (e.g., that of Finnish) the major support for an historically underlying /i̯/ and /e̯/ is precisely the neutrality of/i/ or /e/ in the modern languages. That there is strong historical evidence for the reality of earlier /ɨ/ in the Mongolian languages, for example, does not necessarily apply generally to other language groups (e.g., Uralic).[10]

3.2. Elimination of Front Rounded Vowels. Another very common change is the elimination of the distinction between rounded and unrounded vowels. In the Tungusic languages, according to Poppe (1965) /ö/ has generally become /u/ (through /ü/?); at the same time /ü/ has generally become /i/, the net result being the elimination of front rounded vowels. Thus we have the following cognate sets (from Poppe 1965: 203): Classical Mongolian (Cl. Mo.) *ögede* 'up', Evenki *ugile* 'above'; Cl. Mo. *kötel* 'mountain pass', Lamut *kuter-* 'climb upwards'; Cl. Mo. *örö* 'aorta', Evenki *ur* 'stomach'; Cl. Mo. *ürgü-* 'be frightened', Manchu *fuče-* 'be angry', Ulcha *puču-* 'jump up'; Cl. Mo. *ǰüge-* 'transport', Evenki *ǰugū-* 'transport on sleighs'.

Similar changes are seen as well in Mongolian languages, namely Monguor and a number of other southwestern Mongolian dialects: Cl. Mo. *ödün* 'feather', Monguor (Mgr.) *fōdi*, San-chuan (Sa.) *xotu*, Dunghsiang (Du.), Baoan (Ba.) *xodun*; Cl. Mo. *söni* 'night', Mgr., Sa. *soni*; Cl. Mo. *köl* 'foot', Mgr. *kuor*, Sa. *kor*, Du. *kuan*, Ba. *kul*; Cl. Mo. *törö-* 'be born', Mgr. *turo-*; Cl. Mo. *üge* 'word', Mgr. *uge*, Sa. *ugi*; Cl. Mo. *ükü-* 'die',

[9] Kálmán (1972: 62f.) discusses this change and notes the back vocalism of the modern reflexes of old **ɨ*, e.g., *ír* 'he writes': *írok* 'I am writing'.

[10] Collinder (1960, 1965) argues for **i̯*, **e̯* (his **y*, **õ*) in Proto-Uralic, although "**y* seems to have been of rare occurrence" (1965: 97), and he knows of no reflex in, e.g., Hungarian. Steinitz (1964) proposes **i̯*, but not **e̯*, in Proto-Finno-Ugric.

Mgr. *fugu-*, Sa. *uxu-*, Du. *fugu-*, Ba. *hgude-*; Cl. Mo. *büri-* 'cover', Mgr. *buri-* 'make a cover of leather for a drum'; and Cl. Mo. *ünijen* 'cow', Mgr. *unie* (Poppe 1955: 49ff.; Todaeva 1973: 340, 360, 368, 370).

Loss of front rounding is also reported by Räsänen (1949: 94, 96) for Turkic: Chuvash *kos'* 'eye' (cf. Turkmen *göz*), *kor-* 'see' (cf. *gör-*), *kon-* 'become straight' (cf. *göni-*); East Turki *kop* 'much' < **köp*; Konja Giese Osman *donüp* < *dönüp*; Halič and Lutsk Karaim *egiz* 'ox' < *öküz*, *kez* 'eye' < *köz*; Uzbek *tun* 'night' < **tün*; Halič and Lutsk Karaim *ic* 'three' < **üc*.

Similarly, Vago (1973: 582f.) reports neutralization of *u*, *ü*, and of *o*, *ö* in the Turkish dialect of Vadin on the Danube, as a result of which some stems act as front-vocalic while yet others with the same vowel act as back-vocalic: *buz-da* 'ice (locative)', *oq-ta* 'arrow (locative)', *uş-te* 'three (locative)', *dort-te* 'four (locative)'. He further notes that /k, g, l/ usually become palatalized in the environment of /u/ < /*ü/, but not in that of /u/ < /*u/.

In Uralic too **ü* tends either to unround to /i/ or /e/ or to retract to /u/ or /o/. It is preserved only sporadically outside of Finnish and related Finnic languages and is found as /ö/ in Hungarian (Collinder 1960: 180ff., 1965: 100, 136ff.): Finnish (Fi.) *tyvi* 'butt, base', Hungarian (Hu.) *tő*, Votyak *diń*, Ziryene *din*; Hu. *köd* 'fog, haze', Tavgi Samoyed *kinta* 'smoke'; Fi. *syksi* 'autumn', eastern Cheremis *šižə*; Fi. *yla-* 'over-', Ostyak *elti* 'off, from'; Fi. *nysi* 'handle', Vogul *nɛl*; Fi. *tyma* 'glue', Ziryene, Votyak *l'em*; Fi. *yksi* 'one', Mordvin *vejke*, Votyak *og*; Fi. *syli* 'bosom', Hu. *öl*, Votyak *sul*; Fi. *pyy* 'woodgrouse', Mordvin *povo*, Lule Lapp *boggoi*.

3.3. Umlauting. The shift in value of vowels from marked to unmarked is not the only force that has tended to weaken vowel harmony by creating neutral segments. Another general tendency leading to neutralized contrasts is the assimilation of back vowels to front in the environment of front vocalic segments, usually /i/ or /j/. The result phonetically, if not always phonemically, is usually a partially umlauted vowel, i.e., centralized, or a fully umlauted one, i.e., fronted. Anderson (1980: 3-4) reports that in Modern Uighur /a/ and /ä/ are raised and fronted to [e] in initial unstressed syllables when the following syllable contains /i/: thus, /al+in+mAq/ is realized as *elinmaq* 'to be taken'. Likewise Räsänen (1949: 78ff.) and Tenišev (1984: 82) report many cases of umlaut (palatalisierender Umlaut, *i*-Umlaut) in the Turkic languages: for example, *a* > *e* (Taranchi East Turki *elip*, gerund of *al-* 'take'); *a* > ɛ (Chuvash *sɛjrɛn* ~*sajran* 'appropriate to'; Osman *ɛlma* 'apple' < ? Mongol *alima*); *a* > *ä* (Kazakh *bäri* 'all' < **bar-i*).

Such cases are extremely common in the Mongolian languages. Generally /a o u/ → /ä ö ü/ in Kalmuck (and /o/ to /ö/ in Chakhar), and to central (fronted) varieties in Dagur, Khalkha, Buriat, and other central dialects, before /i/ in the following syllable (Poppe 1955: 26, 28, 31f.): Cl. Mo. *bari-* 'seize', Dagur, Buriat *bári-*, Kalmuck (Klm.) *bär-*; Cl. Mo. *morin* 'horse', Chakhar *möri*, Ordos *mȯri*; Cl. Mo. *qurim* 'wedding party', Klm. *χürm̥*.

In both Mongolian and Turkic such changes generally do not result in neutral vowels. Rather, such phonetically disharmonic segments function phonologically in a regularly harmonic way. In both Buriat and Kalmuck certain dialects reduce diphthongs historically of the form Bi (< Cl. Mo. B*ji*; B = a back vowel, except in Kalmuck where it equals only /a/ or /o/, because Kalmuck /u/ generally remains) to long front "umlaut" vowels: Cl. Mo. *sajin* 'good', Alar Buriat (AB) *hā̈*^{i}*n̲*, Ordos, Kalmuck (Klm.) *sā̈n*; Cl. Mo. *dalai* 'sea', AB, Dörbet Klm. *dalā̈*; Cl. Mo. *oi* 'forest', AB *ȫ*^{i}, Klm. *ȫ* (Poppe 1955: 77, 79). In both languages vowels that at the phonetic level are front monophthongs, but which derive historically from diphthongs, function at the phonological level as back segments (Poppe 1955: 91f.): AB *bā̈*^{i}*γāt* 'having stood' < **baji-*; Dörbet Klm. *ȫγur* 'nearby' < *ör*^{ö} 'near'.[11] In languages in which harmony is moribund such fronted vowels are neutral. Ard (1984: 72), using examples of S. Kałużyński, notes in Sibe assimilatory processes leading to new, fronted vowels: Sibe *ämäs*, Manchu *amasi* 'backwards'; Sibe *dövir'*, Manchu *dobori* 'night'; Sibe *fönǯi-*, Manchu *fonǯi-* 'question'; Sibe *tüč-*, Manchu *tuči* 'come out'.

The fronted monophthongs that have arisen through this process in Kalmuck may induce a secondary fronting of the succeeding vowel: *ȫrd*^{ö}*χə* < *ȫrd*^{ᴅ}*χᴅ* 'to approach' < **ojirad-* (Ramstedt 1935: 305). Similarly the fronting of *a* to *ä* because of a palatal glide *y* may induce in Kirghiz a secondary fronting of *ı* to *i*: *kılbäymin* ~ *kılbäymın* 'I do not make' (Johnson 1980: 97, using data of S. Wurm). Compare Taranchi East Turki *elip*, gerund of *al-*, 'take' (Räsänen 1949: 78). Similar changes are seen in

---

[11] Not all monophthongized diphthongs of the type F: < B*i* are phonologically back. While none is front, some are neutral. Thus AB *ǖ*^{i} < both *ui* and *üi*, e.g., *ǖ*^{i}*lāt* 'having weeped' < **ui-*, but *ǖ*^{i}*lēr* 'by needlework' < **üi-*; Moghol *εi̯*, Monguor *ę̄* < *ai*, *ei*, e.g., Cl. Mo. *arbai*, Moghol *arfεi̯*, Mgr. *ṣbę̄*, Cl. Mo. *isegei* 'felt', Moghol *sisgεi̯*, Mgr. *ṣgę̄* (Poppe 1955: 91-92). Notice that in an abstract treatment the underlying vowels /ui/, /üi/, /ai/, and /ei/ are *not* neutral in these cases.

western Kazakh *ajel* < *ajal* 'woman'; Azerbaijan *öjnämax* 'to play' (Tenišev 1984: 67, 69).

3.4. Schwaification. Norman (1974: 163) noted that in Sibe "when unstressed, the vowels /i/, /u/, and /ə/ are drastically reduced, especially in final position" where they are realized as consonant modifiers. Norman further notes that "in other positions they are reduced but generally retain their syllabicity."

In the Mongolian languages it is generally the case that short unstressed vowels are reduced. Because the first syllable is normally stressed, unless long vowels occur in the word, the effect of this reduction is felt commonly in non-first syllables, and is stronger the further removed the unstressed syllable is from the stressed. This stress reduction can be characterized in terms of a gradual lessening of syllabicity. What was originally a full schwa with vowel coloration has reflexes in such secondary consonantal articulations as palatization or labialization.

These effects are most pronounced in languages like Khalkha (Kh.) and Kalmuck, with strong initial stress, in both of which short unstressed non-initial syllables tend to be reduced in the ways indicated above. In Kalmuck final syllables tend to be lost (Poppe 1951, 1955). Thus Classical Mongolian *naran* 'sun' is Kh. [nɑrɒ], Klm. [nɑrn̥]; *ene* 'this' is Kh., Klm. [enə]; *öndör* 'high' is Kh. [ʊ̈nDᴖr], Klm. [öndr̥]; *bari-* 'seize' is Kh. [barɪ̣], Klm. [bär]; *boro* 'grey' (Middle Mongolian—Muqaddimat al-Adab—*bora*) is Kh. [borɒ], Klm. [bor^{o}], where [ə, ɪ̣, ᴖ, ɒ] are reduced vowels. Ramstedt (1935: xii) offers the Kalmuck alternates [köd^{ü}lm^{ö}š] ~[ködḷm^{i}š] ~ [ködl̥mš̥] 'work'; Poppe (1951: 18) has Khalkha *surgūl^{i}ār* ~*surgūl´ār* 'by, through school'.

In Mongolian languages such as Monguor with end stress, there is a tendency to lose initial syllables. Thus Mgr. *dali* 'like, similar' : Cl. Mo. *adali* (Todaeva 1973: 327); Mgr. *dur* 'day' : Middle Mongolian *ödür*, Cl. Mo. *edür*, Sa. *udur*, Ba. *uder*, Du. *udu* (331f.); Mgr. *(r)džige* 'donkey : Cl. Mo. *elǰige*, Du. *endzege*, Ba. *ndzige* (333); Mgr. *jaga* 'cup' : Cl. Mo. *ayaγa*; Du., Ba. *jiga* (336); Mgr. *nde* 'here' : Cl. Mo. *ende* (349); Mgr. *nt(er)a-* 'sleep' : Cl. Mo. *unt(ar)a-* (352); Mgr. *re-* 'come' : Cl. Mo. *ire-*, Ba. *re-* (356).[12]

[12] Such languages still retain evidence of earlier stages in which they had initial stress: Mgr. *dabse* 'salt'; Cl. Mo. *dabusun*, Moghol *dabsun*, Du. *dansun*, Ba. *dabsoŋ* (Todaeva 1973: 326); Mgr., Ba. *dogloŋ* 'limping':

In some Mongolian languages with inital stress similar effects can be seen when a long vowel causes stress to shift to a non-initial syllable. Thus in Buriat dialects we have: Kachug *taarxaxa*: Literary Buriat *ataarxaxa* 'to envy'; Barguzin *n'een*: Literary Buriat *ün'een* 'cow'; Barguzin *nebšaa*: Literary Buriat *nege bišīxan* 'a bit' (Rassadin 1982: 27f.).

Schwas are purely neutral with regard to vowel harmony. Some scholars have gone so far as to propose phonemicizations in which schwa is a separate, neutral vowel phoneme (for example Street 1962; see also Krueger 1961).

Vowel reduction in Altaic occurs not only in Tungusic and Mongolian, but also in Turkic. The occurrence of schwa-like vowels is noteworthy, for example, in Chuvash. Krueger (1961: 71) writes that:

> The back, low, rounded vowel...is always reduced, and can occur stressed only in the first syllable of a polysyllabic word.... It is fleetingly pronounced, and sometimes so reduced as to sound almost coalesced with the following consonant as in /kăvak/ 'blue', almost > [kvak]... This vowel is an unstable one and drops easily at the end of words, or in compounds, e.g., *tăvat(ă) ura* 'four feet'.

Of the front counterpart, he writes (72) that:

> It too occurs only reduced, and may be stressed only in the first syllable.... It may also virtually disappear between consonants.... It is fleetingly pro-

---

Cl. Mo. *doɣolang* (330). There are numerous Monguor forms with syncope of the middle syllable. That this reflects a period in which initial stress induced vowel loss rather than a period in which end-stress did so is demonstrated by (1) evidence for weakening of the second syllable in disyllabic forms: Mgr. *t'š'iäse̯* (where [e̯] is a mid-central, schwa-like vowel) 'snow': Cl. Mo. *časun* (Poppe 1955: 27); Mgr. *mōdi* 'wood': Cl. Mo. *modun*, Du. *mutun*, Ba. *muto* (Todaeva 1973: 345); (2) the lengthening of /a/ in the initial syllable before /u/ in the second syllable: Mgr. *dālī* 'shoulder': Cl. Mo. *daru-* 'scapula'; Mgr. *dāri-* 'press' (Poppe 1955: 26); (3) rounding assimilation in forms such as Mgr. *sgō-* 'scold': Cl. Mo. *söge-*; Mgr. *murōn* 'river': Cl. Mo. *moren*; Mgr. *gudoli-* 'move': Cl. Mo. *ködel-* (Todaeva 1973: 15, 19, 23); and (4) unrounding in the second syllable in a form like Mgr. *se* : Cl. Mo. *usun* 'water' (Todaeva 1964: 8,9), which could only result under initial, but not final, stress.

nounced, and like /ă/ is unstable in compounds and at the end of words.

The Chuvash schwa can be lost also in the first syllable (Räsänen 1949: 53f.).[13] In Uralic schwaification seems to occur rarely, although apocope is quite common.[14]

3.5. Other Conditioned Changes. Word-final vowels are often vulnerable to changes. In Kalmuck long close vowels in this position tend to open: *irnε̄* ~ *irnǟ* 'comes', Dörbet *būdǟ* ~ *būd'ǟ* ~ *būd'ā* ~ *bǖd'ǟ* ~ *bǖdǟ* ~ (Ölöt) *būdǟ* (Ramstedt 1935: xii). Something similar is seen in the final syllables of Chuvash, especially open final syllables. See Räsänen 1949: 105.

Consonants may have an impact on vowel quality as well. In Kalmuck, velars condition the opening of vowels, especially ε̄ and *ǟ*: *sǟɣār* 'well', *sǟnǟr* 'well'; *temε̄gε̄r* ~ *temε̄ɣε̄r* ~ *temε̄ɣǟr* ~ *temεɣār* 'by camel' (Ramstedt 1935: xiii). The consequence of this opening of vowels when taken in conjunction with the changes suffered by word-final vowels, and with schwaification, is that in some dialects almost all non-initial vowels have disharmonic free variants.

---

[13] While schwaification does occur in other Turkic languages, it apparently is nowhere as advanced as in Chuvash. What is found is vowel loss, i.e., apocope, syncope, etc. While loss of the vowel of the first syllable occurs both in Chuvash (Räsänen 1949: 44f., 53f.) and in other Turkic languages, syncope and apocope are most frequent, as we would expect, in languages with dynamic stress on the first syllable, and Räsänen notes that already in the Runic inscriptions such loss is to be observed, e.g., *oɣ(u)li*, 3rd pers. of 'son'. He cites such examples as Osman *hepsi* 'all of them' < *hepisi*; Taranchi *kiškä* 'to the person' < *kišikä*; Karakirghiz *emki* 'present' < *emiki*. Apocope is expecially common in the formation of compounds, as in Soyon Karakirghiz *karat* 'black horse' < *kara at* and Osman *ne üčün* 'why' > *ničün*.

[14] In Uralic loss of the vowel of the second syllable is quite common with only Finnish and other Finnic languages generally preserving all vowels (Collinder 1960, 1965): Finnish *kala* 'fish', Mordvin *kal*, Cheremis *kol*, Ostyak *kul*, Hungarian *hal*; Finnish *käsi*, *käte-*, 'hand', Mordvin *ked'*, Cheremis *kit*, Votyak, Ziryene *ki*, Vogul *käät*, Ostyak *köt*, Hungarian *kéz*; Finnish *silmä* 'eye', Ziryene *śin*, Vogul *šäm*, Ostyak *sem*, Hungarian *szëm*; Finnish *suoni* 'sinew, tendon', Mordvin *san*, Cheremis *šün*, Votyak *son*, Ziryene *sõn*, Hungarian *ín*, Kamassian *ten*.

Cues for Harmony

We need not have recourse to foreign influence in order to explain the weakening and loss of palatal vowel harmony in Uralic and Altaic languages. Such developments are inherent in systems chaacterized by agglutinative suffixation and root stress, given universal tendencies towards weakening of unstressed vowels, umlauting, and replacement of marked segments by their relatively unmarked counterparts.

As we have seen, a number of phenomena lead to initial syllables that are either neutral or disharmonic relative to the root as a whole. In general such roots do not induce harmonic loss or changes in affixes, since sufficient information in preserved in non-initial vowels to guide the process of harmony. Even when the root is originally monosyllabic (e.g., Hungarian *híd* 'bridge') or monosyllabic through monophthongization or through vowel loss (e.g., AB *hā̈ⁱn* 'good'), or all vowels have been rendered either neutral or disharmonic relative to their etymological harmony (e.g., Da. *bári-* 'seize'; Klm. *χöwị* 'part', cf. Cl. Mo. *qubi*; Klm. *χüwl̥-* 'change appearance', cf. *qubil-*), we must assume no fundamental, underlying change in the harmonic nature of the root in those cases in which affixal harmony continues to operate (cf. AB *bā̈ⁱγāt* 'having been', *ṻⁱlāt* 'having slept' *ṻⁱlēr* 'by needlework').

So long as such derived forms of a root show harmony a root is unlikely to change its underlying harmony. We may compare here the case of Yiddish *avek* 'away'. At one time Yiddish had the same terminal devoicing rule as German; *avek* was {a + veg} (cf. English *a* + *way*). But by the time Yiddish lost this rule, *avek* had been semantically isolated from 'way' and retained the final [k]; hence it now has /k/, not /g/.

Given that such semantic isolation is not in question here, and that these agglutinative languages retain numerous derived stems for each root, how can roots ever change their underlying representatins to neutral or etymologically disharmonic ones? The crucial factor seems to be the phonetic alternation of vowels. We will examine here by way of illustration the case of Kalmuck.

Kalmuck shares the Mongolian **ï > i* change and readily umlauts and monophthongizes. This would be insufficient to disturb affixal vowel harmony were it not for the strong, initial stress of Kalmuck and concomitant loss or weakening of almost all non-initial short vowels. Even so, Kalmuck preserves the distinction of velars (*k*:*x* < *q*; *g*:*g̹*, γ), and it distinguishes according to Ramstedt ɒ (back) and ə (front) as reduced vowels. The problem is that phonetic processes in Kalmuck, have, as we have seen, very nearly obliterated all other distinctions in non-initial syllables, and in some cases even in initial ones. Consequently, even when etymologically harmonic vowels occur in non-initial syllables, these developments have essentially rendered them neutral. Vowel harmony in the Kalmuck language as described by Ramstedt (1935) is only a tendency. In this transitional stage the literary language and the more conservative dialects preserve enough of the distinctions that phonetic effects do not induce underlying phonemic change. But it seems harmony is moribund in Kalmuck, as the surface phonetics of more innovative dialects provide no evidence of differing harmonic vowel sets. Any predictions one can make of the shape of any non-initial vowel depend as much on the consonantism as the vocalism.

Quite natural processes that produce in languages of the Uralic and Altaic type phonetically disharmonic vowels tend over time to induce phonological disharmony through the elimination of cues necessary for the maintenance of the system. It is by predictable language-internal processes, rather than by the contingent accumulation of disharmonic forms or segments, that we can best account for vowel harmony loss, and we may speculate that even those languages furthest removed from foreign influence will eventually lose palatal harmony.

References

Anderson, Stephen R. 1974. *The Organization of Phonology.* New York: Academic Press.

——. 1980. "Problems and Perspectives in the Description of vowel harmony. In Vago 1980c, pp. 1–48.

Aoki, Haruo. 1968. "Toward a typology of vowel harmony." *International Journal of American Linguistics* 34: 142–45.

Ard, Josh. 1981. " A sketch of vowel harmony in the Tungus languages." In *Studies in the Languages of the USSR*, ed. by Bernard Comrie (Edmonton, Alta.: Linguistic Research), pp. 23–42.

——. 1984. "Vowel harmony in Manchu: a critical overview." *Journal of Linguistics* 20: 57–80.

Campbell, Lyle. 1980. "The psychological and sociological reality of Finnish vowel harmony." In Vago 1980c, pp. 245–70.

Cerkasskij, M.A. 1965. *Tjurskij vokalizm i singarmonizm.* Moscow: Nauka.

Collinder, Björn. 1960. *Comparative Grammar of the Uralic Languages.* Stockholm: Almqvist and Wiksell.

——. 1965. *An Introduction to the Uralic Languages.* Berkeley and Los Angeles: University of California Press.

Crothers, John, and Masayoshi Shibatani. 1980. "Issues in the description of Turkish vowel harmony." In Vago 1980c, pp. 63–80.

Gabain, Annemarie von. 1952. "Zur Geschichte der türkischen Vokalharmonie." *Ural-Altaische Jahrbücher* 24: 105–111.

Greenberg, Joseph. 1966. *Language Universals.* The Hague: Mouton.

Hakulainen, Lauri. 1961. *The Structure and Development of the Finnish Language.* (Uralic and Altaic series, 3.) Bloomington: Indiana University.

Jensen, John. 1972. "Hungarian phonology and constraints on phonological theory." Unpublished McGill University Ph.D dissertation.

——. 1978. "Reply to 'Theoretical implications of Hungarian vowel harmony'." *Linguistic Inquiry* 9: 89–97.

Johnson, C. Douglas. 1980. "Regular disharmony in Kirghiz." In Vago 1980c, pp. 89–99.

Kálmán, Béla. 1972. "Hungarian historical phonology." In *The Hungarian Language*, ed. by L. Benko and S. Imre (The Hague: Mouton), pp. 49–83.

Krueger, John R. 1961. *Chuvash Manual.* (Uralic and Altaic series, 7). Bloomington: Indiana University.

Lessing, Ferdinand D. (gen. ed.) 1973. *Mongolian-English Dictionary.* Bloomington: The Mongolia Society. [Corrected reprinting, with a new supplement, of the 1960 edition, Berkeley: University of California.]

Lewis, G.L. 1975. *Turkish Grammar.* Oxford: Oxford University Press. [Corrected reprinting of 1967 edition.]

Lightner, Theodore M. 1965. "On the description of vowel and consonant harmony." *Word* 21: 244–250.

Norman, Jerry. 1974. "A sketch of Sibe morphology." *Central Asiatic Journal* 18: 159–174.

Odden, David. 1978. "Abstract vowel harmony in Manchu." *Linguistic Analysis* 4: 149–165.

Poppe, N. N. 1951. *Khalkha-Mongolische Grammitik.* (Akademie der Wissenschaften und der Literatur, Veröffentlichungen der orientalischen Kommission, 1.) Wiesbaden: Franz Steiner.

——. 1955. *Introduction to Mongolian Comparative Studies.* (Mémoires de la Société Finno-Ougrienne, 110.) Helsinki: Suomalais-Ugrilainen Seura.

——. 1965. *Introduction to Altaic Linguistics.* (Ural-Altaische Bibliothek, 14.) Wiesbaden: Otto Harrassowitz.

Ramstedt, Gustav John. 1935. *Kalmückisches Wörterbuch.* (Lexica Societalis Fenno-Ugricae, 3). Helsinki: Suomalais-Ugrilainen Seura.

Rassadin, V.I. 1982. *Očerki po istoričeskoj fonetike burjatskogo jazyke.* Moscow: Nauka.

Räsänen, Martti. 1949. "Materialen zur Lautgeschichte der türkischen Sprachen." *Studia Orientalia* 15.

Ringen, Catherine O. 1980. "A concrete analysis of Hungarian vowel harmony." In Vago 1980c, pp. 135–154.

Sevortjan, E.V. 1974. *Etimologičeskij slovar' tjurkskix jazykov.* Moscow: Nauka.

Steinitz, Wolfgang. 1964. *Geschichte des finnisch-ugrischen Vokalismus.* Berlin: Akademie-Verlag.

Street, John C. 1962. "Kalmyk schwa." In *American studies in Altaic linguistics* (Uralic and Altaic series, 13), ed. by Nicholas Poppe (Bloomington: Indiana University), pp. 263-91.

——. 1963. *Khalkha structure.* (Uralic and Altaic series, 24.) Bloomington: Indiana University.

Ščerbak, A.M. 1970. *Sravnitel'naja fonetika tjurkskix jazykov.* Moscow: Nauka.

Tenišev, E. R. (gen. ed.). 1984. *Sravnitel'no-istoričeskaja grammatika tjurskix jazykov*. Moscow: Nauka.

Todaeva, B. Kh. 1964. *Baoanskij jazyk*. Moscow: Nauka.

——. 1973. *Mongorskij jazyk*. Moscow: Nauka.

Vago, Robert. 1973. "Abstract vowel harmony systems in Uralic and Altaic languages." *Language* 49: 579–605.

——. 1976. "Theoretical implications of Hungarian vowel harmony." *Linguistic Inquiry* 7: 243–263.

——. 1980a. "A critique of suprasegmental theories of vowel harmony." In Vago 1980c, pp. 151–81.

——. 1980b. "Introduction." In Vago 1980c, pp. xi–xx.

——. 1980c. *Issues in Vowel Harmony*. Amsterdam: John Benjamins.

——. 1980d. *The Vowel Pattern of Hungarian*. Washington: Georgetown University Press.

THE OLD CHINESE TERRESTRIAL RAMES IN SAEK

WILLIAM G. BOLTZ
University of Washington

In a paper prepared for the XVth International Conference on Sino-Tibetan Linguistics held in Peking in the summer of 1982 (Gedney 1982), Professor William J. Gedney made available two different lists of the twelve year animal cycle names, Chinese *ti chih* 地支 'terrestial rames', in the Saek dialect of Tai.[1] The first list is the commonly encountered set that all speakers of Saek seem to know readily, and that can be seen to have been borrowed one way or another from standard Siamese, perhaps via Lao or some dialect in Northeastern Thailand. The second is the linguistically

[1] Saek is a Tai dialect (or language, the two terms are used somewhat promiscuously) spoken in four villages in Nakhon Phanom province in Northeastern Thailand, and across the Mekhong river in a few locations in Laos. It is often classified as a member of the Northern Tai group, in contrast to the Central and Southwest groups, according to the classification scheme proposed in Li 1959, even though it is geographically far removed to the south when compared to the Northern group as a whole. Gedney 1970 speculates on a rather different relation between Saek and the other Tai languages, suggesting that it may have become separated from the Proto-Tai "mainstream" earlier than any other extant Tai language. Virtually all living Saek speakers are bi- or trilingual (in Lao or standard Siamese, or both), and Saek is very much in danger of becoming extinct in a generation or two. It is not a prestigious language for the young speakers, who rather favor Lao.

For other linguistic studies of Saek see Haudricourt 1963 and Gedney 1976.

I have benefitted from the advice and comments of a number of people who read an earlier draft of this paper, especially Jerry Norman, E. G. Pulleyblank, William J. Gedney, and David Strecker. I was also very grateful to receive some notes indirectly from A. Haudricourt via Gedney regarding Gedney's original paper, notes that helped me clarify my thinking on several points, particularly on the question of the relative dates of the borrowings. Outright errors and unfounded speculations remain, of course, entirely my own responsibility.

	Animal	Siamese	Saek set 1	Saek set 2
1.	rat	*chuat*^{3}	*suat*^{5}	*tii*^{6}
2.	ox	*chaluu*^{5}	*să*^{6}*luu*^{1}	*thriw*^{3}
3.	tiger	*khaan*^{5}	*khaan*^{1}	*rin*^{4}
4.	hare	*thɔʔ*^{2}	*thɔʔ*^{4}	*mɛɛw*^{3}
5.	dragon	*marooŋ*^{1}	*mă*^{6}*looŋ*^{4}	*sin*^{4}
6.	serpent	*maseŋ*^{5}	*mă*^{6}*seŋ*^{1}	*tii*^{5}
7.	horse	*mamia*^{1}	*mă*^{6}*mia*^{4}	*ŋɔɔ*^{5}
8.	sheep	*mamɛɛ*^{2}	*mă*^{6}*mɛɛ*^{4}	*muy*^{4}
9.	monkey	*wɔɔk*^{3}	*vɔɔk*^{5}	*thrin*^{1}
10.	cock	*rakaa*^{1}	*lă*^{6}*kaa*^{1}	*raw*^{3}
11.	dog	*cɔɔ*^{1}	*cɔɔ*^{1}	*tut*^{4}
12.	pig	*kun*^{1}	*kun*^{1}	*hɘɘy*^{5}

TABLE I

Notes to Table II (on next page)

1. Yay data are from Gedney 1982: 5–6. This is basically the same language as Li's Dioi in Li 1945.

2. Ahom and Lü data are from Li 1945: 336.

3. Pu-yi data from Chinese Academy of Sciences 1959. In a few of the cases I have had to leave out some minor variants because of the limited space on the chart under the Pu-yi column.

4. Both OC and MC are reconstructed according to the scheme outlined and discussed in Li 1971 (English translation, Li 1975), and Li 1976. The EMC (Early Middle Chinese) is that of Pulleyblank as presented in Pulleyblank 1984.

	Animal		OC	MC	EMC	Saek 2	Yay	Ahom	Lü	Pu-yi
1.	rat	子	tsjəgx	ʻtsï	tsɨˀ	tii^{6}	saɏ^{3}	cheu	tɕai^{3}	ɕaɯ^{3}, ɕai^{3}, saɯ^{3}, tsai^{3}, tsaɯ^{3}
2.	ox	丑	hnrjəgwx	ʻṭhjə̆u	tr'uwˀ	thriw^{3}	pyaw^{3}	plāo	pau^{3}	pau^{3}, piu^{3}, peu^{3}, pjau^{3}, phau^{3}
3.	tiger	寅	rin	˛jin	jin	rɨn^{4}	ɲan^{4}	ngi	ji^{2}	ȵan^{2}, hin^{2}, jin^{2}, ji:n^{2}, ȵen^{2}
4.	hare	卯	mrəgwx	˛mău	mɛʳwˀ	mɛɛw^{3}	maw^{3}	māo	mau^{3}	mau^{3}, mɑu^{3}, mɯ^{3}, mau^{4}, mɑu^{4}
5.	dragon	辰	djən	˛źjĕn	dʑin	sin^{4}	si^{4}	shi	si^{1}	ɕi^{2}, ši^{2}, tsi^{2}, tsei^{2}, ɕei^{2}
6.	serpent	巳	sgjəgx	ʻzjï	zɨˀ	tii^{5}	θɨ^{3}	sheu	sai^{3}	si^{3}, sɯ^{3}, ɬə^{3}, rɯ^{3}, sə^{3}
7.	horse	午	zŋagx	ʻŋuo	ŋɔˀ	ŋɔɔ^{5}	θa^{6}	shi-ngā	sa-ŋa^{4}	sa^{4}, sa^{3}, ɬa^{3}, tsa^{3}
8.	sheep	未	mjədh	mjwĕiʾ	mujʰ	muy^{4}	fat^{1}	mut	met^{6}	fat^{8}, vat^{8}, ve^{6}
9.	monkey	申	hrjin	˛śjĕn	ɕin	thrɨn^{1}	θan^{1}	shan	san^{1}	san^{1}, sin^{1}, ɬan^{1}, sian^{1}
10.	cock	酉	rəgwx	ʻjə̆u	juwˀ	raw^{3}	ru^{6}	rāo	hrau^{4}	zu^{4}, ju^{4}, jəu^{4}, zəu^{4}, su^{4}, zəu^{3}
11.	dog	戌	smjit	sjuĕt	swit	tut^{4}	θit^{3}	mit	set^{5}	sat^{7}, sut^{7}, sɛt^{7}, ɬat^{7}, sie^{5}, rut^{7}
12.	pig	亥	gəgx	ʻɣậi	ɣəjˀ	həəy^{5}	kaɏ^{6}	keu	kai^{4}	kaɯ^{4}, kai^{4}, gai^{4}, ka^{4}, ka^{3}, hai^{4}

Table II

more interesting list. Gedney obtained this set of the animal year names from a nonogenerian informant who apparently thought he was passing on a precious bit of distinctive Saek tradition, something that was virtually unknown among younger generations of Saek speakers. Both lists are given in Table I. The forms in the second list are, as can easily be seen, entirely distinct from those of the first. But they bear in some cases a definite similarity to the same names in other Tai dialects, e.g., Yay, Lü, the Pu-yi dialects, etc. (See Table II.)

In presenting this list Gedney stresses the fact that it is wholly separate from the common Saek set, and asks the question: where did it come from? The answer, as we shall demonstrate below, is that this second Saek set is borrowed from Chinese. The following notes, deliberately modelled on F.K. Li's classic study of the same set of words borrowed into other Tai dialects, and using Li's reconstructions for both Old Chinese (OC) and Middle Chinese (MC), as well as E.G. Pulleyblank's reconstructed Early Middle Chinese (EMC), are intended to show what the reasons are for taking Chinese to be the source of the Saek forms.[2]

A. Tones. Tone distinctions in modern Tai dialects apparently arose in roughly the same way that they did in the modern Chinese dialects, namely, as a function of the kind of initial consonant in an earlier stage of the language. In MC, as is well known, there were four tone categories, three for non-checked syllables and one for checked syllables (i.e., syllables ending in *-p*, *-t*, or *-k*.) Each MC tone category could theoretically give rise to two subsequent categories depending on whether the initial consonant was voiced or voiceless. The Tai case is a bit more complicated, and somewhat more interesting as a result. The Proto-Tai (PT) scheme was about the same as MC, with three tone categories for unchecked syllables, but with two for checked syllables, instead of just one. The distinction between the two is thought to have been one of vowel length. The tones of this PT scheme are generally labelled A, B, C, DS, and DL, respectively.

The devolution of words in these tone categories into modern Tai dialects was governed, as in the case of Chinese, by the kind of initial consonant the word had. But here we find not just a two-way distinction between voiced and voiceless, but a four-way distinction. That is to say, we must recognize four different kinds of initials for each tone category in PT to account for all of the subsequent tonal developments. The two-

[2] For Li's reconstructions see Li 1971, 1975, and 1976. Pulleyblank's EMC reconstructions are outlined and discussed in detail in Pulleyblank 1984. Li's study of the set borrowed into other Tai languages is Li 1945.

way distinction alone between voiced and voiceless initial consonants is not adequate to the task, though voicing is one of the features that characterizes one of the four kinds of initials.

These four kinds of initials are:

i. voiceless fricatives and aspirated stops (e.g., *f-*, *s-*, *ph-*, *th-*, etc.);
ii. voiceless unaspirated stops (e.g., *p-*, *t-*, etc.);
iii. preglottalized stops, including glottal stop;
iv. voiced.

Thus we can draw a chart with the five tonal categories of PT along the horizontal axis, and the four kinds of initials along the vertical, and we would have a total of twenty possible tone distinctions theoretically. No Tai dialect known has anything close to this number; in fact none is known to have more than eight or nine. Table III gives such a chart showing the tonal developments in Siamese (Si), Yay (Y), and Saek (Sk).

Proto-Tai	A	B	C	DS	DL
i. voiceless fricatives & aspirated stops	Si 5 Y 1 Sk 1,2	Si 2 Y 2 Sk 6	Si 3 Y 3 Sk 3	Si 2 Y 3 Sk 4	Si 2 Y 2 Sk 3
ii. voiceless unaspirated	Si 1 Y 1 Sk 1	Si 2 Y 2 Sk 6	Si 3 Y 3 Sk 3	Si 2 Y 3 Sk 4	Si 2 Y 2 Sk 3
iii. preglottalized	Si 1 Y 1 Sk 1	Si 2 Y 2 Sk 6	Si 3 Y 6 Sk 3	Si 2 Y 3 Sk 4	Si 2 Y 2 Sk 3
iv. voiced	Si 1 Y 4 Sk 4	Si 3 Y 5 Sk 5	Si 4 Y 6 Sk 6	Si 4 Y 1 Sk 6	Si 3 Y 5 Sk 5

Table III

Even with only these three dialects we can see that we must have a four-way distinction of initials to account for the modern tonal correspondences. The voiceless friction initials, category i, are distinguished from all other voiceless initials in tone A in Siamese, giving Si tone 5, as opposed to tone

1 for other voiceless initials. Similarly, categories ii and iii are distinguished in tone C by Yay, which has tone 3 in words with originally voiceless initials, except that it has tone 6 in words with originally preglottalized initials.

Because the PT tonal system, and the associated initial consonant types that affected the phonetic evolution of the language, are more complicated than that of MC, we can do little more than to point out indications of originally voiceless versus voiced initials. For this reason initials of the first three categories are often grouped together and treated as a unit, to wit, the voiceless counterpart to category iv, the voiced. The voiceless set is conventionally numbered 1, and the voiced set, 2.

Kurt Wulff in his lengthy study of the relation between Chinese and Tai tried to equate the tone systems of each language family, and the scheme he outlined has been taken as a standard ever since. (Wulff 1934: 166–190) Basically his proposal is that the MC *p'ing* 平, *shang* 上, and *ch'ü* 去 tones match the PT tones A, C, and B in that order, with the MC *ju* 入 tone matching PT tone D, as we would expect. Li (1945) takes this scheme as a given, and discusses the tone correspondences between Chinese and Tai accordingly. We should keep in mind in adopting it that it is still only a premise, and has not been proven in any true sense for a large number of dialects.

The Saek 2 list with the PT tone and initial type (contrasting voiceless and voiced only) is given below. The tone category given in brackets is what the word "ought" to have, assuming it is borrowed from Chinese according to Wulff's proposal above.

1.	*tii*	B1	[C1]*	7.	*ŋɔɔ*	B2	[C2]*
2.	*thriw*	C1	[C1]	8.	*muy*	A2	[B2]*
3.	*rin*	A2	[A2]	9.	*thrin*	A1	[A1]
4.	*mɛɛw*	C1	[C2]*	10.	*raw*	C1	[C2]*
5.	*sin*	A2	[A2]	11.	*tut*	DS1	[DS1]
6.	*tii*	B2	[C2]*	12.	*həəy*	B2	[C2]*

There are two important points to be made. First, although there seem to be seven irregularities vis-à-vis the hypothetical "normal" (those marked with an asterisk *), only two of them involve an irregularity with respect to voicing of the initial in PT, numbers 4 and 10. Number 4 was also indicated as "irregular" in both Lü and Dioi in Li 1945, and has tone C1 in the Puyi data also. So from the Tai perspective we can consider its tone C1 in Saek as perfectly regular; it is only problematical when we look at it in connection with its source in Chinese. Number 10, on the other hand, has the expected tone C2 in both Lü and Dioi, and varies between C2 and C1 in the Pu-yi data. So it is irregular here from both the Tai standpoint and from the perspective of an original Chinese provenance. Except for these two, the correspondences between original voiced and voiceless initials are what they should be if these are in fact Chinese loans in Saek.

The second point has to do with the hypothetical matching of MC and PT tone categories. We mentioned above the assumption the MC *shang* tone is thought to correspond regularly to PT tone C in loanwords from Chinese. But here we have no fewer than four MC *shang* tone words that correspond to Saek tone B (numbers 1, 6, 7, and 12), three of them with originally voiced initials giving Saek tone B2, and one with voiceless giving Saek tone B1. Of the three remaining MC *shang* tone words in the set, we have just discussed two as "irregular" with regard to voicing at the PT stage. The only one left is number 2, which meets the expected requirements of Wulff's hypothesis, having Saek tone C1. On the basis of these data we can at least tentatively suggest that the presumed regular correspondence of MC *shang* tone to PT tone C does not hold universally in the Tai dialects, and in Saek it seems much more likely that the equation should be MC *shang* tone = PT tone B.

B. Initials.

1. The Saek *t-* corresponding to MC *ts-* is reminiscent of the Vietnamese borrowing of this same word, *tử* [tɯ]. In fact there is a somewhat older Vietnamese form *tý* [ti] that matches the Saek form very closely. Cf. also numbers 6, 9, and 11 below.

2. Of the whole set this initial is the most perplexing. Even within Chinese it has long been looked upon as problematical, the 丑 *hsieh-sheng* 諧聲 series including the following members: 紐 MC ˓*njə̆u*, 羞 MC ˓*sjiə̆u*, 狃 MC ˓*ńźjə̆u*, all presumably relatable to the initial of 丑 at the OC stage. Based solely on the internal Chinese data Karlgren reconstructed **t'n-* (*GSR* 107a) to try to account for this alternation. Li has proposed **hnr*, suggesting that the development may have been something like **hnr-* > *hnthr-* > *ṭh-* where the *-r-* is responsible for the retroflection of the MC dental stop.

The point to be noticed is that in the Saek form we have hard, tangible (or at least audible) evidence for the *-r-*, something that was otherwise only a theoretical feature of OC. The evolution may have been something like **hnr-* > *hnthr-* > *thr-* in Saek, very similar to what Li proposed for Chinese. Still, this does not explain the other Tai data. Most striking is the Ahom *plāo*, to which the Yay, Lü and other Pu-yi forms must be related through yodicization of the medial *-l-* (< **-r-*.) This medial *-l-* could readily correspond to the *-r-* of the Saek *thriw* and of OC **hnrjəgwx*.

The equation of *p-* to *th-* (< OC **hn-*) seems at first peculiar, but is not unattested elsewhere. We find, for example, alternations of the following kind between bilabial and dental stops, particularly in clusters with medial *-l-* or *-r-*.

	Saek	Siamese	Yay	gloss
i.	*thrəət*[5]	*phlaat*[3]	*pyaat*[5]	'slip & fall'
ii.	*praak*[3]	*taak*[5]	*taak*[5]	'expose to the sun'
iii.	*preek*[3]	*tɛɛk*[2]	*tek*[3]	'break'
iv.	*pruk*[4]	*tɔɔk*[2]	*tuk*[3]	'bamboo strip'

For i Li reconstructs **bl-*, and for ii, iii, and iv **pr-* (Li 1977: 86–90.) If item number i really represents a pattern (and it is impossible to tell, of course, without more data), then it is conceivable that Sk. *thriw*[3], and Yay *pyaw*[3] are also representative of the same pattern (with the implication that the Siamese would have *phl-* if it existed.) This would then imply a cluster of bilabial + *l/r*, but different from Li's **bl-* for 'slip & fall' because the latter shows the tone for a PT voiced initial, and the former has the tone indicating a PT voiceless inital.

The Saek form *thriw*[3] with tone B1 matches almost perfectly the EMC reconstruction of Pulleyblank, *tr'uwʔ*. Pulleyblank's EMC is representative of a stage of the language somewhat earlier than Li's MC, and probably reflects a time closer to that of the source of these Saek borrowings than Li's MC does. Speaking very speculatively, we may guess that the time of the borrowing was somewhere between the end of the Han and the beginning of the T'ang dynasties, that is, roughly between A.D. 200 and 600. The other Northern Tai forms with initial *p-*, *py-*, and the *pl-* in Ahom may reflect even earlier, independent, borrowings, where the bilabial initial reflects an earlier labio-velar. The original initial of Pulleyblank's OC source for his EMC *tr'uwʔ* is **χr-*, which he thinks became **xw̯r-* regularly before *-ə-*. This labio-velar **xw̯r-* then presumably lost its labialization, giving *xr-* which subsequently fronted to *tr'-*. The bilabials of the Tai forms could be accounted for by a borrowing at the time when the OC word still had an initial **xw̯r-*, prior to the Saek borrowing with *thr-*.

The Vietnamese form has none of the complexity of the Saek, it is simply *sửu* [suɯ], and must be a separate, and later borrowing. It shows that the Saek set as a whole, whatever similarities some of the forms show to Vietnamese, cannot have any direct relation to the Vietnamese borrowings.

3. Li's OC **r-* matches Sk. *r-* perfectly. This initial yodicizes in MC giving *ji-*, and this is the form that must underlie the Vietnamese borrowing, *dần* [jən] in the south, [zən] in the standard language of Hanoi in the north. The

Sk. form shows no trace of the nasalization seen in Yay, Ahom, and some of the Pu-yi forms, and because of which Li speculated on the possibility of a strong nasal quality in the OC initial. (Li 1945: 338) Pulleyblank reconstructs an initial *n̥- for this word in OC, taking into account that nasalization.

4. The Sk. *m-* corresponds to both the *m-* of MC and of EMC. It has been common to assume a cluster of *$m + l$ or r in OC because of the many *hsieh-sheng* derivatives of 卯 that have MC initial *l-*, e.g., 柳 *ljə̆u*, 聊 *ljiə̆u*, etc. While Li reconstructs **mr-* here, he points out in his earlier article that the cluster in OC is very doubtful because there is not a trace of such a cluster in Ahom or Yay, two languages where such clusters are regularly reflected. (Li 1945: 338–339) Pulleyblank has recently also argued against a true cluster in 卯 , and reconstructs it at one stage of OC as **lw̯əlw̯*, derived from an original **ʁəʁ*. He explains the later appearance of both *l-* and *m-* initials in the *hsieh-sheng* series as resulting from the different developments of the **lw̯-* according to the phonetic environment. If the **lw̯-* was heavily labialized, perhaps even with full lip closure as a simultaneous feature of the articulation of the *l-*, it might explain how the initial could have under certain circumstances given rise to an *m-*. Whatever the phonetic vicissitudes of the set, Pulleyblank's reconstruction of a single, heavily labialized, consonant **lw̯-* becoming MC *m-* conforms to Li's observation that the **ml-* that is conventionally inferred on the basis of the Chinese *hsieh-sheng* series is doubtful because of its failure to appear in some form in Ahom and Yay. Saek, which has a rather richer system of initial consonant clusters than most other Tai dialects in general, also fails to show any trace of a cluster in this word.[3]

[3] Pulleyblank's views on the OC for 卯 were a part of a paper presented orally at the February, 1982 meeting of the Chinese Linguistics Circle of the Pacific Northwest, held at the University of British Columbia. Roy Andrew Miller (1951) in discussing the etymology of Chinese *liu* 榴 < **mlôg* 'pomegranate' and its relation to Semitic forms like Hebr. *rimmōn*, Arabic *runmān*, Amharic *rūmān*, Syriac *rumōnō*, etc. was compelled to consider the possibility of a metathesis of the two elements in the OC cluster **ml-*, giving **lm-*. Miller rightly emphasized that we should not automatically predispose ourselves towards any particular order of the consonants in an OC cluster, since there is no firm way to determine what that order may have been. In this case a cluster **lm-* is just as possible as **ml-*. Clearly the **lm-* fits Miller's Semitic data better than **ml-*, and now we can speculate that that **lm-* is a natural consequence of an OC **lw̯-* of

5. Saek *s-* corresponds equally well to Li's MC *ź-* or to Pulleyblank's EMC *dẓ-*. In both cases we have a Chinese palatal as the source for a Sk. dental. For the alternative development of the Chinese dental sibilants, see the next. The tone here, in contrast to the tone in Lü, is that of an originally voiced initial.

6. Sk. *t-* matching Chinese *z-* here looks again like the Vietnamese pattern. For this word Vietnamese has *tị* [ti], almost exactly like the Sk. That the Saek set is not just a direct borrowing from Vietnamese is again confirmed by the fact that although this word matches the pattern of Chinese sibilants corresponding to Vietnamese stops, the preceding word with MC *ź-* (EMC *dẓ-*) is Vietnamese *thần* [tʰən] or *thìn* [tʰin] with a dental stop, whereas the Sk. form, as we saw, had *s-*.

7. The Sk. initial *ŋ-* in the name of the year of the horse is one of the most intriguing of the whole set precisely because it differs so sharply from Yay, and matches both the Chinese and Vietnamese so closely. Pulleyblank's EMC is *ŋɔˀ*, little different from Li's MC *ʻŋuo*, and Vietnamese has *ngọ* [ŋɔ]. Here again we have an indication that the Saek borrowings have to some extent followed the pattern of the Vietnamese in a way that the other Tai dialects have not.

But it is just the other Tai languages that make this word so interesting, as Li already had discussed in 1945. The Ahom *shi-ngā* and Lü *sa-ŋa⁴* both point to an initial cluster **zŋ-* in the OC source, hence our reconstruction of **zŋagx* for OC in Table II. What we find reflected in the Tai borrowings is the kind of bisyllabification, what is often called *dimidiation*, of OC monosyllables with complex initials that occurred on a large scale within the history of the Chinese language proper. The Tai forms with *sa* or *θa*, etc. appear to preserve just the first syllable of the earlier binomial form.

8. The Sk. form with *m-* is a perfect match to the Chinese, both Li's MC *mjwěiʾ* and Pulleyblank's EMC *mujʰ*. The *f-* in Yay has been explained by Li (1945) as probably the result of a dentilabialization within Yay as an independent phonetic development subsequent to the borrowing. Note that in this case Vietnamese has *vị* [vi], also showing a kind of dentilabialization, and again suggesting that the Saek borrowing from Late Middle Chinese *vjì* (Pulleyblank 1982). There is an earlier Vietnamese form *mùi* that is quite clearly the exact counterpart of Saek *muy⁴* and EMC *mujʰ*.

9. In this case the Saek *thr-* shows once again a Vietnamese flavor in that it is a stop corresponding to a Chinese spirant. The Vietnamese is *thân*

---

the type Pulleyblank suggests. This obviates the need to consider any metathesis at all at the OC stage.

[tʰən]. In Li 1971 (p. 49) the OC for 申 is given as **sthjin*, but according to the discussion in Li 1976 this **sthj-* as a source for MC *śj-* (審$_{三}$) could be **hrj-*. This is significant because on the one hand **hrj-* shows the medial *-r-* that turns up in the modern Saek form, and on the other because the *h-* allows the proper homorganic contact with *hsieh-sheng* derivatives like 坤 MC *khwən*. Some modern colloquial readings in the Min dialects show affricate initials corresponding to MC 審$_{三}$ initials, e.g., Foochow *tsui*^{3} 水 'water', and *tshui*^{3} 手 'hand', with unpredictable aspiration. This may be taken to suggest that one possible source for the MC initial was **khrj-*, with a stop rather than a fricative. Conceivably we could postulate **khrjin* for 申, and the Saek *thrin* would be a very late preservation of a transition point between OC **khrj-* and MC *śj-* in an evolution something like **khrj-* > *thrj-* > *hrj-* > *śj-*.

In any case this word, like numbers 2 and 3 above, and the next below, anchors the hypothesized OC *(-)r-* in modern phonetic reality, and for this reason alone is one of the most important in the set.

10. This is a second example of OC **r-* matching Sk. *r-*, and as number 3 above, shows that the borrowing of these words from Chinese into Sk. must have occurred very early, because the **r-* had not yet yodicized in Chinese, a development that must have taken place prior to about A.D. 600.

We should note that none of the Tai data shows any trace in this case of the nasalization that was vestigially in evidence in number 3 above, and that prompted Pulleyblank to reconstruct an OC **ɲ-* in the word for the year of the tiger. For this one Pulleyblank reconstructs OC **j-* > EMC *juwˀ*, which in view of the Tai data with initial *r-* is less satisfactory than Li's **r-*. Vietnamese has *dậu*, northern [zəu], southern [jəu], showing the same reflex as in number 3.

11. Saek again shows the Vietnamese pattern with a stop, *t-* from Chinese *s-* (Li's MC *sjuĕt*, Pulleyblank's *swit*). Vietnamese has *tuất* [tuət]. Li pointed out in 1945 the possibility of an OC **sm-* in this word on the basis of the Ahom *mit*, and the Chinese *hsieh-sheng* derivative 滅 MC *mjät*, and we have reconstructed the OC here accordingly.

12. Sk. *h-* is a precise match for the Chinese ɣ- of both MC and EMC. The majority of other Tai data show a *k-*, only one Pu-yi form preserves the *h-*.

C. Finals. To analyze what hints of a systematic pattern might be observable in so few data as we have in these twelve terrestrial rames we will rewrite the correspondences of finals only (that is, without initials or tones) in Table IV. (The term 'final' is being used in the traditional Chinese sense, that is, all segmental features of the syllable remaining after the initial consonant has been severed. In the strictest sense the Chinese usage includes the tone, but we have discussed tones separately.)

Rime group	Li OC	Li MC	Pulleyblank	Saek	(numbers)
之	-əg	-ậi	-əj	-əəy	(12)
	-jəg	-ï	-ɨ	-ii	(1,6)
幽	-əgw	-ə̆u	-uw	-aw	(10)
	-rəgw	-ə̆u	-ɛʳw	-ɛɛw	(4)
	-rjəgw	-jə̆u	-ruw	-riw	(2)
魚	-ag	-uo	-ɔ	-ɔɔ	(7)
真	(-)rin	-in	-in	(-)rɨn	(3,9)
文	-jən	-jĕn	-in	-in	(5)
脂	-(w)jit	-juĕt	-wit	-ut	(11)
微	-(w)jəd	-jwĕi	-uj	-uy	(8)

Table IV

We can note a few general patterns. The *chih* 之 group, for example, regularly gives a long vowel in Saek. In the division III finals it gives *-ii*, and in division I *-əəy*, both of which are straight-forward reflections of a MC or EMC stage.

Finals of the *yu* 幽 group, always with OC **-gw* (which could be reinterpreted phonemically as simply *-w*), regularly preserve the *-w* in Saek. Li's MC treats all three grades represented here as having *-ə̆u*, , whereas Pulleyblank's EMC distinguishes them, giving in fact a final to 卯 (number 4) that is nearly identical to its Saek value. The Saek borrowings also distinguish them, and thus seem to reflect the EMC stage better than the MC.

The one representative of the *yü* 魚 group, with *-ɔɔ* in Saek, could equally well reflect EMC or MC; there is no essential difference between Li's and Pulleyblank's reconstructions here.

There are two examples of the *chen* 真 group with *(-)r-*, numbers 3 and 9, and both become Sk. *(-)rɨn*. The non-front quality of the Sk. vowel could be due to the *r* directly, or it could be a general feature of borrowings from the *chen* group itself. Without more data it is impossible to say.

The *wen* 文 group is phonetically close to the preceding *chen* 真 group; in Pulleyblank's EMC they coalesce in *-in*, which is exactly the Sk. form. This seems to confirm Pulleyblank's implied claim that already by EMC times the finals of this group had a simple *-i-* head vowel rather than the *-jĕ-* of Li's MC. Notice that Saek is the only Tai form that preserves the *-n*.

The OC finals of both numbers 11 (in the *chih* 脂 group) and 8 (in the *wei* 微 group) are written here with *-(w)-* because they both have an initial *m-*, and this implies an automatic, non-distinctive, labialization of the final. In both cases the Saek form shows this as a rounded vowel, which would be inexplicable if we did not write a *-w-* at the OC stage. This would also be the case for the labialized finals of the MC and EMC values given.

Pulleyblank's EMC seems preferable to Li's MC as the source for Sk. *muy*[4] for number 8 (未) because of the perfect match in head vowel. If the Sk. form reflects an EMC *-uj*, it is unlikely that the Chinese final would have become *-jwĕi* in MC. Notice that the Saek form *muy*[4] does not follow the majority of other Tai dialect borrowings in having *-t*, and therefore does not support Egerod's hypothesis of a distinction between *-d* and *-δ/-j* in OC. (Egerod 1957.) In fact Pulleyblank derives his EMC *muj*[h] from a form **mus* at an only slightly earlier time; and the *-s* of this **mus* would likely account for the *-t* of the Tai forms.

In conclusion we can affirm that Gedney's older generation Saek list of the twelve animal year names is borrowed in its entirety from Chinese, and that the time of the borrowing seems to have been fairly early, probably between A.D. 200 and 600, what Pulleyblank calls the EMC stage. The Vietnamese borrowings of the same set, in contrast, most likely came from the Late Middle Chinese period, as we suggested in connection with numbers 2 and 8 in particular, whereas the borrowings into other Tai languages, e.g., Yay, Ahom, etc., seem to have preceded the Saek borrowings.

In the way it has treated these names Saek continues to maintain its character as an anomalous, in some respects almost "bizarre," Tai language that does not fall into any neat category, or fit into any observed pattern. That is to say, sometimes the borrowings seem to have a Vietnamese flavor, in other cases they are completely different from the Vietnamese. They preserve OC clusters in *-r-* where few, if any, other Tai dialects do, yet in cases like 丑 *thriw*[3] from a putative OC **hnrjəgwx*, the other Tai dialects preserve a bilabial initial, even *pl-* in Ahom, presumably a more archaic feature of the Chinese than either the Sk. or Li's **hnrj-* shows. For 辰 , number 5, Sk. *sin* retains the *-n* of the Chinese where no other recorded Tai form does, and in 午 , number 7, Sk. *ŋɔɔ*[5], it maintains the *ŋ-* when all other Tai forms have *s-* or a presumed derivative of *s-*.

The circumstances and precise time of the borrowings are, of course, not known, nor is the history of the Saek language itself. Even the geographical location of Saek is peculiar for an alleged Northern Tai dialect, and Gedney, following Haudricourt, has speculated that the relation between Saek and the other Tai languages may be something as remote as that that is thought to obtain, for example, between Hittite and Indo-European. (See Gedney 1970.)

References

Chinese Academy of Sciences. 1959. *Pu-yi yü tiao ch'a pao kao* 布依語調查報告. Peking: Chung kuo k'o hsüeh yüan.

Egerod, Søren. 1957. "The eighth earthly branch in Archaic Chinese and Tai." *Oriens* 10: 296–299.

Gedney, William J. 1970. "The Saek language of Nakhon Phanom province." *Journal of the Siam Society* 58: 67–87.

——. 1976. "Saek final *-l*: archaism or innovation?" Unpub. ms. prepared for the IXth International Conference on Sino-Tibetan Languages and Linguistics, Copenhagen.

——. 1982. "The twelve year names in Saek." Unpub. ms. prepared for the XVth International Conference on Sino-Tibetan Languages and Linguistics, Peking.

Haudricourt, A. G. 1963. "Remarques sur les initiales complexes de la langue Sek." *Bulletin de la Société Linguistique de Paris* 58: 56–163.

Li Fang-kuei. 1945. "Some Old Chinese loan words in the Tai languages." *Harvard Journal of Asiatic Studies* 8: 333–342.

——. 1959. "Classification by vocabulary: Tai dialects." *Anthropological Linguistics* 1.2: 15–21.

——. 1971. "Shang ku yin yen chiu" 上古音研究. *Tsing Hua Journal of Chinese Studies* n.s. 9.1–2: 1–61.

——. 1975. "Studies on Archaic Chinese." *Monumenta Serica* 31: 219–287. [= English translation by G.L. Mattos of Li 1971.]

——. 1976. "Chi ko shang ku sheng mu wen t'i 幾個上古聲母問題." In *Tsung t'ung—Chiang Kung shih shih chou nien chi nien lun wen chi* 總統—蔣公逝世週年紀念論文集. Taipei, pp. 1143–1150.

——. 1977. *A Handbook of Comparative Tai*. Honolulu: University of Hawaii Press.

Miller, Roy Andrew. 1951. "The etymology of Chinese *'liu* 'pomegranate'." *Language* 27: 154–158.

Pulleyblank, E.G. 1984. *Middle Chinese: A Study in Historical Phonology*. Vancouver, B.C.: University of British Columbia Press.

Wulff, Kurt. 1934. *Chinesisch und Tai: Sprachvergleichende Untersuchungen. (Det Kgl. Danske Videnskabernes Selskab. Historisk-filologiske Meddelelser XX, 3). Copenhagen: Levin and Munksgaard.*

DIACHRONIC ASPECTS OF REGULAR DISHARMONY IN MODERN UYGHUR

Reinhard F. Hahn
University of Washington

0. Introduction. Palato-velar harmony is a law that requires value agreement among vowels with regard to the feature [Back]. It is common to all Turkic languages and is usually accompanied by language-specific types of consonantal harmony based upon the features [Back] or [High]. Labial harmony requires value agreement among vowels with regard to the feature [Round]. In Turkic it is languages-specific in occurrence and diverse in manifestation. The fact that all Turkic languages have harmonic principles but at the same time seem to tolerate various types and degrees of disharmony has been complicating the formulization of harmonic rules in specific Turkic languages.

The basic argument offered in the following[1] is that Turkic harmony applies regularly and that the apparent violation of harmonic rules is "regular" in the extended sense of Johnson's (1980) term. Regular disharmony will be shown to be due to any of four main factors among which one constitutes a regular response to lexicalized disharmony, one is a superstratal (or postlexical) process, and two define applicability.

Moreover, it will be shown implicitly that results of synchronic, language-specific analyses can be confirmed by means of comparative and etymological data. Diachronic data may help to corroborate the synchronically based identification of remaining underlying distinctions. A comparative approach enables one to gain a clearer insight into the evolution and development of harmonic systems, particularly within a language group that is as close-knit as Turkic.

Modern Standard Turkish has hitherto received by far the greatest amount of attention in Western publications dealing with Turkic harmony.

---

[1] This presentation is a revised version of a manuscript cited in Hahn 1991, forthcoming, Lindblad 1990, and Zhao & Hahn 1990: 282. Ablahat Ibrahim and Litip Tohti occasionally served as Uyghur language informants, and Vern Lindblad shared some of his research findings with me and made some valuable suggestions.

Here, Modern Uyghur[2] data are entered into the discussion, since this language on the one hand is relatively conservative with regard to suffix creation and labial harmony development but on the other hand is innovative with regard to phonological neutralization, both of which characteristics contribute to a considerable degree of apparent disharmony. Data taken from other Turkic languages serve to illustrate developmental tendencies and scopes.

1. Harmonic Principles

1.1. Vowel Phoneme Distinctions. The vowel phonemes of Standard Uyghur are divided into two identically structured main groups that are distinct on the basis of the feature [Back]. Each of these two groups has three height levels and is subdivided into two vertical columns that are distinct on the basis of the feature [Round]. Furthermore, the phonemes have binary quantitative distinction.[3]

(1) Modern Uyghur vowel phonemes (extended inventory)

[−Back]				[+Back]			
[−Round]		[+Round]		[−Round]		[+Round]	
[−Long]	[+Long]	[−Long]	[+Long]	[−Long]	[+Long]	[−Long]	[+Long]
i	ii	ü	üü	ı	ıı	u	uu
(e)	(ee)	ö	öö	(ɤ)	(ɤɤ)	o	oo
ä	ää			a	aa		

[2] Modern Uyghur (formerly "East(ern) Turki") serves as a first-learned language primarily in China's Xinjiang Uyghur Autonomous Region (formerly "Eastern Turkestan" or "Chinese Turkestan"), to a lesser extent in the neighboring Soviet republics, Afghanistan and Outer Mongolia. In Xinjiang, it also serves as an official lingua franca among many of those non-Uyghur inhabitants whose first-learned language is not Chinese. In the following, "Modern Standard Uyghur" (hereafter "(Standard) Uyghur") collectively refers to the standard "literary" variety of China and of the Soviet Union, unless specified otherwise.

[3] (Hahn 1991, forthcoming, Hašim & Mixri 1986, Polat 1984.) None of the modern orthographies observes this underlying quantitative distinction; e.g., /tär/ = *tär* 'sweat' vs. /täär/ = *tär* 'complexion'. (Although its word-initial status remains debatable, a glottal stop (/ʔ/ = ') is here assumed to be phonemic in all positions.)

The native vowel phoneme inventory has been augmented by means of the loan-specific phoneme pairs /e/ ≠ /ee/ and /ɤ/ ≠ /ɤɤ/.[4] (In native contexts, [e] can occur only as a distributional variant of any unrounded vowel; Hahn 1986: 43–48; 1991; forthcoming; Zhang & Meng 1982: 59; see also 2.2.3.). Other Turkic vowel phoneme inventories have been augmented differently,[5] if at all. In a few Turkic languages, the distinction in the non-high front (usually /e(e)/ ≠ /ä(ä)/) also applies in what appear to be

---

[4] I follow Lindblad 1990: 8–9 in assuming a back counterpart to /e(e)/ to account for back-vocalic response to what is orthographically represented as *e* in certain loanwords; e.g., Chinese *gōngshè* > Uyghur *guŋše* 'commune' → *guŋše+da* (not **guŋše+dä*) 'at the commune', Russian *universitet* → Uyghur *'uniwersitet* 'university' → *'uniwersitet+ta* (not **'uniwersitet+tä*) 'at the university'.

[5] In Modern Standard Turkish, for example, loan roots may contain vowels that orthographically equal back vowels but trigger off front-vocalic harmony response. Among these vowels, only *a* = [ɑ]~[a] may differ phonetically from back *a* = [ɑ]; e.g., Arabic *ḥāl* > *hal* = [ha:l] 'condition' → *hali* = [ha:lı] (not **halı* = *[hɑɫɨ]) 'its condition' (cf. *dal* = [dɑɫ] 'branch' → *dalı* = [dɑɫɨ] 'its branch'). Yavaş (1980) argues that in this case front-vocalic response is due to the palatality of an adjacent consonant (i.e., /haali/ vs. /dalı/). While this seems justified at least regarding initial anaptyxis (e.g., French *club* = [klüb] > /klüb/ → *kulüp* = [kulüp] 'club'), it is disproven where front-vocalic response to *a* occurs across other kinds of consonants in non-initial anaptyxis as well as in suffixation; e.g., Arabic *qabr* > *kabir* (not **kabır*) 'tomb' → *kabri* (not **kabrı*) 'his tomb' (Lewis 1978: 19), Arabic *zirā'at* > *ziraat* = [zırɑ:ɑt] 'agriculture' (cf. Uyghur /ziraa'ät/ → *zira'ät* 'agricultural product') → *ziraati* (not **ziraatı*) 'its agriculture'. Thus, the only possible solution seems to be to assume loan-specific phonemes, such as /ȧ(ȧ)/, which are treated front-vocalically like /ä(ä)/, as distinct from back-vocalic /a(a)/: /kȧbr/, /ziraa'ȧt/ etc. (Alternatively, one might represent the set /ä(ä)/ ≠ /ȧ(ȧ)/ ≠ /a(a)/ as /e(e)/ ≠ /ä(ä)/ ≠ /a(a)/ respectively.) Loan-specific rounded vowel phonemes cannot be posited, since front-vocalic response after *u* and *o* appears to be consistently due to consonant feature assimilation (e.g., after front /l/), as suggest by Yavaş (1980); e.g., Arabic *nukūl* 'denial' > /nüḱuul/ → *nükûl* 'retraction' → *nükûlü* 'its retraction' (cf. Arabic *nufūs* 'souls' > /nüfuus/ → *nüfus* 'population' → *nüfusu* 'its population'), French *rôle* > *rol* 'role' → *rolü* 'its role' (cf. French *record* > *rekor* 'record' → *rekoru* 'its record').

native roots,[6] which appears to represent a secondary development.[7]

In the absence of augmentation and quantitative distinction, the Standard Uyghur vowel phoneme inventory is that shared by all known Turkic languages. It has only two height levels. The mid-level and the low level together constitute a single low level.[8] This basic low-level structure is perfectly symmetrical in conjunction with the high-level structure in an inventory each of whose three categorial criteria rely upon binary distinction.

(2) Modern Uyghur vowel phonemes (basic inventory)

	[−Back]		[+Back]	
	[−Round]	[+Round]	[−Round]	[+Round]
[−Low]	i	ü	ı	u
[+Low]	ä	ö	a	o

It is this simple inventory and its distinctive feature categorization that constitutes the basis for Turkic suffix vowel assignation.

1.2. Harmonic Processes. In all Turkic languages, native morphological derivation and syntactic function marking rely solely upon postpositive devices, namely upon the adding of postpositions, compound elements, enclitics and suffixes to roots and stems. With regard to vocalic structure, postpositions, compound elements and enclitics are discrete units, while suffixes must be adapted to the roots and stems to which they are attached

[6] For example, in Qazaq (Kazakh), native (and Common Turkic) /ä/ (→ *e* = [e]) is distinct from /à/ (→ *ä* = [æ]; alternatively /e/ ≠ /ä/). The latter occurs in a few kinship terms, otherwise in loanwords; e.g., Arabic *hawā'* > *äwa* 'air', Farsi *har* > *är* 'each', Russian *pal'to* > *palto* ~ [p'ælte] 'overcoat' (Geng & Li 1985: 205, 207, 215). In Azerbaijani, this distinction exists within the native lexicon; e.g., *el* 'nation' vs. *äl* 'hand' (Amirpur-Ahrandjani 1971: 46–47, Poppe 1960: 105).

[7] Poppe (1960: 102–106) assumes that the development of mid-level /e/ took place in both Mongolic and Turkic after the separation of these two Altaic branches, since /e/ ≠ /ä/ distinctions do not correspond between them. He considers it possible that /e/ was derived from /ä/ under the influence of an adjacent palatal and a following (subsequently deleted) vowel.

[8] Based upon the commonly held assumption that [+Low] is marked, and taking into account Uyghur vowel raising as a manifestation of reduction in light syllables (i.e., [+Low] → [−Low]), mid- and low-level vowels are here combined under the label [+Low] rather than under the label [−High].

and with which they form units that upon the basis of their phonological integrity are defined as "words." Suffix adaptation is characteristically based upon harmonic principles that determine feature value assignation to all vowels and to certain consonants. Harmonically responsive segments are assumed to be derived from archiphonemes (i.e., underspecified phonemes) and as such are here and elsewhere represented by means of capital letters. Vocalic archiphonemes are minimally distinct in height. Harmonic backness value assignation applies mandatorily and uniformly during suffixation in all Turkic languages, while harmonic roundness assignation is language-specific regarding applicability and conditioning.

1.2.1. Palato-Velar Harmony. The term "palato-velar harmony" denotes the concomitance of vocalic backness harmony with one of several backness-conditioned consonantal harmony variants. Palato-velar harmony manifests itself in virtually all known Turkic languages. More precisely stated, it applies consistently in all modern spoken Turkic languages (with a few exceptions, such as certain varieties of highly Iranized urban Uzbek) and in most modern written Turkic languages. Certain remnants of it survive in those varieties that have been regarded as having lost harmony. Palato-velar harmony is attestable in all known pre-modern Turkic languages as far back as in the varieties recorded in the earliest extant Early Written Turkic (i.e., Kök Turkic and Old Uyghur) documents. Distinctions both among vowel symbols and among certain consonant symbols serve as clear indicators in Old Uyghur manuscripts from as early as the ninth century C.E. (Gabain 1974, Nasilov 1963). Categorial distinction among vowel-carrying consonant symbols has been observed in the "runic" Turkic epitaph inscriptions of the Orkhon and Yenessei areas, which go back to the seventh century C.E. and possibly much earlier. These orthographic differentiations are understood as indicating the existence of harmonic backness distinction in the earliest known varieties of Turkic (Abduraxmânov & Rustamov 1982, Ajdarov 1971, Erimer 1969, Gabain 1959, 1974, Malov 1951, Meyer 1965). There ought to be little doubt about this distinction being vocalic, since rounded back and front vowels are distinguished also in the absence of vowel carriers, and vocalic backness harmony is attestable only some one hundred years later. If and to what degree this distinction was also consonantal (namely affecting *b, d~t, s, n, l, r, g~k* and *y*) remains to be determined.

1.2.1.1. Palato-Velar Vowel Harmony. As mentioned earlier, in the Turkic languages at least height value is predetermined in vocalic archiphonemes that undergo backness harmony assignation: high /I/ (→ non-labial /i/ ~ /ı/, labial /ü/ ~ /u/) and low /A/ (→ non-labial /ä/ ~ /a/, labial /ö/ ~ /o/). Within a language-specific, synchronic context, this could be argued to be the case in languages such as Turkish, namely in languages in which labial harmony applies consistently to all high vowels. Vocalic archiphonemes may have predetermined roundness value as well: /I/, /U/, /A/, /O/; e.g., Standard Uyghur /I/ → /i/ ~ /ı/, /U/ → /ü/ ~ /u/, /A/ → /ä/ ~ /a/. This is most clearly evident in Turkic languages in which a suffix may have an inherently round vowel that does not undergo delabialization where labial harmony applies; e.g., Qirghiz (Kirghiz) /I/ → /i/ ~ /ı/ ~ /ü/ ~ /u/, /U/ → /ü/ ~ /u/, /A/ → /ä/ ~ /a/ ~ /ö/ ~ /o/, /O/ → /ö/ ~ /o/. Fundamentally, namely in the absence of superstratal disharmonization and root-internally tolerated disharmony, all vowels within and not beyond the boundaries of a word (#) agree with each other in backness value:

(3) Palato-velar vowel harmony

$$\# \; C_0 \begin{bmatrix} V \\ \alpha\text{Back} \end{bmatrix} \left(C_1 \begin{bmatrix} V \\ \alpha\text{Back} \end{bmatrix} \right)_0 \; C_0 \; \#$$

1.2.1.2. Palato-Velar Consonant Harmony. Within native contexts, consonantal harmony requires certain consonantal phonemes to conform to the backness value of the assigned vocalism within a word. In Karaim, this applies to all consonants (Musaev 1966, Pritsak 1959a). In Southwestern Turkic languages, such as Gagauz (Pokrovskaja 1966), Azerbaijani (Amirpur-Ahrandjani 1971, Gadžieva 1966) and Western Turkish dialects, velars associate with back vowels, while their palatal or palato-alveolar counterparts associate with front vowels (/l(′)/ ≠ /ł/, /ǵ/ ≠ /g/, /ḱ/ ≠ /k/). In most other Turkic languages (including Modern Uyghur), palatalization may be encountered as a secondary feature, the basic manifestation of consonantal harmony being harmonic distinction among back consonants, namely between velars and uvulars (/g/ ≠ /ɢ/, /k/ ≠ /q/, /ŋ/ ≠ /ɴ/).[9]

(4) Palato-velar consonant harmony

$$\begin{bmatrix} C \\ \alpha\text{Back} \end{bmatrix} \% \begin{bmatrix} V \\ \alpha\text{Back} \end{bmatrix} \quad \text{or} \quad \begin{bmatrix} C \\ -\alpha\text{High} \end{bmatrix} \% \begin{bmatrix} V \\ \alpha\text{Back} \end{bmatrix}$$

---

[9] A back nasal pair (always η in the official orthographies) is here assumed included in the harmony-sensitive series. (The allophone [ɴ] occurs with back vowels and uvulars.)

Under (5), regular manifestations of palato-velar harmony are illustrated by means of corresponding morphemic forms in Turkish and Qazaq (Geng & Li 1985, Kenesbaev and Karaševa 1966, Xinjiang Weiwuer Zizhiqu Wenzi Gongzuo Weiyuanhui 1983).

(5) Regularly applying palato-velar harmony

Turkish	Qazaq	
#ǵiy-im+i+n+dän#	#kiy-im+i+n+nän#	'from his clothing'
#kız+ı+n+dan#	#qız+ı+n+nan#	'from his daughter'
#äšäḱ+lär+imiz+ä#	#äsäk+tär+imiz+gä#	'to our donkeys'
#ayak+ɫar+ımız+a#	#ayaq+tar+ımız+ɢa#	'to our feet'

1.2.2. Labial Vowel Harmony. The term "labial (vowel) harmony" collectively denotes all variants of a law that requires word-internal vocalic roundness agreement. This type of harmonic agreement shares its domain of application partially[10] or entirely with palato-velar harmony, but usually does not exceed it.[11] Although the application of labial harmony in its various forms tends to be more prevalent in one Turkic subgroup than in another, and the possibility that language contacts account for its spread

[10] Menges (1947: 61) describes a Qaraqalpaq dialect in which labial harmony does not apply beyond the first controlled syllable; e.g., *köllöründä* (cf. Qirghiz *köldöründö*) 'in its lakes', *tömändägi* (cf. Ili Turki *temändägi* [Zhao & Hašim 1985: 28]) ~ *tömöndägi* (cf. Qirghiz *tömöndökü*) '(that) which is (shown) below' ("on the above, on high" [sic.], Menges 1947: 61).

[11] A rare instance of low labial harmony applying in the absence of palato-velar harmony is found in Ili Turki (Hahn 1990, Zhao & Hašim 1985), for example with regard to the collective numerative marker ...*(a)w* ~ ...*(ȯ)w* (cf. Old Uyghur ...*(ä)gü* ~ ...*(a)ɢu*, Xinjiang Qazaq ...*(ä)w* ~ ...*(a)w*). In Ili Turki, unrounded non-high vowels are phonetically distinct with regard to backness, while the rounded vowels surface neutralized as medial allophones. Attached to a root whose last vowel is unrounded, the morpheme in question acts like an enclitic in that it remains back-vocalic even after front-vocalic stems (e.g., *beš+aw* 'the five of them together'), but it does respond to labial harmony (e.g., *üč+ȯw* 'the three of them together'). Another such rare instance is the Turkish attributive marker ...*ki* which acts like a postposition (i.e., does not undergo harmony and voicedness assimilation); e.g., *šimdiki* (not **šimdigi*) 'current', *yarınki* (not **yarıngı*) 'tomorrow's'. However, it does respond to front labial influence; e.g., (#bu##ǵün##ḱi# 'this day's' >) *bugünkü* (not **bugünki*) 'today's'.

cannot be ruled out, its presence and typology do not appear to be definable as solely genealogically or areally based. Labial harmony and its typology can be dialectally based and can be quite diverse within the same genealogically defined language, as is the case for example in Modern Uyghur (Cheng 1984, Ğappariwa 1980, Hahn 1986: 36–42, Jarring 1933: 67–89, Li 1986, Mixri 1984, Osmanop 1983, Pritsak 1959b, Sadvakasov 1970, 1976, Tenišev 1963) and in Qazaq (Geng & Li 1985: 4, Poppe 1960: 150). So far, the two main types "high labial harmony" and "general labial harmony" have been discussed in some detail in relevant publications.

1.2.2.1. High Labial Harmony. The type of labial harmony that consistently and exclusively affects the realization of high vowels has been analyzed and discussed mainly within the context of Turkish (e.g., Clements & Sezer 1982, Crothers & Shibatani 1980, Kardestuncer 1982a, 1982b, 1983, Lees 1961, 1966a, 1966b, Pierce 1966, Zimmer 1967). This type applies also in other Turkic languages, primarily in those used on the western periphery of the Turkic-speaking area, for example in Azerbaijani (e.g., Amirpur-Ahrandjani 1971: 69–73, Gadžieva 1966), Turkmen (e.g., Azimov et al. 1966, Hanser 1977), Gagauz (e.g., Pokrovskaja 1966), Kumyk (e.g., Magomedov 1966), Karachay-Balkar (e.g., Xabičev 1966), Karaim (e.g., Musaev 1966, Pritsak 1959a) and Chulym Turki (Dul'zon 1966). Early tendencies toward this type are evident in medieval Eastern Turkic literature, including the Qarakhanid text *Qutaḍɢu bilig* of the eleventh century C.E. (Doerfer 1985: 19–20, Minzu Wenxue Yanjiusuo 1984), as well as in Qypchaq and Ottoman literary works from between the 13th and 18th centuries C.E. (e.g., Doerfer 1985).

Under (6), this type of roundness agreement of every high vowel with the nearest vowel (usually with the immediately preceding vowel in iterative application) is illustrated in the case of Standard Turkish, juxtaposed with cognate forms in Written Qazaq, a language in which no type of labial harmony applies.

(6) Extent of high labial harmony

Turkish	Qazaq	
#ǵöl+ümüz+ün#	#köl+imiz+diŋ#	'of our lake'
#ǵöl+lär+imiz+in#	#köl+där+imiz+diŋ#	'of our lakes'
#koł+umuz+un#	#qol+ɪmɪz+dɪɴ#	'of our arm'
#koł+łar+ɪmɪz+ɪn#	#qol+dar+ɪmɪz+dɪɴ#	'of our arms'
#ǵün+ümüz+ün#	#kün+imiz+diŋ#	'of our day'

#ǵün+lär+imiz+in#	#kün+där+imiz+diŋ#	'of our days'
#kuš+umuz+un#	#qus+ımız+dıɴ#	'of our bird'
#kuš+łar+ımız+ın#	#qus+tar+ımız+dıɴ#	'of our birds'

1.2.2.2. General Labial Harmony. In another major type of labial harmony, roundness agreement affects also low vowels under various language-specific constraints. Low labial harmony has been assumed to be a relatively more recent development than is high labial harmony from which it has been traditionally distinguished by means of the label "labial attraction" (e.g., in Menges 1947: 60–64, and Poppe 1959: 675, 1960: 150). A simultaneous rule application treatment has been proposed for Qirghiz (Johnson 1980; see 1.3.).

In this type of labial harmony, high vowels are ordinarily affected consistently. Usually, all low vowels can be labialized as well, except where /a/ is controlled by /u/, which is the case for instance in Qirghiz (e.g., Axmatov 1970, Axmatov et al. 1975, Hebert & Poppe 1963, Hu 1986, Junasaliev 1966), as illustrated in juxtaposition with Turkish cognates under (7).

(7) Extent of general labial harmony

Qirghiz	Turkish	
#köl+übüz+dön#	#ǵöl+ümüz+dän#	'from our lake'
#köl+dör+übüz+dön#	#ǵöl+lär+imiz+dän#	'from our lakes'
#qoł+ubuz+dan#	#koł+umuz+dan#	'from our arm'
#qoł+dor+ubuz+dan#	#koł+łar+ımız+dan#	'from our arms'
#kün+übüz+dön#	#ǵün+ümüz+dän#	'from our day'
#kün+dör+übüz+dön#	#ǵün+lär+imiz+dän#	'from our days'
#quš+ubuz+dan#	#kuš+umuz+dan#	'from our bird'
#quš+tar+ıbız+dan#	#kuš+lar+ımız+dan#	'from our birds'

The same rule applies in Lopnori (which is officially considered a Modern Uyghur dialect)[12] and in certain dialects of Altay (Menges 1947: 60,63,

[12] Ğappariwa 1980: 25–26, Hahn 1986: 38, Mixri 1984, Osmanop 1983, Pritsak 1959a: 540, Tenišev 1963: 147–150, Zhao & Zhu 1985: 200–201; e.g., #köl+lör# (cf. Standard Uyghur #köl+lär#) 'lakes', #qoy+lor# (cf. Standard Uyghur #qoy+lar#) '(various) sheep', #üz+zör# (cf. Standard Uyghur #yüz+lär#) 'faces', but #lop++tuq+tar# (cf. Standard Uyghur #lop++luq+lar#) 'people of Lop' (Mixri 1984: 57,59).

Pritsak 1959c: 577–578). In Yakut, low vowels can be labialized only by a preceding non-high, short, rounded vowel.[13] In Bashqir—a language in which, as in its close relative Tatar (Chen & Ilčen 1986, Zakiev 1966), most Common Turkic high- and mid-level vowels have switched levels—low labial harmony is confined to the mid-level and is controlled by non-high vowels (Juldašev 1966, Poppe 1965: 182). Its passive constraints thus, strictly speaking, equal those of high labial harmony, since common Turkic high suffix vowels have been lowered, and low suffix vowels are exempted from labial harmony. Its causative constraints, however, belong to the same category as those in Yakut. In Standard Altay, underlying high vowels tend to be labialized within lexicalized stems only and then only after a high round vowel; e.g., #sülizin# ~ #sülüzün# 'fox' (Pritsak 1959c: 577). However, usually only underlying low vowels are labialized by preceding non-high vowels; e.g., #qol+dor# 'arms', vs. #qol+ı# 'his arm' (Poppe 1965: 183, Baskakov 1966). Certain non-standard varieties of Shor show a tendency toward general labial harmony, but low labialization is restricted to front-vocalic sequences.[14] A rare case of unrestricted general labial harmony application is found in spoken Standard Turkmen; e.g., *ulumsıramak* = [ulumθuromoq] '(process of) boasting' (Hanser 1977: 15).

1.3. Formulization. Vowel harmony in Altaic (i.e., Turkic, Mongolic and Tungusic) and Uralic (i.e., Finnic, Ugric and Samoyedic) languages has been widely regarded as being generated by means of iteratively applying metaphonic or specificatory rules. In recent years, models for simultaneous rule application have been proposed, such as Clements' autosegmental treatment (e.g., Clements 1976, 1980, Clements & Sezer 1982), and these have been variously rejected within a Ural-Altaic context (e.g., Anderson 1980, Johnson 1980: 93–94, Vago 1980b).

It is not intended to enter into any lengthy discussion about various descriptive approaches within the limited scope of this presentation. The definition of the domain of mandatory harmony application and the identification of regular disharmonizing processes and conditions presented here implicitly point toward the consistent application of harmonic rules in Turkic, and they throw further doubt upon the practice of positing disharmony

[13] For instance #börö+lör# 'wolves', #o+lor# 'those', but #uu+lar# 'waters', #tül+lär# 'dreams', #uol+lar# 'sons', #küöl+lär# 'lakes' (Poppe 1959: 676).

[14] For instance #sös+täŋ# ~ #sös+töŋ# 'from the word', #kör−−zä# ~ #kör−−zö# 'if he sees' (Pritsak 1959d: 632).

labels and opaque constituents such as those used particularly in simultaneous application models. *Ipso facto*, they contribute to the invalidation of hitherto expressed objections to linear application models, at least within a Turkic context.

For the purpose of the present discussion then, it is assumed that Turkic harmony manifests itself by way of feature value assignation rules that operate on a co-occurrence restriction basis and apply progressively, i.e., cyclically, to their own output: an added suffix is assimilated to the nearest relevant segment. Crothers & Shibatani's (1980) basic analysis within a Turkish context is here taken as being fundamental also within a more general Turkic context. In this analysis, morpheme structure constraints and phonetic constraints are assumed to be, by and large, identical co-occurrence restrictions, the former defining well-formed lexical representations, and the latter defining well-formed words (Crothers & Shibatani 1980: 77). Native and fully nativized roots and lexicalized stems have undergone harmonizing processes in this fashion, while phonological adaptation of loanwords as Turkic roots does not include internal harmonic assimilation. All roots are lexicalized fully specified with regard to level, backness and roundness, be they internally harmonic or disharmonic. Only a root- or stem-final syllable is relevant to further harmonization in that it initially determines at least the backness category of the remainder of a word. Suffixes used for free derivation and for syntactic function marking contain segments with archiphonemic representation that undergo feature value assignation rules. This implies a greater degree of abstractness than in Kiparsky's (1973) model in which also vowels in productive suffixes are fully specified in their "least marked" form before they undergo harmonic assimilation.

This model appears to be viable at least within a synchronic context. For example, it allows palato-velar harmony (1.2.1.) and high labial harmony (1.2.2.1.) applying to underlying vowels to be captured within one conflated rule statement, assuming that there are only the two vocalic archiphonemes whose backness and roundness values are to be determined.

(8) Palato-velar harmony and high labial harmony

$$\begin{bmatrix} \text{V} \\ \emptyset\text{Back} \\ \left\langle \begin{matrix} +\text{High} \\ \emptyset\text{Round} \end{matrix} \right\rangle \end{bmatrix} \rightarrow \begin{bmatrix} \alpha\text{Back} \\ <\beta\text{Round}> \end{bmatrix} / \begin{bmatrix} \text{V} \\ \alpha\text{Back} \\ <\beta\text{Round}> \end{bmatrix} \text{C}_0 \;\underline{\qquad}$$

Vowels within roots and lexicalized stems cannot undergo this rule, since they are fully specified, namely have no blanks (∅). Alternatively, morpheme boundary specifications would have to be incorporated into the rule, which would be problematic, because within contemporary, synchronic contexts suffixes may be disyllabic as a result of contraction (e.g., Turkish /-IǰI+#/[15] discussed below).

In most Turkic languages, only the feature [Back] has indeterminate value, while labial harmony involves labialization but not delabialization (see 1.2.1. above). Thus, the vowel in the Qirghiz habitual participial suffix /-čU+#/,[16] for example, undergoes palato-velar harmonization but retains its inherent roundness under all conditions; e.g., #min-čü# '(habitually) riding', #bar-ču# '(habitually) going (and arriving)' (Hu 1986: 121). In contrast, the vowels in the Turkish equivalent /-IǰI+#/ (< */-A#čI+#/ < */-A#čU+#/?) surface in two unrounded and two rounded variants; e.g., #äz+iǰi# 'crushing', 'overwhelming', #ak-ıǰı# 'fluent', #ǵüldür-üǰü# ("causing to laugh" =) 'amusing', #uyuštur-uǰu# ("benumbing" =) 'intoxicating' (Hatiboğlu 1974: 75–76, Lewis 1978: 220). Johnson (1980: 91), assuming iterative rule application, captures Qirghiz general labial harmony (see 1.2.2.2.) within a single labialization rule according to which non-application of low labialization after /u/ constitutes a case of regular labial disharmony.

(9) Johnson's Qirghiz labialization rule

$$V \rightarrow [+\text{Round}] \;/\; \begin{bmatrix} \text{V} \\ \alpha\text{High} \\ \beta\text{Back} \\ +\text{Round} \end{bmatrix} \; C_0 \; \left[\overline{\gamma\text{High}}\right]$$

Condition: $(\alpha,\beta,\gamma)\neq(+,+,-)$

1.4. Diachronic Implications.

Assuming on the basis of language-specific data that labial harmony is a labialization process within the entire Turkic context would be too sweeping a generalization, even though comparative and historical data strongly tempt one to regard labialization

---

[15] Consistently with Western Turcological conventions (Gabain 1974), the symbols + and - in morphemic representations indicate nominal and verbals suffix boundaries respectively. In this presentation (as in Hahn 1991), this has been extended to final position where further suffixing is possible. Further suffixing is mandatory in the absence of a final word boundary (#).

[16] Cf. Traditionally Written Mongolian imperfect converbial *-ǰü* ~ *-ǰu* ~ *-čü* ~ *-ču*; e.g., *kele-ǰü* 'saying', *abču* 'taking', (Gabain 1974: 116, Poppe 1964: 96).

of fully specified unrounded phonemes as being an earlier developmental stage whose principle is still underlying. Within a purely Turkish context, for example, such diachronic considerations ought not stand in the way of capturing the utmost degree of abstractness, as that of the archiphonemic Turkish suffix vowel inventory /I/, /A/. In analyzing harmonic systems within purely synchronic contexts, only language-specific domanial constraints, degrees of abstractness and rule statements are relevant.

Within a comparative, diachronic context, a significant implication of the development from specification to underspecification regarding roundness, in conjunction with the identification of historically word- and enclitic-derived suffixes (see 2.1.), is that Turkic suffixization is essentially an abstraction process. If one goes along with Crothers and Shibatani's defense of the permissibility of blanks in harmonic system descriptions (Crothers & Shibatani 1980: 70–72, Shibatani & Crothers 1974: 268), one would have to conclude that this type of affixization, as an essential part of a development from phonological discreteness to phonological dependency, signifies the loss of unconditional feature value specification and thus the evolution of archiphonemes.

Consistently with this conclusion, one would not simply state that an inherently rounded vowel in a word- and clitic-derived suffix has undergone delabialization in a language without labial harmony and still undergoes delabialization where in a labial harmony system non-labial variants are required. Rather, one would have to state that the positive roundness feature value has been deleted and a blank has been created in the course of affixization. For example, in some Turkic languages, the Early Written Turkic aoristic verb form #tur-°r# 'stand(s)', 'persist(s)' (Gabain 1974: 126, Lewis 1978: 96, Räsänen 1957: 172–173) has been developed into a literary or categorical statement expression or into a progressive tense marker. In certain languages it developed into an enclitic;[17] e.g., in Troki (Lithuanian) Karaim (Musaev 1966: 264), Western Uyghur ("Yellow Uyghur," Chen & Lei 1985) and Modern Uyghur (*#tur-°r# > /...#dur#/). In other languages, such as Turkish, it developed into a prestressed suffix (Lewis 1978: 96–98, *#tur-°r# > /...++dIr#/).[18] As an enclitic, it undergoes voicedness assimilation but does not undergo harmonic assimilation. As a suffix, it is affixed after stress assignment, but it still undergoes harmonization, surfacing either in two variants (i.e., where labial harmony does not apply) or in four variants

[17] A single word boundary (#) separates a clitic (Kardestuncer 1982b; see 2.4.).

[18] A double suffix boundary separates a prestressed suffix (see 2.4.).

(i.e., where labial harmony applies to underlying vowels).

(10) Enclitic vs. suffix

Uyghur	Turkish	
#gǘl#dur#	#ǵǘl++dür#	'is (indeed) a flower'
#ʔót#tur#	#ót++tur#	'is (indeed) an herb'
#ʔä́r#dur#	#ä́r++dir#	'is (indeed) a male'
#ʔát#tur#	#át++tır#	'is (indeed) a horse'

Recognition of this evolutionary process in conjunction with comparative analyses within a Turkic and generally Altaic context may facilitate and corroborate the identification of words as sources of enclitics and suffixes. This might prove to be beneficial also to language-specific, synchronic analyses, given the fact that suffixes that can be attested as being word-derived tend to be phonologically distinguished from other suffixes.

2. Regular Disharmony. The Modern Uyghur harmony system has been described as being inconsistent and thus as occupying in this respect a categorial position somewhere between that of a "harmonic" language, such as Qirghiz, and that of a "non-harmonic" language, such as Uzbek (Kajdarov 1966: 368). Evidently, this view is based solely upon phonetic surface manifestations and variously distorting orthographic conventions. Harmonic processes apply underlyingly in virtually all Turkic language, even though it might be true to say that the system is moderately to highly flawed in a few varieties, such as Standard Uzbek (Sjoberg 1962). With regard to alleged harmonic inconsistencies in Modern Uyghur, it is possible to argue that whatever appears to be disharmonic is attributable to specific, regular constraints and processes that are identified as follows:

(11) Disharmony factors in Modern Uyghur

- (1) Root-final disharmony
- (2) Phonological neutralization
- (3) Labialization constraints
- (4) Domanial constraints

Orthographic disharmony cannot be dismissed as entirely irrelevant in all cases, considering that, due to a usually high degree of prestige of the written language, orthographic conventions tend to become interpreted as generally prescriptive and thus tend to influence spoken forms to various degrees. This is the case in Modern Uzbek where a written Iranized urban dialect with a somewhat abstract orthography tends to reinforce phonetic neutralization in prestigeous spoken varieties (Menges 1968: 79–80).

2.1. Root-Final Disharmony. As mentioned earlier (1.2.1.), disharmony is tolerated inside a Turkic root. The type of disharmony one encounters in a few apparently native roots, particularly in kinship terms and onomatopoetic forms, tends to be limited to a vowel and a consonant belonging to different harmonic categories; e.g., Uyghur *'aka* (not **'äkä* or **'aqa*) 'elder brother'. Any type of harmony violation may be encountered within roots that have been derived from foreign words; e.g., Chinese *dàxué* > Uyghur /#daašöö+#/ → *dašö* '(Chinese) college', Farsi *qabrestān* > Uyghur /#qäbristaan+#/ → *qäwristan* 'graveyard'. What determines the harmonic category of the remainder of a given word is the root-final syllable, in the vast majority of cases the final vowel; e.g., *'aka+da* 'by the elder brother', *dašö+dä* 'at the (Chinese) college', *qäwristan+da* 'at the graveyard'. Where in Uyghur a vowel happens to be followed by a root-final consonant of the opposite harmonic category, and the following suffix begins with a harmonically sensitive consonant, suffix-internal disharmony is created, since the root vowel determines the suffix vowel category, while the root-final consonant determines the category of the immediately adjacent suffix consonant (Hahn (forthcoming), Lindblad 1990: 28–29). This is most clearly illustrated by means of the dative-directive suffix /+GA+#/, which under ordinary circumstances has the front allomorphs /+gä+#/ ~ /+kä+#/ and the back allomorphs /+ɢa+#/ ~ /+qa+#/, but which under certain conditions may also have the disharmonic allomorphs /+qä+#/ and /+ka+#/.

(12) Suffix-internal disharmony in Uyghur

Arabic *xalq*	>#xälq+#	'nation'	→#xälq+qä+#	'to the nation'
Farsi *kāvāk*	>#kawak+#	'pit'	→#kawak+ka+#	'to the pit'
Arabic *šarq*	>#šärq+#	'east'	→#šärq+qä+#	'to the east'
	#taktak+#	'clapper'	→#taktak+ka+#	'to the clapper'

2.2. Phonological Neutralization. Among the Turkic languages, vowel neutralization is an innovative, apparently eastern areal feature. In Modern Uyghur, neutralization is created by fronting. The innovative features of umlauting and raising in conjunction with fronting lead to regular occurrence of any unrounded vowel as *i* or *e* in light syllables. As in generally better-known cases such as Standard Russian and Iberian Portuguese, Uyghur vowel raising is associated with weakness and thus may be considered a manifestation of "vowel reduction."

Certain types of superstratal neutralization seem to have existed already in early Eastern Turkic varieties, probably as early as in Old

Uyghur dialects (Gabain 1974: 45–46), thus a good millenium ago. Menges (1968: 79) assumes it to have existed also in Chaghatay ("Old Uzbek," which served as a literary language between the 15th century C.E. and 1921), but this has not been recognized by others (e.g., Eckmann 1966, Ščerbak 1962). Menges generally attributes neutralization to foreign influences, particularly to Iranization, namely to a Tajik stratum. Vowel neutralization and signs of perhaps more deep-seated harmonic pertubations are well-known characteristics of modern urban Uzbek varieties, including Standard Uzbek (in which neutralization has been artificially enhanced by way of orthographic rules). These characteristics too have been attributed to a significant Iranic stratum, not only to external Iranic influences (i.e., Tajik language proficiency among Uzbeks) but also to the adoption of Uzbek among former Tajik speakers. Vowel neutralization appears to occur as an areal feature among the Turkic languages. It is more or less restricted to the eastern regions of Central Asia, and it has affected also Turkic varieties, such as Salar dialects,[19] that had been imported from Western Turkic regions in which neutralization never gained a foothold.

2.2.1. Fronting. Outside neogrammarian circles, neutral vowels in Turkic languages have been widely regarded as being indicative of fundamentally flawed harmonic systems. Zhao & Zhu (1985: 20–21), for example, appear to interprete phonologically neutralized vowels in Modern Uyghur as phonemes (*yinwei*). Unlike for instance in certain Uralic languages and in post-medieval Mongolic varieties, accept Moghul (Poppe 1960: 112–113), neutralization in Turkic is, by and large, attributable to superstratal (or postlexical) rules, namely they are preceded by harmonization. In Standard Uyghur, the high unrounded vowels are neutralized (i.e., fronted) to *i*, but any following morpheme is predictably harmonic.

(13) High-level fronting and harmony in Uyghur

	#kiši+#	#qıs-m+#	#jäŋ++čI+#
V.Harmony			#jäŋ++či+#
Anaptyxis		#qıs-ım+#	
Plural	#kiši+lAr+#	#qıs-ım+lAr+#	#jäŋ++či+lAr+#
V.Harmony	#kiši+lär+#	#qıs-ım+lar+#	#jäŋ++či+lär+#

---

[19] Linguistic evidence points toward Salar belonging to the Western or Oghuz Turkic group. Salar acquired various Eastern strata in the wake of its speakers' eastward migration into areas located in today's Xinjiang, Qinghai and Gansu. Neutralization in Salar may be attributable to medieval Chaghatay-Turkic influence (Hahn 1988).

Fronting		#qis-im+lar+#	
	kišilär	*qisimlar*	*ǰäŋčilär*
	'people'	'sections'	'warriors'

Neutralization by way of fronting takes place also on the mid level, which, as noted above, is occupied by loan-specific front /e(e)/ and back /ɤ(ɤ)/, both being orthographically rendered as *e*.

(14) Mid-level fronting and harmony in Uyghur

	#täybey+#	#gunšɤɤ+#	#xɤɤbɤy+#
Locative	#täybey+dA+#	#gunšɤɤ+dA+#	#xɤɤbɤy+dA+#
V.Harmony	#täybey+dä+#	#gunšɤɤ+da+#	#xɤɤbɤy+da+#
Fronting		#gunšee+da+#	#xeebey+da+#
	Täybeydä	*guŋšeda*	*Xebeyda*
	'at Taibei'	'at the commune'	'at Hebei'

The label "fronting" may be considered somewhat too general. This type of neutralization, in which back vowels come to share a set of allophones with its front counterpart, takes place only in neutral types of environments, namely in environments in which either front vowels or back vowels may occur. Back-vocalic allophones still occur in typically back-vocalic environments, namely adjacent to uvulars.

2.2.2. Vowel Raising. In the standard dialect and in other northern dialects of Modern Uyghur, the low unrounded vowels (i.e., /ä/ and /a/) are transformed into high unrounded vowels (i.e., *i* and *ı* respectively) in non-initial and non-final light (i.e., unstressed CV-type) syllables. This is represented consistently in the official orthographies, except where it applies word-finally in connected speech. Vowel raising follows harmonization and precedes neutralization (see 2.2.1.); i.e., raised vowels are neutralized to *i*, and a following suffix is predictably harmonic.

(15) Uyghur vowel raising

#bala+lar+ı+##käl--mä-di#	→	[balilirikälmidi]
#child+PL+3+##come--NEG-PAST3#		'His children did not come.'

#ʔišäg+i+gä+##bar-–sa-NIZ+#	→	[ʔišiɣiɣiβársiŋiz]
#donkey+3+DAT+##go--COND-2POL+#		'if you go to his donkey'

2.2.3. Umlauting. In many Uyghur dialects, including the standard dialect, vowel raising and fronting are preceded by an umlauting rule that creates what is orthographically represented as *e*: in a word-inital light syllable followed by a syllable with /i/ or /ɪ/, a low unrounded vowel (i.e., /ä/ or /a/) is raised to mid-level (i.e., to *e* or *ɤ* respectively).

(16) Uyghur umlauting (I)

#kälin+gä+#	→	#kelin+gä+#	→	*kelingä*	'to the bride'
#balɪɢ+ɢa+#	→	#bɤlɪɢ+ɢa+#	→	*beliqqa*	'to the fish'
#ʔät+i+dä+#	→	#ʔet+i+dä+#	→	*'etidä*	'in its flesh'
#ʔat+ɪ+da+#	→	#ʔɤt+ɪ+da+#	→	*'etida*	'in its name'
#bär-iš+mäg+#	→	#ber-iš+mäg+#	→	*berišmäk*	'giving together'
#bar-ɪš+maɢ+#	→	#bɤr-ɪš+maɢ+#	→	*berišmaq*	'going together'

Being of the type VV (i.e., V_iV_j, where i = j) and thus rendering a syllable "heavy," long vowels cannot be umlauted.

(17) Uyghur umlauting (II)

#tär+i+#	→	*teri*	'his sweat'
#täär+i+#	→	*täri*	'his complexion'

Rather than writing a single umlauting rule that raises and fronts, Lindblad (1990: 9–12) describes umlauting as "initial vowel raising," which precedes fronting. His solution has been facilitated by his identification of a back mid-level vowel phoneme.

2.3. Labialization Constraints. At first glance, labial assimilation among vowels in Standard Uyghur appears to be inconsistent in comparison with its manifestations in most other Turkic languages. Uyghur roundness response most closely resembles the type of high labial harmony that is prevalent among Western Turkic languages (see 1.2.2.1.), but since roundness is archiphonemically specified (i.e., /U/), this response would, theoretically, be identifiable as a high-level labialization process (i.e., [−Round] → [+Round]) rather than as a truly harmonizing, namely feature-specifying, process (i.e., [∅Round] → [±Round]). What tends to baffle the casual observer about Standard Uyghur vowel labialization is that only certain morphemes within the harmonization domain (see 2.4.) take on rounded vowels.

(18) Labialization in Uyghur

(1)	#yol+um+#	'my way'	#ɢaaz+im+#	'my goose'
	#köl+üm+#	'my lake'	#xälq+im+#	'my nation'
	#tuz++luq+#	'salty'	#qar++liq+#	'snowy'
	#süt++lük+#	'dairy ...'	#tääm++lik+#	'tasty'
(2)	#yol+umiz#	'our way'	#ɢaaz+imiz+#	'our goose'

	#köl+ümiz+#	'our lake'	#xälq+imiz+#	'our nation'
	#ʔon+unči#	'tenth'	#toqsaan+inči+#	'eightieth'
	#ʔüč+ünči+#	'third'	#bäš+inči+#	'fifth'
(3)	#yol+niɴ+#	'of the way'	#ɢaaz+niɴ+#	'of the goose'
	#köl+niŋ+#	'of the lake'	#xälq+niŋ+#	'of the nation'
	#tuz++siz+#	'salt-free'	#qar++siz+#	'snow-free'
	#süt++siz+#	'non-dairy'	#tääm+siz+#	'tasteless'
(4)	#yol+i+#	'its way'	#ɢaaz+i+#	'its goose'
	#köl+i+#	'its lake'	#xälq+i+#	'its nation'
	#tuz+ni+#	'the salt' acc.	#qar+ni+#	'the snow' acc.
	#süt+ni+#	'the milk' acc.	#tääm+ni+#	'the taste' acc.

Groups (18.1) and (18.2) contain only very small samples to illustrate that labialization response after a stem-final rounded vowel occurs only in certain cases. In suffixes of the type shown in Group (18.2) (i.e., /±VCVC(±)#/, e.g., #yol+umiz+#), the first vowel is represented as *i* in the official orthographies (e.g., *yolimiz*), but most speakers labialize it after a rounded stem vowel (e.g., [yolumiz]). Some speakers will apply labialization to suffixes of the type shown in Group (18.3) (i.e., /±CVC(±)#/, e.g., #yol+nuɴ#), but this is hardly acceptable in the standard language. Labialization will never be applied to suffixes of the type shown in Group (18.4) (i.e., /±(C)V(±)#/, e.g., **yolu*), except in dialects that are considered far removed from Standard Uyghur.

The degree of what at first seems to be inconsistency among the Uyghur data becomes all the more apparent in juxtaposition with cognates in Literary Qazaq and Uzbek, in which labialization does not apply, as well as with cognates in Modern Standard Turkish, in which labial harmony applies to any high vowel.

(19) Labialization in Qazaq, Uzbek, Uyghur and Turkish

	Qazaq	Uzbek	Uyghur	Turkish	
(1)	*ǰolım*	*yolim*	*yolum*	*yolum*	'my way'
	kölim	*kolim*	*kölüm*	*gölüm*	'my lake'
	tuzdı	*tuzli*	*tuzluq*	*tuzlu*	'salty'
	sütti	*sutli*	*sütlük*	*sütlü*	'dairy . . .'
(2)	*ǰolımız*	*yolimiz*	*yolumiz*	*yolumuz*	'our way'
	kölimiz	*kolimiz*	*kölümiz*	*gölümüz*	'our lake'
	onınši	*oninči*	*'onunči*	*onunǰu*	'tenth'
	üšinši	*učinči*	*'üčünči*	*üčünǰü*	'third'

(3)	*ǰoldıŋ*	*yolniŋ*	*yolniŋ*	*yolun*	'of the way'
	köldiŋ	*kolniŋ*	*kölniŋ*	*gölün*	'of the lake'
	tuzsız	*tuzsiz*	*tuzsiz*	*tuzsuz*	'salt-free'
	sütsiz	*sutsiz*	*sütsiz*	*sütsüz*	'non-dairy'
(4)	*ǰolı*	*yoli*	*yoli*	*yolu*	'its way'
	köli	*koli*	*köli*	*gölü*	'its lake'
	tuzdı	*tuzni*	*tuzni*	*tuzu*	'the salt' acc.
	sütti	*sutni*	*sütni*	*sütü*	'the milk' acc.

Standard Uyghur vowel labialization can be explained reasonably only on the assumption that it applies exclusively to epenthetic vowels, specifically to anaptyctic vowels,[20] namely to vowels that are inserted to create a desirable CVC-type sequence (e.g., *tuz+um* 'my salt') where the union of two morphemes would otherwise create an undesirable CC-type sequence (e.g., **tuz+m*). The only inherent feature specification of an epenthetic vowel (which we represent as /°/) is [–Low]; in other words, it is high, and the respective values of its features [Back] and [Round] come to be harmonically specified upon its insertion. In contrast, an underlying high vowel—in fact any underlying vowel—in a suffix comes prespecified with regard to the features [Low] and [Round] (i.e., /I/, /U/, /A/), and only the value of its feature [Back] comes to be harmonically specified (i.e., /I/ → /i/ ~ /ı/, /U/ → /ü/ ~ /u/, /A/ → /ä/ ~ /a/).

This analysis is, by and large, consistent with the identification of what is commonly known as "linking vowels" (German *Bindevokale*) among Turcologists. In fact, the same type of harmonic labialization applied already in Old Uyghur (Gabain 1974: 47–48, Poppe 1960: 150), a language from which Modern Uyghur descended partly.

Since CC-type suffixes do not exist (e.g., *#tuz++lq+#), and there is no need for anaptyxis between a consonant and a CV-type sequence (e.g., #köl+din+# (not **köl+üdin*) 'from the lake'), a problem appears to exist *vis-à-vis* suffixes of the types /±CVC(±)#/ (e.g., #tuz++luq+# 'salty') and /±VCVC(±)#/ (e.g., #köl+ümiz+# 'our lake'). These types of suffixes, though being considered indivisible in the modern language, may be fairly safely assumed to be compounds of two or more suffixes. For example, the attributive suffix /++l°G+#/ (as in #tuz++luq+#) seems to be composed of adjectival /++l+#/ and /+G+#/ (Gabain

[20] In Uyghur, other types of epenthetic vowels do not undergo labialization; i.e., prosthesis: Russian *sport* > Uyghur *isport* (neither **usport* nor anaptyctic **suport*) 'sport'; post-final epenthesis: Russian *Tomsk* > Uyghur *Tomski* (neither **Tomsku* nor anaptyctic **Tom(u)suk*) 'Tomsk'.

1974: 60,65,76), and the third person plural possessive marker /+°mIz+#/ (as in #köl+ümiz+#) appears to be derived from first person singular possessive /+m+#/ (as in #köl+üm+# 'my lake') and the ancient dual or plural marker (/+r_2+#/ >) /+z+#/, i.e., from /+m+z+#/, in which case the second anaptyctic vowel became underlying and the first remained anaptyctic.

The identification of anaptyxis is corroborated by the fact that the type of vowel in question occurs, wherever possible, in alternation with zero; e.g., #yol+um# 'my way' vs. #bala+m+# 'my child'. Most convincingly, the same type of labialization and V~∅ alternation occurs where anaptyxis converts attestable foreign CC-type sequences to Uyghur CVC-type sequences.

(20) Uyghur anaptyxis

			'eGiz	'mouth'	(*'aGzim*	'my mouth')
			köŋül	'heart'	(*köŋlüm*	'my heart')
			'oGul	'son'	(*'oGlum*	'my son')
Arab.	*šukr*	>	*šükür*	'gratitude'	(*šükrüm*	'my gratitude')
Arab.	*mulk*	>	*mülük*	'property'	(*mülküm*	'my property')
Russ.	*litr*	>	*litir*	'liter'	(*litri*	'liter of it')
Russ.	*traktor*	>	*tiraktor*	'tractor'		
Russ.	*truba*	>	*turuba*	'pipe'		

At this juncture, there appears to be no definitive answer to the question in which direction Turkic vowel assimilation has been developing: toward labialization or away from it. As with most problems in diachronic Turkic phonology, Early Written Turkic documents (i.e., Kök Turkic and Old Uyghur inscriptions) and virtually all other pre-contemporary written Turkic works do not provide sufficient relevant data: they represent only a small handful of varieties at relatively late historical stages, and their orthographies do not provide for consistent vowel representation. If the development is assumed to have moved *toward* labialization, the type of labial assimilation we have identified in Modern Standard Uyghur would represent the earliest stage: anaptyctic labialization. Labial harmony of high underlying vowels would represent a major intermediate stage, and the various types of general labial harmony together would represent the latest major stage. Epenthetic labialization, or labial assimilation applying to underlying and epenthetic high vowels, is assumed to be contained in high and general labial harmony systems. On the basis of this general model, degree of power to cause and resist labialization is found to be dependent upon degree of specification and markedness: minimal /°/ ([−Low, ∅Back]), and maximal /a/ ([+Low, +Back]).

(21) Types of Turkic labial vowel assimilation

Labialization Type	Vowel Labializing	Vowel Labialized	Sample Language
(1) —	none	none	Uzbek
(2) Anaptyctic	any	°	Uyghur
(3) High	any	high	Turkish
(4) General	(1) any	high	Yakut
	low	low	
	(2) any	high	Qirghiz
	any but *u*	low	
	(3) any	any	Turkmen

2.4. Domanial Constraints. Above (1.2.1., 1.3.) it has been mentioned that Turkic harmony is restricted in applicability to the span of a word, or, more precisely stated, to all derivative and syntactic suffixes up to the nearest following word boundary. Disharmony has come to be tolerated on the root level, being common in foreign words that have been converted to Turkic roots. In any case, it is the stem-final syllable that determines the harmonic category of the remainder of a given word, disharmony being created only where the final vowel and consonant belong to different categories (see 2.1.). Under ordinary circumstances, this applies also to labial harmony, except that in this case a non-qualifying segment (e.g., /a/ after /u/) may terminate the process before the nearest word boundary has been reached.

Given this analytical model, any morpheme that does not conform to the palato-velar harmony specification of an immediately preceding morpheme and whose nonconformity cannot be attributed to superstratal (or postlexical) factors is identified as being preceded by at least one word boundary. Two discrete words are separated by two word boundaries, across which only syntactically conditioned connected speech rules apply. Compound elements and enclitics are separated from a preceding word by a single word boundary, which permits the application of voicing assimilation, devocalization and vowel truncation but not the application of harmonic assimilation. Within the framework of lexical phonology, these sets of processes would be attributed to different strata.

This basic analysis is, also within a general Turkic context, consistent with the one Kardestuncer (1982a, 1982b, 1983) proposes specifically for Turkish. On this basis, the Turkish gerundive marker ...*iyor(...)*, for example, which in other analyses is considered a disharmonic, opaque suffix (e.g., Clements 1980, Clements & Sezer 1982), is identified as being an enclitic ("gerundive compound component," Kardestuncer 1983) whose palatal glide raises the converbial suffix (/-A#/ →) *-ä* ~ *-a*; e.g., #ǵäl-ä#yor# → *geliyor* 'is coming' consistent with #ǵäl-ä#bil-ir# → *gelebilir* 'can come'. Compared with the potential marker *...bilir(...)*, which is derived from the aorist form of the verb *bil-* 'to know', it appears that *...yor(...)* lacks the aorist suffix (/-°r+#/ →) *-ur*, besides the fact that in Modern Turkish **yor-* does not exist as a verb from which a gerundive marker could have been developed. Further research indicates that *...yor(...)* is a contracted form of gerundive #yor-°r# (consistent with #tur-°r#, see 1.4.), and that *yor(ı)-* is attested as an Early Written Turkic verb denoting 'to walk', 'to go on', 'to progress' (Gabain 1974: 388, Lewis 1978: 108, Räsänen 1957: 224–225, 1969: 207), being preserved in the causative form for instance in Old Ottoman Turkish (*yort-* 'to cause (animals) to go' >?) 'to go (on)', 'to travel', Dilçin 1983), Modern Uzbek (*yort-* 'to travel at a steady, fast pace') and Modern Uyghur (*yort-* 'to trot').

Kaisse (1986) has identified in Turkish another morphemic stratum between the suffix and enclitic strata. Such "prestressed suffixes" (or "non-harmonizing enclitics") exist also in Modern Uyghur and other Turkic languages. Morphemes agglutinated on this stratum are within the harmonization domain but outside the word stress assignment domain; i.e., they surface as harmonic but never take on primary stress.[21]

(22) Prestressed suffixes

Turkish	Uyghur	
#ǵä́l−−mä-∅#	#kä́l−−mä-∅#	'don't come!'
#ká́ł−−ma-dim#	#qá́l−−mi-dim#	'I did not stay'
#sǘt++lü+#	#sǘt++lük+#	'containing milk'
#túz++suz+#	#túz++siz+#	'salt-free'

The identification of this prestressed stratum is relevant also within a comparative Turkic context. Certain prestressed suffixes in one language correspond to enclitics in another language, and some of these enclitics appear to be word-derived. This leads to the conclusion that Turkic affixization, specifically suffixization (i.e., the development of a bound morpheme or even a separate heteromorphic structure into an underspecified,

---

21 Primary stress is assigned to the last heavy syllable (i.e., CVV, CVC, CVVC, CVCC) in ultimate or penultimate position; where no such syllable is encountered, primary stress is assigned to any final syllable (Hahn 1991, forthcoming).

harmonizing suffix in the process of changing into a bound morpheme), involves the shift from the word stratum via the enclitic stratum to the prestressed suffix stratum. Movement from the prestressed suffix stratum to the stressed suffix stratum does not seem to be attestable, unless one considers for instance the development of prestressed negative /−−mA-/ (e.g., Uyghur #bar−−mA-d°m# → *bármidim* 'I did not go') to stressed /-mAy#/ in the course of fusing with /-A#/ (i.e., */−−mA-A#/ > /-mAy#/, e.g., Uyghur #bar-mAy#män# → *barmáymän* 'I do not go').

(23) Turkic cliticization and affixization[22]

Morpheme	*Boundary*	*Phonology*	*Development*
1. Root		foot-formation	
2. Suffix 1	+ ~ −	word stress	
3. Suffix 2	++ ~ −−	harmony	(↑)
4. Enclitic	#	connected speech rules 1	↑
5. Word	##	connected speech rules 2	↑

The entire attestable development can be followed in the case of the Early Turkic verb *il-* 'to attach', whose converbial form *il-ä* came to serve as a comitative or instrumental marker. In Modern Standard Turkish, it is used both as a postposition (i.e., word) and as a prestressed suffix. Tabrizi Azerbaijani (Householder & Lotfi 1965) treats it as an enclitic, while Soviet Standard Azerbaijani (Gadžieva 1966, Householder & Lotfi 1965: 79) treats it as a prestressed suffix that differs from its Turkish counterpart in that vowel truncation is complete.

(24) Development of **il-ä* 'attaching' > 'with'

(1) Word-level:

Turkish:	#át##ilä#	'with the horse'
	#atá##ilä#	'with the father'

(2) Enclitic-level:

Tabrizi Azerbaijani:	#át#ilä#	'with the horse'
	#atá#ylä#	'with the father'

(3) Prestressed-suffix-level:

Turkish:	#át++la#	'with the horse'
	#atá++yla#	'with the father'
Soviet Azerbaijani:	#át++la#	'with the horse'
	#atá++la#	'with the father'

[22] Roughly based upon Kaisse's stratification model (1986: 237).

Modern Uyghur retains on the enclitic level a number of morphemes that in other Turkic languages have progressed to the prestressed suffix level. This will be illustrated by means of the following example.

The prestressed equative suffix /++dAy+#/ in some Turkic languages corresponds in Standard Uyghur to the enclitic /#däg+#/ after nominals and to the prestressed suffix /++dAG+#/ after pronominals.[23]

(25) Equative marking

(1) Nominal

Uyghur	*Qazaq*	
#küz+#däk#	#küz++däy#	'autumn-like'
#čüš+#täk#	#tüs++täy#	'dream-like'
#qár+#däk#	#qár++day#	'snow-like'
#qúš+#täk#	#qús++tay#	'bird-like'

(2) Pronominal

Uyghur	*Qazaq*	
#qá+n++daq#	#qá+n++day#	'like what?'
#šú+n++daq#	#só+n++day#	'like that'

In the wake of re-nativization efforts among language planners, the cognate equative enclitics /#däg+#/ and /#dägin+#/, still being used in certain dialects, have been promoted to replace the postposition (Arabic *qadr* 'equivalent' >) *kadar* as the Standard Turkish equative marker (Lewis 1978: 88). Gabain (1974: 64,146) recognizes the suffix /++dAG#/ in Old Uyghur but also identifies *täg* as a separately written postposition. It is tempting to follow Zhao (1984) in linking these forms to the verb *täg-* 'to approach', 'to reach' (*> 'similar', 'equal'). Yet, just as well worth considering within an Altaic context are the Mongolian forms *teg* 'level (place)' > *tegši* 'equal'. In any of these cases, a suffix ought to be assumed dropped (e.g., converbial /-n+#/ or locative /+n#/; Gabain 1974: 141–142, 392–393), being preserved in the dialectal Turkish forms. Alternatively, one might go along with the theory that this marker has been derived from the verb *tä-* 'to say' (which as converbial /#dä-b+#/ → *däp* is extensively used as a marker of purpose) nominalized by /-G+#/ (see e.g., Räsänen 1957: 71–72).

[23] Voiced consonants are assumed to be underlying in cases of [±Voiced] alternation, since only devoicing, not voicing, is attestable in Uyghur (Hahn 1991).

Verbal cliticization occurs in Modern Uyghur verb compounding, specifically in the use of aspectual verbs, like Turkish /...A-#yor-/ mentioned above. For example, the verb *yat-* 'to settle down', 'to be settled', 'to be in a prone position', has come to serve as a cliticized aspectual verb denoting progression.

(26) Uyghur *yat-* as an aspectual enclitic

#sözlä-b#yat-A#män# → {Khotan *sözläwyátimän* / Standard *sözläwátimän*}
#speak-CONV#ASP-V#1SG#
'I am speaking.'

By contrast, cliticization is absent where, in the same type of converbial construction, *yat-* occurs in its original function as an independent verb.

(27) Uyghur *yat-* as an independent verb

#sözlä-b##yat-A#män# → *sözläp yátimän*
#speak-CONV##lie-V#1SG#
'I speak and lie down.'

Thus, strictly speaking, apparent disharmony that is due to domanial constraints does not fully qualify as a form of disharmony. A lack of conscious awareness of these domanial definitions and a lack of orthographic distinctions have led to the widespread perception of it as disharmony.

2.5. Conditional Transparency. The general argument so far has been that in Modern Uyghur, as in virtually all other Turkic languages, harmony may be observed to apply quite regularly once seemingly perturbing superstratal (or postlexical) processes and domanial (or stratal) definitions have been identified. The implication has been that the inherent degree of feature specification within a given morpheme on a given level is constant. This is correct in all cases examined so far. However, one exception deserves some mention at this point: the Modern Uyghur postnominal enclitic /#čä+#/, whose function might be summarized by the label "modal" (e.g., manner: *'uyGurčä* '(in the) Uyghur (manner/language)', equative: *taGčä* '(one) as big as a mountain', diminutive: *kitapčä* 'booklet', approximative: *'ončä* 'about ten').[24] Quite predictably, this enclitic triggers front-vocalic response in a following suffix, as long as the /ä/ does not occur in an open

[24] Initial /č/ does not alternate. In Uyghur, suffix- and enclitic-initial voicing assimilation involves only the native pairs /d~t/, /g~k/ and

syllable, i.e., does not undergo raising to *i*. As soon as it is raised, it turns transparent, namely it ceases to function as a harmonic determinant, the result being that any following suffix harmonizes with the syllable preceding /+čä+#/ (Hahn 1991, Lindblad 1990: 44–48, Šinjaŋ 'Uygur 'Aptonom Rayonluq Millätlär Til-Yeziq Xizmiti Komiteti 1985: 25–27).

(28) Transparency of ...*čä* in Uyghur

(1)	/#näy+#čä+m+dA+#/	→ *näyčämdä*	'in my little flute'
	/#kitaab+#čä+m+dA+#/	→ *kitapčämdä*	'in my booklet'
(2)	/#näy+#čä+dA+#/	→ *näyčidä*	'in the little flute'
	/#kitaab+#čä+dA+#/	→ *kitapčida*	'in the booklet'

It might be proposed that this is a case of feature erasure, namely a type of rule that changes the specification [−Back] to [∅Back] (i.e., /ä/ to /A/) after raising has changed /ä/ to *i*. It is tempting to regard this case of conditional underspecification—namely a case in which a morpheme wavers between two levels—as affording us a glimpse at history in the making: a shift from the enclitic stage to the prestressed suffix stage, which is a development that in other Turkic languages has been completed; e.g., Turkish *türkčä* (cf. Uyghur *türkčä*) 'Turkish', *uygurǰa* (cf. Uyghur *'uyɢurčä*) 'Uyghur'. However, considering that it is a language-specific rule (i.e., vowel raising) that provides the condition in this unique case of "conditional transparency" (or "quasi-transparency"), serious consideration seems to be due to Lindblad's (1990: 47–48) proposed explanation: upon raising, /#čä+#/ comes to be indistinguishable from the agent marker /++čI+#/, which, being a prestressed suffix, is harmony-sensitive (e.g., /#xizmät++čI+lAr+#/ → *xizmätčilär* 'service employees', /#čarwa++čI+lAr+#/ → *čarwičilar* 'herders').

2.6. Conclusion. By outlining harmonic principles within a general Turkic context and by identifying four factors that create what on the surface appears to be disharmony, the Modern Uyghur harmony system

---

/ɢ~q/. (Labial stops do not occur in such positions.) The phonemes /ǰ č/, /z s/ and /ž š/ do not function as pairs (i.e., /č/, /s/ and /š/ do not undergo alternation), because the respective voiced counterparts are loan-specific as onsets. Other Turkic languages have extended their alternation systems to include some or all of these; e.g., */süt++čI+#/ > Turkish *sütčü* (cf. Uyghur *sütči*) 'milk vendor', */ʔaab++čI+#/ > Turkish *avǰı* (cf. Uyghur *'owči*) 'hunter', */kör−−sA+#/ > Shor *körzä* (cf. Uyghur *körsä*) 'if he sees'.

has been described as being a regularly applying set of processes whose evolution can be understood by means of comparative data.

Uyghur disharmony occurs within roots that have been based upon phonologically adapted loanwords, in which cases nativization does not involve harmonization. Where a root-final VC-type sequence happens to consist of two segments of opposite harmonic categories, an immediately following suffix beginning with a CV-type sequence will be disharmonic if both segments are harmony-sensitive.

Uyghur vowel neutralization consists of a set of superstratal (or postlexical) rules of raising and fronting. In non-final light (i.e., CV-type) syllables, low, unrounded vowels are raised. In initial light syllables, they are shifted to the mid level by a following high, unrounded vowel. In any non-initial light syllable, they shift to the high level. All unrounded non-low vowels are then fronted to *e* and *i* respectively.

Labial harmonization in Uyghur has been shown to be restricted to anaptyctic vowels. Assumedly, this is the earliest type of labial harmony in Turkic; high labial harmony represents an intermediate stage, and general labial harmony represents the final stage in this development. The degree of vocalic labialization in Turkic has been identified as being related to the degree of feature specification: the more specified and marked a vowel, the greater its power to cause and resist labialization.

One of the reasons why traditional analyses created the common impression that the Uyghur harmony system is greatly flawed is that domanial constraints (i.e., rule applications on various morphological strata) had not been understood. We have identified three types of agglutinative morphemes in Uyghur, and this may well be extensible to other Turkic languages: (1) suffixes, (2) prestressed suffixes (or "non-harmonic enclitics"), and (3) enclitics. In the course of outlining this argument, some evidence has been presented to show that Turkic bound morphemes may develop from being phonologically discrete to being phonologically dependent by way of cliticization and affixization. Affixization—which in Turkic is restricted to suffixization—has been argued to be a type of abstraction process that involves a shift from full specification to underspecification, namely a shift from resistance to susceptibility in terms of harmonization.

References

Abduraxmânov, Ğ., and A. Rustamov. 1982. *Qadimgi turkiy til.* Tashkent: «Oqituwči».

Ajdarov, Gubajdulla. 1971. *Jazyk orxonskix pamjatnikov drevnetjurkskoj pis'mennosti VII veka.* Alma-Ata: Izdatel'stvo «Nauka» KazSSR.

Amirpur-Ahrandjani, Manutschehr. 1971. *Der aserbaidschanische Dialekt von Shahpur: Phonologie und Morphologie.* Freiburg im Breisgau: Klaus Schwarz.

Anderson, Steven R. 1980. "Problems and perspectives in the description of vowel harmony." In: Vago 1980a: 1–48.

Axmatov, Toktosun K. 1970. *Zvukovoj stroj sovremennogo kirgizskogo literaturnogo jazyka.* Frunze: «Mektep».

——, et al. 1975. *Kirgizskij jazyk: Učebnik dlja russkix grupp vuzov Kirgizskoj SSR.* Frunze: «Mektep».

Azimov, P., Dž. Amansaryev, and K. Saryev. 1966. "Turkmenskij jazyk." In: Vinogradov 1966: 91–111.

Baskakov, Nikolaj A. 1966. "Altajskij jazyk." In: Vinogradov 1966: 506–22.

Chen Zongzhen, and Ilčen. 1986. *Tataeryu jianzhi* (Zhongguo shaoshu minzu yuyan jianzhi congshu). Beijing: Minzu.

Chen Zongzhen, and Lei Xuanchong. 1985. *Xibu Yuguyu jianzhi* (Zhongguo shaoshu minzu yuyan jianzhi congshu). Beijing: Minzu.

Cheng Shi. 1984. "Weiwueryu Kashi-shi fangyan yuyin tedian." *Xinjiang Daxue xuebao* 4: 100–107.

Clements, George N. 1976. "The autosegmental treatment of vowel harmony." In: W.U. Dressler & O. Pfeiffer, eds., *Phonologia 1979* (Innsbrucker Beiträge zur Sprachwissenschaft 19), 11–119.

——. 1980. *Vowel Harmony in Nonlinear Generative Phonology: An autosegmental model* (1976 version). Bloomington: Indiana University Linguistics Club.

——, and Engin Sezer. 1982. "Vowel and consonant disharmony in Turkish." In: H. van der Hulst & N. Smith, eds., *The Structure of Phonological Representations* (2) (Dordrecht: Foris), 213–55.

Crothers, John, and Masayoshi Shibatani. 1980. "Issues in the description of Turkish vowel harmony." In: Vago 1980a: 63–88.

Deny, Jean, et al., eds. 1953. *Philologiæ turcicæ fundamenta* (2), Wiesbaden: Franz Steiner.

Dilçin, Cem, ed. 1983. *Yeni Tarama Sözlüğü.* Ankara: Türk Dil Kurumu Yayinlari.

Doerfer, Gerhard. 1985. *Zum Vokalismus nichterster Silben in altosmanischen Originaltexten* (Veröffentlichungen der Orientalischen Kommission, Akademie der Wissenschaften und der Literatur, Mainz). Wiesbaden: Franz Steiner.

Dul'zon, Andrej P. 1966. "Čulymsko-tjurkskij jazyk." In: Vinogradov 1966: 446–66.

Eckmann, Janos. 1966. *Chaghatay Manual* (Research and Studies in Uralic and Altaic Languages 77). Bloomington: Indiana University, The Hague: Mouton.

Erimer, Kayahan. 1969. *Eski Türkçe Göktürk ve Uygur yazı dili.* Ankara: Türk Dil Kurumu.

Gabain, Annemarie von. 1959. "Das Alttürkische." In: Deny et al. 1959: 21–45.

——. 1974 (1950). *Alttürkische Grammatik.* Wiesbaden: Otto Harrassowitz.

Gadžieva, Ninel' Z. 1966. "Azerbajdžanskij jazyk." In: Vinogradov 1966: 66–90.

Geng Shimin, and Li Zongxuan. 1985. *Hasakeyu jian zhi* (Zhongguo shaoshu minzu yuyan jianzhi congshu). Beijing: Minzu.

Ğappariwa, Aminä. 1980. "Lun xiandai Weiwueryu fangyan ji minzu wenxue yuyan de jichu fangyan he biaozhunyin." *Minzu yuwen* 2: 24–30.

Hahn, Reinhard F. 1986. "Modern Uighur language research in China: Four recent contributions examined." *Central Asiatic Journal* 30.1–2: 35–54.

——. 1988. "Notes on the origin and development of the Salar language." *Acta orientalia academiæ scientiarum hungaricæ* 42.2: 235–75.

——. (1990). "An annotated sample of Ili Turki." *Acta orientalia academiæ scientiarum hungaricæ* 44.

——. (1991). *Spoken Uyghur.* Seattle: University of Washington Press.

——. (forthcoming). "Modern Uyghur *y*∼*r*-insertion: Nativization through analogical extension."

Hanser, Ottokar. 1977. *Turkmen Manual: Descriptive grammar of contemporary literary Turkmen: Texts, glossary* (Beihefte zur Wiener Zeitschrift für die Kunde des Morgenlandes 7). Vienna: Verlag des Verbandes der Wissenschaftlichen Gesellschaften Österreichs.

Hašim, and Mixri. 1986. "Weiwuer kouyu li de chang duan yuanyin." *Minzu yuwen* 3: 39–43.

Hatiboğlu, Vecihe. 1974. *Türkçenin ekleri.* Ankara: Türk Dil Kurumu.

Hebert, Raymond J., and N. N. Poppe. 1963. *Kirghiz Manual* (Uralic and Altaic Series 33). Bloomington: Indiana University Publications.

Householder, Fred W. Jr., and Mansour Lotfi. 1965. *Basic Course in Azerbaijani.* Bloomington: Indiana University, The Hague: Mouton.

Hu Zhenhua. 1986. *Ke'erkeziyu jianzhi.* (Zhongguo shaoshu minzu yuyan jianzhi congshu). Beijing: Minzu.

Jarring, Gunnar. 1933. *Studien zu einer osttürkischen Lautlehre.* Lund: Borelius, Leipzig: Otto Harrassowitz.

Johnson, C. Douglas. 1980. "Regular disharmony in Kirghiz." In: Vago 1980a: 89–99.

Juldašev, Axnef A. 1966. "Baškirskij jazyk." In: Vinogradov 1966: 139–93.

Junasaliev, Bolot M. 1966. "Kirgizskij jazyk." In: Vinogradov 1966: 482–505.

Kaisse, Ellen M. 1986. "Toward a lexical phonology of Turkish." In: M. Brame, H. Contreras, and F.J. Newmeyer, eds., *A Festschrift for Sol Saporta* (Seattle: Noit Amrofer), 231–39.

Kajdarov, Abdu-Ali T. 1966. "Ujgurskij (novoujgurskij) jazyk." In: Vinogradov 1966: 363–403.

Kardestuncer, Aino B. 1982a. "Theoretical Implications of Turkish Vowel Harmony." University of Connecticut unpublished Ph.D. dissertation.

——. 1982b. "A three-boundary system for Turkish." *Linguistic Analysis* 10.2: 95–117.

——. 1983. "Vowel harmony and gerundive compounds in Turkish." *Acta linguistica hafniensia* 18.1: 55–64.

Kenesbaev, Smet, and N.B. Karaševa. 1966. "Kazaxskij jazyk." In: Vinogradov 1966: 320–339.

Kiparsky, Paul. 1973. "Phonological representations." In: O. Fujimura, ed., *Three Dimensions of Linguistic Theory* (Tokyo: TEC).

Lees, Robert B. 1961. *The Phonology of Modern Standard Turkish* (Uralic and Altaic Series 6). Bloomington: Indiana University Publications.

——. 1966a. "On the interpretation of Turkish vowel alternation." *Anthropological Linguistics* 9: 32–39.

——. 1966b. "Turkish harmony and the phonological description of assimilation." *Türk dili araştırmaları yıllığı.* Ankara: Belleten Üniv.

Lewis, Geoffrey L. 1978 (1967). *Turkish Grammar.* Oxford: Oxford University Press.

Li Sen. 1986. "Weiwueryu zhongxin fangyan de zhuyao tedian: jian lun xiandai Weiwuer wenxue yuyan de jichu fangyan." In: Li P.Y., ed., *Zhongguo minzu yuyan lunwenji* (Chengdu: Sichuan-sheng Minzu), 341–65.

Lindblad, Vern M. 1990. "Neutralization in Uyghur." University of Washington M.A. Thesis.

Magomedov, A. G. 1966. "Kumykskij jazyk." In: Vinogradov 1966: 194–213.

Malov, Sergej E. 1951. *Pamjatniki drevnetjurkskoj pis'mennosti: Teksty i issledovanija.* Moscow, Leningrad: Izdatel'stvo Akademii Nauk SSSR.

Menges, Karl Heinz. 1947. *Qaralqapaq Grammar: 1. Phonology.* Morningside Heights, N.Y.: King's Crown Press.

——. 1968. *The Turkic Languages and Peoples: An Introduction to Turkic Studies.* Wiesbaden: Otto Harrassowitz.

Meyer, Iben R. 1965. "Bemerkungen über das Vokal- und Schriftsystem des Runentürkischen." *Acta orientalia (havniæ)* 29: 183–202.

Minzu Wenxue Yanjiusuo, eds. 1984. *Yusup Xas Hajip: QutadGu bilik.* Beijing: Minzu.

Mixri. 1984. "Weiwueryu Luobuhua mingci fushu xingshi fenxi." *Minzu yuwen* 1: 57–59.

Musaev, K. M. 1966. "Karajmskij jazyk." In: Vinogradov 1966: 260–79.

Nasilov, Vladimir M. 1963. *Drevneujgurskij jazyk.* Moscow: Izdatel'stvo Vostočnoj Literatury.

Osmanop, Mirsultan. 1983. "Hazirqi zaman 'uyğur tiliniŋ Lopnor diyalekti (Qisqičä tonušturuš)." In: Zayit Rähim, ed. *Türki tillar tätqiqati* (2) (Beijing: Minzu Chubanshe), 45–89.

Pierce, Joe E. 1966. "Some problems in understanding consonantal conditioning of Turkish vowels." *Anthropological linguistics* 8: 25–29.

Pokrovskaja, Ljudmila A. 1966. "Gagauskij jazyk." In: Vinogradov 1966: 112–138.

Polat, Aabdurup. 1984. "'Uyğur tilidiki 'uzun sozuq tawušlar häqqidä." In: Xämit Sultan, ed., *'Uyğur tili mäsililiri* (Türki tillar tätqiqati 3) (Urumchi: Šinjaŋ 'Uyğur 'Aptonom Rayonluq Millätlär Til-Yeziq Xizmiti Komiteti), 711–28.

Poppe, N. N. 1959. "Das Jakutische." In: Deny et al. 1959: 671–684.

——. 1960. *Vergleichende Grammatik der altaischen Sprachen: Vergleichende Lautlehre* (1). Wiesbaden: Otto Harrassowitz.

——. 1964. *Grammar of Written Mongolian.* Wiesbaden: Otto Harrassowitz.

——. 1965. *Introduction to Altaic Linguistics.* Wiesbaden: Otto Harrassowitz.

Pritsak, Omelijan. 1959a. "Das Karaimische." In: Deny et al. 1959: 318–40.

——. 1959b. "Das Neuuigurische." In: Deny et al. 1959: 525–63.

——. 1959c. "Das Altaitürkische." In: Deny et al. 1959: 568–98.

——. 1959d. "Das Abakan- und Čulymtürkische und das Schorische." In: Deny et al. 1959: 598–640.

Räsänen, Martti. 1969. *Versuch eines etymologischen Wörterbuchs der Türksprachen* (1,2). Helsinki: Suomalais-ugrilainen seura.

——. 1957. *Materialien zur Morphology der türkischen Sprachen* (Studia Orientalia 21). Helsinki: Societas Orientalis Fennica.

Sadvakasov, Gožaxmet. 1970. *Jazyk ujgurov Ferganskoj doliny: Očerk fonetiki, teksty i slovar'* (1). Alma-Ata: Izdatel'stvo «Nauka» KazSSR.

——. 1976. *Jazyk ujgurov Ferganskoj doliny: Leksika, morfologija i jazykovaja interferencija* (2). Alma-Ata: Izdatel'stvo «Nauka» KazSSR.

Ščerbak, Aleksandr M. 1962. *Grammatika starouzbekskogo jazyka.* Moscow, Leningrad: Akademii Nauk SSSR.

Shibatani, Masayoshi, and John Crothers. 1974. "On the status of blank features in phonology." *Glossa* 8.2: 261–70.

Šinjaŋ 'Uygur 'Aptonom Rayonluq Millätlär Til-Yeziq Xizmit Komiteti, eds. 1985. *Hazirqi zaman 'uyɢur 'ädibiy tiliniŋ 'imla luɢiti.* Urumchi: Xinjiang Minzu.

Sjoberg, Andrée F. 1962. *Uzbek Structural Grammar* (Uralic and Altaic Series 18). Bloomington: Indiana University Publications.

Tenišev, Ėdgem R. 1963. "O dialekte ujgurskogo jazyka Sin'czjana." In: A.K. Borovkov, ed., *Tjurkologičeskie issledovanija* (Moscow, Lenigrad: Izdatel'stvo Akademii Nauk SSSR), 136–51.

Vago, Robert M., ed. 1980a, *Issues in Vowel Harmony* (Proceedings of the CUNY Linguistics Conference on Vowel Harmony, May 14, 1977). Amsterdam: John Benjamins.

——. 1980b. "A critique of suprasegmental theories of vowel harmony." In: Vago 1980a: 155–82.

Vinogradov, Viktor V., ed. 1966. *Jazyki narodov SSSR: Tjurkskie jazyki* (2). Moscow: Izdatel'stvo «Nauka».

Xabičev, M. A. 1966. "Karačaevo-balkarskij jazyk." In: Vinogradov 1966: 213–33.

Xinjiang Weiwuer Zizhiqu Wenzi Gongzuo Weiyuanhui, eds. 1983. *Qazirgi qazaq tili.* Beijing: Minzu.

Yavaş, Mehmet. 1980. "Vowel and consonant harmony in Turkish." *Glossa* 14.2: 189–211.

Zakiev, Mirfatyx Z. 1966. "Tatarskij jazyk." In: Vinogradov 1966: 139–54.

Zhang Hongyi, and Meng Dageng. 1982. Qian shuo xiandai Weiwueryu yuanyin /i/ ji qi bianti. *Minzu yuwen* 5: 58–61.

Zhao Xiangru. 1984. "Hanyu *di* he Weiwueryu *tɛg* de guanxi chutan: jian ji Hanyu yinsheng-yun de fuyinwei." *Yanbian Daxue xuebao* 4: 87–98.

——, and Reinhard F. Hahn. 1990. "The Ili Turk people and their language." *Central Asiatic Journal* 33.3–4: 260–89.

——, and Hašim. 1985. "Xinjiang Yili diqu Tuerkehua de tedian." *Minzu yuwen* 5: 26–35.

——, and Zhu Zhining. 1985. *Weiwueryu jianzhi* (Zhongguo shaoshu minzu yuyan jianzhi congshu). Beijing: Minzu.

Zimmer, Karl E. 1967. "A note on vowel harmony." *International Journal of American Linguistics* 33: 166–71.

VLAX PHONOLOGICAL DIVERGENCE FROM COMMON ROMANI: IMPLICATIONS FOR STANDARDIZATION AND ORTHOGRAPHY

IAN HANCOCK
The University of Texas at Austin

Since the late nineteenth century, Romanologists have been attempting to classify the dialects of Romani spoken throughout Europe. This has not been an enterprise of interest only to professional linguists and philologists, but has had practical implications for many people concerned with the various aspects of Romani culture and society, especially in view of the emergence of Romani civil and political rights movements, and the increasing participation of the Romani people in national and international affairs. One particular problem facing the Romani Union's language planning committee (*O Kolo le Alomasqe la Rromana Ćhibaqe*) is that with respect to overall numbers and geographical distribution a Vlax-based dialect is the obvious choice as a standard language; yet it is precisely the Vlax dialects that have diverged the most radically in their phonology from common Romani.

A number of classifications of the Romani dialects may be found in Hancock (1988). Nearly all of the earliest have attempted to group them according to geographical criteria. In 1882, for example, Elysseeff, perhaps the first to do so, divided the population thus (Kounavin 1882):

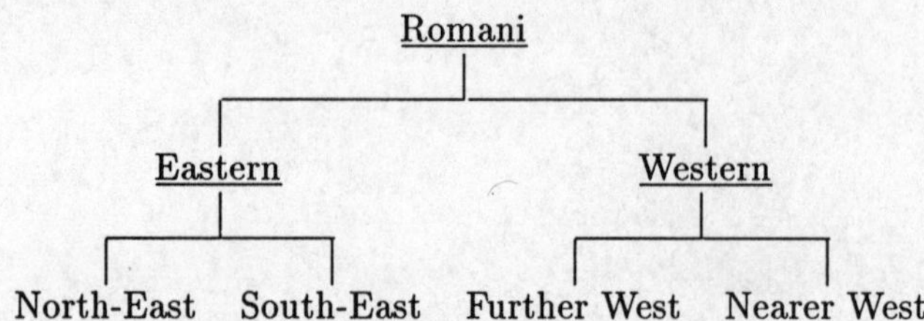

In this classification Elysseeff placed both the Greek and the British Gypsies together in the "Nearer West" group, and included speakers of the Russian dialects under the same heading with those of Iran and the Caucasus as "South-Eastern." Our contemporary linguistic knowledge of the dialects of these populations leads us to group them differently.

Later classifications have been based upon shared lexical and phonological features, although the names for the sixty or so dialects still tend to be geographical in origin. The most generally accepted genetic classification is that of Kaufman (1979, and in Hancock 1988), reproduced here in much simplified form:

Romani

Balkan	Northern	Vlax
Black Sea	Central	Ukrainian
Erli	Sinto	Central
Greece	Nordic	Lovari
Bulgaria	British	Southern
Hungary	Baltic	South-Western
etc.	etc.	etc.

One particular problem in retrieving information on population movement, and hence on external influences which have shaped these dialects, is the non-retention of information about their own migrations among Romani speakers themselves. Although there are several hundred thousand Vlax speakers in the United States, who began arriving here in the decades following the abolition of slavery in the mid–19th century, no one is aware now of the five centuries of enslavement, nor of the Vlaxs' having spent that length of time in what is today Rumania. Even the word *řobo*, originally 'slave' now means in this country 'one unwilling to work', and *řobija* means 'imprisonment'. In Europe the situation is different; there, knowledge of that period of Romani history is widespread. One Romano writer, Matéo Maximoff, has even written a novel about it (1947), and it is also dealt with in the works of Roleine (1978) and Hancock (1987).

This non-awareness is not a recent phenomenon. Seventy-five years ago Winstedt's report on a community of Kalderash Vlax Rom which arrived in Britain, speaking a heavily Rumanian-influenced dialect, made it clear that they had no idea that they were just fifty years from Wallachia and slavery. They identified themselves as Hungarian Gypsies and spoke "good Russian" (Winstedt 1912). It is unlikely that this was mere smoke-screening; there would have been no need to hide an origin in Rumania, and there is a well-established tradition of Gypsies identifying themselves in terms of the place they last were. The names "Tatar" and "Bohemian" and possibly the very name "Gypsy" are examples of this. In the United States there are Vlax-speaking groups identifying themselves as Argentinians, Serbians, Greeks and so on. It is also possible that there has been a complete, purposeful obliteration of the memory of the centuries of slavery, which would account for its general non-retention in this country.

Wherever Romani dialects have been spoken for any length of time they have undergone phonological and other modification as a result of contact with surrounding languages. Thus, in English-speaking countries such as the United States and Canada, the phonemic distinction between aspirated and non-aspirated voiceless stops is becoming lost for some younger speakers. In Finnish Romani the voiced/voiceless distinction is becomming neutralized as a consequence of Finnish proper which lacks that as a significant contrast. In Greece /c/ (i.e., [ts]) and earlier /č/ are collapsing to /c/ under influence from Greek, which lacks /č/. It is phonological changes of this kind that have influenced the Vlax, i.e., "Wallachian" or Rumanian dialects, sometimes referred to as the "Danubian" group, most extensively.

The features I want to examine here are the development of the stops /d/ and /t/, and of the affricates /dž/ and /čh/ in the environment of high and mid-high front vowels, not only in native (i.e., Indo-Aryan derived) items, but in any item containing them traceable to the period up to the time of contact with Rumanian. This would include words from Persian, Armenian, Byzantine Greek, southern Slavic, as well as other languages; for example *tiro* 'your', which is Indic, *luludi* 'flower', from Greek, *pativ* 'honor', from Armenian, and so on.

As a result of prolonged contact with Rumanian, the stops /d/ and /t/ in the Vlax dialects have gone though a succession of changes as shown here, every stage of which is found occurring in some modern dialect:

/d/ → /dj/ → /dž/ → /gj/ → /g/
/t/ → /tj/ → /č/ → /kj/ → /k/

Basing ourselves on Kaufman's classification (1979), the most comprehensive treatment of the Romani dialects available, and using *buti* (Sanskrit *vṛtti*, Prakit *vutti*) 'work' and *stadi* (Greek *skiádi*) 'hat' as examples, we can illustrate the distribution of these sounds as follows:

Group I

1. Bukovina *bući*, *stađi* (Miklosich 1874)
2. Serbia *bući*, *stadji* (Miklosich 1874)
3. Serbia (Macvano) *buči*, *stadži* (Hancock)
4. Bosnia *bući*, *stadji* (Uhlik 1983)
5. Kalderash (Russian) *buki*, *stagi* (Hancock)
6. Kalderash (Yugoslav) *bukji*, *stagji* (Hancock)
7. Kalderash (Swedish) *butji* ~ *buči*, *stadži*

(Gjerdman, et al. 1963)

8. Kalderash (Russian?) *buči*, *stadži* (Ackerley 1914)
9. Russian *buţi*, *staḑi* (Barannikov 1933)
10. Hungarian *butji*, *stadi* (Vekerdi 1983)
11. Hungarian (Lovari) *buči*, *stadži* (Hancock)
12. Polish (Lovari) *bući*, *stadźi* (Pobożniak 1964)
13. Galicia *buki*, *stagi* (Miklosich 1874)

(See Map 1.)

In dialects outside the Vlax group the original values of these phonemes have been retained, or have been modified differently as a result of independent factors:

Group II

14. Balkan (Erli) *butin*, *stadi* (Calvet 1957)
15. Hungarian (Romungro) *buti*, *stadi* (Vekerdi 1983)
16. Northern (Sinto) *buti*, *stadi* (Bischoff 1827)
17. Northern (British) *buti*, *stadi* (Sampson 1926)
18. Northern (Finnish) *butti*, *stadi* (Valtonen 1972)
19. Northern (Polish) *buty*, *stady* (Miklosich 1872)
20. Northern (N. Italy) *buti*, *stadi* (Zatta 1984)
21. Carpathian (Bornemisza) *buti*, *stadin* (Miklosich 1872)
22. Baltic (Latvian) *buti*, *stadik* (Kochanowski 1963)

(See Map 2.)

Allowing for differences in each reporter's orthographic representation, and on the basis of the availability of native speakers of different Vlax dialects in the United States (forms from this source are marked "Hancock"), we can assume that the transcriptions in group I are meant to indicate affrication or palatalization of the earlier dental stops. In two cases (Nos. 5 and 13), retraction has gone completely to a velar articulation. The development of the affricates in Spanish Romani *buchi* and *estache* (Jung 1972) are the result of contact with Spanish, and the same rule has operated in that language upon non-Romani items (cf. *leche* 'milk'). The Iberian branch is in any case not Vlax, its speakers having descended from the first diaspora.

Given that with very few accountable exceptions, it is only the Vlax group of dialects that has developed these affricated forms, we can assume that they are the result of varying lengths of contact with the Rumanian language. In Standard Rumanian, /d/ and /t/ remain unaffected in the environment of /i/ or /e/, although /g/ and /k/ become palatalized before these sounds, which may have influenced the second shift discussed below.

When we examine the Rumanian dialect of the Bayash, however, we find that the feature is widespread. The Bayash descend from the house slaves whose prolonged contact with the non-Gypsy house-holders led to their losing Romani altogether, and acquiring a form of Rumanian natively (Acton 1986). From the studies of the Bayash Rumanian dialect that we have at our disposal (Calotă 1971, Papp 1982a, 1982b, Hasler 1985), and from native speakers in the United States, it is evident that regional, non-standard varieties have served as the model, especially varieties spoken in the western part of Rumania, Banat in particular. Papp provides regional forms together with the Standard Rumanian equivalents in his dictionary, and represents the Bayash pronunciations in phonemic transcription. Other treatment of non-standard Rumanian forms are Gamillscheg (1936), Puşcariu (1943), Pop (1966) and Cazacu (1967); the following examples are from Papp:

Bayash	Rumanian	
alče	*alte*	'other'
beče	*bete*	'intoxicated'
bolînše	*bolînde*	'crazy'
flămînǵe	*flămînde*	'hungry'
ǵes	*des*	'thick'
ǵinče	*dinte*	'tooth'
lače	*late*	'windy'
muratače	*muratate*	'pickled'

It would therefore seem to be the case that the extent of this feature reflects the extent of contact between Rumanian speakers and Gypsies in Moldavia and Wallachia. Kaminski (1980:149–50), in his enormously valuable study of Carpathian and Vlax Romani migrations out of southeastern Europe, adds a further social factor to this:

> ... this linguistic labyrinth should start with the two major dialect subgroups of the Vlachs: the Kalderasha and Lovara. While in Rumania, these two groups specialized in different occupations, and thus came under different spheres of linguistic influence. The Kalderasha, working mainly as coppersmiths, had most of their outside contact with the local peasantry, and for this reason their dialect is heavily influenced by Rumanian. the Lovara, on the other hand, specialized in horse-dealing. Their business was conducted primarily in urban markets, where Hungarian was the dominant language. Thus their vo-

cabulary shows more professional words with a Hungarian etymology.

All Vlax dialects have been affected by this kind of contact; not one has preserved the underlying, historical values of these phonemes in these positions. In addition a degree of free variation is characteristic of some dialects. Gjerdman and Ljungberg (1963), for example, include variant pronunciations such as /dji/ ~ /dži/ 'stomach' in the speech of the same informant; Ackerley (1912) does the same.

In areas where the greatest contact with non-Gypsy languages took place this feature has gone yet further, affecting the articulation of the existing, historical /dž/ and /čh/ producing the retroflex fricatives [ʐ] and [ʂ] (here written /ś/ and /ź/) in all positions. Examples of this include:

džav	*źav*	'I go'
dženo	*źeno*	'person'
živindo	*źivindo*	'alive'
džov	*źov*	'oats'
džuv	*źuv*	'louse'
čhav	*śav*	'boy'
čhel	*śel*	'smallpox'
čhinav	*śinav*	'I cut'
čhon	*śon*	'month'
čhut	*śut*	'vinegar'

Recently adopted items beginning with /dž/ are not subject to this shift; e.g., *džežeš* 'train', *džanta* 'inkstand', etc.

In Bosnian Romani, while the above shifts have not operated, underlying /g/ and /k/ have become palatized to /dj/ and /tj/, while /kh/ has gone to /čh/ (Uhlik 1941): *gili* 'song', *kerko* 'bitter', *kher* 'house' have become *djili*, *tjerko*, and *čher* respectively; also *mange* 'to me', *tuke* 'to you' have become *mandje*, and *tutje*. For some speakers of American Mačvano Romani, these are *mandže*, and *tuče*. In the Kalderash dialect represented by that spoken by Matéo Maximoff /th/ has gone to /č/; e.g., *them* -> *čem* 'country'.

The changes discussed here can be summarized in the following table:

Historical	*t* → *č*	*buti* → *buči*	
Historical	*d* → *dž*	*stadi* → *stadži*	
	d → *dž* → *g*	in Eastern Kalderash: *stagi*	
	t → *č* → *k*	in Eastern Kalderash: *buki*	
	dž → *ź*	in var. dialects:	
			gadžo → *gaźo* 'non-Gypsy'
	čh → *ś*	in var. dialects: *lačho* → *laśo* 'good'	

kh → *čh* in Mačvano: *kher* → *čher* 'house'
th → *č* in some Kalderash:
them → *čem* 'country'
d → *dž* in Mačvano:
g → *dž* in Mačvano: } Collapse of *mange, mande* → *mandže*
t → *č* in Mačvano:
k → *č* in Mačvano: } Collapse of *tuke, tute* → *tuče*

This kind of extensive sound shift is typical of the dialects of Romani that developed in western Rumania, and may be specifically associated with that of the Mačvaya and some varieties of Churari. The particular dialect called Coppersmith, i.e., Kalderash, by Gjerdman and Ljungberg (1963) is more like a form of Churari, and the existence of this characteristic, as well as certain lexical features, identify it as the latter, even though the speaker of the dialect described identifies himself as Kalderash. Unlike Mačvano, which is a geographical designation relating the population to a specific area in Serbia, "Coppersmith" or "Kalderash" is an occupational name, and applies to speakers of various dialects, not all of whom practice coppersmithing as a profession. It would be extremely valuable for this kind of study to investigate the speech of the descendants of the Netotsi, or slaves who escaped from the Rumanians to live in the mountains. Supposedly these features would be far less in evidence. By determining the extent to which these Rumanian-based changes have affected the various dialects of Vlax Romani, we will be able to estimate the degree of contact with Rumanian, and as a result the degree of assimilation to Rumanian culture attending it. In the extreme case of the Bayash, the language has been lost altogether. On the other hand, those dialects most drastically affected by Rumanian phonology are among the lexically richest and most viable in Europe today.

Distribution of Dialect Groups

A. Southern

1. All Vlax Romani dialects developed in the Wallachia-Moldavia-Transylvania area, beginning in the 14th century, and since that time have spread into adjoining regions, namely, Yugoslavia, eastern Hungary, the Ukraine, and parts of Czechoslovakia, Poland, Bulgaria and Greece. There are large migrant Vlax-speaking populations in the rest of Europe, and Vlax is the best represented of all varieties of Romani spoken overseas.

2. The Greek and Balkan groups fall into a number of non-contiguous dialects spoken in Bulgaria, Greece, parts of Turkey and in Macedonia, Bergenland, the Crimea and southern Italy. The Iberian dialects, now restructured on Spanish, Catalan and Portuguese, may also be related to these branches.

B. Central

Central dialects form a transitional group between the Northern and the Southern, but are somewhat closer to the latter, and are found in Czechoslovakia, and parts of Hungary, Germany, Austria and Italy. Much linguistic work has been done on dialects belonging to the Central group.

C. Northern

1. The Baltic dialects are spoken in parts of Poland, Lithuania, Estonia, Latvia and northern Russian. Their speakers suffered particularly badly under Nazism, and today these dialects are no longer numerically well-represented. The Romano linguist Kochanowski has proposed that a Baltic Romani dialect be cultivated as the international standard, his claim being that it remains closest to the original Romani language (Kochanowski 1986).

2. Sinti and Manush are closely-related branches of Northern Romani as it developed on the Continent. The British dialect, now spoken only in Wales and by a steadily diminishing number, has developed separately from it over the past four centuries. Other northern dialects are spoken in Norway, Sweden and Finland. Geographically, this group has traditionally been the most widely spoken throughout Europe, although they have been superceded during the past century by Vlax. Many northern speakers also perished during the period 1933–1945. Nevertheless, Romani activism is particularly strong among the Sinti and the Manush, and the possibility of both a Northern and a Southern Romani standard being developed bears consideration.

In a number of cases dialects spoken in the areas remotest from the Balkans have become restructured, giving rise to varieties which have retained a basic Romani lexicon, but whose phonology, morphology, syntax and idiom are those of the surrounding language. This has happened in Portugal, Spain, Scandinavia and the British Isles. The dialect of the latter has spread to former British territories overseas, and is particularly well represented in North America and Australia.

The distribution of the Romani dialects discussed above is shown on Map 3.

Selection of a Standard Dialect

The varieties of Romani used most extensively for purposes of documentation are Central Vlax (i.e., Kalderash), the Erli dialect of Balkan Romani, and the Slovak variety of Central Romani. The Balkan dialect, spoken in south-eastern Yugoslavia, supports a considerable local literature and the Romani translation of *The Destiny of Europe's Gypsies* (Kenrick & Puxon 1971) has been made using it. It is also used as the written dialect of Romani Union representatives in that part of Europe. The Central dialect does not support an extensive literature, but it is used as the written medium by a number of Romani Union representatives, including the President of the U.N. Praesidium Dr. Jan Cibula, in Switzerland. Elsewhere in Europe, and in North and South America, Vlax Romani is the most commonly-used dialect for correspondence. All Romani-language publications in North America are in Kalderash Vlax, as are most of those currently being published in western Europe as well. There are more contemporary grammars and dictionaries available for Vlax than for other dialects, and more unpublished theses. It is quite clear that for the most widely-applicable practical use, a Kalderash-based dialect would be the logical choice for a standardized dialect.

Balkan dialects differ from Vlax more than conservative Central dialects do, and their geographically restricted use argues against their being cultivated as the basis for an international standard. Differences between Vlax and Central Romani can be minimized with only a small risk of creating an artificial dialect which is native to no one, differences which are primarily phonological and lexical. It is not my intention to address the latter here. Lexical problems are the result of non-shared words for the names of concepts met with after separation in Europe, and have been dealt with by Kochanowski and others. Phonological problems, including problems of differences in stress, a significant factor in reducing intelligibility between dialects, are more easily addressed when dealing with the written, rather than the spoken, word. These may be overcome in part by devising an orthography that uses a fixed set of graphemes interpretable and pronounceable by speakers of both Central and Vlax Romani according to their own phonology, but which at the same time allows the written word to remain constant.

Although Vlax dialects are characterized in particular by the kind of affrication described above, the retention of two /r/ phonemes, and by extensive centralization and palatalization of the vowels, these features are neither exclusive to them nor consistent with them. Typically, extreme differences between the two are of the following type:

	Vlax	Central	
1	[śon]	*čhon*	'moon/month'
2	[ga'źo]	*'gadžo*	'man'
3	[raj]	*raj*	'gentleman'
4	[ʁaj]	*raj*	'twig'
5	[bar]	*bar*	'fence'
6	[baʁ]	*bar*	'rock'
7	[sə]	*si*	'is/are'
8	[kə'rəs]	*'keres*	'you do'
9	[kər'ɟan]	*'kerdan*	'you did'
10	[ʎa(s)]	*las*	'he took'

For 1 Vlax makes no phonemic distinction between aspirated and non-aspirated [č], a contrast maintained in the Central dialects. The grapheme <čh>, therefore, can be retained for either [čh] or [ʂ], or even for [š] where the shift has gone this far. Items also occur in such dialects, e.g., in some varieties of Lovari or Kalderash, which contain an historical /š/, and the symbol <š> should be retained for these only. For all dialects, /č/ exists as an independent phoneme. For item 1, then, the written form <čhon> would be pronounced variously as [čhon], [čon], [ʂon] or [šon] depending upon the dialect of the speaker.

For item 2 /dž/ also exists as an independent phoneme for all dialects, but this can go to [ʐ] or [ž] in Vlax (corresponding to the voiceless shift of [čh] to [ʂ]), suggesting an underlying, but unattested, /*džh/ phoneme.

For items 3, 4, 5 and 6 only Vlax and the Balkan dialects retain the voiced uvular fricative, as well as the flapped /r/, the latter retaining in addition a third lateral retroflexed [ɽ]. Use of the wedge accent <ř>, rather that a separate symbol, would retain the grapheme and make use of a written diacritic mark already existing.

For items 7 and 8 there is no need to indicate centralization since this is not phonemic. For items 9 and 10, palatalization operates following /d/ and /l/ in several Slavic-influenced dialects, both Vlax and Central, though not uniformly in either. In some items this is phonemic, e.g., Vlax *la* 'she', *lja* (or *la*) 'he took'. One way of providing one letter having both values has been used by Barthélémy (1976), who has introduced the grave accented <à>, to be read as /a/ or /ja/ depending upon the dialect of the reader. If it were felt necessary to use only one written diacritic for the whole language, this could also be a wedge diacritic.

At the present time orthographies tend to be those based upon the national languages of the countries in which Romani is spoken, Thus in the United States and Canada, /čh/ and /š/ are both usually written

<sh>. Aspiration tends not to be distinguished orthographically because of confusion with English spelling conventions, and no satisfactory way exists to represent the fricatives /x/ and /ř/, which are sometimes written <k> ~ <h> and <g>. Until a uniform international orthography, and its formal teaching, is instituted, however, Romani will continue to be written in a variety of orthographies.

Map 1.

Balkan area in which the Vlax dialects developed after ca. 1860.

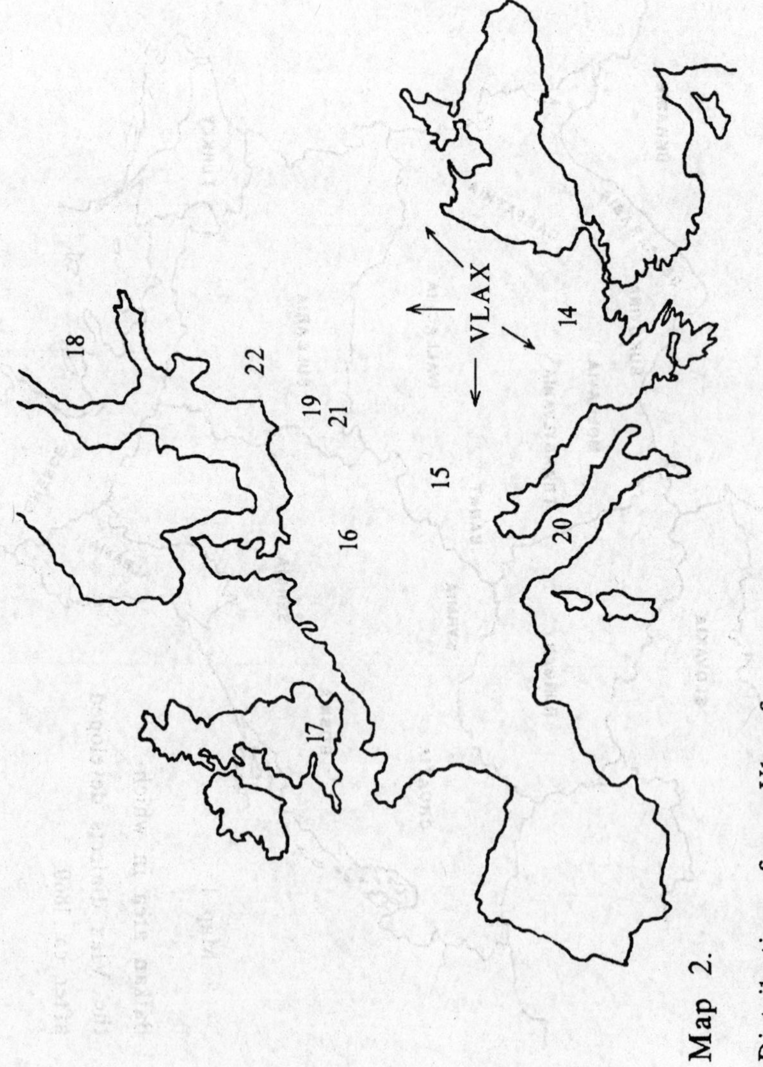

Map 2.

Distribution of non-Vlax forms retaining /t/ and /d/.

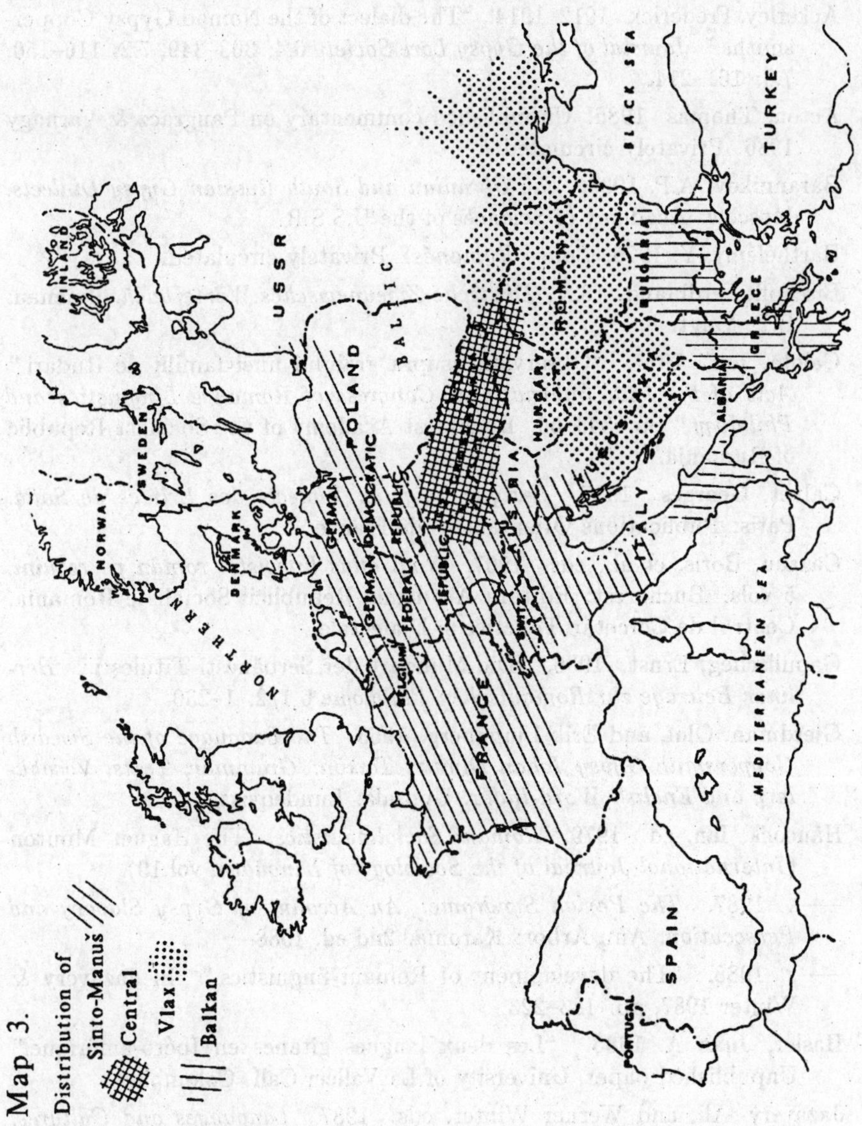

Map 3.
Distribution of
Sinto-Manuš
Central
Vlax
Balkan

References

Ackerley, Frederick. 1912–1914. "The dialect of the Nomad Gypsy Coppersmiths." *Journal of the Gypsy Lore Society* 6.4: 303–349, 7.2: 116–150, 7.3: 161–214.

Acton, Thomas. 1986. Unpublished commentary on Pangracz & Varnagy 1986. Privately circulated.

Barannikov, A.P. 1933. *The Ukranian and South Russian Gypsy Dialects.* Moscow: Academy of Sciences of the U.S.S.R.

Barthélémy, Y. 1976. *Źaneś Ṟomanés?* Privately circulated.

Bischoff, Ferdinand. 1827. *Deutsche-Zigeunerisches Wörterbuch.* Ilmenau: B.F. Voigt.

Calotă, Ion. 1971. "Observaţii asupra graiului unei familii de Rudari." *Acts of the 12th International Congress of Romance Linguistics and Philology,*" pp. 343–50. Bucharest Academy of the Socialist Republic of Rumania.

Calvet, Georges. 1957. *Lexique Tsigane: dialecte des Erlides de Sofia.* Paris: Publications Orientalistes de France.

Cazacu, Boris, et al., eds. 1967. *Noul atlas lingvistic român pe reguini.* 5 vols. Bucharest: Editura Academia Republicii Socialiste România. Centrul de Cercetări Fonetice şi Dialectale.

Gamillscheg, Ernst. 1936. "Die Mundart der Serbănesti-Tituleşti." *Berliner Beiträge zur Romanischen Philologie* 6.1/2: 1–230.

Gjerdman, Olof, and Erik Ljungberg. 1963. *The Language of the Swedish Coppersmith Gypsy Johan Dimitri Taikon: Grammar, Texts, Vocabulary and English Word-Index.* Uppsala: Lundeqvist.

Hancock, Ian, ed. 1979. *Romani Sociolinguistics.* The Hague: Mouton (*International Journal of the Sociology of Language*, vol.19).

——. 1987. *The Pariah Syndrome: An Account of Gypsy Slavery and Persecution.* Ann Arbor: Karoma. 2nd ed. 1988.

——. 1988. "The development of Romani linguistics." In Jazayery & Winter 1987, pp. 183–223.

Hasler, Juan A. 1985. "Les deux langues gitanes en Ibéro-amérique." Unpublished paper, University of La Vallée, Calí, Colombia.

Jazayery, Ali, and Werner Winter, eds. 1987. *Languages and Cultures: Studies in Honor of Edgar C. Polomé.* The Hague: Mouton.

Jung, Christof. 1972. *Wortliste des Dialekts der spanischen Zigeuner.* Mainz: Flamenco-Studio.

Kaminski, Ignacy-Marek. 1980. *The State of Ambiguity: Studies of Gypsy Refugees.* Göteborg: Kompendiet Förlag.

Kaufman, Terrence. 1979. Review of W.R. Rishi, *Multilingual Romani Dictionary* [Chandigarh: Roma Publications (1974)]. In Hancock 1979: 131–144.

Kenrick, Donald, and G. Puxon. 1971. *The Destiny of Europe's Gypsies.* London: Heinemann.

Kochanowski, Jan. 1963. *Gypsy Studies.* New Delhi: The International Academy of Indian Culture. [In two parts.]

Kochanowski, Vanya de Gila. 1986. *Problems of the Common Romani.* Paris: Romano Yekhipe.

Kounavin, M. 1882. [Summary of Kounavin's Romani Research], *Izvestiya Imperatorskavo Russkavo Geograficheskavo Obshchestva* 17: 20–44.

Maximoff, Matéo. 1947. *Le prix de la liberté.* Paris: Flammarion.

Miklosich, Franz. 1872–1881. *Ueber die Mundarten und Wanderungen der Zigeuner Europa's.* Vienna: Alfred Hoelder. [In twelve parts.]

Papp, Gyula. 1982a. "A Beás Cigányok román nyelvjárása." *Tanulmányok* 5: 1–173.

——. 1982b. "Beás-Magyar szótár." *Tanulmányok* 6: 1–199.

Pobożniak, Tadeusz. 1964. *Grammar of the Lovari Dialect.* Krakow: Polska Akademia Nauk.

Pongrácz, Eva and E. Varnagy. 1986. "Communication without writing: Pictorial art and the education of Gypsy children." Paper presented at the International Symposium of Romani Language and Culture. Sarajevo, June 9–12, 1986.

Pop, Sever. 1966. *Receuil posthume de linguistique et dialectologie.* Gembloux: Éditions Duculot.

Puşcariu, Sextil Iosif. 1943. *Die rumanische Sprache.* Leipzig: Harrassowitz.

Roleine, Roberte. 1978. *Le prince d'un été.* Paris: Tallandier.

Sampson, John. 1926. *The Dialect of the Gypsies of Wales.* Oxford: The Clarendon Press.

Uhlik, Rade. 1941. "Bosnian Romani: Vocabulary." *Journal of the Gypsy Lore Society* 20: 78–84, 100–140; 21: 24–55, 110–141; 22: 38–47, 107–190.

——. 1983. *Srpskohrvatsko-Romsko-Engelski Rečnik.* Sarajevo: Svjetlost.

Valtonen, Pertti. 1972. *Suomen Mustalaiskielen etymologinen sanakirja.* Helsinki: Suomalaisin Kirjallisuuden Seura.

Vekerdi, Jozsef. 1983. "A magyarországi Cigány nyelvjárások szótára" *Tanulmányok* 7: 1–246.

Winstedt, Eric O. 1912–13. "The Gypsy Coppersmiths' Invasion of 1911–1913." *Journal of the Gypsy Lore Society*. 6.4: 244–303.

Editors' Note: Since the publication of this paper, the language commission of the International Romani Union, which met in Warsaw in the Spring of 1990, has reached a consensus on a standard orthography for Romani. This orthography incorporates some of the features described in this paper.

DIALECTS, DIGLOSSIA, AND DIACHRONIC PHONOLOGY IN EARLY INDO-ARYAN

HANS HENRICH HOCK
University of Illinois at Urbana-Champaign

1. Introduction. Most discussions of early Indo-Aryan, and especially Sanskrit, diachronic phonology sooner or later invoke dialectal differences to account for certain changes that are considered to be otherwise difficult, if not impossible, to explain. In Sanskrit the most notorious of these changes is the development of a contrast between dental and retroflex consonants, which will feature prominantly in the present discussion. Some of these developments may be attributed to contact with other languages, but will be ignored in the present paper. For recent discussions, see Emeneau 1980, Hock 1975, 1984.

While in many Indo-European languages such dialectological arguments are fairly straightforward, in early Indo-Aryan they are not: First of all, some scholars (such as Mansion 1931 and Renou 1957 [note 80]) would like to deny that the early Sanskrit developments that are often considered dialectal must be attributed to fully differentiated dialects. Secondly, linguists claiming dialectal influence on early Sanskrit do not necessarily agree as to whether we are dealing with geographical or social dialect differences. More commonly, reference is made to social dialect differences, i.e., between a highly standardized and conservative Sanskrit and the more vernacular and innovative Prakrits; e.g., Edgerton's (1930) and Emeneau's (1966) papers on dialects in Old Indo-Aryan. It is convenient to refer to this kind of social differentiation as DIGLOSSIC, thus distinguishing it from geographically defined, DIALECTAL differences, although for early Indo-Aryan the term may not be entirely appropriate. Some scholars, on the other hand, may posit geographical dialect differences instead of, or in addition to, the diglossic ones; e.g., Fortunatov 1881, and Chatterji 1960. Another, partly related argument is that a shift in the geographic basis of Sanskrit accounts for many changes in the history of the language; e.g., Zimmer 1879. Finally, it has been argued that many of the developments claimed to exhibit dialectal or diglossic influence on early Sanskrit should instead be viewed as something like corruptions in the oral transmission of the early Sanskrit texts. These are said to reflect features in the native dialect of the persons in charge of the oral transmission, features that differ from the early Sanskrit norm and come closer to the later Prakrit norms. See Deshpande 1978 for the most recent discussion.

In this paper I attempt to provide a critical review of these different hypotheses by: (i) determining the extent to which the arguments decided in their favor can be considered established; and (ii) examining whether the phonological changes for which they have been invoked require the assumption of one or another of these views. Moreover, I will investigate to what extent dialectological or diglossic differences can help explain developments for which they have not so far been invoked. In the process I will draw on pertinent textual passages, the evidence of ancient Indian phonetic treatises, the dialect-geographical data provided by the Aśokan inscriptions, as well as the evidence of phonological change within Indo-Aryan, especially Sanskrit.

2. Textual passages. Let me begin with the testimony in early Sanskrit texts that has been invoked as evidence for dialectal differences.

2.1. A famous and often-quoted passage from the Kauṣītaki-Brāhmaṇa appears to establish that "northern [or northwestern] speech" was considered especially prestigious and correct; see numbers (1) and (2) below. Taken by themselves, these statements might not be considered particularly enlightening. In conjunction with other evidence they can be interpreted as indicating that the Sanskrit of this area was especially conservative. Thus it has been noted that the northwestern versions of the Mahābhārata and the Pañcatantra are considerably more conservative than the more eastern and southern versions; and that the northwestern dialects and languages of Middle and Modern Indo-Aryan preserve features of Old Indo-Aryan more faithfully than their more eastern or southern counterparts. For a good summary, see Renou 1956: 10, 103.

(1) *tasmād udīcyāṁ diśi prajñātatarā vāg udyata* (|) *udañca u eva yanti vācaṁ śikṣituṁ* (|) *yo vā tata āgacchati tasya vā śuśrūṣante...eṣa hi vāco dik prajñātā*
'In the northern region, speech is spoken particularly distinct(ly). People go to the north to learn speech. Or if someone comes from there, they like to hear/learn from him. For this is known as the region of speech.' (Kauṣītaki Brāhmaṇa 7.6)

(2) *údīcīm evá díśam* (|) *pathyàyā svastyā́ prā́jānaṁs* (|) *tásmād átrottarā́hi vā́g vadati kurupañcālatrā́* (|) *vā́g ghy*

èṣā́ nidā́nena

'Through Pathyā Svasti they recognized the northern quarter/region. Therefore there speech speaks northwards/better, among the Kuru-Pañcālas. For she is really speech.' (Śatapatha-Brāhmaṇa 3.2.3.15)

2.2. This description of "northern" speech has been contrasted with the speech of the easterners, as it is said to be characterized in the passages cited in (3) and (4). Cf. especially Chatterji 1960.

(3) *té 'surā ā́ttavacaso he 'lávo he 'láva íti vádantaḥ párābabhūvuḥ* (|) *tátrainām ápi vā́cam ūduḥ* (|) *upajijñā́syām̐* (|) *sá mléchas* (|) *tásmān ná brāhmaṇó mleched* (|) *asuryà haiṣā́ vā́g*

'The asuras, deprived of (proper) speech, saying *he 'lavo he 'lavaḥ* [instead of the correct *he 'rayo he 'rayaḥ*] were defeated. At that time they spoke that speech, (which was) unintelligible. That is a barbarism. Therefore a brahmin should not speak like a barbarian. That speech is of the asuras.' (Śatapatha-Brāhmaṇa 3.2.1.23-4)

(4) *aduruktavākyaṁ duruktam āhur...adīkṣitā dīkṣitavācaṁ vadanti*

'Speech which is not difficult they consider difficult ...even though they are not consecrated, they speak the language of the consecrated' (Pañcaviṁśa- Brāhmaṇa 17.9)

Again, these citations require interpretation and supporting evidence to become intelligible:

In the passage cited in (3), one of the asuras' mistakes lay in pronouncing an *l* where they should have used *r*. This use of *l* is characteristic of eastern or "Magadhan" speech in later Indo-Aryan. Moreover, there is independent evidence that this *l*- variety of Indo-Aryan, as well as the people from Magadha held a relatively low prestige. Thus the word *kalma-*, an *l*-variety of *karma-* 'action, deed', has the negative meaning 'ill-begotten deed'. The word *puṁścalī* 'whore (who runs after men)', which is derived from *pum(an)s-* 'man' and the root *car-/cal-* 'move, run', significantly is attested only with *l*. (For further discussion and references, see Hock and Pandharipande 1976: 127.) And the vidūṣaka, the fool of Sanskrit drama, who although being a brahmin, cannot converse in Sanskrit, speaks a (stage) variety of Magadhi. In addition there is further textual evidence in early Sanskrit which supports an equation of the asuras with the easterners and a view of Magadhans as being associated with inferior people; cf. (5) and (6). Interestingly, the latter passage contains a variant of the word *puṁścalī*.

(5) *tásmād yā́ daívyāḥ prajā́ś cátuḥsraktīni tā́ḥ śmaśānā́ni kurvaté 'tha yā āsuryā̀ḥ prācyā́s tvad yé tvat parimaṇḍalā́ni té*

'Therefore those people who are godly make their burial grounds four-cornered, but those who are of the asuras, either the easterners or whoever, (make them) round.' (Śatapatha-Brāhmaṇa 13.8.1.5)

(6) *māgadhaṁ ca puṁścalūṁ ca dakṣiṇe vedyante mithunīkārayanti*

'They make a Magadhan and a whore copulate to the south of the altar' (Jaiminīya-Brāhmaṇa 2.404)

The dialectological interpretation of the passage in (3), thus, can be considered fairly well established.

The situation is less certain for the passage cited in (4): It comes from a description of the "vrātya" rite and appears to indicate that the vrātyas did not speak proper Sanskrit. In fact, Chatterji interprets the term "difficult speech" to refer to the complex consonant clusters of Sankrit which in the Prakrits are simplified (such as in example (7)). Underlying Chatterji's interpretation is the assumption that the vrātyas were easterners and that eastern speech exhibited the Prakritic process of cluster simplification at a much earlier time than did the more western varieties of Old Indo-Aryan.

(7) Skt. *sapta* > MIAr. *satta* 'seven'

Given these asumptions, the passage appears to provide excellent and even more concrete evidence for early dialectal differentiation. However, Chatterji's interpretation lacks cogency for several reasons: First, the identity (social, geographical, or ethnical) of the vrātyas is still a matter of controversy. Secondly, and more specifically relevant, a fuller version of the passage in (4) is as in (4') below. While the exact significance of the additional textual material is not entirely clear, it suggests that the complete passage may not so much refer to linguistic features of the vrātyas' speech, as to certain ritually incorrect actions and to the function of speech in that context. This interpretation is reflected in the gloss of (4'). It is further supported by the parallel passage of the Jaiminīya-Brāhmaṇa, given in (8), which states that the vrātyas use speech for ritually impure purposes.

(4') *garagiro vā ete ye brahmādyaṁ janyam annam adanty* (|) *aduruktavākyaṁ duruktam āhur* (|) *adaṇḍyaṁ daṇḍena ghnantaś caranty* (|) *adīkṣitā dīkṣitavācaṁ vadanti*

'They who eat foreign food (?) as brahmin food are eaters of poison. Speech that is not badly spoken they consider badly spoken. They go around punishing/keep punishing who is not to be punished. Even though they are not consecrated, they (dare to) speak the language of the consecrated' (Pañcaviṁśa-Brāhmaṇa 17.9)

(8) *vācā hy avratam amedhyaṁ vadanti*

'By means of speech they speak something not in accordance with religious duties, something ritually impure' (Jaiminīya-Brāhmaṇa 2.222)

2.3. The passage in (4) thus must be considered of dubious relevance, and we are left with two very general statements to the effect that northern (or northwestern) speech is purer or more conservative, and a passage suggesting that the use of *l*-forms, an eastern or Magadhan feature, is considered barbaric. The textual evidence for geographical dialect differentiation thus is quite meager.

On the other hand, given the contexts in which the passages in (1), (2), and (3) are embedded, as well as the general tradition to which they belong, the social element of "purity" vs. "corruption" appears to be much more relevant than geographical considerations. Note that even the passages in (4/4') and (8) can be considered to be concerned with linguistic—and ritual—purity. In fact, the concern for linguistic and ritual purity can be traced back as far as Rig-Vedic times; cf. Hock and Pandharipande 1976 with references. Given this background, then, the problem of barbaric speech adressed in (3) may be considered at least as much one of diglossia (between a conservative standard and a vernacular standard) as one of dialectal differentiation.

3. The evidence of the phonetic treatises. More concrete evidence for some kind of dialectal diversification can perhaps be gleaned from the phonetic treatises that were developed to asure proper recitation of the Vedic texts, namely the Prātiśākhyas.[1]

---

[1] For modern summaries and interpretations of these texts, see Whitney 1862, 1863, Varma 1929, Allen 1953, and Mishra 1972. The last-mentioned

In the following, I will limit myself to a discussion of what is important for the subsequent discussion. Note from the outset, however, that here too we need to resort to a fair amount of interpretation in order to understand the import of the statements made in these treatises.

First of all, it is important to keep in mind that except for the Pāṇinīya-Śikṣā, these treatises attempt to describe (or prescribe) the correct pronounciation for particular branches (śākhās) of the Veda. To the extent that they offer varying accounts for particular segments, these variations therefore refer to differences in the recitation of different Vedic traditions or SCHOOLS. They do not necessarily refer to geographical differences, although it is possible that the starting point for the different traditions of recitation lay in geographically distinct variants of Sanskrit. Still, whether the variations are attributed to geographical dealects, to geographically based differences between Vedic schools, or to some other factors, there is no reason against accepting them as genuine phonetic differences across different varieties of Sanskrit.

3.1. There is a considerable amount of variation or disagreement between the different Prātiśākhyas as far as the phonetic characterization of the dentals, *r*, and the retroflex consonants is concerned. The different characterizations are summarized in Table I, which also gives a key to the abbreviations used in this section.

The description in VP, AP, and TP of the retroflex consonants as being articulated with the tongue curled back is interesting mainly for its fine phonetic observation. There is no compelling reason for assuming a different articulation for the domals in the other Vedic branches or for the language described by the Pāṇinīya-Śikṣā.

For the dentals, however, there is an interesting difference: While most of the Prātiśākhyas, as well as the Pāṇinīya-Śikṣā, describe them as articulated against the teeth, two texts (RP and TP) characterize them as being produced at the root of the teeth (*dantamūla*), suggesting a slightly more retracted pronunciation. Variation of this sort is entirely credible and has parallels in the varying pronounciation of "retroflex" stops as alveolars or strongly retracted segments in different varieties of Modern Hindi-Urdu. (The alveolar articulation seems to be especially favored by Muslims).

---

of these books, in its first part, extensively repeats Varma 1929 (generally without attribution); the second part appears to contain more original material.

	RP	VP	AP	TP	RT	PS
Retroflex	domal	domal with tongue curled back	domal with tongue curled back	domal with tongue curled back	domal	domal
Dental	tooth-root	dental	dental	tooth-root	dental	dental
r	tooth-root/ alveolar	tooth-root	tooth-root	behind teeth	dental/ tooth-root	domal
l	tooth-root	dental	dental	tooth-root behind teeth		dental
ṛ	velar partly [r]	velar [ªrª]	partly [r]	alveolar	velar	domal
ḷ	velar	dental	partly [l]	alveolar		dental

(Abbreviations: RP = Rik-Prātiśākhya; VP = Vājasaneyi-Prātiśākhya, AP = Atharva-Prātiśākhya; TP = Taittirīya-Prātiśākhya; RT = Rik-Tantra; PŚ = Pāṇinīya-Śikṣā. The term "domal" translates the Sanskrit *murdhanya-* 'located at the dome or roof of the mouth'.)

Table I: Dentals and retroflexes in phonetic treatises

3.2. Also for the liquids *r* and *l*, we find varying descriptions. The general pattern is as follows: *l* almost invariably is described in the same way as are the dental stops, and it is almost always characterized as more dental than *r*. (The only exception is TP.) And *r* is usually described in the Prātiśākhyas as farther back than the dental stops, but not as far back as the retroflex stops. RP and RT, to be sure, offer this postdental articulation only as an option. However, given that an *r* is difficult, if not impossible to articulate against the teeth (or even against the base of the teeth), one suspects that what is offered as an option actually is the phonetically more accurate account.

An apical postdental articulation, i.e., farther back than the normal articulation for the dentals (whether that is fully dental or "tooth-root") is further suggested by the fact that, like postdental retroflex *ṣ*, *r* has triggered a change of *n* to *ṇ* under certain conditions; cf. the formulation and examples in (9). The synchronic alternations left behind by this *n*-retroflexion had to be accounted for by Pāṇini's grammar. And it is no doubt in this synchronic phonological context that the generalization that postdental/alveolar *r* and postdental/retroflex *ṣ*—both apical—trigger *n*-retroflexion was captured by labeling both segments as retroflex (or "domal"). This PHONOLOGICAL, rather than phonetic, characterization then must be considered to have entered the Pāṇinīya-Śikṣā, the phonetic treatise of the Pāṇinians. (See also Hock 1979, 1984, To Appear.)

Some scholars, such as Varma (1929: 53), to be sure, prefer to see in the retroflex characterization of *r* further evidence for dialectal diversification. But this interpretation is unnecessary and dubious as well, given that no attested varieties of Indo-Aryan offer any direct phonetic evidence for a retroflex articulation of *r*.

(9) $$\mathrm{n} > \underset{.}{\mathrm{n}} / \left\{ \begin{matrix} \mathrm{r} \\ \underset{.}{\mathrm{s}} \end{matrix} \right\} (\mathrm{V}) \left(\left\{ \begin{matrix} \mathrm{C, +grave} \\ \mathrm{y, v, h} \end{matrix} \right\} \right) (\mathrm{V}) \_\_\_ \dots$$

varna- > *varṇa-* 'color, variety, etc.'
viṣnu- > *viṣṇu-* 'Vishnu'
kṛpāna- > *kṛpāṇa-* 'lamenting'
coṣkūyamāna- > *coṣkūyamāṇa-* 'tearing'

3.3. Summarizing our findings up to this point as in Table II, we can see that there are two varieties of Vedic recitation whose relationship to each other is such that the dentals of one variety are articulated roughly in the same position as the postdental *r* of the other variety. As a consequence, the cut-off point between dental and postdental (indicated by ||) differs between the two traditions. Assuming that these differences rest on some kind of genuine dialectal distinction in Vedic Sanskrit (whatever the original geographical or social basis), we can draw on them in our later discussion to propose a posible new explanation for certain phonological developments which have again and again intrigued historical linguists and led them to postulate a large variety of different explanations.

	Dental	Tooth-root	Alveolar	Domal
RP/TP		"dentals'	‖*r*	"retroflexes"
Others	"dentals'	‖*r*		"retroflexes"

Table II: Places of articulation for dentals, retroflexes, and [r] in Vedic recitation (Summary)

3.4. What is more problematic is the interpretation of the statements concerning syllabic *ṛ* and *ḷ*. The fact that certain Prātiśākhyas refer to one of both of them as velar has given rise to a number of different interpretations; cf. e.g., the discussion in Whitney 1862, 1868, Varma 1929, Allen 1953, Mishra 1972. I believe Cardona (personal communication, 1980) is correct in resolving the issue by arguing that "velar" here refers to the fact that, at least in some traditions of Vedic recitation, these segments were pronounced as in (10a); cf. e.g., the characterization of syllabic *ṛ* in VP, as well as the fact that in Avestan, a closely related ancient Iranian language, the counterparts of those segments are commonly written as in (10b). (Avestan lacks forms with *l*.)

Support for this analysis may be seen in the fact that in the grammars of post-Vedic Sanskrit, [a] is classified as a velar. For the Prātiśākhyas, to be sure, there is the difficulty that *a* seems to be classified as glottal (together with *h* [ɦ] and visarga [h]), rather than velar. Still, given that one of the treatises that classify syllabic *ṛ* as a velar also characterizes it as mixed with *a* and that the other (as well as AP) makes a statement eminently compatible with that description, the analysis in (10a) appears to be preferable to such alternatives as postulating for certain branches of the Veda a velar—or rather, uvular—syllabic *Ṛ* and a velarized syllabic *ḷ*. For while the change of alveolar *r* to uvular *R* is not at all uncommon in the world's languages, I know of no case in which it has been confined to syllabic *ṛ*. Similarly, the change of dental or "clear" *l* to velarized or "dark" *ł* is quite common, but again, I am not aware of it ever being restricted to syllabic *ḷ*. Moreover, the fact that syllabic *ṛ* serves just as much as a trigger for *n*-retroflexion as non-syllabic *r* (cf. the third example in (9)) would be accounted for more easily by assuming that its *r*-element has the same apical and postdental articulation as non-syllabic *r*. This issue is taken up in greater detail in Hock 1987. (The fact that syllabic *r̥* triggers *n*-retroflexion is of course responsible for its classification as retroflex in the Pāṇinīya-Śikṣā.)

(10) (a) VP [^{a}r^{a}], [^{a}l^{a}]
(b) Avestan [^{ə}r^{ə}]

3.5. Two further observations of the ancient Indian phonetic treatises will be important for our discussion. One concerns the articulation of intervocalic voiced retroflex stops; the other addresses the issue of "gemination."

3.6. The Rik-Prātiśākhya, following the established text of the Rig-Veda and the Brāhmaṇas belonging to it, teaches that the voiced retroflex stops are articulated as retroflex laterals *ḷ*, *ḷh* in intervocalic position. This pronunciation receives support from a commentary on AP and an optional rule of the VP, to the extant that for intervocalic *ḍ*, *ḍh* one must avoid "heavy contact," that instead they are to be articulated with a "gentle effort."

3.7. All the Prātiśākhyas agree on prescribing gemination of consonants in certain contexts. And as Varma (1929, Chapters 2 and 5) has pointed out, examples of such gemination are found in certain manuscripts; cf., e.g., (11).

(11) (a) yukktāḥ = yuktāḥ 'yoked ones'
(b) dakkṣāyāḥ = dakṣāyāḥ 'of the active one'
(c) addya = adya 'today'
(d) puttra- = putra- 'son'
(e) ghanasppati- = ghanaspati- [read *vanaspati*- 'tree'?]
(f) asmmin = asmin 'in that one'
(g) dīrggha- = dīrgha- 'long'

What the Prātiśākhyas do not entirely agree on are the specific contexts in which gemination takes place. Thus, AP prescribes it for final consonants, but none of the other Prātiśākhyas adhere to this view. AP, VP, and TP exclude gemination before homorganic consonants; RP has no such restriction. And so on. What remains are some general tendencies. The most widely accepted case of gemination is that of consonants before or after *r*. But even here, AP, TP, and Pāṇini agree on ruling out gemination of sibilants after *r*, and RP proscribes any sibilant gemination.

3.8. These geminations are of interest to linguists working of the historical phonology of early Indo-Aryan in so far as they have been claimed to be the antecedents of Prakit developments of the type illustrated in (7). (This example is repeated here for convenience.)

(7) Skt. sapta > MIAr. satta 'seven'

While according to a traditional view, espoused for instance by Mayrhofer (1951) and Hock (1986a), changes of this sort are to be attributed to large-scale assimilations, Varma (1929) and following him, Murray (1982) have argued that they reflect earlier geminated clusters, as in (12). This view requires the assumption that the triggering environment dropped out in Prakrit, presumably through cluster simplification.[2]

(12)	Original	Geminated	Prakrit
(b)	dakṣa-	dakkṣa-	dakkha-
(c)	adya	addya	ajja
(d)	putra-	puttra-	putta-
(e)	ghanaspati-	ghanasppati-	ghanapphati
(f)	asmin	asmmin	ammi
(g)	dīrgha-	dīrggha-	diggha-

While certainly attractive, this "geminatory" explanation of the Prakrit developments of Old Indo-Aryan clusters suffers from a number of weaknesses.

One is the appearance of aspiration in the Prakrit outcomes of (12b) and (e). Murray (1982: note 13) admits that the development on these examples is "problematic," but the solution that he proposes is rather opaque. One of the processes it seems to require is a regular, but unmotivated metathesis of the sibilant with the following (geminated) stop for examples like (12e).

I have argued elsewhere (1985), that the development in (12e) should be considered in conjunction with the USUAL Prakrit development of clusters of the type (12f), a development which is not as indicated in example (12f) but rather as in (12'f). What we find here is that *s* has

[2] The data in (12) are subcategorized by environment in the same manner as (11), with (b)–(d) covering stop before a consonant that is a trigger for gemination, and (e)–(f) giving stops after such triggers. The data have been rearranged so as to give a clearer picture of the putative historical developments. Moreover, the account has been simplified by giving stems, rather than longer inflected forms. In a few cases, Prakrit equivalents are given that are not directly documented but that would have the indicated shape if they were attested. (Note that (11a) has no counterpart in (12) since its behavior is quite different; cf. (12'a–a''') below.)

gone to *h*, which like inherited *h* has metathesized with the nasal. Note that unlike Murray's scenario, this metathesis is motivated—as a means of eliminating post-vocalic, syllable-final *h*. (Cf. Hock 1985.)

Given the precedent of the nasals, it is then possible to argue for the development in (12'e), involving a similarly motivated metathesis. (For clarity's sake, aspiration and segmental *h* are here distinguished as [ʰ] vs. [h].) The only difference between (12'f) and (12'e) is that since Indo-Aryan has stop aspirates of independent origin and does not tolerate clusters of stop plus *h*, the segment *h* fuses with a preceding stop into an aspirate. Gemination of the aspirate, then, compensatorily preserves the quantity of the earlier cluster. (In (12'f), on the other hand, such a development does not take place, since there are no independent aspirated nasals. The *h* of such Prakrit forms is solidly segmental.)

Forms of the type (12b) seem to require weakening of sibilant to *h* AFTER stop, i.e., a mirror image of the weakening in (12'e). From that point onward, however, the development would be entirely parallel to the post-metathesis changes in (12'e). See the formulation in (12'b). While such post-consonantal weakening is not as common as syllable-final weakening, it can be found elsewhere. Compare e.g., Italian **dopplo* > *doppio* [doppi̯o] 'double'.

Further problems result from the fact that the gemination of stop before stop in (11a) would predict the Prakrit outcome in (12'a). What we find instead is the development in (12'a'). Varma, fully aware of this difficulty, postulated the developments in (12'a''). However, his account involves a complex scenario of syllable-final weakening, followed by assimilation—IN ADDITION to gemination.

Now, syllable-final weakening is a well-established phenomenon in Sanskrit, vouched for by the Prātiśākhyas, where it is referred to as *abhinidhāna*. (Where necessary, weakened segments are indicated by a following [˺] in the examples below.) But the Prātiśākhyas—and universal principles—tell us that in (12'a''), the syllabification must be as in (12'a'''). It is difficult to see how in this configuration, syllable-final *k* could assimilate to anything but the following syllable-initial *k*. The outcome, then, should still be an incorrect *yukka-**. Under these circumstances, the traditional assimilation approach, probably preceded by a certain amount of syllable-final weakening, would appear to be much more straightforward.

(12')	(a)	*yukta-*	> *yukkta-*	> *yukka-**	
	(a')	*yukta*		> *yutta-*	
	(a'')	*yukta-*	> *yuk˺kta*	> *yutta*	> *yutta-*
	(a''')	*yuk $ ta-*	> *yuk˺$kta-*	> *yuk $ kta-*	> *yukka-**

(b) *dakṣa-* > *dakha-* > *dakk^{h}a-*
(e) *g^{h}anahpati* > *g^{h}anaphati-* > *g^{h}anapp^{h}ati-* > *g^{h}anapp^{h}ati-*
(f) *asmin* > *ahmi(n)* > *amhi*
cf. *brāhmaṇa-* > *bamhaṇa-* 'brahmin'

Supporting evidence for the traditional assimilation approach comes from developments like the ones in (13). The various outcomes of *ātman-* 'soul, self' can be best accounted for as reflecting the intermediate stage in the second column, with partial assimilation of *m* to the preceding voiceless oral stop *t*. (Varma was able to account for some of these outcomes, in terms of the notion *yama* employed in the Prātiśākhyas. However, for *atpa-/appa-* his account would run into the same difficulties as his explanation for *yutta-* in (12'a'').)

(13) *ātman-* > *atpa(n)-* (Aśoka) > *atta-* (Aśoka and later IA)
appa- (later Indo-Aryan)

3.9. If the arguments just presented are correct, then Sanskrit gemination and the geminates of Prakrit cannot be considered directly related. However, this does not rule out an INDIRECT relationship: In Hock 1976 I have presented cross-linguistic arguments for a relationship between syllable-final weakening, "resyllabication," and gemination. For syllable-final weakening, cf. (12'a'') above and the Spanish example in (14) below. Examples of resyllabication, a process in which a syllable-final consonant is shifted into the onset of the next syllable, are given in (15). (Thus, in (15a), the RP form exhibits resyllabication vis-à-vis the TP form.) I will forgo repeating the fairly complex arguments of Hock 1976. Suffice it to state that I proposed to see in gemination a compromise betweeen the two different patterns of syllabication that are found in (15). Compare the formulation in (16).

(14) Span. [at \$ las] > [at˺ \$ las] > [aθ \$ las] > [aδ \$ las] > [a∅ \$ las] 'atlas'

(15)	"Normal" Skt.	TP	RP
(a)	*yuk \$ ta-*	*yuk \$ ta-*	*yu \$ kta*
(b)	*dak \$ ṣa-*	*da \$ kṣa*	*da \$ kṣa*
(c)	*rat \$ na-*	*rat \$ na-*	*ra \$ tna-*
(d)	*put \$ ra-*	*pu \$ tra-*	*pu \$ tra-*
(e)	*ad \$ ya*	*a \$ dya*	*a \$ dya*

(16) *yuk \$ ta-* X *yu \$ kta-* = *yuk \$ kta-*
put \$ ra- X *pu \$ tra-* = *put \$ tra-*
etc.

What is important in the present context is that the Prātiśākhyas provide evidence for all three of these related phenomena: *Abhinidhāna* or syllable-final weakening is prescribed (with various restrictions) by the Rik-, Vājasaneyi-, and Atharva-Prātiśākhyas. Resyllabication is enjoined or permitted as an option in the Rik- and Taittirīya-Prātiśākhyas. And gemination of some kind is taught by all of the Prātiśākhyas.

4. Direct evidence in early Sanskrit texts. As noted in Hock and Pandharipande 1976: 125, "[l]ittle conclusive evidence for dialectal variation can be found for the Vedic period. Most of the evidence usually adduced in favor of geographical dialect mixture is ambiguous at best."

4.1. For instance, in the area of morphology, we find numerous doublets, such as the ones in (17). These have been taken as evidence for dialectal diversity; cf., e.g., Emeneau 1966: 126–7. However, the doublets patently result from anological changes. Their coexistence thus can be accounted for entirely by "internal" developments, without resorting to "outside," dialectological explanations. In the case of (17a) the inherited ending is *-ā̆*, while *-āni* is an innovation. Similarly, in (17b), *-ās* is the original ending, *-āsas* an innovation. The situation is more complex for the endings in (17c): One originally seems to have belonged to the pronouns, the other to the nouns. Still, the Vedic competition between the two forms in both inflectional classes results from analogical transference, which in this case went in both directions.

(17) (a) *a*-stem Nom./Acc. pl. neut.: *-ā̆* beside *-āni*
(cf. *yugā̆*: *yugāni* 'yokes')
(b) *a*-stem Nom. pl. masc.: *-ās* beside *-āsas*
(cf. *devās*: *devāsas* 'gods')
(c) *a*-stem Instr. pl. masc./neut.: *-ebhis* beside *-ais*
(cf. *devebhis*: *devais* 'with the gods')

4.2. Specifically phonological evidence has been argued to be found in the expression of (18). For in this construction, *sū́re* often is analyzed as resulting from *sū́ras*, genitive singular of the word for 'sun', with a non-Sanskrit dialectal development of final *-as* to *-e* before voiced consonants. The normal Sanskrit outcome would be *-o*; the development to *-e* is in the Prakrits limited to the eastern dialects. (For this argument see for instance Wackernagel 1896: xxi.) However, the form is amenable to a number of different, non-dialectological interpretations which include its analysis as a dative or locative singular. Compare the discussion and references in Mehendale 1969.

(18) *sū́re duhitā́* 'daughter of the sun' vs. normal *sū́ro duhitā́*

4.3. More cogent phonological evidence for dialectal diversification may perhaps be seen in the fact that, as noted in 3.6 above, the Rig-Veda and the Brāhmaṇas belonging to it exhibit the development of intervocalic voiced retroflex stops into retroflex laterals. (The same phenomenon is found in some of the branches of the White Yajur-Veda and of the Sāma-Veda.) In this development, then, some of Vedic Sanskrit seems to agree closely with the Prakrits which likewise exhibit lateral outcomes. Cf., e.g., the examples in (19).[3] Notice however that in weakening intervocalic voiced retroflex stops to laterals, the Rig-Vedic tradition is not affiliated with any particular geographical dialect, but with the Prakrits as a whole. This raises the possibility that a different, "diglossic " interpretation may be required. This alternative possibility will be discussed further below. What complicates matters is that a similar weakening of intervocalic voiced retroflex stops has been observed for other branches of the Veda. In fact, Whitney (1862: 359) surmises that it is "altogether probable" that in these branches, too, "the resulting sound is...of the nature of an *l*."

(19) "Normal Sanskrit"	Rig-Veda (etc.)	Pali/Prakrit	
nīḍa-	*nīḷa-*	*nīḷa/nīla-*	'abode'
gūḍha-	*gūḷha-*	*gūḷha/gulha-*	'hidden'

4.4. Fairly uncontroversial evidence for dialectal difference is found in the fact that in the Rig-Veda, forms like the one in (20) have a long syllabic *r̥̄*, where elsewhere the *r̥* is short.[4] An explanation for this dialectal diversity has been suggested in Hock 1986b: The length of the Rig-Vedic *r̥̄* resulted from compensatory lengthening, a process that also changed earlier *i*, *u* into *ī*, *ū*; cf. (21a). Now, while in the Rig-Vedic dialect, compensatory lengthening applied without restrictions, in the dialects that formed the basis of the non-Rig-Vedic traditions it appears to have been restricted to those segments that had counterparts with independently established length. Such counterparts were found for the *i-* and *u-* vowels; cf. (21b). On the other hand, there is a good reason for assuming that at the relevant

---

[3] For the Pali reflexes, cf. Mayrhofer 1951: 49 with 33; for the later Prakrits, see Pischel 1900: 162, 168–70. In the later Prakrits, lateral outcomes appear to be rare for the aspirate.

[4] The writing with short *r̥* in the extant text of the Rig-Veda no doubt the reflects the practice of the later language which does not lengthen *r̥*. The evidence of the meter shows that in the language of the Rig-Veda, the segment that is written *r̥* was in fact long in these forms.

point in time, syllabic *ṛ* lacked such a counterpart.[5]

		Pre-Skt.		Rig-Veda	Elsewhere	
(20)		**mṛẓḍa*		*mṝḍa*	*mṛ̆ḍa*	'be gracious (to us)'
		**dṛẓḍha-*		*dṝḍha-*	*dṛ̆ḍha-*	'firm'
(21)	(a)	**niẓḍa-*	>		*nīḍa-*	'abode'
		**guẓḍha-*	>		*gūḍha-*	'hidden'
	(b)	**pīto-*	>		*pīta-*	'drunk'
		**bhūto-*	>		*bhūta-*	'been'

It is generally agreed that the Rig-Veda originated in the extreme north-west of India. It is therefore possible that the compensatory lengthening of *r* was a dialectal feature of that area. Corroborative evidence for dialectal differences between northwestern Sanskrit and the Sanskrit of the central area, the "MADHYADEŚA," may be found at a later period, in the area of syntax: As noted in Hock 1981, the later Vedic (as well as post-Vedic) Sanskrit conventions for causee marking differ considerably from what we find in the northwestern language of Pāṇini. Similarly, Deshpande (1983) has argued that certain embedded structures postulated in Pāṇini's grammar and absent from madhyadeśa texts do appear in Sanskrit documents from the northwest.

4.5. A feature of more controversial interpretation is the distribution of *l*- vs. *r*- forms in Vedic: In the earliest, Rig-Vedic layer of the language, Proto-Indo-European (PIE) **r* and **l* usually are both reflected as *r*; cf. (22a). Forms with *l*, such as the ones in (22b), are exceedingly rare. Moreover, they tend to ocur more commonly in the notoriously late portions of the Rig-Veda, especially in book 10; cf., e.g., *lohitá-* 'red'. However, beginning with late Rig-Vedic, we find a steady increase in *l*- forms. Often these replace, or coexist with, earlier *r*- forms whatever their source; cf. e.g. the data in (23a). The incidence of *l* appears to be especially high in words that have no known Indo-European etymology, including words that are probable borrowings from one of the pre-Indo-Aryan languages; cf. (23b/c).[6] The later the text, the higher the incidence of *l*. The extent of this increase can be seen from the fact that (i) in the latest parts of the

[5] The *ṝ* found in the accusative and genitive plural of *r*- stems appears to be a fairly late development, built on the analogy of parallel forms in the *i*- and *u*- stems. Cf. Hock 1974b with references.

[6] On the question of early borrowings from pre-Indo-Aryan languages see Hock 1975, 1984, and the literature cited there.

Rig-Veda, *l* is eight times more common than in the oldest parts, and (ii) the ratio between *l* and other segments is 17 : 5000 for the entire Vedic language vs. 52 : 5000 in post-Vedic; cf. Wackernagel 1896: 215–6.

(22)	PIE *r	PIE *l
(a)	**rewdh-* > *rohitá-* 'red'	**ḱlew/ḱlu-* > *śro/śru* 'hear'
(b)	**rewdh-* > *lohitá-* 'red'	**ḱlow-ko-* > *ślo-ka-* 'fame'

(23) (a)	PIE *r:	early RV	*rohitá-*	late RV	*lohitá-*	'red'
		RV	*riś-*	AV	*liś-*	'tear up'
		RV	*kṣar-* 'flow'	ŚB	*kṣāláyati*	'rinse'
	PIE *l:	early RV	*rabh-*	late RV	*labh-*	'seize'
		RV	*cárati-*	AV	*cálati-*	'moves'
		RV	*rih-*	JB	*lih-*	'lick'
	PIE *r or *l (?):					
		RV	*pāṁsura-*	SV	*pāṁsula-*	'dusty'
	cf. also	RV	*miśra-*	beside RV	*-miśla-*	'mixed'
(b)	Uncertain origin:					
		RV	*mruc-*	AV	*mluc-*	'go down'
(c)	Borrowing:					
		RV	*lā́ṅgala-*	'plough'		

(Abbreviations: AV= Atharva Veda, JB= Jaiminīya-Brāhmaṇa, RV= Rig-Veda, ŚB= Śatapatha-Brāhmaṇa, SV= Sāma-Veda.—In the last two examples of (a), the suffix could be either **lo-* or **ro-*).

4.6. A variety of different explanations have been proposed for the increase of *l-* forms in early Sanskrit. A common view is that they belong to a more "popular" layer of Sanskrit that contrasts with a "hieratic" *r-* dialect. According to some, it is this popular variety of Sanskrit that served as a vehicle for borrowings of the type (20c). Compare for instance Ammer 1948, Bloch 1934, Renou 1956, Thieme 1955, Wackernagel 1926.

4.7. According to a second view, the *l-* forms (other than the type (23c)) are the result of dialect borrowing. Note that this view is not necessarily mutually exclusive with the preceding one. For instance, Thieme (1955) relates "popular" Rig-Vedic *l* to the asuras' regional and non-standard *he 'lavo he 'lavah* in example (3). What is attractive about this correlation between social and regional dialects is that it makes it possible to establish very plausible correlations between several otherwise seemingly unrelated phenomena. These are as follows:

The first is the dialectal distribution of *r*- and *l*- forms, in Indo-Aryan and in the larger, Indo-Iranian family to which Indo-Aryan belongs: In early Iranian, Indo-European **r* and **l* had completely merged into *r*. On the other extreme, in the eastern Aśokan inscriptions from Magadha, as well as in the stage-Magadhi of Sanskrit drama, the contrast between **r* and **l* (to the extent that the segments have not been lost) is neutralized in favor of *l*. This dialectal setting helps explain the fact that the Rig-Vedic dialect, being closest to Iranian, normally shows *r* for both **r* and **l*. Moreover, it provides a good motivation for the increase of *l*- forms in the later language: As noted for instance by Zimmer (1879: 38–9), the historical increase in *l*- forms appears to go hand in hand with a shift of the linguistic and literary core area of Sanskrit from the extreme northwest to the central area of madhyadeśa. This shift moves the core area closer to the eastern *l*-dialects and thus permits the introduction of a larger number of borrowings from those dialects.

Secondly, the fact that the pure *l*-dialects, even after this shift, still lie outside the core area of Sanskrit, helps explain the sociolinguistic connotations of the *l*-forms in Sanskrit. On one hand, this scenario would predict that from the puristic point of view, *l*-forms would be considered corruptions. (Recall that in Sanskrit drama, the vidūṣaka, an ignorant brahmin, speaks a variety of Magadhi, an eastern form of Prakrit.) This attitude would account for the negative connotations of some of the *l*-forms. On the other hand, the scenario is consonant with the fact that *l*-forms are characteristic of the "popular" language, if by "popular" we mean "vernacular." What we need to assume is that the speakers of "popular" Sanskrit were less averse to dialect borrowing than those of the more conservative and puristic, "hieratic" variety of the language.

4.8. While few, if any, linguists would take issue with the view that in early Indo-Iranian, the western, Iranian, dialects had completely neutralized the PIE contrast between **r* and **l* in favor of *r*, and the eastern Indo-Aryan, Magadhan, dialects had neutralized it in favor of *l*, there is some disagreement as to whether there may have been a third, Indo-Aryan, dialect which retained the contrast between **r* and **l*. And this difference turns out to be of crucial importance for the evaluation of certain claims concerning the diachronic phonology of early Indo-Aryan retroflexion. (See 7.1 below.)

Linguists who argue in favor of such a third dialect claim that in early Rig-Vedic (and/or later), *l*- forms more commonly are found for words with PIE **l* than with **r*. While forms with *l* for *r* do occur in the Rig-Veda (cf. the examples in (22) and (23)), they are said to be limited to "labial"[7] environment; cf., e.g., (22a), as well as (24).[8] That is, their *l* is attributed to a special, conditioned development. The implicit assumption is that *l*- forms reflecting PIE **l* cannot be explained by such a special phonological conditioning. As a consequence, then, they must be attributed to borrowing from a dialect that retained the original contrast between **r* and **l*. Compare for instance Fortunatov 1881, 1900, Wackernagel 1896: 217, Arnold 1893, 1897: 259. See also 7.1 below.

(24) PIE **r*:

kruś-	'shout'	:	*klośa-*	'a shout'
rup-	'rip off'	:	*lopāśa-*	'jackal'
jalgul-	'swallow'	:	*jargur-*	'swallow'
upala-	'upper grinding stone'	:	*upari-*	'above'
vala-	'cave'	:	*var/vṛ-*	'enclose'

4.9. In an important, but largely ignored paper, Bartholomae (l896) has demonstrated that the argument for a third dialect area with retention of the contrast between *r* and *l* is dubious. For as he noted, a large number of the Rig-Vedic words with supposedly retained *l* likewise show that segment in "labial" environment; cf., e.g., the examples in (25), as well as in (22). In fact, whether in labial or in non-labial environment (for which see some of the examples in (23)), no appreciable difference seems to exist between the number of *l*-forms reflecting PIE **l* and those which go back to **r*.

(25) PIE **l*:

ruc-	'shine'	:	*loka-*	'world'
pru-	'spring'	:	*plu-*	'flow'
puru-	'much'	:	*pulu-*	'much'
rabh-	'seize'	:	*labh-*	'seize'

[7] Note than just as in the works of the Sanskrit grammarians and phoneticians, the term "labial" here includes both rounded vowels and labial consonants. Moreover, the cited examples suggest that these "labials" do not have to occur directly next to the liquid.

[8] The etymologies in this example, as well as in (24), may not always be self-evident. Some of them nevertheless are quite sound. For instance, the semantic specialization by which **lou-ko-* comes to mean 'world' has parallels in Lat. *lūcus* 'grove', Lith. *laukas* 'field', Eng. *lea* 'meadow'. The starting point seems to have been something like 'clearing in the forest', hence 'grove', 'meadow', 'field', or 'area fit for habitation, (inhabitable) world'.

The evidence of early Indo-Aryan, then, does not support the assumption of a dialect in which the PIE contrast between **r* and **l* was retained. Rather, it appears that ALL of Indo-Iranian neutralized the contrast. For even though the large central area, between the extreme west and the extreme east, offers both *r* and *l*, each of the two segments may indiscriminately reflect either **r* or **l*. That is, here too, the PIE contrast is in effect neutralized. Under these circumstances, and given the absence of any direct evidence in its favor, the assumption of a dialect area that retained the PIE contrast between **r* and **l* would seem to be a gross violation of Occam's Razor. (See also Edgerton 1946: 17–19, Hock & Pandharipande 1976: 125–6.)

The Sanskrit coexistence of *r* and *l*, combined with the predominance of *r* and with the increase of *l*-forms as the core area of Sanskrit shifts more to the east, then, is more plausibly attributed to dialect borrowing from the eastern *l*-dialects into a western *r*-dialect area.

4.10. There is, to be sure, a possible alternative interpretation of the Vedic evidence. But like the borrowing analysis, it does not require setting up a dialect which retained the contrast between **r* and **l*.

In Hock 1979 I have shown that the gradual elimination in Vedic Sanskrit of morphophonemic retroflexion processes across word boundary proceeded via variable rules. And in Hock 1980 I have demonstrated that a Vedic change of *iy* to *y* before vowel was eliminated through a variable rule. This independent evidence for variable processes in Vedic Sanskrit strengthens an argument that I first presented in Hock & Pandharipande 1976 (note 10): We need to start again with the assumption that the contrast between **r* and **l* was at first neutralized to **r* in ALL of Indo-Iranian. Now, recall that in the Rig-Veda, PIE **r* and **l* appeared as *l* mainly in "labial" environments. Against this background, it is possible to speculate that the change of **r* to **l* began as a variable rule of COMMON Indo-Aryan, initially triggered by "labial" environments. While the process evidently was completed in the eastern Middle Indo-Aryan dialects, in the central area—and especially in the northwestern dialects—it appears to have been aborted in mid-stream, presumable due to the sociolinguistically negative value which tended to be attached to the *l*-variants in this dialect area.

5. Evidence from Middle Indo-Aryan: A number of the phonological developments that differentiate Prakrit or Middle Indo-Aryan from Sanskrit have already been mentioned. These include the pervasive reshaping of consonant clusters (cf. (7) and (12')); the neutralization of the contrast between *r and *l in the eastern, Magadhi, dialects; and the intervocalic weakening of the voiced retroflex stops ḍ and ḍh to lateral ḷ and ḷh.

5.1. Associated with this latter development is a pervasive tendency to weaken all non-geminate intervocalic stops.[9] Cf. the examples in (26). While weakening is the norm for the classical Prakrits, the early Middle Indo-Aryan of Pali and of the Aśokan inscriptions shows the development much more sparingly. Nevertheless, even here we may find occasional examples of weakened intervocalic stops, especially for the voiced aspirates, where Sanskrit preserves the unweakened pronunciation. Compare the Pali examples in (27), where the items in (a) exhibit weakening, while those in (b) represent the more common, unchanged outcomes. Examples of the type (23a) are often interpreted as dialectal borrowings or "Prakritisms"; cf., e.g., Mayrhofer l951. However, they may just as well be considered early results of a variable proess of intervocalic weakening, a change in progress that was to be successfully completed in most of the "classical" Prakrits.

(26)		Sanskrit	Prakrit	
		mukha-	*muha-*	'face, head'
		megha-	*meha-*	'cloud'
		āgata-	*āgada-*, *āyaya-*, *āaa-*	'arrived'
(27)		Sanskrit	Pali	
	(a)	*laghu-*	*lahu-*	'light'
		-ebhiḥ	*-ehi*	(Instr. pl. ending)
		pṛṣata-	*pasada-*	'spotted antelope'
		khādita-	*khāyita-*	'eaten'
	(b)	*khādita-*	*khādita-*	'eaten'
		tathāgata-	*tathāgata-*	(epithet of the Buddha)
		labhati	*labhati*	'obtains'
		sīdati	*sīdati*	'sits (down)'

5.2. A development more or less parallel to the intervocalic weakening of non-geminate oral stops is the tendency for medial dental *n* to change into a

[9] Geminates generally persist in Middle Indo-Aryan, although short vowel + geminate may interchange with long vowel + single segment—in either direction. For a recent discussion of this non-weakening development, see Hock 1986a: 161 and 1986b. Genuine, weakening, in the form of degemination with compensatory lengthening, is found only in early Modern Indo-Aryan; cf. Miranda 1984 and Hock 1986b.

segment that is written as retroflex *ṇ*; cf., e.g., (28a). Schwarzschild (1973) has argued that in certain varieties of Middle Indo-Aryan, this change was part of a neutralization between dental *n* and retroflex *ṇ*, such that the dental appeared word-initially, the retroflex medially in non-geminates, while medial geminates varied in their transcription between retroflex and dental. Concerning the interpretation of the medial non-geminate retroflex nasal, it is possible to go beyond Schwarzschild: Given the fact that in modern Sanskrit, medial retroflex *ṇ* is pronounced as a retracted nasalized flap [ṛ̃], it is possible to speculate that the retroflex transcription of medial non-geminate apical nasal in Middle Indo-Aryan dialects likewise referred to a retracted nasalized FLAP [ṛ̃], that is, that the transcription with retroflex nasal indicated intervocalic weakening.[10]

What is important for the present argument is Schwartzschild's claim that in the early Prakrits this development is characteristic of the northwestern Aśokan inscriptions (as well as of the extremely northwestern Niya-Prakrit), while the eastern Aśokan dialects do not exhibit the change.

This claim must be qualified to some extent. For in the northwestern Aśokan inscriptions, *ṇ*-forms of this type are quite rare, the normal representation being *n*. (In fact, after an incomplete but fairly extensive cross-check of Bloch's (1950) edition of the Rock inscriptions, I have come up only with the two examples in (28a).) However, it is possible that many of the *n*-spellings reflect the influence of the eastern model from which the northwestern inscriptions may have been translated. Independent evidence for this assumption can be seen in the fate of original retroflex *ṇ*: The eastern dialects regularly show dental [n] for this segment, while the northwestern inscriptions generally retain *ṇ*; cf. (28b). In a fairly large number of cases, however, they offer the "eastern" *n* instead; cf. (28c). (For other "easternisms," cf. Bloch 1951: 47.) If this explanation is correct, then the lower frequency of *ṇ* for words with original dental *n* could be accounted for by the assumption that the change from *n* to *ṇ* was still in progress, with many instances of *n* not yet affected.

5.3. A development shared by all of Middle Indo-Aryan is the replacement of syllabic *ṛ* by vowels or combinations of non-syllabic *r* + vowel. Compare

[10] This interpretation may perhaps be supported by the fact that Modern Indo-Aryan provides evidence for the weakening also of non-geminate [m]; cf. Skt. *kamala-* vs. dial. Hindi [kā̃βal] 'lotus'. An intermediate stage probably was [kaβ̃al-]. Cf. Hamp 1974, Hock 1986b: 82. (The present speculation has been anticipated in Bloch 1919: § 81, but with focus mainly on Marathi.)

(28)	Sanskrit	Northwest Aśokan	East Aśokan	
(a)	*devānām*	*devaṇa/devana(ṁ)*	*devānaṁ*	'of the gods'
	ānṛṇyam	*aṇaṇiyaṁ/anaṇiyaṁ*	*ananiyaṁ*	'unindebtedness'
(b)	*brāhmaṇa-*	*bramaṇa-*	*bābhana-*	'brahmin'
	śramaṇa-	*śramaṇa-*	*samana-*	'monks'
	prāṇa-	*praṇa-*	*pāna-*	'animate being'
(c)	*agreṇa*	*agrena*	*aggena*	'initial (Instr.)'
	ākāreṇa	*akarena*	*ākālena*	'appearance (Instr.)'

the examples in (29) which come from the north-central area. Linguists subscribing to the neogrammarian doctrine of the regularity of sound change would obviously like to attribute these quite diverse developments to originally different environmental or dialectal conditions. But the nature of the evidence has so far defied any attempt at such an explanation that would account for all of Middle Indo-Aryan. At best it is possible to point to certain tendencies, such as outcomes with *u* next to labials. Compare, e.g., (29a). However, as the alternative form of this item, as well (29b–c) show, other outcomes are possible even in labial environment. And yet further variations are found in other environments. (Berger (1955), to be sure, has argued that it is possible to posit regular developments for Pali, if proper allowence is made for analogy and carry-overs from the original, eastern speech of the Buddha. Perhaps his approach is correct for Pali. However, the number of special assumptions and developments required to account for apparent exceptions appears extremely large. Moreover, the situation in the other Middle Indo-Aryan dialects is not accounted for.)

(29)	Sanskrit	Middle Indo-Aryan	
(a)	*vṛddhi-*	*vaḍḍhi-/vuḍḍhi-*	'growth'
(b)	*mṛta-*	*maṭa-*	'dead'
(c)	*mṛga-*	*miga-*	'antelope'
(d)	*kṛta-*	*kaṭa-/kiṭa-*	'done'

5.4. The final phonological feature on Middle Indo-Aryan to be examined is the fate of the Old Indo-Aryan/Sanskrit configurations of (i) vowel + *r* + dental stop and (ii) syllabic *ṛ* + dental stop. As (29a, b, d) illustrate, a common outcome presents retroflex stops where Sanskrit had dentals. However, beside or instead of such forms with retroflex we may find words with dentals; cf., e.g., (30).

(30)	Sanskrit	Middle Indo-Aryan		
(a)	*kṛta-*	*kata-* :	*kaṭa-*	'done'
(b)	*kīrtti-*	*kitti-* :	*kiṭṭi-*	'fame'
(c)	*artha-*	*attha-* :	*aṭṭha-*	'purpose'

As for the dialectal distribution of these forms in early Middle Indo-Aryan, a wide-spread view holds that retroflexion is a dialectal, eastern, development; cf., e.g., Bloch 1919: 117, Chatterji 1926: 44–6, 1960: 61–2, and the discussion and references in Deshpande 1978: 244–5. In 1934, Bloch stated the matter somewhat differently, claiming that the dental outcome seems more common in the southwest; cf. also Deshpande (ibid.).

In a number of publications, one or another of these statements of the dialectal distribution of retroflex and dental outcomes has served as the basis for arguments concerning the relationship between the Prakrits and Sanskrit; cf. e.g. Chatterji and Deshpande. However, given the fact that the core area of Sanskrit at an early time was in the northwest, and later in the central area of madhyadeśa, statements concerning the eastern and the southwestern dialects of Middle Indo-Aryan may not be the most relevant for an investigation of early Sanskrit. Fortunately, the Aśokan inscriptions provide evidence for the northwest and north-central areas as well. And as it turns out, the dialect map which we can distill from the inscriptions is less clear cut than Bloch's combined statements might suggest. Rather, we find that both the northwest and north-central areas exhibit a considerable MIXTURE of retroflex and dental outcomes. Interestingly, the northwest shows a stronger preference for retroflex outcomes than the north-central inscriptions. In the latter area, retroflex regularly appears for syllabic *r̥* + single dental, but dentals seem to be preferred in other environments. compare the summary in Table III which is based on the evidence of the major Rock inscriptions.[11]

6. The question of Prakritisms and diglossia in Vedic. After this rather extensive survey of Vedic and Middle Indo-Aryan evidence, we can more meaningfully explore the question of whether it is legitimate to postulate an influx of Prakritic elements into Vedic Sanskrit. An allied question concerns the nature of the relationship between Prakrit and Sanskrit during

---

11 Note that in the northwestern dialects, we may frequently find orthographic clusters of dental or retreflex stop + *r*. It is not entirely clear whether these should be read as an alternative method of transcribing retroflex stops, or whether they should be interpreted as genuine clusters. Representations of this type are given in square brackets.

Sanskrit	‖ Southwest	Northwest	North-Central	East
vart-	*tt*	*ṭ(t)*	*ṭṭ/tt*	*tt*
kartavya-	*tt*	*ṭ*	*ṭṭ*	*ṭṭ*
(-)artha-	*tth*	*ṭh (th)* [thr]	*ṭṭh/tth*	*ṭṭh*
vardh/vṛddh-	*ḍḍh/ddh*	*ḍh/dh* [dhr]	*ḍḍh/ddh*	*ḍḍh*
kīrti-	*tt*	*ṭ* [ṭr]	*tt*	*ṭṭ*
(-)vṛtti		*ṭ*	*tt*	
vṛtta-	*tt*	*ṭ(t)*	*tt*	*tt*
vṛddha-	*ḍḍh*	*ḍh (dh)*	*ddh*	*ḍḍh*
kṛta-	*t*	*ṭ* [ṭr]	*ṭ*	*ṭ*
bhṛta-	*t*	*ṭ*	*ṭ*	*ṭ*
**sṛta-*(?)	*ṭ*	*ṭ*	*ṭ*	*ṭ*
-stṛta-	*t*	*ṭ*	*ṭ*	
mṛta-		*ṭ*	*ṭ*	

(Notes: "Southwest"= inscriptions mainly from Girnar; one example from Sopara; "Northwest"= Shahbazgarhi and Mansehra; "North-Central" = Kalsi; "East"= mainly Dhauli, supplemented by Jaugada.—*ḍḍh/ddh* etc.= "retroflex and dental are both common"; *ṭh (th)* = "retroflex is more common than dental." For [thr] or [ṭhr] see note 11. Blanks indicate that no relevant attestation was found for the area in question.)

Table III: Middle Indo-Aryan reflexes of Sanskrit dental +[r/ṛ]

the Vedic period. Was it comparable to the heavily polarized relationship that we find in Classical Sanskrit (cf. Hock and Pandharipande 1976, Hock 1986: 429–32)? That is, was it diglossic in the sense of Ferguson 1959? Or was it more similar to, say, the relationship between standard and vernacular in modern American English?

As noted in the introduction, some scholars have denied that the early Sanskrit developments which are often considered dialectal must be attributed to fully differentiated dialects. Rather, they would advocate considering them something like forerunners of later Middle Indo-Aryan changes; cf. Mansion 1931, Renou 1956. The notion of Vedic dialects is in effect rejected also by Deshpande (1978) who argues that many of the claimed Vedic Prakritisms, as well as the contrast between dental and retroflex which is generally acknowledged to go back to the earliest Vedic period, are to be attributed to something like corruptions in the oral transmission of the early Sanskrit texts. These are said to reflect features in the native dialect of the persons in charge of recitation, features that differ from the early Sanskrit norm and come closer to the later Prakrit norms.[12]

On the other side there is a tradition, going back as far as Pott (1833), according to which certain developments are indubitably—or ar least, most likely—to be attributed to Prakrit evidence. (Other early advocates of such a scenario are Benfey 1859 and Weber 1851.) A minority of scholars (such as for instance Tedesco 1947) has carried this approach to the extreme, tending to posit Prakrit origin for almost anything that is not explainable by straight-line developments from PIE or Proto-Indo-Iranian.

To avoid getting bogged down in what sometimes probably are unresolved controversies, I will limit my discussion to those phenomena whose interpretation I believe to be reasonably well established.

6.1. Several lexical items that make their appearance in Vedic Sanskrit exhibit features that link them with Middle Indo-Aryan, rather than Sanskrit.

One such innovation, recognized already in Wackernagel 1896: xviii–xix, is the replacement of the Rig-Vedic, inherited present stem of the verb 'to do' by a stem that is best explained as derived from the corresponding Middle Indo-Aryan form(s); cf. (31a). The Prakrit forms can be straightforwardly derived from their inherited Sanskrit counterparts via the well-established substitution of *a* or *u* for syllabic *ṛ*. The innovated Sanskrit stems, then, are plausibly accounted for as regularizations, introducing the *r* that is found in other forms of the verb; cf. (31b).[13]

(31) (a) Inherited stem Innovated stem Prakrit stem
kṛṇo- *karo-* *(*)kaṇo-*
kṛṇu- *kuru-* *(*)kuṇu-* (cf. *kuṇa*)
(b) inf. *kar-tum*, desiderative *ci-kīr-ṣati*, etc.

A second word indicative of Prakrit influence on Vedic Sanskrit is *muhuḥ* 'suddenly, quickly'. As Bloch (1929) demonstrated, this word can be given a credible etymology if it is considered a borrowing of the Middle Indo-Aryan reflex of Proto-Indo-Iranian **mṛjhu-*; cf. (32). Previously proposed etymologies, on the other hand, leave a lot to be desired; cf. Mayrhofer 1953–61: s.v.

---

[12] This latter view has been discussed and refuted in Hock 1979. Additional difficulties have been pointed out by Polomé (1963).

[13] A different interpretation is found in Schmid 1960. A refutation of Schmid's view is given in Hock & Pandharipande 1976 (note 3).

(32) PIIr.	Avestan	Expected Skt.	Attested Skt.	Expected Pkt.
**mṛjhu-*	*mərᵊzu-*	**mṛhuḥ-*	*muhuḥ*	*muhu-*

A third item with Middle Indo-Aryan development of syllabic *ṛ* is the word for 'gambler'. As Wackernagel (1932) has shown, the form is most plausibly explained as the Prakrit equivalent of expected Sanskrit *kṛtavant-* 'who has (or hopes to have) the *kṛta-* or lucky throw'. Compare (33).

(33) Expected Skt.	Attested Skt.	Expected Pkt.
kṛtavant-	*kitava-*	*kitava-/katava-/kiṭava*, etc.

Finally, the neuter interrogative pronoun *kim* provides evidence for Prakritic morphological influence; cf. Tedesco 1945. The expected Sanskrit form is *cid* (cf. Avestan *ciṯ*), of which *kad* is an early, pre-Vedic replacement. Both of these forms contain the normal Sanskrit pronominal nominative/accusative singular neuter ending *-d*. The form *kim*, on the other hand, which begins to appear in the Rig-veda and quickly ousts the old *kad* (except in a few marginal uses), contains the usual Middle Indo-Aryan pronoun ending *-m*; cf. (34) and (35). And as (35b) shows, this *m-* is an innovation, built on the model of the nouns.

(34)	Proto-IAr.	Expected Skt.	Expected Pkt.	Attested Skt.
	**cid*	(*cid*) *kad*[14]	*kiṁ*[14]	*kim* (*kad*)
(35) (a)	Proto-IAr	Skt.	MIAr.	
	**tad*	*tad*	*taṁ*	'that'
	**yad*	*yad*	*yaṁ*	'which (rel.)'

(b)	Stem		Nom./Acc.neuter	
Noun	*deva-*	:	*deva-ṁ*	'god'
Pronoun	*ta-*	:	X = *ta-ṁ*	
	ya-	:	Y = *ya-ṁ*	

Two of the forms just discussed, the innovated present stem of 'do' and the new interrogative pronoun *kim*, are of considerable significance for an interpretation of the relationship between Prakrit and Sanskrit during early Vedic times. For while many of the phonetic Prakritisms could perhaps be explained as having arisen as mistakes in the later transmission of the Vedic texts, such an account is inadequate for *kuru-* and *kim*, since it would not be able to account for the chronology of the forms.

14 Note that both Vedic Sanskrit *kad* and Prakrit *kim* are analogical replacements of the original *cid* which serves only in marginal function, as a particle of emphasis, etc.

As is well known, the stem *kuru-* first appears in the notoriously late tenth book of the Rig-Veda. In the Atharva-Veda, the new stem has become more productive than the old one. And by the time of the Brāhmaṇas, the old stem *kṛṇu-* survives only in citations from the earlier Vedic texts. The form *kim* follows a similar development, except that the change appears to have begun earlier. Throughout the Rig-Veda it is in competition with inherited *kad.* In the tenth book *kim* predominates; the later language, by contrast, uses *kim.* This chronology is perfectly compatible with the assumption that the words were borrowed from Prakrit during the Rig-Vedic period and that subsequently they slowly replaced their native Sanskrit counterparts. On the other hand, an approach trying to account for them as mistakes in the later oral transmission of the texts would be unable to explain why, for example, *kuru-* replaces *kṛṇu-* in the tenth book of the Rig-Veda, but not earlier, or why it becomes the norm for the Atharva-Veda, etc. Mistakes in recitation should be distributed in a more random fashion.

We can therefore conclude that the forms discussed in this section are in fact borrowings from Prakrit and thus provide evidence for an early Vedic coexistence of a more conservative variety of language—Sanskrit—with more developed varieties—early forms of Prakrit. These Prakrits should, of course, not be conceived of as identical with the later Middle Indo-Aryan dialects, attested in the Aśokan inscriptions or even later. Still, as the evidence discussed has shown, some of the features that separate the later Prakrits from Sanskrit are found as early as in Vedic. These include the replacement of syllabic *ṛ* by vowel and the development of a new, innovated ending for the neuter nominative/accusative singular of the pronouns.

The early Prakrit borrowings are interesting for another, sociolinguistic reason: They suggest that at this early stage of the language, there has not yet been any attempt on the side of Sanskrit to differentiate itself from the Middle Indo-Aryan vernaculars. For borrowings like *kim* are accepted, even though they belong to the basic vocabulary of the language and affect its grammatical structure. At this stage, therefore, the relationship between Prakrit and Sanskrit is not yet polarized or diglossic (in the sense of Ferguson 1959).

6.2. A number of phonological developments that are more or less contemporary with the lexical/morphological changes just discussed likewise are commonly attributed to Prakrit influence or borrowing. These include a wide-spread weakening of voiced aspirates to *h*.

For one segment, pre-Sanskrit **jh* (reflecting PIE **ǵh* or palatalized **g(ʷ)h*), the change is completely regular; cf., e.g., the examples in (36a). Elsewhere, the change is highly sporadic; cf. (36b). What is important is that, as in the case of *kuru-*, forms with *h* often replace earlier forms with aspirated stop within the observable history of Vedic Sanskrit. Compare for instance (36c), where the form with *bh* represents the Rig-Vedic norm, while forms with *h* are rare and generally late in the Rig-Veda; cf., e.g., Debrunner 1957: 139. In post Rig-Vedic, on the other hand, *h*-forms become the norm.

(36)		PIE	(Rig-)Vedic	
	(a)	**ǵhew/ǵhu*	*ho-/hu-*	'pour libations'
		**gʷhen-ti*	*han-ti*	'slays'
	(b)	**-medhə*	*-mahi*	(first pl. mid. ending)
		**rewdh/rudh-*	*rohitá-*	'red'
	vs.	**rewdh/rudh-*	*rudhira-*	'red'
		**widhewā*	*vidhavā*	'widow'
	(c)	**ghrebh/ghr̥bh-*	*gr̥bhṇāti*	
			→ *gr̥hṇāti*	'seize'

According to Bradke (1886), the change from voiced aspirated stop to *h* must be due to vernacular, Prakritic influence. This view has been widely accepted; cf., e.g., Edgerton 1946, Emeneau 1966. Meillet (1912/13), on the other hand, claims that the change was more or less regular within the northwestern speech that forms the basis of the Rig-Vedic language. However, as the basis of Sanskrit shifted to an area that did not participate in the change, the speakers of that area began to substitute their own voiced aspirates for the *h* of the Rig-Vedic texts. In many words they succeeded, but in some words, and especially in inflectional endings (such as the *mahi-* of (36b)), they failed to do so. Also Meillet's view has found adherents; cf., e.g., Bloch 1919.

Of these two different arguments, Bradke's is clearly superior. For not only do lexical/morphological loans like *kim* provide independent evidence for the possibility of borrowing. We also know that the change of voiced aspirates to *h* is a wide-spread and eventually regular Middle Indo-Aryan development. But perhaps most importantly, the chronological development of forms like the ones in (36c) is compatible with Bradke's analysis, but not with Meillet's scenario. As in the case of the lexical/morphological borrowings, a hypothesis postulating substitutions (of aspirated stops for Rig-Vedic *h*) in the later transmission of the Vedic texts would be unable to account for this chronology.

Note however that given the nature of the Middle Indo-Aryan evidence, an alternative analysis is possible. Under this interpretation, the Vedic development of voiced aspirates to *h* is an early stage in the variable-rule processes which eventually, in the "Classical" Prakrits, converted all intervocalic aspirates to *h*. The fact that, as noted earlier, the change appears to have still been in progress in Pali may be taken as corroborative evidence. Further supporting evidence for such a variable-rule weakening may possibly be seen in the Rig-Vedic (and perhaps more wide-spread) development of intervocalic voiced retroflex stops to retroflex laterals.[15]

At present I can think of no strong evidence or arguments to decide between the Prakrit-influence and variable-process accounts. But no matter which of them should turn out to be more accurate, both are consonant with a non-polarized relationship between early Vedic Sanskrit and Prakrit. On the other hand, if the variable-process interpretation is correct, then the fact that later Sanskrit no longer participates in the change, while the Prakrit do, would constitute further evidence for a diglossic polarization at that time.[16]

6.3. The fact that the Middle Indo-Aryan weakening of intervocalic voiced aspirates to *h* thus is found also in Vedic Sanskrit lends further support to what I have argued elsewhere (Hock and Pandharipande 1976) to be the best analysis for one of the developments frequently labeled "spontaneous retroflexion." This is the intervocalic change of *n* to *ṇ* outside the environment that conditions regular *n*-retroflexion (for which see example (9) above). Instances of this change appear as early as the Rig-Veda; cf., e.g., (37a). Interestingly, like the weakening of voiced aspirates, this change may occasionally affect new items in post-Rig-Vedic, as in the example under (37b).

---

[15] Note that this analysis is eminently compatible with Mansion's (1931) and Renou's (1956) argument that the alleged Vedic Prakritisms are something like forerunners of later Middle Indo-Aryan changes. However, for borrowings like *kim and kuru-*, such an interpretation would not be appropriate.

[16] Some scholars, notably Wackernagel (1942), find evidence also for the early voicing of medial voiceless stops, as in the river name *vibālī́-* (RV 4.30.12) = earlier **vi-pārī́-* 'the one whose shores are far apart'. If this interpretation is correct, we would have further evidence for Prakritic borrowing or for an incipient sound change that gets regularized in the Prakrits. For post-Rig-Vedic examples whose interpreation is more certain, see also Edgerton 1930.

(37) (a) Proto-Indo-Iranian Avestan Rig-Vedic Skt.

**st(h)ūnā-*	*stūnā-*	*sthū́ṇā*	'pillar'
**mani-*	*-maⁱni-*	*maṇí-*	'necklace'

(b) Rig-Vedic Skt. Later Skt.

mānavá-	*māṇava*	'human; young man'

The issue of "spontaneous retroflexion" has given rise to a plethora of different explanations which have been reviewed in Mayrhofer 1968. Mayrhafer argued that none of these is cogent. Instead, anticipated by Bloch (1934: 57), he claimed that the Rig-Vedic change constitutes the initial stage of the more wide-spread Middle Indo-Aryan development of *n* to *ṇ*. That is, in more "up-to-date" terminology, we are dealing with the early phase of a variable rule. What makes this analysis especially attractive is the fact that as noted earlier (section 5.2), the Prakritic "weakening" of *n* to *ṇ* is characteristic of the northwestern dialects, i.e., of the area closest to the dialectal basis of early Vedic.

Now, as noted in 4.10 above, Hock 1979, 1981 provides independent evidence for variable phonological processes in Vedic Sanskrit. Given that evidence, as well as the suggestive evidence presented in this paper in favor of variable-rule approaches for the Vedic *l*-forms and the weakening of voiced aspirates to *h*, Mayrhofer's proposal is eminently plausible. However, just as in the case of these other Vedic phonological developments, the possibility of Prakritic borrowing cannot be excluded.

6.4. While the developments so far discussed are "convergent" with Middle Indo-Aryan changes, there is some evidence that the diglossic polarization which characterizes the classical language had its beginnings in Vedic. Recall first of all the passage in example (3), where the asuras' dialectal (whether Prakritic or regional Sanskrit) pronunciation of *l* for *r* is considered a barbarism. Secondly, developments of a morphological sort suggest that Sanskrit and Middle Indo-Aryan began to develop in very different directions.

Thus from early Rig-Vedic to the later prose of the Taittirīya Saṁhitā, there is a steady reduction in the morphological variations listed in example (17), reproduced below for convenience. Compare the ratios in (38) which are taken from Debrunner and Wackernagel 1930: 100, 103, 105–6.

On the other hand, although Middle Indo-Aryan was for some of these forms developing in the same direction, traces of the endings *-ā* and *-āsas* are found in Pali (cf. Mayrhofer 1951: 83, 84) and even as late as the "classical" Prakrits (cf. Pischel 1900: 254, 255, 258). Through its much

(17) (a) *a*-stem Nom./Acc. pl. neut.: *-ā̆* beside *-āni*
(cf. *yugā̆*: *yugāni* 'yokes')
(b) *a*-stem Nom. pl. masc.: *-ās* beside *-āsas*
(cf. *devās*: *devāsas* 'gods')
(c) *a*-stem Instr. pl. masc./neut.: *-ebhis* beside *-ais*
(cf. *devebhis*: *devais* 'with the gods')

(38)	*-āni* : *-ā*	*-ās* : *-āsas*	*-ais* : *-ebhis*
RV	2 : 3	2 : 1	666 : 543
AV	4 : 3	24 : 1	263 : 53
TS	∅	∅	∅

faster elimination of the alternative endings *-ā̆* and *-āsas*, then, Vedic Sanskrit comes to DIVERGE from Middle Indo-Aryan.

The most striking divergence, however, consists in the fact that for the instrumental plural ending, Sanskrit generalizes *-ais* (except in one pronominal relic, *ebhis*), while all of Middle Indo-Aryan opts for *-ehi(ṁ)*, the Prakrit counterpart of Skt. *-ebhis*. As Meillet (1910) suggested, this highly divergent pattern of generalization can be attributed to an anti-Prakrit attitude on the part of the speakers of Sanskrit. (The issue is developed further in Hock and Pandharipande 1976: 113.)

7. Retroflexion: Dialectology and diglossia. The aspect of Indo-Aryan diachronic phonology which has received the largest number of different explanations no doubt is the issue of retroflexion, both as a regular development and as a sporadic phenomenon, the so-called spontaneous retroflexion. I have treated the general issue, as well as some aspects of spontaneous retroflexion elsewhere; cf. Hock 1974a, 1975, 1979, 1984, as well as Hock 1986a: 77–9. Rather than repeating myself, I will confine my discussion to issues for which dialectological arguments (both geographic and social) are relevant.

7.1. There are a fair number of Vedic examples of the type (39), with retroflex where a cluster of *r* or *l* plus dental stop might be expected. Concerning their interpretation, there are two major views (disregarding attempts to identify some or all of these words as borrowings from non-Indo-Aryan languages). On one side are scholars like Wackernagel 1896: 167–71 (with earlier references) and Bartholomae 1896, who consider these words to be borrowings from Prakrit. On the other side, beginning with Fortunatov 1881, 1900, and continuing to the present day (cf. e.g. Burrow 1972, Hamp 1983), it is claimed that some or all of the forms are to be explained within Sanskrit, by means of a conditioned change whereby the combination of PIE *l + dental yields a retroflex.[17]

(39) Skt.	*jaṭhara-*	'womb'	: Goth.	*kilþei*
	pāṇi-	'(inside of) hand'	: OEngl.	*folm*
	paṭa-	'cloth'	: Goth.	*falþan*
	hāṭaka-	'gold'	: OEngl.	*gold*

Those who do not accept Fortunatov's Law argue that original r + dental also can yield retroflex, as in the examples in (40). Cf., e.g., Bartholomae 1894, 1896, Wackernagel 1896, Meillet 1903.

(40) Skt.	*niṇyá-*	'intimate, etc.'	: Gk.	*nérteros*			
	káṭuka-	'bitter'	: Lith.	*kartus*			
	víkaṭa-	'enormous'	: Skt.	*vi-kṛta-*	'changed'	Lith.	*kùr-ti*
	kāṭá-	'depth'	: Skt.	*kartá-*	'cavity'	Lith.	*kert-ù*

Words like *kuru-*, *muhuḥ-*, and *kitava-* provide independent evidence that Rig-Vedic could borrow Prakritic words which had undergone the replacement of syllabic *ṛ* by vowel. Examples like *víkaṭa-* : *vikṛta-* can be taken to follow the same pattern. But while *kitava-* exhibits the Middle Indo-Aryan option with DENTAL after the *ṛ*, *víkaṭa-* has the RETROFLEX alternative. Recall that this option exists especially in the northwestern Aśokan inscriptions, i.e., in the area closest to the northwestern basis of Rig-Vedic.

In putative words with original vowel + liquid + dental, to be sure, there is the difficulty that (i) we seem to find no early examples with retroflex geminates and (ii) in cases like *pāṇi-*, *hāṭaka-*, and *kāṭa-* there is an unexplained length. However, the coexistence of forms with and without length before the non-geminate retroflex is a problem also for those who advocate a Fortunatov's Law solution. Moreover, in the Prakrit-borrowing approach, the first of these two difficulties can be taken care of quite easily by assuming that the words in question reflect not vowel + liquid + dental, but the "0-grade" form with SYLLABIC liquid + dental. (Thus, *káṭuka-* 'bitter' would go back to **kṛtu-*, not the *kortu-* suggested by Lithuanian.) And given Middle Indo-Aryan alternations like Pali *nĭḍḍa-* beside *nīḷa-* 'abode' vs. Skt. *nīḍa-*, it is at least possible that the length plus single stop in forms like *kāṭa-* is a similar alternant for the short vowel plus geminate (*kaṭṭa-*) expected as the ordinary Prakrit counterpart of Skt. *karta-*.

The most fatal flaw common to Fortunatov's original "law" and to all later attempts to revive it is that they must assume the existence of

[17] For the most recent review of the issue, see Collinge 1985: 41–6.

a Sanskrit dialect that retained the PIE contrast between *r and *l. As noted in section 4.9, this assumption is not supported by any independent evidence. Given the possibility of alternative, Prakritic, explanations for the forms in (39) and (40), as well as the independent evidence for Prakritic developments in early Sanskrit, Fortunatov's Law must therefore be considered highly dubious.

7.2. While many retroflexes that cannot be explained by straight-line developments from PIE can thus be attributed to borrowing from Middle Indo-Aryan or to phonological developments shared with Prakrit, there remains a certain residue of forms with "spontaneous retroflexion" for which such explanations do not seem to work.

A fair number of these can be explained in terms of special, notoriously sporadic developments, such as dissimilation, analogy, and morphological reanalysis.[18] Thus, Thieme (1942) has argued that developments like the ones in (41a) can be accounted for as resulting from the dissimilation of the first of two dental stops. Wackernagel (1896: 172) has suggested that the final *ṭ* in the sacrificial or ritual exclamations *vauṣaṭ*, *śrauṣaṭ* of (41b) may be analogical to *vāṭ*, another sacrificial exclamation. Perhaps, however, forms of this type should be explained as exhibiting something akin to tabooistic distortion. For not only does the final consonant exhibit an unexpected development (of retroflex to dental), also the medial retroflex sibilant (for **kṣ* or **ś*) is difficult to account for. Moreover, as (41c) shows, the Vedic literature offers a number of other examples of "ritualistic" distortion in sacrificial exclamations. These are especially common in the Brāhmaṇas of the Sāma-Veda. And as (41d) illustrates, they may affect not just sacrificial exclamations, but longer passages of ritual text. Finally, Wackernagel (1942) has explained the change in (41e) as resulting from generalization of the retroflex initial that would be expected after the preverb *nis-*.

However, a fairly large residue remains of forms like (41f) which defy any explanation of this sort.

(41) (a) RV *atati* : Class. Skt. *aṭati* 'wanders'
Skt. *patati* : Magadhi *paḍadi* 'falls'
(b) Ved. *váṣaṭ* < *vákṣat* < **vaṭṣat* (?) 'he will bring hither'
śrauṣaṭ < **śroṣat* (?) 'he will hear'
cf. *vāṭ*, *vaṭ* < **vāṭṣ* 'he has brought hither'

[18] Hoffman (1961) adds the possibility of onomatopoetic motivations for retroflex consonants.

(c) cf. *vauṣaṭ* < *vā́ṣaṭ*
vaujhak < *vauṣaṭ*
vauk < *vāk* 'speech' X *vauṣaṭ*
vét < *vā́ṣaṭ* (X *(a)vet* 'knew'?)

(d) *o yirā yirā cā dākṣāsā iti yad girā girā ca‿iti brūyād agnir vaiśvānaro yajamānaṁ gired* '(He should say) "*o yirā yirā cā dākṣāsāi.*" If he said "*girā girā cā*...," Agni Vaiśvānara would swallow the sacrificer.' (Jaiminīya-Brāhmaṇa 1.175–8)

(e) RV *dī-* : Class. Skt. *ḍī-* 'fly'
cf. **nis-dī-* > **nī-ḍī-*

(f) RV	*naḷá-*, AV *naḍá-*	: *nadá-* (1x); cf. Avest.	*naδa-*	'reed'
Skt.	*kuṇṭha-*	: NPers.	*kund*	'blunt'
	piṇḍa-	: Arm.	*pind*	'lump/compact'

Bailey (1961, 1963) and following him, Burrow (1971) have proposed to see in examples of the type (41e)—as well as in many other instances of "spontaneous reflexion"—a "fission" in "colonial speech" of original dental into dental and retroflex. Bailey (1963) adds that "the cause of the fission may be beyond recovery but possibly contact with other people is suggested" by similar fissions in Ossetic.

Given the evidence of the Prātiśākhyas on the pronunciation of the dentals, it may perhaps be possible to give an alternative and more satisfactory account for variations of the type (41e): As noted à-propos table II, the Prātiśākhyas suggest that there were two varieties of Vedic Sanskrit, one in which the dentals were pronounced as pure dentals, the others in which they had "tooth-root" articulation. Now, the latter variety's articulation coincided (or nearly coincided) with the pronunciation of postdental/alveolar *r* in the second variety. This raises the possibility of the latter group mistaking the first group's dental stops etc. as POSTDENTAL and therefore RETROFLEX, much as the postdental/alveolar stops of modern English are mistaken as retroflex in Hindi and other South Asian languages.[19]

[19] This account is reminiscent of Emeneau's bilingual scenario (1974 = 1980: 198). However, that analysis lacks the specific phonetic motivation postulated in the present account. Moreover, and more importantly, even with that phonetic motivation, one would have to ask why the dialectal Vedic postdental "tooth-root" segments were not rendered as alveolars, given that early Dravidian had a contrast between dental, alveolar, and retroflex stops. In early Indo-Aryan, on the other hand, there was a choice

While clearly speculative, this hypothesis seems to provide a better explanation than the mere label "spontaneous retroflexion," or Bailey and Burrow's unmotivated "colonial fission." In addition, it provides a final illustration of the extent to which the dialectology (both geographic and social) of early Indo-Aryan may be drawn upon to account for developments in diachronic phonology that otherwise are difficult, if not impossible, to explain.

---

only between dental and retroflex stops. Misassignments of postdentals could only yield retroflex segments.

References

Allen, W. Sidney. 1953. *Phonetics in Ancient India.* London: Oxford University Press.

Ammer, Karl. 1948. "Die *l*-Formen im Ṛgveda." *Wiener Zeitschrift für die Kunde des Morgenlands* 51: 116–37.

Arnold, E.V. 1893. "*l* in the Rig-Veda." In *Festgruß an Rudolf von Roth* (Stuttgart: Kohlhammer), pp. 145–46.

——. 1897. "Sketch of the historical grammar of the Rig and Atharva Vedas." *Journal of the American Oriental Society* 18: 203–353.

Bailey, H.W. 1961. "Arya III." *Bulletin of the School of Oriental and African Studies* (University of London) 24: 470–83.

——. 1963. "Arya IV." *Bulletin of the School of Oriental and African Studies* (University of London) 26: 69–91.

Bartholomae, Christian. 1894. "Zur *l*-Frage." *Indogermanische Forschungen* 3: 157–97.

——. 1896. "Beiträge zur altindischen Grammatik." *Zeitschrift der Deutschen Morgenländischen Gesellschaft* 50: 674–735.

Benfey, Theodor. 1859. "*Perna* in *pérnēmi* und sanskritisch *paṇ*, *paṇi* und verwandtes." *Zeitschrift für vergleichende Sprachforschung* 8: 1–20.

Berger, Hermann. 1955. *Zwei Probleme der mittelindeschen Lautlehre.* München: Kitzinger.

Bloch, Jules. 1919. *La formation de la langue marathe.* Paris: Champion. (English translation 1970, Delhi: Motilal Banarsidass.)

——. 1929. "Deux adverbes moyen-indiens en védique." In *Donum natalicium Schrijnen* (Nijmegen & Utrecht: Dekker & van de Vegt), pp. 369–70.

——. 1934. *L'indo-aryan du véda aux temps modernes.* Paris: Adrien-Maisonneuve.

——. 1950. *Les inscriptions d'Asoka.* Paris: Les Belles Lettres.

Bradke, P. von. 1886. "Beiträge zur altindischen Religions- und Sprachgeschichte." *Zeitschrift der Deutschen Morgenländischen Gesellschaft* 40: 655–98.

Burrow, T. 1955. *The Sanskrit Language.* London: Faber and Faber.

——. 1971. "Spontaneous cerebrals in Sanskrit." *Bulletin of the School of Oriental and African Studies* (University of London) 34: 538–59.

——. 1972. "A reconsideration of Fortunatov's Law." *Bulletin of the School of Oriental and African Studies* (University of London) 35: 531–45.

Chatterji, Suniti Kumar. 1926. *The Origin and Development of the Bengali Language.* 3 vols. Calcutta: University Press. Reprinted 1970 (London: Allen & Unwin).

——. 1960. *Indo-Aryan and Hindi.* Second edition, Calcutta: Mukhopadhyay.

Collinge, N.E. 1985. *The Laws of Indo-European.* Amsterdam: Benjamins.

Debrunner, Albert. 1957. *Nachträge* [to the 1957 reissue of Wackernagel 1896]. Göttingen: Vandenhoeck & Ruprecht.

——, and Jacob Wackernagel. 1930. *Altindische Grammatik*, 3. Göttingen: Vandenhoeck & Ruprecht.

Deshpande, Madhav M. 1978. "Genesis of Ṛgvedic Retroflexion: A Historical and Sociolinguistic Investigation." In *Aryan and non-Aryan in India*, ed. by M. M. Deshpande and P. E. Hook (Ann Arbor: The University of Michigan Center for South Asian and Southeast Asian Studies), pp. 235–315.

——. 1983. "Pāṇini as a frontier grammarian." In *Papers from the 19th Regional Meeting of the Chicago Linguistic Society*, pp. 110–116.

Edgerton, Franklin. 1930. "Dialectic phonetics in the Veda: Evidence from the Vedic variants." In *Studies in Honor of Hermann Collitz*, reprinted 1969 (Freeport, NY: Books for Libraries Press), pp. 25–36.

——. 1946. *Sanskrit Historical Phonology.* New Haven: American Oriental Society.

Emeneau, Murray B. 1966. "Dialects of Old Indo-Aryan." In *Ancient Indo-European Dialects*, ed. by H. Birnbaum and J. Puhvel (Berkeley: University of California Press), pp. 123–38.

——. 1974. "The Indian linguistic area revisited." *International Journal of Dravidian Linguistics* 3: 92–134.

——. 1980. *Language and Linguistic Area: Essays by Murray B. Emeneau*, selected and introduced by Anwar S. Dil. Stanford: Stanford University Press.

Ferguson, Charles A. 1959. "Diglossia." *Word* 15: 325–40.

Fortunatov, Ph. 1881. "*L* + dental im Altindischen." *Beiträge zur Kunde der indogermanischen Sprachen* 6: 215–20.

——. 1900. "Die indogermanischen liguiden im Altindischen." *Zeitschrift für vergleichende Sprachwissenschaft* 36: 1–37.

Hamp, Eric P. 1974. "Reassignment of nasality in early Irish." *Papers from the Parasession on Natural Phonology*, Chicago: Linguistic Society, pp. 127–30.

——. 1983. "A revised amendment to Fortunatov's Law." *Indo-Iranian Journal* 25: 275–6.

Hock, Hans Henrich. 1974a. "Historical change and synchronic structure: The case of the Sanskrit root nouns." In *Toward Tomorrow's Linguistics*, ed. by R.W. Shuy and C.-J. W. N. Bailey (Washington, D.C.: Georgetown University Press), pp. 329–42.

——. 1974b. "On the Indo-Iranian accusative plural of consonant stems." *Journal of the American Oriental Society* 94: 73–95.

——. 1975. "Substratum influence on (Rig-Vedic) Sanskrit?" *Studies in the Linguistic Sciences* 5.2: 76–125.

——. 1976. "Final weakening and related phenomena." *Mid-America Linguistics Conference Papers*, 1975, edited by F. Ingemann (Lawrence: University of Kansas. Department of Linguistics), pp. 215–59.

——. 1979. "Retroflexion Rules in Sanskrit." *South Asian Languages Analysis* 1: 47–62.

——. 1980. "Archaisms, morphophonemic metrics, or variable rules in the Rig-Veda?" *Studies in the Linguistic Sciences* 10.1: 59–69.

——. 1981. "Sanskrit causative syntax: A diachronic study." *Studies in the Linguistic Sciences* 11.2: 9–33.

——. 1984. "(Pre-)Rig-Vedic convergence of Indo-Aryan with Dravidian? Another look at the evidence." *Studies in the Linguistic Sciences* 14.1: 89–108.

——. 1985. "Regular metathesis." *Linguistics* 23: 529–40.

——. 1986a. *Principles of Historical Linguistics.* Berlin: Mouton de Gruyter.

——. 1986b. "Compensatory lengthening: In defense of the concept 'mora'." *Folia Linguistica* 20: 431–60.

——. To Appear. "Syllabic ṛ and ḷ in early Sanskrit: A critical study of the Prātiśākhyas and Śikṣās." *Phonetic Studies*, 1 (Mysore, India).

——, and Rajeshwari Pandharipande. 1976. "The socio-linguistic position of Sanskrit in pre-Muslim South Asia." *Studies in Language Learning* 1.2: 107–38 (Urbana: University of Illinois).

Hoffmann, Karl. 1961. Review of the 1957 reissue of Wackernagel 1896. *Zeitschrift der deutschen Morgenländischen Gesellschaft* 110: 175–82.

Mansion, Joseph. 1931. *Esquisse d'une histoire de la langue sanscrite.* Paris: Geuthner.

Mayrhofer, Manfred. 1951. *Handbuch des Pali*, 1. Heidelberg: Winter.

——. 1953–61. *Kurzgefaßtes etymologisches Wörterbuch des Altindischen*, vol. 1 and 2. Heidelberg: Winter.

——. 1968. "Über spontanen Zerebralnasal im frühen Indo-Arischen." *Mélanges d'indianisme à la mémoire de Louis Renou* (Paris: Boccard), pp. 509–17.

Mehendale, M.A. 1969. "*Sū́re duhitā́.*" In *Proceedings of the 26th International Congress of Orientalists* (New Delhi, 1964), 3.1: 105–8. Pune: Bhandarkar Oriental Research Institute.

Meillet, Antoine. 1903. "Sur l'étymologie de l'adjectif védique *niṇyáḥ*." In *Album Kern* (Leiden: Brill), pp. 121–2.

——. 1910. Review of A.A. Macdonnell's *Vedic Grammar*. *Journal asiatique* 1910.2: 179–87.

——. 1912–13. "Des consonnes intervocaliques en védique." *Indogermanische Forschungen* 31: 120–5.

Miranda, Rocky V. 1984. "Temporal compensation and phonetic change: the case of compensatory lengthening in Hindi." In *Papers from the Minnesota Regional Conference on Language and Linguistics* (Minneapolis: University of Minnesota, Department of Linguistics), pp. 91–104.

Mishra, Vidhata. 1972. *Sanskrit Phonetics.* Varanasi: Chowkhamba Sanskrit Series.

Murray, Robert W. 1982. "Consonant cluster developments in Pāli." *Folia Linguistica Historica* 3: 163–84.

Pischel, R. 1900. *Grammatik der Prakrit-Sprachen.* (*Grundriß der Indo-Arischen Philologie und Altertumskunde*, 1: 8.) Straßburg: Trübner.

Polomé, Edgar. 1983. "Bilingualism and language change as reflected by some of the oldest texts in Indo-European dialects." *NOWELE* 1: 9–30.

Pott, August Friedrich. 1833. *Etymologische Forschungen auf dem Gebiete der indogermanischen Sprachen.* First edition, vol. 1. Lemgo: Meyer.

Renou, Louis. 1956. *Histoire de la langue sanskrite.* Lyon: AIC.

——. 1957. "Introduction générale" [to the 1957 reissue of Wackernagel 1896]. Göttingen: Vandenhoeck & Ruprecht.

Schmid, Wolfgang P. 1960. "Zum Problem *kṛṇoti—karoti.*" *Indogermanische Forschungen* 65: 235–48.

Schwarzschild, L.A. 1973. "Initial retroflex consonants in Middle Indo-Aryan." *Journal of the American Oriental Society* 93: 482–7.

Tedesco, Paul. 1945. "Persian *čīz* and Sanskrit *kím.*" *Language* 21: 128–41.

——. 1947. "Sanskrit *mālā-* 'wreath'." *Journal of the American Oriental Society* 67: 85–106.

Thieme, Paul 1942. "Merkwürdige indische Worte." *Zeitschrift für vergleichende Sprachforschung* 67: 183–96.

——. 1955. Review of Burrow 1955. *Language* 31: 428–88.

Varma, Siddheshwar. 1929. *Critical Studies in the Phonetic Observations of Indian grammarians*. Reprinted 1961, Delhi: Munshi Ram Manohar Lal.

Wackernagel, Jakob. 1896. *Altindisch Grammatik*, 1. Göttingen: Vandenhoeck & Ruprecht.

——. 1926. "Kleine Beiträge zur indischen Wortkunde." In *Festgabe H. Jacobi* (Bonn, pp. 1–17). Reprinted in Wackernagel 1953.

——. 1933. "Indoiranica." *Zeitschrift für vergleichende Sprachforschung* 59, 19–30. Reprinted in Wackernagel 1953.

——. 1942. "Indoiranica." *Zeitschrift für vergleichende Sprachforschung* 67: 154–82. Reprinted in Wackernagel 1953.

——. 1953. *Kleine Schriften*, 1. Göttingen: Vandenhoeck & Ruprecht.

Weber, Albrecht. 1851. "Analyse der in Anquetil du Perron's Uebersetzung enthaltenen Upanishad." *Indische Studien* 2: 1–111.

Whitney, William Dwight. 1862. "The Atharva-Veda Prātiśākhya...." *Journal of the American Oriental Society* 7: 333–615.

——. 1868. *The Taittirīya-Prātiśākhya.* Reprinted 1973, Delhi: Motilal Banarsidass.

Zimmer, Heinrich. 1879. *Altindisches Leben*. Berlin: Weidmann.

THE EMERGENCE OF THE SYLLABLE TYPES OF STEMS (C)VCC(V) AND (C)V̄C(V) IN INDO-ARYAN AND DRAVIDIAN: CONSPIRACY OR CONVERGENCE?

Bh. Krishnamurti
University of Hyderabad and Osmania University

1. Introduction.* M. B. Emeneau, the proponent as early as 1955 of an Indian "Sprachbund," made the following observation in his paper "The Indian linguistic area" ([1971], 1980: 175):

> Other traits have been suggested as belonging to the Indian linguistic area but have not been investigated, usually because data and analysis are not yet under control. Examples are the phonological development of syllabic structure and phoneme distributions that is seen in proceeding from OIA to MIA, with an end result that is sus-

---

* Earlier versions of this paper were presented at a National Seminar on "The Syllable in Phonetics and Phonology" held at Osmania University, Hyderabad, on January 17–18, 1986, as well as presented before the Departments of Linguistics at the State University of New York at Stony Brook and Cornell University.

The following sets of abbreviations are employed in this paper:

Indo-European Languages: A.=Assamese; Av.=Avestan; B.=Bengali; Bhoj.=Bhojpuri; G.=Gujarati; K.=Kashmiri; Ko.=Konkani; Ku.=Kumauni; L.=Lahnda; M.=Marathi; Marw.=Marwari; MIA=Middle Indo-Aryan; Mth.=Maithili; N.=Nepali; NIA=New Indo-Aryan; OIA=Old Indo-Aryan; Or.=Oriya; P.=Panjabi; Pa.=Pali; Pk.=Prakrit; RV=Rig Veda; S.=Sindhi; Si.=Sinhala; Skt.=Sanskrit; W.Pah.=West Pahari.

Dravidian Languages: Br.=Brahui; CDr.=Central Dravidian; Ga.=Gadba; Go.=Gondi; Ka.=Kannaḍa; Ko.=Kota; Koḍ.=Koḍagu (Coorg); Kol.=Kolami; Kur.=Kuru<u>kh</u>; Ma.=Malayalam; NDr.=North Dravidian; Nk.=Naikṛi; Nk.(Ch.)=Naiki of Chanda; Oll.=Ollari; PDr.=Proto-Dravidian; Pa.=Parji; SCDr.=South-Central Dravidian; Ta.=Tamil; Te.=Telugu; To.=Toda; Tu.=Tuḷu.

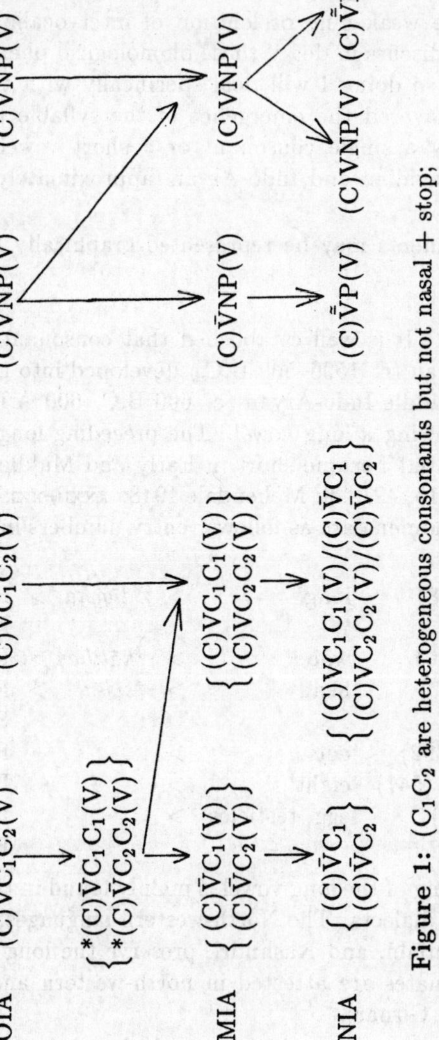

Figure 1: (C_1C_2 are heterogeneous consonants but not nasal + stop; N = homorganic nasal; P = stop/obstruent, voiced or voiceless

piciously close to the structure of PDr., as represented fairly closely by old or literary Tamil....

In making these remarks Emeneau was evidently referring to processes which are the subject matter of this paper as well as to other phonological changes between OIA and MIA (e.g., simplification of consonant clusters word-initially, the weakening or lenition of intervocalic stops). It is my intention here to discuss in detail these phonological phenomena alluded to by Emeneau. In so doing I will deal specifically with those phonological processes which favored the emergence of the syllable types with a long vowel followed by a single consonant or a short vowel followed by two consonants in Dravidian and Indo-Aryan, approximately within the same time frame.

The developments may be represented graphically for Indo-Aryan in Figure 1.

2. Indo-Aryan. It is well established that consonant clusters of Literary Old-Indo-Aryan (c. 1500–500 B.C.) developed into geminates through assimilation in Middle Indo-Aryan (c. 600 B.C.–600 A.D.) and were then degeminated following a long vowel. The preceding long vowel sometimes remained in Pali but became short in Early and Middle Prakrits (Turner [1966] 1975: 405–15, 421–29; Mehendale 1948: xxxii–xxxiii, 21–27). Examples of these phenomena are as follows (entry numbers in CDIAL are given in parentheses):

OIA *dīrghá* (6368)	'long'	>	**dīggha*	>	Pa. *dīgha*, Pk. *diggha*
OIA *kāṣṭhá* (3120)	'wood'	>	**kāṭṭha*	>	Pa., Pk. *kaṭṭha*
OIA *śīrṣa* (12497)	'head'	>	**sīssa*	>	Pa. *sīsa(ka)*, Pk. *sissa/sīsa*
OIA *kárman* (2892)	'act'	>			Pa., Pk. *kamma*
OIA *aṣṭá*, *aṣṭáu* (941)	'eight'	>			Pa., Pk. *aṭṭa*
OIA *aṇḍa* (1111)	'egg, testicles'	>			Pa. *aṇḍa*, Pk. *aṃḍā*

The shortening of the long vowel is mainly found in the Central, Southern, and Eastern dialects. The North-western languages, viz. Sindhi, Lahnda, Western Panjabi, and Kashmiri, preserve the long vowels. The long vowels and geminates are attested in north-western and western Aśokan inscriptions (e.g., Girnar).

A further development which started about the second centry A.D. (as evidenced from Sinhala) was the simplification of the geminates with compensatory lengthening of the preceding vowel in all NIA languages with the exception of Sindhi, Lahnda, and Panjabi (Beames, 1872–79, I: 73–85; Bloch 1965: 92; Turner [1967] 1975: 405, fn. 8; Arun 1961: 93–121). The change was well under way by the ninth or tenth century A.D.:

Pa., Pk. *kamma* 'work' > (a) K. *kam*, S. *kamu*, L., P. *kamm*, WPah. *kamm*: (b) Ku., N., A., B., Mth., Bhoj. H., Marw., M. *kām*, Or. *kāma*, G. *kam*/*kāmũ*, Ko. *kāma*, Si. *kama*.

Pa., Pk. *aṭṭha* 'eight' > (a) S. *aṭha*, L. *aṭṭh*, P., WPah. *aṭṭh*: (b) Ku., N., A., Mth., Bhoj., Aw., H., Marw. *āṭh*, G., M. *āṭh*, B. *āṭ*, Or., *āṭha*, Si. *aṭa*.

Pa., Pk. *kaṭṭha* 'wood' > (a) S. *kāṭhu*, L., P. *kāṭh*, *kāṭṭhī*: (b) Ku., N., A., B., Mth., Bhoj., Aw., H., G. *kāṭh*, M. *kāṭhī*, Or. *kāṭha*, *kāṭhi*; Si. *kaṭa*.

Both Bloch and Turner remark that assimilation and compensatory lengthening can be observed in isolated words even from a pre-Sanskritic or Early Old Indic stage: e.g., Skt. *majjati* 'dive' < **madj-* (cf. *madgu*); *uccá* 'upwards' from *ut-* (cf. Av. *usča*) (Bloch 1965:80); pre-Vedic **niẓ-d* > RV *nīḍa* 'nest' (Turner [1967] 1975: 422); RV *vrīhi* (< **vriṃhi*; cf. Pers. *birinj*). Turner ([1967] 1975: 429) observes that "the process of simplifying a consonant group or shortening a long consonant with accompanying lengthening of the preceding vowel, which had begun in the pre-Sanskritic stage, was continued throughout the history of Indo-Aryan."

Beames (1872–79, Book I, Chapter IV) presents a very useful typology of assimilative changes, progressive and regressive, in terms of the relative strength of the segments involved in consonant groups. With a few exceptions, his theory works and anticipates recent studies in the dimension of strength/weakness of segments in phonological processes (e.g., Hyman 1975: 161–69).

According to Beames, if the cluster has a nasal + stop, it is not assimilated in Pa. and Pk. In NIA the preceding vowel gets lengthened and nasalized in languages which apply the degemination rule. The cluster also remains in the north-western languages. One exception is the cluster *mb*, which becomes *mm*, followed by degemination and lengthening of the preceding vowel (p. 295) Indo-Aryan data drawn from Turner 1966 (=CDIAL) that illustrate the phenomena pointed to by Beames are the following:

kaṇṭa, *káṇṭaka* 'thorn' (2668): Pa. *kaṇṭa*, *kaṇṭaka*, Pk. *kaṃṭaya* > (a) S. *kaṇḍo*, L., P. *kaṇḍā*, WPah. *kaṇṭā*: (b) Ku. *kāno*, N. *kā̃ṛo*, B. *kā̃ṭā*, Or. *kaṇṭā*, Aw., H. *kā̃ṭā*, G. *kā̃ṭɔ*, M. *kā̃ṭā*, *kāṭā*, Ko. *kāṇṭo*; Si. *kaṭuwa*.

jambú, *jambū́* (5131) 'rose apple tree (Eugenia jambolana)' > Pa. *jambu*, Pk. *jaṃbū* > (a) S. *jamū̃*, L. *jamū̃*, P. *jammū*, WPah. *jEmmu*: (b) N. *jāmu*, A. *zāmū*, B. *jām*, Or. *jāmba*, *jāma*, *jāmū*, H. *jām*, G. *jām*, *jā̃bu*, *jā̃buṛī*, M. *jā̃b(h)*, Ko. *jā̃mba*, Si. *dam̆ba*; S. *jāmu*, Or. *jāmbu/jāma* 'the guava'.

2. Dravidian. There are parallels to the above phonological processes in Dravidian from an early time. Attention to the alternation between a long vowel + C and a short vowel + CC was drawn in Krishnamurti 1961 (p. 125), in explaining the alternation between **kāṇ* and **kaṇ(ṇ)* 'to see' in Dravidian. For Proto-Dravidian (PDr.) we can set up the following types of stem morphemes (CC = geminate or nasal + stop):

(1)	a.	(C)VC(V)	b.	C($\bar{V}$)C(V)
(2)	a.	(C)VCC(V)	b.	(C)$\bar{V}$CC(V)

In (2a) and (2b), CC may represent a PDr. obstruent geminate or a sequence of N (homorganic nasal) + P (voiceless stop, phonetically voiced).

Where the final vowel is the non-morphemic *u*, it is difficult to establish contrast between C and CC following a short vowel; thus, **cupp/*cup* 'salt'; when followed by a vowel, the form is **cuw-a-*. The type (C)$\bar{V}$CCV/(C)$\bar{V}$CV with grammatical alternation (**māṯṯu* 'to change' [v.tr.]: **māṯu* 'to change' [v.i.]) involves a morph boundary, i.e., **māṯ* + *tt-* > **māṯ-ṯṯ-* > *māṯṯ-*. It is also possible to set up a type *(C)VCCC for PDr., where CCC=NPP, but there is definitely a morph boundary here, descriptively +NP +P (transitive) as opposed to +NP (intransitive); e.g., **kānku* 'to boil (v.i.)': **kānkku* 'to boil (v.tr.)'.

The following syllable changes are established as part of the morphophonemics of PDr. (Krishnamurti 1961, Zvelebil 1970, Subrahmanyam 1983):

$$\left\{ \begin{array}{c} (C)\bar{V}C \\ (C)VCC \end{array} \right\} \rightarrow (C)VC/\underline{\qquad} +V$$

The next question that arises is the extent of the occurrence of the alternation (C)VCC(V)/(C)$\bar{V}$C in Dravidian. Zvelebil (1970: 185) has discussed this problem, providing two pertinent examples from Tamil, namely the contrast between *meṭṭu* 'mound'and *mēṭu* 'height, hillock', as well as between *yāṉ* 'I' and *eṉṉ-ai* 'me (acc.)'. Zvelebil also notes the existence of the alternations of Ta. *pāṭu* 'sing' with *pāṭṭu* 'song' and Ta. *āṟu* 'river' with *āṟṟu* 'of river'. He observes (p. 187) that these phenomena occur in place of the expected proto-forms **paṭṭu* and **aṟṟu*. He cautions, however, that these phenomena require further investigation.

The following data, drawn from Burrow and Emeneau 1984 (=DEDR) demonstrate the existence in Dravidian of the patterns V̄C/VCC, although they are irregularly distributed:

DEDR 765. Ta. *ekku* 'to pull cotton with fingers', Ma. *ekkuka*, Ka. *ekku* 'to separate cotton', Tu. *ekkuni* 'to gin': Te. *ēku*, Pa. *ēk* 'to pick and throw away woods', Kui *ēspa* 'to unravel'.

DEDR 2715. Ta. *cuṟṟu* 'to revolve, spin', Ma. *cuṟṟuka*, Ka. *suttu*, Koḍ. *cutt*, Tu. *suttuni*, Te. *cuṭṭu*, Nk. *sutt*, Gad. *cuṭṭ*, Go. *cuṭṭ*, Kui *huce*: Ta. *cūṟai* 'whirlwind', Kuvi *sūt* 'to roll up', *hūc* 'to put on clothes'.

DEDR 3323. Ta., Ma. *tuppu* 'to spit; spittle', Koḍ. *tuppu-*, Te. *tuppuna* (imitative adverb), Pe. *cup*, Kur. *tupp* (v.), *tuppalxō* 'saliva', Malto *tup* 'to spit', *tupglo* 'spittle': Ka. *tūpu*, Kui *sūpa* (v. and n.), Kuvi *hūp* (v.), *hūpka* (n. pl.).

DEDR 3570. Ta. *nakku* 'to lick, lap', Ma. *nakkuka*, Ka. *nakku*, *nekku*, Kod. *nakk-*, Tu. *nakkuni*, *nekkuni*: Te. *nāku*, Kol., Nk. *nāk-*, Pa. *nēk*, Ga. *nāk*, Go. *nāk-*, Konḍa *nāk-*, Pe. *nāk-*, *nāng-*, Manda *nēk*, Kui, Kuvi *nāk* (? related to PDr. **nā* 'tongue' [DEDR 3633]; cf. Ga. *nāŋ* (< **nālnk-*/**nālnkk-* 'tongue'), Te. *nā(lu)ka)*.

DEDR 4167. Te. *pittu* 'break wind', Go. *pitt*/*pihk*: *pīt* (n.) 'fart', Konda *pīt-*, Kui, Kuvi *pīt-*, Pe., Manḍa *pīt-*, Kur. *pītna* (*pittyas* v.), Malto *pīto* (cf. PDr. **pī* 'excrement' [DEDR 4210]).

DEDR 5401, Ta. *vittu*, *viccu* 'to sow seed', (n.) 'seed', Ma. *vittu* (n.), Ka. *bittu* (v. and n.), Koḍ. *bitt* (v.), *bittï* (n.), Tu. *bittuni* (v.), *bittu* (n.), Te. *vittu* (v. and n.), Nk. *vit*, Pa. *vit* (v.), *vittid* (n.), Ga. *vit* (v.), Go. *wit*, Konḍa *vit* (v.), *vitu* (n.), Kui *vitka* (n.): Oll. *vīti* 'seed', Go. *wīt*, Kuvi *vīcana* 'semen', Malto *bīc* (Kuvi, Malto < IA *bīja*).

DEDR 5117. Ta. *mottu* 'strike, beat (n.), *mōtu* id., Ma. *mōtuka*, Ka. *mōd*, Te. *mottu* 'to strike', also *mōdu*.

The above cases indicate two points: (1) the alternation (C)VCC/(C)V̄C is not reconstructable to PDr.; and (2) the forms with compensatory lengthening appear, by and large, in SCDr., CDr. and NDr., where they are in contact with Indo-Aryan. Less regularly distributed, the alternation is found in different languages. Subrahmanyam (1983: 169–71) cites thirty-two cases, which he states constitute "more or less a complete list of such instances for the operation of this process." Of these, thirteen are restricted to Tamil alone, one occurs only in Malayalam, three only in Kannada, and one only in Telugu. In eight instances a language of SCDr. or CDr. shows compensatory lengthening corresponding to the structural pattern (C)VCC of SDr.

During the historic period of each of the Dravidian languages certain phonological changes led to the emergence of two patterns, (C)VCCV and (C)V̄CV, at the expense of (C)V̄CCV. This is not a case of compensatory lengthening, but rather one of the creation of two complementary patterns, whereby two syllabic types have come to be favored.

In Kannada and Telugu (C)V̄CCV became (C)V̄CV; in other words, geminate stops (always voiceless) became degeminated following a long vowel. This change goes back to the prehistoric period of these two languages. The same development is also seen in all the other languages except Tamil and Malayalam. Examples of this phenomenon are given below:

DEDR 347. PDr. **āṭu* (v.) 'move, dance, play', **āṭṭu*, **āṭṭam* (n.) 'play' (< *āṭ* + *ttu*, *āṭ* + *ttam*):

Ta., Ma.	*āṭu* (v.):	*āṭṭam*, *āṭṭai* (n.)
Ko.	*āṛ* (v.)	*āṭ* (n.)
To.	*āṛc* (v.)	*āṭ* (n.)
	ōḍ (v.)	*ōṭ* (n.)
Ka.	*āḍu* (v.)	*āṭa* (n.)
Koḍ.	*āḍ* (v.)	——
Tu.	*āḍuni* (v.)	*āṭa* (n.)
Te.	*āḍu* (v.)	*āṭa* (n.)
Kol.	*āḍ* (v.)	——
Nk.	*āṛ* (v.)	——
Go.	——	*āṭa* (n.)

DEDR 4834. PDr. **māṯu* 'change' (v.i.); *māṯṯu* (v.tr.); *māṯṯam* (n.) 'diversity, exchange, word, reply':

Ta., Ma.	*māṟu*	*māṟṟu*	*māṟṟam* (n.)
Ko.	*mār*	*māt*	*mānt* (n.)
To.	*mōr*	——	*mōt* (n.)
Ka.	*māru*	——	*mātu* (n.)
Te.	*māṟu*, *māru*	——	*māta*
Go.	*māri*	——	*māndi*, *māṭa* (lw. < Te.)

Koṇḍa	*mār*	——	*māṭa* (lw. < Te.)
Kui	*māsk*	——	——
Kuvi	*māsk*	——	——

DEDR 2019. PDr. **kēṯ* 'to winnow' : **kēṯṯam* 'winnowing basket'

Ma.	*cēṟuka* (v.)	——
Ko.	*kēṟ*	——
To.	*kȫṟ*	——
Ka.	*kēṟu*	——
Te.	*cerugu*	*cēṭa* (< **cēṭṭa* < **kēṯṯa*)
Kol.	*kēd*	*kēt*
Nk.	*kēd*	*kēt*
Pa.	*kēd*, *kēḍ*	*kēti*, *kēṭi*
Gad.,Oll.	*kēy*	*kētin*, *kēten*
Go.	*hēc*, *hēh*, *ēc*	*sēti*, *hēti*, *ēti*
Koṇḍa	——	*sēRi*
Pe.	*jēc*	*hēci*
Manḍa	——	*hēci*
Kui	——	*sēsi*
Kuvi	——	*hēci*
Kur.	*kē̃s* (*kisyas*)	*kēter*
Malto	*kēs*	*kētnu*

In To., Ko. and all languages of SCDr., CDr., and NDr. even geminates after short vowels became degeminated, and the contrast between -C- and -CC- of identical consonants seems to have been lost in SCDr. and CDr.:

DEDR 1147. PDr. **kaṭṭ* (v.), *kaṭṭay* (n.) 'knot, dam, bank'. All languages show double consonants, except Ko. *kaṭ* (v. and n.), To. *kaṭ* (v. and n.), Kol. *kaṭ* (v.), *kaṭṭa* (n.), Nk.(Ch.) *kaṭ*/*kaṭṭ* (v.), Oll. *kaṭ* (v.), Go. *kaṭ* (n.), Koṇḍa *kaṭ* (v.), *kaṭa*, *gaṭu* (n.), Pe. *kaṭa* (n.), Kui *kāṭ* (v.), Kuvi *gaṭu* (n.), Malto *gaṭa*.

It is significant that the contrast in PDr. of C vrs. CC (single vrs. double) has come to be maintained as a contrast of voice vrs. voiceless following a long or short vowel (i.e., **āṭ(u)* [āḍ(u)]: **āṭṭa* [āṭṭa] > *āḍ(u)*: *āṭa*) in most of the languages; so also **kaṭṭa* > *kaṭa* in SCDr. languages.

The only other consonant group allowed within a stem is N (=homorganic nasal) + (=stop) in the following sequences:

(1) (C)VNP(V) phonetically [(C)VNB]
(2) (C)V̄NP(V) phonetically [(C)V̄NB]

(3) (C)VNPP(V)
(4) (C)V̄NPP(V)

Pattern (1) is, by and large, preserved in all languages. Toda loses the nasal before P, which appears as B. In Malayalam, NP > NN through progressive assimilation in the velar, palatal, dental, and alveolar series. In the labial series in all languages except Ta. and Ma. **mp* > *mm*:

DEDR 4469. PDr. **poṅku* 'to spoil': Ta. *poṅku* 'to boil, bubble up', Ma. *poṅṅuka*, Ko. *poŋg*, To. *pïg* (with loss of *n*), Ka. *poŋgu*, Koḍ. *poŋŋ*, Tu. *boŋguni*, Te. *pongu*, Kol. *poŋg*, Nk. *poŋk*, Go. *pōŋ*, Koṇḍa *poŋi*, Kuvi *poŋg*, Malto *pongje*.

Type (2) is preserved only in Tamil, Malayalam, and CDr. Many languages simplify V̄NB by the loss of N with or without nasalization of the preceding long vowel. This is very systematic in Telugu (datable to Early Telugu, 7th or 8th century A.D.) and Kannada; cf. **mūṉṯu* 'three' > Te. *mūṉṟu* > *mūṇḍu* > *mū̃ḍu* > *mūḍu*; Ka. *mūṟu* (already in Pampa Bharata of the 10th century [Ramachandra Rao 1972: 27, 28, 514]); *tōḍu* (< **tōṇṭu*) 'to burrow, dig' [Ramachandra Rao, 1972: 382). *NPP following V or V̄ is simplified as NP or PP in different languages (Kumaraswami Raja 1969). Consider the following examples:

PDr. **tūnku* (v.i.) 'to hang, swing': **tūnkku* (v.tr.) 'to suspend, swing': **tūnkk-am* (n.) 'balance, sleep'

Ta.	*tūṅku* (v.i.)	*tūkku* (v.tr.)	*tūkkam* (n.)
Ma.	*tūṅṅuka*	*tūkkuka*	*tūkkam*
Ko.	*tūg*	*tūk*	——
To.	*tūx*	*tūk*	——
Ka.	*tūgu*	*tūnku*	*tūka*
Koḍ.	*tūng*	*tūk*	——
Tu.	*tūnguni* (v.i./tr.)	*tūnkuni* (v.i.)	*tūnki*, *tūnka*, *tūku* (n.)
Te.	*tūgu*	——	*tūkam*
Koṇḍa	*dūŋ*	*dūk*	——
Pe.	*tūŋ(g)*	*tūk*	——
Kui	*dūŋg*	——	——
Kuvi	*tūŋg*	*tūk*	——
Kur.	——	——	*tūngul*
Malto	——	——	*tūngle*
Brah.	——	——	*tūgh*

From the above data we notice that most Dravidian languages have evolved toward the pattern (C)VCC/(C)V̄C, where CC/C is historically traceable to geminates following a short and long vowel; where the older sequences were *NP (following a V̄), and *NPP (following a V/V) there was a regular loss of the N of the *NP sequence and loss of *P of the *NPP sequence in Telugu and Kannada. Assimilation of NP to a single segment, as illustrated by the changes *ng* > *ŋ* and *mb* > *m*, occurs in many CDr. and SCDr. languages.

There is, however, no case where, as in the case of Indo-Aryan, assimilation is followed by compensatory lengthening in the proceding vowel:

> DEDR 3178. Ka. *taggu* 'to be lowered, to diminish' (< **taẓunku*) can never become **tāgu*.
>
> DEDR 690. Ta. *uẓuntu* 'blackgram', Ma. *uẓunnu*, Ka. *urdu*, *uddu*, Tu. *urdu*, To. *uddulu*, Kol. *urunde*, Nk. *urndal* (< **uẓuntu*).

For the most part Ka. and Te. show reduction of trisyllabic bases through the loss of the unstressed vowel followed by consonantal assimilation (c. 10th A.D.). In the CDr. and SCDr. languages assimilation does not take place in sequences of liquid and following stop:

> DEDR 485. PDr. **iruppay* 'mahua tree, Bassia longifolia': Ta. *iruppai*, Ma. *irruppa*: Ka. *ippe*, Tu. *ippe*, *irippe*, Te. *ippa*, Kol. *ippa* (< Te.), Nk. (Ch.) *irpu*, Pa. *irpa*, Gad. *irpa*, Koṇḍa *ipa* (< Te.), Go. *irup*, *irp(i)*, Kui *irpi*, *ripi*, Kuvi *irpi*.

3. Discussion. The most important question raised by the facts presented above is whether the occurrence in Indo-Aryan of a process whereby consonantal assimilation led to the emergence in MIA of geminates can be ascribed to Dravidian influence.

Caldwell (1875: 53) supports the hypothesis that "the North Indian vernaculars had been dervied from Sanskrit, not so much by the natural process of corruption and disintegration, as through the overmastering, remoulding power of the non-Sanskritic element contained in them." While dealing with assimilation, Beames (1872–79: 282–3) rejects Dravidian influence, saying that similar cases of assimilation are also found in Italian.[1]

---

[1] The following defensive remarks made by Beames (Bk.I: 282–3) in this connection are amusing:

> It is, however, held by some writers, who are never easy unless they can drag in some kind of non-Aryan influence to account for changes which require no such explanation,

Chatterji (1926: Vol.1,p.171) takes the position that simplification of consonant clusters was a parallel development in Indo-Aryan and Dravidian. He states that

> in the matter of simplification of OIA consonant groups by assimilation which gave rise to MIA it was probably internal, as it took place also in Italic among other IE languages, but here, IA reached that stage at least a thousand years before Italic; contact with Dravidian, as well as the adoption of the Aryan speech by Dravidians early in the history of IA has probably something to do with it.

The reduction of geminates following a long vowel is a change in pre-Telugu and pre-Kannada, going to the pre-Christian era, about the time that a similar change was developing in Pali and early MIA (Bloch 1965: 89), e.g., *śīrṣa* > **sīssa* > Pa. *sīsa*; *pārśva* > **pāssa* > Pk. *pāsa*; *siṃha* > *sīha*. Bloch observes (p. 92) that "the Middle Indian word contains strong consonants only when initial or geminate and has none in final position and in which hiatuses occur frequently."

There is, therefore, a clear case of phonological convergence in the emergence of (C)VCC(V) and (C)V̄C(V) as the favored types of nominal and verbal stems in Indo-Aryan and Dravidian. Even in modern spoken Tamil and Malayalam, V̄CC can be interpreted as V̄C, i.e., there is a

---

> that the weakness of Dravidian enunciation, which forbids the use of any complex accumulation of consonants, is parallel to the weakness which led the Prakrits to assimilate **kt** into **tt**. As, however, the Italians do precisely the same, it is not evident why non-Aryan intervention should be suggested. There is a process in Prakrit, carried on into the moderns, which certainly does resemble Dravidian customs, namely, that of splitting up a nexus by the insertion of a vowel; when the custom is discussed it will be seen how far this supposition is true; at any rate it has become of late years quite a nuisance, this perpetual suggestion of non-Aryans here, there, and everywhere; one will soon have to believe that the Aryans did not know how to speak at all till the Dravidian taught them the use of their tongue, and that the Vedas are a mangled copy of some ancient Tamil liturgy!

quantitative reduction of long consonants after long vowels (e.g., Ta. *mūṇï* 'three' (*mūṇṇï* < **mūṉṟu*); *pāṭï* 'song' (< *pāṭṭu*). Both Dravidian and Indo-Aryan also agree in progressive assimilation and gemination of *ng* > *ŋŋ* > *ŋ* and *mb* > *mm* > *m*.

4. General Observations. The shortening of a long vowel before a consonant cluster or when more than two syllables follow is observed in several languages of the world. Kiparsky (1968: 179–81) formulates a rule for such changes occuring in Old and Middle English:

$$\text{V} \rightarrow [\text{-long}] \;/\; \underline{\quad\quad}\text{CC}$$

$$\ldots\text{V}\ldots\text{V}$$

The Modern English alternations of *keep* and *kept*, *severe* and *severity*, as well as that of Old English *gōdspel* with Modern English *gospel* and Early Middle English *hūsband* with Modern English *husband* are accounted for by this rule.

Stampe (1979: 47–49) questions both the form of the rule as well as the arguments given in favor of its psychological reality for speakers of English, and asserts that the reduction of vowel length here is a "process" within the framework of Natural Phonology. This rule is stated by Stampe as follows:

$$\text{V} \rightarrow [\text{-long}]/ \underline{\quad\quad}\text{CC\$} \quad \text{(for Old English)}$$

$$\text{V} \rightarrow [\text{-long}]/ \underline{\quad\quad}\text{C\$} \quad \text{(for Middle English)}$$

\$ = syllable boundary

In the Indian linguistic area these developments seem to be based on the placement of stress on the initial syllable of a word and the balancing of length between the stressed vowel and the following consonant. In both Dravidian and Indo-Aryan it appears that it is the vowel which wins out in this balancing game. Compensatory lengthening occurs in languages that lose the final vowel.

These developments also suggest the syllable division for forms like Te. *nakku* 'to hide' and *nāku* 'to lick' as shown in Figure 2.

Mohanan (1986: Chap. 4), following the theory of the syllable outlined in Halle and Vergnaud (1980), proposes for Malayalam and Dravidian in general a so-called "no coda hypothesis" according to which he advocates a syllable division of the form *na-kku* (instead of *nak-ku*). Mohanan's arguments are not convincing. Although I will not present a detailed refutation of Mohanan's views here, I can state that my analysis simplifies the definition of a metrical long syllable. I claim that it is possible to describe a long syllable as simply a syllable that has a branching rime.

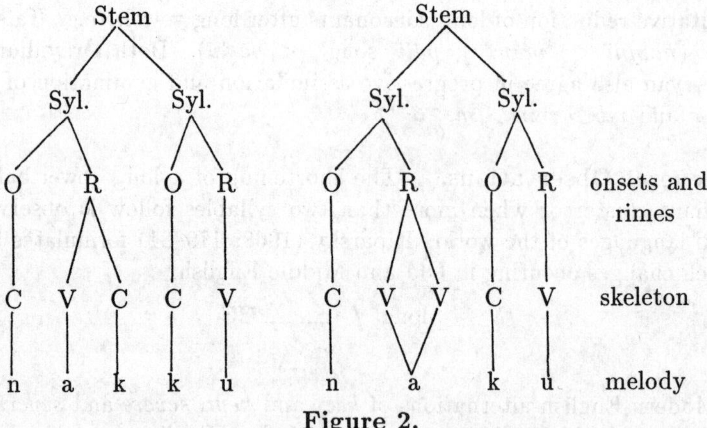

Figure 2.

Then the change of *nakku* to *nāku* can be stated as a change affecting the constituents of the rime of a syllable instead of the rime of one syllable and the onset of the next. The change is therefore confined to lower levels of structure, viz. the skeleton and melody. The reduction of (C)V̄CCV to (C)V̄$CV in Dravidian and to (C)VC$CV in Indo-Aryan also supports the division of the former as (C)V̄C$CV, because the extra long syllable V̄C (i.e., V̆ + V̆ + C) has dropped a V̆ or C to bring about parity of syllable weight between (C)V̄$CV and (C)VC$CV. Hock (1986) explains compensatory lengthening as a result of adjustment of morae representing the segments of successive syllables.

5. Conclusion. The reduction of extra-long syllables to long (i.e., V̄C$CV to V̄$CV)) took place in OIA and Dravidian at about the same time, viz. centuries immediately before the beginning of the Christian era. In early MIA this development was preceded by assimilation of heterogenous consonants into geminates, irrespective of the quantity of the preceding vowel. This appears to be quite similar to constraints of Proto-Dravidian phonotactics, which allowed only geminates and NP(P) sequences within stems. The development of OIA V̄C-CV to VC-CV was an early Middle Indic development which probably spread throughout the Indo-Aryan area. This was followed by the loss of the final vowel, leading to degemination and compensatory lengthening of the preceding vowel in South, East, and Western NIA languages. Kashmiri, Sindhi, Punjabi, Lahnda, and West Pahari, which preserve the geminates, also preserve the final vowel or vowel release.

The alternation of VCC(V)/V̄C(V) is found in Dravidian only sporadically, and is not traceable to Proto-Dravidian. However the types VCC(V) and V̄C(V) emerged as the favored syllable types in Dravidian to the exclusion of V̄CCV and V̄̆NPPV.

Turner traces the two "tendencies," i.e., assimilation of heterogenous consonants and compensatory lengthening of the preceding vowel, to Early Old Indic, suggesting a gradual areal and lexical diffusion of these changes into MIA and NIA stages. The development of these "tendencies" into general rules into MIA (particularly assimilation) must have been triggered by intimate contact with the Dravidian languages spoken in the Indo-Gangetic plains.

Vowel nasalization eliminating a preconsonantal nasal in Indo-Aryan (i.e., V̄NP > V̄̃P; VNP > V̄̃P [where P = voiceless/voiced obstruent]) compares favorably with nasal loss in Dravidian (i.e., V̄NP > V̄̃B > V̄B; V̄NPP > V̄̃NP > V̄̃P > V̄P; VNPP > VNP/VPP [where P is a voiceless obstruent and B its voiced counterpart]) to produce the favorite stem types V̄C/VCC. To the Dravidian examples of this phenomenon, given above in section 2, may be added the following from Indo-Aryan:

> OIA *kā́ṇḍa* (CDIAL 3023) 'single joint of a plant' > MIA: Pa. *kaṇḍa*, Pk. *kaṃḍa* > NIA: B. *kā̃ṛ* 'arrow', H. *kā̃ṛī* 'yolk', M. *kā̃ḍ* 'trunk', etc.
>
> OIA *pañca* (CDIAL 7655) 'five' > MIA: Pa., Pk. *pañca* > NIA: S. *pañja*, L. *panj*; B. *pā̃c*, H. *pā̃c*, M. *pā̃ċ*, etc.

It is true that changes resulting in the balancing of weight between vowels and consonants in successive syllables are well attested in languages other than those of South Asia. However, we have noted that successive changes in MIA and Dravidian have produced the same end result of shaping within the same time frame V̄C(V)/VCC(V) patterns into favorite stem types. This does not seem to be the result of an accident of phonological conspiracy. Judged from the other evidence supporting structural convergence in morphology and syntax, etc., the emergence of these syllable types point to a phonological phenomenon which must have resulted from a very intimate contact between speakers of Dravidian and Indo-Aryan for over a millllennium prior to the emergence of MIA.

References

Arun, Vidya Bhaskar. 1961. *A Comparative Phonology of Hindi and Panjabi*. Ludhiana: Panjabi Sahitya Akademi.

Beames, John. 1872–79. *A Comparative Grammar of the Modern Aryan Languages of India*. Reprinted edition [Delhi: Munshiram Manoharlal, 1970].

Bloch, Jules. 1965. *Indo-Aryan from the Vedas to Modern Times*. Translation by Alfred Master from original French. Paris: Adrien Maisonneuve.

Burrow, T. and M. B. Emeneau. 1984. *A Dravidian Etymological Dictionary*. 2nd ed. Oxford: Oxford University Press.

Caldwell, Rev. Robert. 1875. *A Comparative Grammar of the Dravidian or South Indian Family of Languages*. 3rd edition. Reprinted edition [Madras: University of Madras, 1956].

Chatterji, S. K. 1926. *The Origin and Development of the Bengali Language*. 3 vols. Reprinted edition [London: George Allen & Unwin, 1970].

Emeneau, M. B. 1971. "Dravidian and Indo-Aryan: The Indian linguistic area." Reprinted in *Language and Linguistic Area: Essays by Murray B. Emeneau*, selected and edited by Anwar S. Dil (Stanford: Stanford University Press [1980], pp. 167–96).

Halle, M. and J. R. Vergnaud. 1980. "Three dimensional phonology." *Journal of Linguistic Research* 1.1: 83–105.

Hock, Hans Heinrich. 1986. "Compensatory lengthening: In defence of the concept 'mora'." *Folia Linguistica* 20: 432–60.

Hyman, Larry M. 1975. *Phonology: Theory and Analysis*. New York: Holt, Rinehart and Winston.

Kiparsky, Paul. 1968. "Linguistic universals and linguistic change." In Emmon Bach and Robert T. Harms (eds.), *Universals in Linguistic Theory* (New York: Holt, Rinehart and Winston), pp. 170–202.

Krishnamurti, Bh. 1961. *Telugu Verbal Bases: A Comparative and Descriptive Study*. (University of California Publications in Linguistics, No. 24). Berkeley and Los Angeles: University of California Press.

Kumaraswami Raja, N. 1969. *Post-nasal Voiseless Plosives in Dravidian*. (Department of Linguistics Publication No. 18). Annamalainagar: Annamalai University.

Mehandale, M. A. 1948. *Historical Grammar of Inscriptional Prakrits*. Poona: Deccan College Postgraduate and Research Institute.

Mohanan, K. 1986. *The Theory of Lexical Phonology*. Dordrecht: D. Reidel.

Nara, Tsuyoshi. 1979. *Avahaṭṭa and Comparative Vocabulary of New Indo-Aryan Languages.* Tokyo: Institute for the Study of Languages and Cultures of Asia and Africa.

Ramachandra Rao, B. 1972. *A Descriptive Grammar of Pampa Bhārata.* Mysore: University of Mysore.

Stampe, David. 1973. "A dissertation on natural phonology." Unpublished Ph.D. dissertation, University of Chicago.

Subrahmanyam, P.S. 1983. *Dravidian Comparative Phonology.* Annamalainagar: Annamalai University.

Turner, R. L. 1966. *A Comparative Dictionary of the Indo-Aryan Languages.* 3 vols. London: Oxford University Press.

——. 1967. "Geminates after long vowel in Indo-aryan." *Bulletin of the School of Oriental and African Studies* 30.1: 73–82. Reprinted in *Collected Papers 1912–1973* (London: Oxford University Press [1975], pp. 405–15).

Zvelebil, Kamil. 1970. *Comparative Dravidian Phonology*. The Hague: Mouton.

HOW MANY VERNER'S LAWS DOES AN ALTAICIST NEED?

ROY ANDREW MILLER
Honolulu, Hawaii (USA)

Writing in the journal *Language* shortly after the publication of Miller 1971, John Street expressed himself upon the question of the genetic relationship of Japanese in the following terms:

> Poppe mentions that some scholars still doubt the Altaic hypothesis. Such scholars will have to come up with some entirely new theory of language history if they can maintain their doubt in the face of evidence presented by Miller 1971; this book, in my opinion, proves with absolute conclusiveness that Japanese is an Altaic language, and—en passant—that there *is* an Altaic language family (Street 1972: 212, note 1, emphasis in original).

Subsequent to the appearance of Miller 1971, really no more than the starting point for current interest in the Altaic linguistic relation of Japanese, the field has seen a considerable amount of important publication, much of it gratifyingly encompassing new etymological materials and fresh historical-linguistic formulations over and above the data and hypotheses advanced in 1971.[1]

Less than a decade later, and despite the progress and refinement exhibited by subsequent studies, we find Street sounding another and curiously different note. In the concluding section of a paper that he presented at an International Symposium held in Kyoto, October 10-13, 1980, he averred:

> Unless there are major new discoveries in the phonological comparison of Japanese with Altaic, I very much fear that it will never be possible to convince the scholarly community that Japanese is genetically related to the

[1] One indication of this is the fact that for the Japanese translation of Miller 1971 by Nishida Tatsuo et al. (Miller-Nishida 1981), it was already necessary to rewrite a number of sections of the original book substantially in order to keep its argumentation *au courant* of the many swiftly moving developments in this field. For this reason it is better today to cite Miller-Nishida 1981 rather than Miller 1971, though few in the field do so.

> Altaic language family. Indeed, because of the phonological under-differentiation of Old Japanese with respect to proto-Altaic, proto-Dravidian, proto-Austronesian, etc., and because of the paucity of morphological irregularities in Old Japanese, I am now somewhat pessimistic about the possibility of ever actually proving genetic relationship between Japanese and any other language group (Street 1981: 304).

This thoroughly startling, not to mention discouraging, *volte face* in his position on the relation of Japanese to Altaic was prefaced with a related discussion in which Street concluded *inter alia* that we (himself included apparently!) had until now been going about this entire business of the comparison of Japanese with other languages in precisely the wrong way. And he promised that he himself would take the lead in a new approach that "starts with raw data from Turkic, Chuvash, Mongolian, and Tungus, and attempts to collect the maximal set of etyma exhibiting some specific phonological feature of Proto-Altaic" (Street 1981: 303).

The great virtue of this new approach is alleged to lie in the detail that "since here one is working from Altaic to Japanese, rather than from Japanese to Altaic—that is, from the more differentiated to the less differentiated phonological system—there is greater likelihood that one may discover phonological splits, rather than remaining bogged down in phonemic losses and mergers. *With luck, someone may eventually come up with historical statements as strong and persuasive as Verner's Law in Germanic*" (Street 1981: 304, emphasis added).

Street's contention that it is now suddenly incumbent upon us to "work...from Altaic to Japanese, rather than from Japanese to Altaic" is more than a little puzzling, if only because his own work heretofore has displayed a somewhat greater familiarity with the literature, especially with that portion of it for which Miller is responsible, than this particular statement would indicate.

The goal of Miller's work all along has been to propose comparisons between the Altaic linguistic unity on the one hand and Japanese materials on the other, in a word, to "work...from Altaic to Japanese" precisely in the fashion that Street now hails as being the yet untried, but essential methodological approach.

Street's otherwise somewhat inexplicable statement may actually be due to a derivative reflection of an objection earlier raised against Miller's work by G. Doerfer. But our esteemed German colleague's principal concern, and also his major misunderstanding, was not particularly with the direction of the comparisons, rather with the specific identity of the elements being compared:

> Miller verglicht ja im Grunde das Japanische nicht mit "dem" Altaischen, sondern mit dem Türkischen, Mongolischen und Tungusischen, ihm stehen also drei separate Wortschätze zur Verfügung. (Doerfer 1974: 137)[.] ...Es ist nach der Methode "Man nehme zwei Wörterbücher und vergleiche drauf los" gearbeitet worden (1974: 141).

We have specifically answered these charges elsewhere (see e.g., Miller 1976), hence their details need not concern us further here, except as they bear on Street's subsequent viewpoint. Examples in various books and papers of Miller that show the comparative approach being utilized so as always to associate (a) Altaic on the one hand, i.e., the Altaic linguistic unity as represented in the form of the individual, specific reflexes of the elements in that now-lost unity as they survive in their putative cognates in the various languages, and (b) Japanese on the other, are so numerous that one wonders how Doerfer, and now in his turn Street, could possibly have overlooked them.

The difficulty appears to arise out of a failure to understand that the linguist most effectively and economically cites an earlier, now-lost linguistic entity, e.g., Proto-Altaic, or Proto-I.E., or proto-anything, not merely by citing reconstructed forms, but rather by citing the reflexes in the attested languages upon which the reconstructions can and must be based. One customarily speaks of comparing Lat. *pater* with Skt. *pitár-*, Gr. *patḗr*, Gothic *fadar*, and other specific, attested forms. The sense of such statements is of course that one is comparing all the forms cited, Latin as well as all the others, with I.-E. **pətēr*, the existence of which is attested to by the individual language citations given.

Similarly, then, when one speaks or writes of the comparison of Old Japanese *isi* 'stone' with Trk. *tāš*, Mo. *čilagun*, Tg. *žolo*, Kor. *tol*, and other specific attested linguistic forms, the comparison proposed is not actually being undertaken with each or every individually cited form; nor has one (to paraphrase Doerfer's colorful phrase) seized upon the two dictionaries nearest at hand and forcibly placed into juxtaposition what one finds there. Moreover, in the case of the Altaic languages, where so many details of reconstruction are still to a greater or lesser degree uncertain, it is frequently advisable to cite the reflexes rather than the reconstructions in order to avoid the discursive trails down which the premature introduction of certain details of any given reconstruction of proto-Altaic would, at the present time at least, necessarily lead us.

A specific case in point is provided by the earliest recoverable form for the word meaning 'stone' in all Altaic languages. Reconstructed in widely different ways at different times in different segments of the Altaic literature, this word nevertheless provides, within its historical phonological paradigms, a conspectus of many of the essential issues in comparative Altaic linguistics. Yet there is still no substantial degree of agreement among those who have concerned themselves with this problem about how best to write the most satisfactory reconstruction of the shape of the original form. Forms as widely different as Proto-Altaic *$t\bar{a}l_2$ and *$t\hat{\underset{\frown}{i}}\bar{a}l_2$ are among those that have been suggested. Most recently, we have presented at some length our arguments for reconstructing the original in question as *til_2.-*a*-, and in the process analyzing this prototype for the attested forms as a deverbal noun upon the so-called cooperativum in original *l_2 parallel with *til_1- 'cut, split', plus the original, inherited *.*a*- thematic vowel, as best accounting for the attested data (Miller 1985c: §2.5.2, 206 sqq.; 1986: §4.4.1, 197–8; these two papers were actually published in 1986 and 1987, resp.). But no matter how we write this, or any other, reconstruction, the essential data are those of the later attested forms for which we are providing an accounting, not the specific or particular marks that we chose to make on paper when we write our reconstructions.

In this fashion, then, even though some, indeed many of the individual segments of the historical-comparative phonology of the proto-Altaic word for 'stone' are thus still open to fruitful discussion, at the heart of the matter lies one of the basic assumptions of the Altaic hypothesis, or at the very least of the historical-phonological dimension of that hypothesis. This is the thesis that in the original language there were four distinct and contrasting liquid phonemes. These, following Ramstedt, and in his turn Poppe, we routinely reconstruct as *l, *l_2, *r, and *r_2. The first represents the correspondence of *l* in all the languages, the second the correspondence of *l* in all the languages except non-Chuvash Turkic, where this phoneme is instead represented by *š*, the third *r* in all the languages, and the fourth similarly except for non-Chuvash Turkic where it appears as *z*.[2]

[2] In a recent publication Street (1985) now even more surprisingly suggests that the entire four liquid formulation for Proto-Altaic is to be set aside—and with it, presumably, what little we have learned over the past half-century about the original Altaic linguistic unity. Street 1985 raises many questions and problems that can only be discussed in detail else-

The forms cited above for 'stone' show us at once that we are dealing here with a putative instance of a morpheme that in the original language must necessarily have contained Proto-Altaic $*l_2$. This is because of the correspondence of *l* in all the languages, including Chuvash, with Turkic *š*, together with, as we have now suggested in the literature on this subject for two decades, the *s* in Old J. *isi*, New J. *ishi* 'id.'

Whether we overtly write our present hypothesis for the shape of the entire Proto-Altaic morpheme involved in this etymology, or whether we simply write the attested forms in the various languages, the point at issue remains the same. We are not proposing comparing Japanese *ishi* directly with Turkic *tāš*, or with Mongolian *čilagun*, or with any other attested form or forms from any other specific and single language. The comparison has always been carried out between Japanese and Altaic, as it must be.

Two other points must here be made about the further implications of this particular lexical comparison for the historical inheritance of the Proto-Altaic four-liquid system into Proto-Japanese and Proto-Korean. The first is that only when we assume a Proto-Altaic linguistic unity, and then next assume also that in the case of this particular morpheme the comparison hinges upon the proposal of an original phoneme $*l_2$, are we able in turn to postulate Old Japanese (and New Japanese) *s* as being at least two of the reflexes for this phoneme—or more precisely, two of the later descendants of the reflex for this original Altaic phoneme $*l_2$ in Proto-Japanese.

This last assumption is substantiated to a significant extent when we note (see Miller 1971: 114-5, 123) that *s* is neither the sole nor the unique reflex of $*l_2$ in Japanese. We also find an additional reflex *r* for $*l_2$ in precisely describable contexts, viz., when in the original language the $*l_2$ in question was immediately preceded by another consonant, e.g. Proto-Altaic $*\tilde{n}\breve{i}ml_2ak$, reflected in Tkc. *jïmšaq* 'weak', but yielding Japanese *yawaraka* 'soft, pliant' as a consequence of the original $*ml_2$- configuration internal to the morpheme.

The second point is closely tied to the first. The above hypothesis for the several developments of $*l_2$ in Japanese simultaneously provides further evidence for the essential correctness of the reconstruction of this

where; for the moment it is sufficient to note that he particularly errs (a) in discussing only the $*l_2$ problem, as if this could usefully be treated in isolation from the reconstruction of the other three original liquids; and (b) in relying upon second- and third-hand sources for his Japanese lexical data, which renders most of his own attempts to denigrate well-established Japanese-Altaic comparisons out of the question.

particular element as $*l_2$, i.e., as some distinctive variety of an *l*, and not, for example, as some variety of **s* or other sibilant. Had $*l_2$ actually been **s* or the like in the earliest recoverable stages of the original language–as has so frequently been alleged in the Turkological literature in particular–there would have been no historical-phonological motivation for the appearance of the $l > r$ reflexes in Japanese for those instances where $*l_2$ in the original morphological configuration occurred immediately preceded by another, and consequently assimilatory, consonant.

The evidence from Japanese is of particular importance not only for the historical study of Japanese but also for the overall formulation of Altaic phonology, because it provides some of the most decisive data available for solving a number of the critical issues still surrounding the reconstruction of the four Altaic liquids, the specific sector of the phonology that serves as a veritable keystone for the entire problem of the recovery of the structure of the original language. Similarly, it is also worth noting that the same methodological principle, i.e., the principle of beginning with the more-differentiated and working from there to the less-differentiated phonological system, again with particular application to the highly differentiated four liquid system of original Altaic, has also been employed to suggest a solution for one of the long-standing problems in the historical phonology of Korean (Miller 1979).

The Old Korean written records have been transmitted in a complex orthography that, like the Old Japanese *Man'yōshū* texts, employs Chinese characters used both as phonograms and logographs, together with occasional rebus writings. In these texts the Chinese phonogram 尸, which in terms of Chinese historical phonology could only have been an orthographic device for writing *s* or *š*, has in modern Korean scholarship consistently been understood instead as a writing for some earlier form of the later New Korean generalized liquid phoneme ㄹ, i.e., the phoneme that we shall here transcribe as *l*, to be understood as representing the realization of /l/ as a phone [l] when morpheme-final, but as a phone [r] in other environments.

For this apparent orthographic anomaly in the Old Korean texts of 尸 *s* or *š* writing /l/ such empty explanations as "scribal caprice" were earlier all that might be suggested. But the entire phenomenon now finds a straight-forward and indeed elegant explanation in terms of overall Altaic comparative phonology. The now-traditional "reading" for this phonogram as Korean ㄹ /l/ is, we must also keep in mind, neither actually very old nor truly very "traditional." It was given wide circulation by Japanese scholars of Korean only in the first decades of the present century. And, in doing this, those same pioneering Japanese scholars were not really making any specific allegations about Old Korean phonology at all. They were simply carrying over, quite mechanically, the late Middle Korean, or even at times merely the putative New Korean, equivalents for Old Korean words in the texts written with the phonogram 尸, implementing in the process their unverbalized assumption that Old Korean was in its phonology precisely the same as late Middle and New Korean—a hypothesis that is, on the face of it, unlikely. Nevertheless, these Middle and New Korean equivalents with their own very late *l* have all but universally found their way into our editions of Old Korean materials for virtually every instance of the phonogram 尸.

Once we opt to proceed along the lines of the assumption that Old Korean, like Middle and New Korean in their turns, was actually an Altaic language, then a new and exciting possibility for solving the problem of these writings with the phonogram 尸 is immediately opened before us. In these Old Korean texts where the *s* or *š* written with 尸 obviously corresponds to Middle and New Korean *l*—more precisely expressed, in the lexical items in Old Korean where the words with this phonogram have clear cognates with Middle and New Korean forms identical in phonological configuration except for the substitution of their *l* for the *s* or *š* of the Old Korean documents—what we have is an important new variety of historical-linguistic evidence documenting that among these three different historical stages of Korean—Old, Middle, and New—a rather more complex relationship must originally have obtained than had until recently been understood.

We can see in most of the examples of Old Korean available to us a variety of Altaic in which, as in non-Chuvash Turkic at the one extreme of the Altaic domain and in Old Japanese at the other, original $*l_2$ was inherited as a sibilant, *s* or *š*. At the same time this further implies that we have a later, secondary re-Altaicization on the Korean peninsula, that is, the Old Korean sibilant *s* or *š* became /l/, reverting to a form similar in manner of articulation to the original Altaic $*l_2$ whence it derived. This postulated re-Altaicization must have been the result of contact with Tungusic languages to the north, where $*l$ and $*l_2$ both become *l*, and $*r$ and $*r_2$ both become *r*. In other words, Korean abutted upon a linguistic region where the configuration for the Proto-Altaic liquids shows a close parallel with the liquid-structuring of Middle and New Korean. There only remains to single out for particular attention the one important further refinement that, subsequent to this secondary re-Altaicization of the Korean linguistic area from the north, and sometime between the Old and Middle Korean periods, the two surviving Tungusic liquids *l* and *r* were, on the peninsula, de-phonemicized and reordered into the two allophones *l* and *r* of the single surviving Middle and New Korean liquid /l/.

Here we are able to observe the comparative method of the neogrammarians fully operative and elegantly performing what it was originally devised to do. By referring (as e.g., Miller 1979) to the more highly differentiated Altaic system of the phonology of the liquids, and coordinating this with, on the one hand, the phonogram orthography of the Old Korean written records, and on the other, with the phonological structure of Middle and New Korean, we have been able to recover many of the details of an important scenario for the historical development of linguistic systems on the Korean peninsula that otherwise would have been lost—the series of events in which the three principal varieties of Old Korean known to us from texts were displaced under the impact of successive incursions from the Tungus-speaking northern marches, eventually to be replaced on the peninsula by the equally Altaic, but structurally quite different varieties of language that eventually provide us with our attested Middle and New Korean.[3]

The single most important lesson to be learned from all this is that the work of historical-linguistic recovery can be achieved only when, as has always been true, we operate in the direction that points from the more differentiated toward the less differentiated systems, in other words, when

[3] Misunderstandings also cloud much of the literature on this issue. Janhunen & Kho 1982, for example, profess to find it "absurd" even to attempt to identify phonological patterns for the reflexes of Proto-Altaic $*l_2$ in languages as geographically separate as Turkic on the one hand and Old Korean on the other. For them Tkc. *š*, despite its clear correlation with words that show it to correspond to *l* in the other languages, is not a phenomenon that may be treated in terms of comparative Altaic phonology, but merely a "distinctive inter-Turkic development," and hence without significance for the comparison of any other languages elsewhere in the world, Korean of course included. Their joint misunderstanding of this point is rooted in nothing more substantial than the *a priori* denial of any possibility of genetic relation between any of the languages commonly denominated "Altaic." Since Janhunen & Kho begin by denying even the possibility of ever reconstructing an original Altaic linguistic unity, they are of course left with nothing but discrete, language-specific linguistic phenomena to deal with. In any such system it is only to be expected that as a consequence nothing can be found to correspond to or to correlate with anything else.

and only when we follow precisely the same path that Street 1981 now enjoins upon us all.

Street appears willing to allow a position that is, for all its problems, still refreshingly different from that of the anti-Altaicists who presume *a priori* that the Altaic languages simply are not and cannot ever have been related. Street is at least not of their camp. As he, however reluctantly, puts it, "with luck, someone may eventually come up with historical statements [relating Japanese to Altaic] as strong and persuasive as Verner's Law in Germanic" (1981: 304).

Street's evocation of Verner's Law in this passage has the merit of relating the discussion about Japanese and the Altaic languages to received assumptions about the comparative method and its implications for the postulation of linguistic relations. "Strong and persuasive" are indeed fit and proper terms to use when speaking of Verner's Law. But the question must be asked, strong in what respect, and persuasive concerning what specific question? The implication of Street's remarks is that Verner's Law is "strong and persuasive" as a proof for the genetic relation obtaining among the Indo-European languages as a group, or perhaps "strong and persuasive" for the relation of Germanic to the other Indo-European groups.

Refreshing our memories on the details of the complex set of phonological relations subsumed under the term "Verner's Law," we are at first tempted, along with Street, to interpret its formulations as "strong and persuasive" arguments for genetic relations. There can be no question but that the hypothesis of an earlier Indo-European linguistic unity was much strengthened by the discovery "in 1876 [by] Karl Verner (1846-1896), a Danish linguist, [who] showed that in a number of cases where Germanic has the troublesome [d] [i.e., a [d] such as that in the word 'father', which appeared to be anomalous in Proto-Germanic for showing [d] instead of the [θ] expected in terms of Grimm's Law], this consonant falls upon a vowel or dipthong which is unstressed in Sanskrit and Greek; this correlation occurs in enough instances, and in the morphologic structure, systematically enough, to exclude the factor of accident... Since the place of the word-accent is determined by the primary phonemes in Italic, Celtic, and Germanic, we can easily believe its position in each of these languages is due to later change. Sanskrit and Greek, moreover, agree so often, although the place of the accent in both is highly irregular, that we do not hesitate to attribute this feature to the parent language." (Bloomfield 1933: 308-9, § 18.7)[4]

---

[4] The original statements of "Verner's Law" were published by Karl

But is Street actually correct in suggesting that the principal utility of Verner's Law in Indo-European studies is to be identified in the "strong and persuasive" argument it presents for the hypothesis of an earlier Indo-European linguistic relation, and hence also in his implication that for any thesis relating Japanese to the other Altaic languages we too must somehow come up with our own "Verner's Laws"? No, unfortunately, he is not—as it becomes clear after re-reading Bloomfield's classic presentation of Verner's Law, and his interpretation of its significance for historical linguistics:

> As to the correction of our correspondence-groups by a careful survey of the residual cases, the neogrammarians soon got a remarkable confirmation of their hypothesis in Verner's treatment of Germanic forms with discrepant [b, d, g] in place of [f, θ, h].... This was so striking a confirmation of the hypothesis of regular sound-change, that the burden of proof now fell upon the opponents of the hypothesis: if the residual forms can show such a correlation as this, we may well ask for very good reasons before we give up our separation of forms into recognized correspondences and remainders, and our principle of scanning residual forms for new correspondences....The assumption of regular (that is, purely phonemic) sound-change is justified by the correlations which it uncovers; it is inconsistent to accept the results which it yields and to reject it whenever one wants a contradictory assumption ("sporadic sound-change") to "explain" difficult cases. (Bloomfield 1933: 357, 359, 360, § 20.8).

Street has muddied the historical-linguistic waters by virtue of his genial assumption that the principal utility of Verner's Law for the Indo-Europeanist is to be identified in the "strong and persuasive" fashion in which the statements that comprise that "Law" "prove" the genetic relationship of the Indo-European languages. Bloomfield's account of the matter, concise and elegant as always, immediately shows that this is not and never was the case. For the classical Indo-Europeanists, Verner's Law provided the then-still-necessary additional dollop of evidence that pretty

---

Verner under the title, "Eine Ausnahme der germanischen Lautverschiebung," in *Kuhns Zeitschrift*, vol. 23, p. 27 sqq., in 1877. They are summarized, with references to other primary literature on this formulation, in Prokosch 1939: 60–68, 20.

well persuaded most people in the field that the doctrine of the "Invariability of Sound Laws" (*Ausnahmslösigkeit der Lautgesetze*) was a useful, practical, and probably also a historically valid working-hypothesis for conducting etymological studies. In actual point of fact Verner's Law tells us absolutely nothing about the historicity of the genetic relations presumably obtaining among the Indo-European languages. Instead, simply because it supplied additional "strong and persuasive" evidence arguing in favor of the invariability of sound-laws, it provided a rigorous standard for the regular formulation of a number of important new etymologies that until then had remained unaccounted for, i.e., what in etymological studies constitute a "residue." But it no more "proved" the Indo-European linguistic relations than Grimm's Law had. With or without either Grimm or Verner, that relation, like all early linguistic relations, was and still is a theoretical construct not susceptible to proof. In this respect, it only remains to be added, Indo-European is precisely comparable to Altaic.

It is all but impossible to extricate from Street's apparent misunderstanding of the nature and utility of Verner's Law his insistence upon the importance of phonological splits as against loss or merger in the collective etymological evidence that figures in any argument for the genetic relationship of Japanese to the Altaic languages. In 1981 he addresses himself to the task of refuting the implications of the bulk of the earlier literature on this question of splits versus mergers. A case in point is the formulation of a striking instance of phonological split documented by the Japanese lexical evidence for the reflexes of Altaic $*r_2$ (first set out in detail in Miller 1971: 146–53, § 4.4 then supplemented by many additional examples, with a number of attendant phonological refinements, in Miller 1975). Altaic $*r_2$ appears as *r* in all the languages except in non-Chuvash Turkic, where it is *z*. Its Old Korean reflexes remain obscure (though Miller 1979: 35–40; and 43 note 165 has assembled some tentative evidence on this point). But in Old Japanese, as well as in the later stages of Japanese, this phoneme was the victim of an interesting, significant, and phonologically unambiguous split, yielding Japanese *r* except when the initial phoneme of the morpheme in question was a continuant, in which circumstances it yielded Japanese *t*. Numerous examples of this split have already been cited in the literature; typical is OJ *natu* 'summer', going regularly with Proto-Altaic $*\tilde{n}\bar{a}r_2$, Tkc. *jaz* 'spring', Kor. *yŏlŭm* 'summer'.

Street is not only familiar with this formulation, he has himself invoked it on at least one occasion (Street 1979: 69). This was an attempt to provide an Altaic etymology for OJ *Fituzi* 'sheep' that would relate the *-t-* in this form to original $*r_2$. Unfortunately this particular etymological suggestion is unlikely on the basis of extra-linguistic evidence. The historical record shows that sheep were introduced quite late into Japan from the Old Korean kingdom of Paekche, so that the word in question is almost surely not a regular development of any inherited Altaic etymon, but rather a fairly recent loanword from Paekche Old Korean into Old Japanese.

Despite the inadequacies of this particular etymology, Street (1979) has correctly understood, and attempted to apply, the principle at issue in Miller's formulation of the Old Japanese reflexes of Altaic $*r_2$. Consequently it is all the more surprising to find him writing in 1981 in the following fashion:

> ...if we examine the sound-changes that have thus far been hypothesized on the basis of lexical comparisons between Japanese and Altaic, we find that most if not all of them involve either phonological loss or merger, total or partial. Professor Miller in his *Japanese and the Other Altaic Languages* suggested only about a dozen phonological developments which imply systematic phonemic splits, and so far as I am able to determine, all of these involve loss or merger in their products, and none seems to have brought about systematic morphophonemic alternations. Rather typical is Miller's suggestion involving a purported split of the proto-Altaic phoneme $*r_2$: it was hypothesized that this phoneme became Japanese *r* in some positions but *t* in others. But Japanese r resulted also from proto-Altaic $*l_1$ and $*r_1$, and Japanese *t* came also from one or more of the proto-Altaic stops, so that both of the products of this split merged with other elements. And even the possibility of any morphophonemic alternation between these products is prohibited by the nature of the factor supposed to have conditioned the split. In short, then, *what phonological splits have been hypothesized for the prehistory of Japanese seem to be of a rather uninteresting sort* (Street 1981: 298–99, emphasis added).

Throughout his 1981 paper, Street stresses—and rightly so—the power of conviction that demonstrations of phonological splits in etymologically documented sound correspondences carry in questions of the genetic relationships of languages, in contrast to phonological mergers. He also recognizes that such splits have indeed been demonstrated to be operative within the parameters of certain of the correspondences proposed thus far as illustrating the inheritance of Altaic lexical materials by Japanese. But then he deftly deflects any argumentative impact that such splits might otherwise have by his declaration that these earlier demonstrated (not "hypothesized"!; it is the relations they imply that are hypothesized, not the splits themselves, which are matters of attestable fact) are "of a rather uninteresting sort."

This particular anathema has at least the recommendation of novelty and originality. One cannot recall ever having seen the putative "interest" or "lack of interest" of a historical sound change called into question in earlier literature as a significant criterion in connection with problems of genetic relations. Unfortunately, Street does not make it clear what he considers to be an "interesting" variety of phonological split, or by that same token what he finds "uninteresting," except of course that under this latter devasting rubric it is clear that he subsumes Miller's formulation of the Old Japanese reflexes of Altaic $*r_2$.

Largely by reading between the lines of his contribution, we can get at least a hint of what has impelled him toward this highly idiosyncratic value judgement. Apparently he finds the phonological split earlier demonstrated for the Japanese reflexes of Altaic $*r_2$ "rather uninteresting" because each of the Japanese developments of this original phoneme, i.e., OJ *t* and OJ *r*, "resulted also in other etyma and under other conditions from still other Altaic phonemes," i.e., OJ *t* is not only the development, in certain circumstances, of Altaic $*r_2$, but also of Altaic **t* and **d*, while OJ *r* may also result from Altaic **l* and, in a small number of, again, strictly demarcated phonological contexts, Altaic $*l_2$. What Street seems to find "rather uninteresting," and hence by his implication of little or no value for discussions of genetic relation among the languages at issue, is the fact that the end products of the demonstrated $*r_2$ split in Japanese are not unique elements in the subsequent phonological system, but instead co-exist there together with other end-products of other original phonemes. In other words the split in question, demonstrated and clear though it may be, is complicated at the same time by the simultaneous occurrence of merger(s).

Essentially mistaken though this particular point of Street's is, it is not necessarily or completely misleading. No one would question the proposition—if indeed such is Street's contention—that a phonological split completely and totally unsullied by the simultaneous operation of mergers within the same system is, hands down, the most impressive sort of evidence in this particular sector of historical phonology. But as much as we would all like to have evidence of such a vivid variety in discussing problems relating to the historical relations among the languages of Central and North Asia, we are well advised to ask how frequently such a clear-cut proposition can be established in other, better studied historical-linguistic systems, before we dismiss out of hand as "rather uninteresting" hard-won evidence for splits that also happens to include subsidiary and not entirely irrelevant evidence for mergers.

The single most curious fact about Street 1981 is that, for all his talk of Verner's Law, Street appears to have had in mind not actually that formulation at all, but rather the still earlier Indo-Europeanist canon of phonological changes usually known as Grimm's Law. One arrives at the inevitable conclusion that it is the Law named for Grimm and not that for Verner that he would admit to be "interesting," as specifically incorporating splits of the non-contaminated variety.

In the shifts of the Indo-European consonants into Proto-Germanic that Grimm's Law describes there are, to be sure, a limited number of cases where the context-sensitive developments of the consonants (Bynon 1977: 84) do indeed result in splits yielding newly phonemicized elements within the phonology, resulting in elements that did not merge with any pre-existing phonological entities in the system. But even in this instance, such splits unsullied by mergers are true of only a fraction, roughly one-third, of the total evidence. This means that if we were to follow Street, Grimm's Law too would, in a majority of its specific etymological applications, be "rather uninteresting."

At issue here are the developments, e.g., of IE **t* into Proto-Germanic. In obstruent clusters, this **t* falls together with ("merges" with) the regular Proto-Germanic reflex of IE **d*, and—by Verner's Law!–under other particular phonological constraints involving word-accent it also falls together with the regular reflexes of IE **dh*. It is only in those actually rather special circumstances when neither of these two other specific phonological contexts is at issue, that the non-merger-tainted Proto-Germanic reflex as θ is to be found. Thus, if we were to apply Street's categorization, only about one-third of the instances of Grimm's Law are "interesting," in the sense that only about one-third of them offer Germanic split reflexes that are not simultaneously involved in mergers.

And what may thus be set forth for Grimm's Law holds even truer for Verner's Law, where, *pace* Street, all the end products of its split operation are phonemes that simultaneously participate in mergers elsewhere within the system, precisely as do OJ *r* and *t* when treated in the light of Altaic $*r_2$. It was, after all, the problem presented by "the word father, [which] together with some others, is anomalous in Primitive Germanic in containing [d] instead of [θ]" (Bloomfield 1933: 308, § 18.7) that was solved by the formulation of Verner's Law, since it provided a regular phonological-contextual framework in terms of which the appearance of this [d] might regularly be predicted. But this Germanic *d* was not, by any means, a newly phonemicized segment of the phonology, nor was it a newly independent entity not capable of identification with, or structural contamination by, any like-looking phonological segment. In other words it was never totally isolated from any independent evidence for the simultaneous operation of mergers. Among its other sources, this Germanic *d* whose appearance, until then believed to be sporadic, was regularly explained by Verner's Law, was at the same time the regular development in Germanic of IE **-dh-* (cf. Lat. *vidua*, Skt. *vidhávā*, NE *widow*; IE **widhewa-*, or Lat. *medius*, Skt. *mádhya-*, Goth. *midjis*, *miduma*, NE *middle*, IE **medhi-*).

Thus, the end products of the split that is described under the rubric of Verner's Law also participated in mergers, just as did the end-products of the split that may be described, in terms of its OJ reflexes, for Altaic $*r_2$. If the latter is "of a rather uninteresting sort," then so also must be the former.

Essentially mistaken, though not necessarily or completely misleading, then, is at the same time the best and the worst that may be said of Street's dictum in this connection. It is not totally misleading, because no one would wish to deny the obvious fact that, as we go about our work of historical linguistics, we frequently come upon individual languages that have, in the course of their change through time, undergone a considerable degree of phonological merger, at times a degree so extensive as to alter their entire phonological-structural aspect markedly. And when these mergers are massive, the situation often develops in which the very nature of the latter, changed linguistic forms with which we must deal makes it difficult to cite forms and comparisons that are, on their surface at least, as convincing or striking as those that may be cited in instances where more splits have produced unique, newly phonemicized end-products. This is particularly so when such unique end-products are in good supply *vis-à-vis* the end-products of splits that have simultaneously participated in mergers. If the massive presence of mergers were actually able to render questions of genetic relation between languages impossible to argue with conviction, then the Indo-European relation of, e.g., the Tocharian languages would necessarily remain obscure.

The development of the Tocharian consonantism can only be described as the result of massive mergers that threw together the most disparate segments of the original system. IE **reudh-* yielded Toch. A *rtär*, Toch. B *ratre* 'red', IE **dhughəter-* appears as Toch. A *ckācar*, Toch. B *tkācer* 'daughter', IE _*pətēr-_ as Toch. B _pātär-_, 'father', IE _*bhrāter-_ as Toch. B _protär-_ 'brother', and IE _*māter-_ as Toch. B _mātär-_ 'mother' (further examples in Winter 1980). In this far from uncommon variety of historical phonological development, massive evidence for mergers always threatens to wipe out whatever evidence may once have existed for splits. And this is _mutatis mutandis_ precisely the variety of historical-phonological development that we have to reckon with, not only in formulating those sound-correspondences that relate Japanese to Altaic, but also those that relate Korean to Altaic.

The case of Korean is particularly to the point. In at least one sense it would by no means be an overstatement to regard Korean as the Tocharian of the Altaic linguistic domain. Both Korean and Tocharian have reached us in written records that already show enormous shifts and changes in phonology between the time of our earliest texts and that of the most recent stages, changes and shifts so sweeping that they often obscure almost entirely the nature of the linguistic relation involved. Normally we begin the work of Korean-Altaic comparisons from the data of our earliest integral Korean written records, the not-very-old documentary remains of "Middle Korean" from the mid-15th century. In this Middle Korean we are immediately confronted by the system of a greatly simplified consonantism: only _p t k_, _m n ñ_, _č s z_, and _l y w h_ (several of which unitary phonemes also entered into clusters with one another, thus _pk-_, _psk-_, _pt-_, _pč-_, _čč-_, etc.) survived from the far-richer Proto-Altaic consonantism. Old Japanese of course had also considerably simplified its consonantism in comparison with the original Altaic language, but by no means as much as Korean, since it preserved (albeit not in completely free contextuality) both _F_ and _b_, _t_ and _d_, and _k_ and _g_. Perhaps—probably, one is tempted to say—Old Korean too, like Old Japanese, represented an intermediate stage in this process of simplification-by-merger, and had had a somewhat more elaborate consonantal structure. But unfortunately, because of the extreme philological difficulties of the Old Korean written records, we are not able, at least for the present, to speak with authority concerning most of the details of its consonantism.

As we have already seen, we have in the Old Korean written records incontravertable documentary evidence for the _s_ or _š_ with which most of the Old Korean languages corresponded to Altaic $*l_2$, in the form of overt phonogram scriptions with the graph 尸. Again, this Old Korean _s_ or _š_ also had other sources, especially in Altaic _*s_, so that this too was not a unique split end-product uncontaminated with the evidence of mergers (and the same is also true of the OJ _s_ reflexes from $*l_2$). Nevertheless, these Old Korean and Old Japanese reflexes for *l are of unique—might one add, "strong and persuasive"?—value, not because they are not themselves somewhat obscured by mergers, but because these formulations of *l_2 (and so also for *r_2) are themselves prime examples of splits with unique end-products elsewhere in Altaic (e.g., Tkc. *š* and *z*, resp.). It would hardly be inaccurate, and not in the least misleading, to characterize the two decades of Japanese-Altaic comparative studies that have followed upon the publication of *Japanese and the Other Altaic Languages* as having been a period that has demonstrated the importance of context-sensitive splits as a powerful factor working toward the eventual clarification of the precise details of the scenario that connects Japanese with other languages.

Time and time again these studies have shown that what initially appear to be scattered sets of anomalous phonological correspondences fall neatly into place as soon as we recognize the possibility that they are not random or sporadic variants, but instead the remnants of a once regular pattern of context-sensitive splits within the phonological structuring of the original language, or in some cases, within the phonological structuring of the Pre-Japanese stage that must be interposed between our earliest written records for Old Japanese on the one hand and the most recent stages that we can reconstruct for Proto-Altaic on the other.

It will be useful to illustrate the point with a small selection of examples, drawing in all cases upon recently published materials not available to Street in 1981. Perhaps if these data had been at hand he would not have so rashly, and pessimistically, generalized upon the lack of examples involving Japanese with Altaic that also bring into evidence the phenomenon of phonological split:

(1) In 1971 it was not possible to formulate the reflexes of Proto-Altaic **ä* rigorously in Old Japanese. We could only state in very general terms that, by and large, this original vowel appeared to correspond to OJ *a* (thus Miller 1971: 306, § 2.41). But even then it was clear that this statement did not take proper account of a significant portion of the phonological residue, e.g., it did not accomodate such important etymologies as OJ *we* 'food for domesticated animals', Proto-Tungus **bä* 'bait, lure, food for animals.'

Subsequent re-study of this question, and re-formulation based upon the evidence of additional etymologies not at hand in 1971, have since made it feasible to re-investigate this problem. As a result we can now demonstrate with a considerable body of evidence that the developments of **ä* in Japanese are capable of completely rigorous statement, and in fact that these developments represent the results of a context-sensitive phonological split that took place somewhat subsequent to the last stages that may be reconstructed for the original language, and probably just prior to the earliest written records from the archipelago:

> pA *ä was inherited directly, and more-or-less unaltered, as OJ *e* when it appeared in an original, inherited morpheme that (a) was a monosyllable, and (b) did not end in a final consonant... It was the original environment of pA *ä...that determined the later developments of this phoneme in Old Japanese (Miller 1985: 78, §8, "Phonological Excursus: The Old Japanese Reflexes of pA *ä").

Thus, we now understand how and why it is that, as a result of these context-sensitive split phenomena, we find OJ *e* under the circumstances of original monosyllables not ending in a final consonant (as in OJ *we* 'food for animals', pTg *bä, cited supra), but when the original form was either (a) monosyllabic but with a final consonant, or (b) was polysyllabic, *ä was then regularly inherited not as OJ *e* but as OJ *a*, thus yielding, e.g., OJ *Fara* 'belly, womb', from pA *bǟl 'midsection of the body'; OJ *kani* 'crab (marine)', pTk. *känä 'parasites, ticks, etc.' (i.e., 'crab (lice)'); finally, "the apparent anomaly presented by a [further small] residue of forms that refuse to be accomodated under the above stipulations, showing as they do OJ *ö* for expected *a* from *ä, are capable of rigorous statement once we note that this development occurs only in the vicinity of a labial consonant, and hence represents another example of the well-known assimilatory process commonly encountered among all the Altaic languages, and generally designated 'labial attraction'," e.g., OJ *omö*, pTg. *ämä*, Ma. *eme* 'mother'; OJ *töb-* 'to fly (of birds), to flutter or move in the air (of objects)', pA *däb-, 'to fly' (cf. further relevant etymologies and details in Miller 1985: 78-83).

In other words, this new formulation for the Japanese reflexes of Proto-Altaic *ä not only makes it possible for us to regularize a number of important etymologies that have until now appeared to involve anomalous phonological elements in their historical development; it also provides a large set of interrelated examples all documenting the operation of an early context-sensitive split in the phonological structure of Proto-Altaic just prior to the development of the Pre-Japanese that underlies our earliest written records.

(2) As it happens, evidence for yet another context-sensitive split has been preserved, *inter alia*, in the etymologies cited immediately above, where the attentive reader will by now have noticed an apparent anomaly in the Japanese reflexes for original Proto-Altaic *b. In certain examples it is alleged that this phoneme developed into OJ *w* (as in the word for

'food for animals, bait'), but in others into OJ *F* (as in the word for 'belly, midsection of the body'). Here too a contact-sensitive split is involved: "the rule is that original **b* became OJ *w-* except when the word or morpheme with this initial had internal **-r-* or **-l-* or **-r_2-* or **-l_2-*, in which cases instead it appeared as OJ *F-*." Thus we are now able to explain, in terms of a regular development of this split, such otherwise superficially anomalous etymologies as OJ *Far-* 'draw a bow', against pTg **bäri* 'a bow' (cf. additional details in Miller 1985: 82).

This particularly well documented case of a Pre-Old Japanese split is not only important for regularizing a number of hitherto anomalous Japanese-Altaic etymologies; it also provides important evidence bearing upon one of the oldest, and most frequently debated, issues in general Altaic historical phonology as well, viz., the phonetic identity of what is reconstructed as **-l_2-*.

Much lively discussion has taken place in Altaistic circles about the phonetic nature of the original phoneme we reconstruct as **l_2*. In effect, most of the questions raised in this connection ask whether or not this phoneme was "some kind of an *l*," in the sense of having perhaps been some special variety—palatalized, unvoiced, etc.—of a liquid, or whether it was instead some variety of a hushing sibilant. Questions of this sort are actually of relatively little moment for the solution of the larger problems in Altaic historical linguistics. Once we recognize the clear necessity for reconstructing four separate and distinct "Lateral- und Zitterlaute" (Poppe 1960: 72) for the original language, it hardly matters very much just what particular phonetic value we assume for each to flesh out this structural scheme. Here, as always, it is the structure and the system, the phonemes and not the phones, that ultimately matter. But since these and similar questions on the level of articulatory phonetics continue to be asked, it is probably helpful to note that in this specific instance, the clarification of the early Japanese split of **b-* before all representations of the original "Lateral- und Zitterlaute" set does incidently demonstrate that **l_2* was indeed phonetically "some sort of *-l-*." This is because the Japanese cognates for forms with internal **-l_2-*, which in Old Japanese as in Turkic appears as a sibilant, nevertheless show the same context-sensitive split of an initial **b-*, e.g., OJ *Fasira* 'pillar, column', cognate with OTk. *bāš* 'head', i.e., Proto-Altaic **bāl_2* .[5] Had original **l_2* not been "some sort of *-l-*," it

[5] This important etymology Street would now dismiss, on the grounds that according to Murayama Shichirō "OJ *Fasira* means 'pillar', not 'main pillar', which destroys the semantic basis for this comparison" (1985: 647).

could hardly have participated in the viccissitudes of this particular split in company with the other, "ordinary" *l*.

(3) Perhaps the most elaborate, and by that token also probably the most convincing variety of evidence for a context-sensitive split between Altaic and Japanese is that involving Proto-Altaic **x*-. This phoneme was an original velar spirant that was lost ("merged with zero") early in the history of the so-called "inner Altaic" languages (Turkic and Mongolian), and survived only in the Tungus domain and on the Japanese archipelago. Its developments, therefore, may be accounted for by a set of regular correspondences between Proto-Tungus on the one hand and Old Japanese on the other. But this is merely a matter of convenience for statement and description, since there is evidence for the early membership of this phoneme in the inventory of the original language. In other words, even though the historical-comparative accounts of **x*- may most expeditiously be stated as correspondences between Tungus and Japanese, it must also be kept in mind that actually these are in fact descriptions of the historical development of an original Altaic phoneme in both Tungus and Japanese.

In these terms, then, the statements for the pattern of context-sensitive splits undergone by **x*- in pre-Old Japanese, and documented as such in the written records of Old Japanese, are as follows: we find OJ *F* as representing **x*- before the OJ reflexes of pTg *ā̆, *ū̆, *ō̆, and *ȫ̆; but OJ *w* as representing **x*- before *ǟ̆ and *ǖ̆; and OJ *s* as representing **x*- before *ï̄̆ and *ī̆.

It will be sufficient here to give the following eight representative etymologies in order to demonstrate the variety of lexical evidence now available for this hypothesis. They have been selected from among a total

On his p. 651, Street cites the standard and reliable Sanseidō dictionary of Old Japanese, but apparently he did not use it. It he had, he would have found that Murayama's claims about this word are totally without foundation. The dictionary specifically defines *Fasira* as 'the most important structural member in the construction of a house' (*kasaku ni oite mottomo shuyō na mono* [p. 578c., *s.v.*]). Similarly without basis in fact, but similarly repeated uncritically by Street, are Murayama's *dicta* on the morpheme-division of OJ *yasirö* 'cult site' (Street 1985: 640 note 21; see Miller-Nishida 1981: 97, 133 for the correct analysis of this word, for which Murayama was only repeating a centuries-old folk etymology known to every Japanese schoolboy), and his totally irresponsible analysis of OJ *tas*- as "a late abbreviation [sic!] from...*tar-a-su*" (Street 1985: 638 note 11). For this not a shred of evidence is or indeed can be cited, since none exists.

of thirty-six new Japanese-Altaic comparisons published in detail for the first time in Miller 1987: (1) DIG OUT: pA *$\textit{xär}_2$- > pTg *xär-, Ev. *er-* 'to dig (snow), excavate (earth)', Orok. *xeri-* 'to dig (snow)', Olc. *xeru-*, Neg. *xeruči-* 'id.', Ma. *eri-* 'to sweep (a floor)', WMo. *erü-* 'dig, cut, hack', Chag., Osm. *äz-* 'rub, grate', Poppe 1960: 103, OJ *wer-* 'engrave, incise (on wood, stone); dig out (a hole in the ground)'; (2) BARK: pTg **xūra(.kta)*, Ev. *ủra-* 'cover (of a tent, etc.)', *ủran* 'summer tent of skins or bark', Orok. *xủrakta*, Olc. *xorakta*, Na. *xorakta* 'bark', Ma. *umriha*, *uriha* 'membrane, inner bark on trees, skin on walnuts and hazelnuts', early MJ *Foro* 'supplementary armor worn on the back by a mounted warrior to ward off arrows', WMo. *urača* 'Laubhütte, konische Hütte aus Birkenbast, Art Wigwam', Yak. *urasa*, *uraha* 'id.', Poppe 1960: 80; (3) FINGER: pTg **xunia*, Ev. *un´akan*, *un´akāsān* 'index finger', Orok. *xủná*, 'spoon', *xủn´aptủ(n-)* 'finger ring', Olc. *xon´a(n-)* 'spoon', Na. *xon´ã* 'spoon', *xon´aka* 'finger ring', OJ *Fone* 'bone' (cf. the semantics of MLG *knockel* 'bone, knuckle', against Dan. *knokkel* 'bone', NHG *bein* 'leg', cognate with OE *ban*, NE *bone*); (4) ENJOY: pTg **xäpī-*, Ev. *ewī-*, Orok. *xupi-*, Olc. *xupi-*, Na. *xupi-*, Ma. *efi-* 'play, enjoy oneself; act', OJ *weF-* 'be intoxicated', OJ *werak-* 'laugh aloud with pleasure (esp. when drunk)'; (5) FLOWER, ORNAMENT: pTg **xïlaga*, Ev. *ilaga*, Orok. *silla*, Olc. *irga* 'ornament', *sila* 'flower', Na. *elga* 'ornament', *sela* 'flower', *sīla-* 'to bloom', Ma. *ilha*, *ilga* 'flower, blossom; patterned, colored', Ma. *ilgari*, *ilhari* 'paper strips attached to a willow branch used as an offering to spirits', OJ *siraka* 'ornament or device (of obscure construction but involving paper or other white material), employed in the worship of autochthonous deities'; (6) SNOW: pTg **xïman.sa*, Ev. *ïmanna* 'snowfall', Orok. *sïmata* 'snow', Olc. *sïmata*, Ma. *nimangi* 'id.', OJ *simo* 'frost', Ryūkyū *simu* 'cold winter rain'; (7) TAIL: pTg **xürgü*, Ev. *irgi*, Orok. *xudu*, Olc. *xủjủ*, Na. *xujgu* 'tail' OJ *worö* 'tail (of mountain bird)', OJ *woröti* 'the great serpent (in the myth)', cf. Ev. *irgiči* 'wolf (lit., the tailed one')', Kor. *ilhŭi* 'wolf'; (8) STAR: pTg *xōsï(.kta)*, Ev. *ōsīkta*, Orok. *wasikta*, Olc. *xosta*, Na. *xosekta*, Ma. *usiha* 'star', OJ *Fosi* 'star' (and as a consequence not cognate with its frequently cited semantic and phonetic "look-alike" NKor. *pyŏl* 'star', which goes instead with pTg **pälä(n)* 'elk', Na. *peule* 'Ursa Major', Ev. *heglun*, *hoglan*, *heglen*, *evlen* 'id.', *lit* 'young of the elk').

This scheme of reflexes can hardly be the result either of chance or of borrowing. As a consequence it speaks persuasively on behalf of ultimate genetic relationship.

(4) Finally, we may summarize briefly still another variety of phonological split, now also better understood as a result of recent studies. Old

Japanese frequently displays voicing dissimilation of certain consonants in successsive syllables. In Japanese historical linguistics these phonematic operations are generally referred to as "Lyman's Law," named after the American geologist Benjamin Smith Lyman (1835-1920) who first drew attention to this feature of the language, though he himself was unable to provide a satisfactorily rigorous account of the phenomenon.

Vance 1982 incorrectly concluded that this phenomenon was and always had been totally sporadic. Actually, it is now clear that the phenomenon of "Lyman's Law" originally operated according to a rigid pattern of regular phonological constraints strikingly analogous to Grassman's Law for Indo-European, or Dahl's Law for the Bantu languages. Moreover, a recent contribution (Miller 1985b) has now offered evidence, chiefly through the analysis of twenty-seven new Japanese-Altaic etymologies, that further argues for interpreting this phenomenon of "Lyman's Law" as a direct inheritance from Proto-Altaic. That article documents a complete analysis of the "Lyman's Law" set of splits, together with all the etymological evidence necessary to establish its operation. The following five selected examples are representative:

(1) MOUTH: pA **güdi*, WMo. *güǯege* 'belly, stomach of animals, rumen', Ev. *gudigə̄*, *gudī* 'peritoneum, stomach, entrails', Ma. *guwejihe* 'stomach' (Poppe 1969: 24, 53,133, 135), further cognate with pTg **güdä* 'a hole', **güdä-* 'break, tear, rupture,' as in Oroc. *gudə-* 'break, tear', but Orok., Na. *gudə̄* 'a hole':: OJ *kuti* 'mouth (body part) (esp. as an organ for eating and speaking)', MKor. *´kut* 'hollow, cavity'. The semantic dimension of this etymology exactly parallels that of Gk. *stómakhos* as a derivative from *stóma*, originally 'throat, gullet' as the passage from the mouth, subsequently 'orifice of the stomach', and finally 'stomach' (Buck 1949: 253a). (2) YOUNG: pA **baga*, WMo. *baga* 'young, small, junior':: OJ *waka.* 'young, immature'. (3) HEIGHTS: pA **dāga*, WMo. *taiga* 'thick coniferous forest, the taiga', OTk., Uig., MTk. etc. *tağ* 'mountain', Yak. *tya* 'forest', Tkmn. *dāğ*, pTg **dāga-* 'cross over', Ev. *dag-*, Lam. *daw-*, Na. *dā-*, Ma. *doo-* 'id.' :: OJ *taka.* 'high (in elevation, geog.), OJ *takë* < **taka.i* 'mountain heights'. On the semantics, with 'cross over' :: 'mountain pass' :: 'mountain', cf. pA **daba-*, cognate with OJ *yama* 'mountain' (Miller 1971: 85–86), Ev. *dawa-* 'move, transfer a burden (across a mountain ridge or range)', but also Olc. *dawa* 'mountain chain, ridge'. (4) REAR: pA **gädä*, WMo. *gede* 'nape, back of neck; occiput', *gedei-* 'to bend backward', *gedeski-* 'to make a sudden movement backward' (a denominal verb in **-ki*, cf. Miller 1983), Ev. *gətkən* 'nape', Tk. **ki* 'rear', mostly in ancient petrified case forms, e.g. OTk. *kidin* 'to the rear', *kin* 'after', *kinintä*

'later', *kirü* 'to the rear', cf. MMo. *gerü* 'rear; shadow, shaded side (of a mountain etc.)' :: late OJ *kita* 'north', NJ *ketu* 'buttocks' (Poppe 1971: 24,53, 105, 125, 135, 145, 155–56). The first syllable vowel in Japanese *kita* 'north' is analogical, after the vowel in the prototype of Tkc. **ki* 'rear', reflecting the influence of an early south-oriented system of directions (cf. Kononov 1977). NJ *ketu*, a modern vulgar body-part term, is not attested in earlier texts because of its meaning, but the formation is obviously old, since it preserves the prototype's first vowel intact, and also displays a petrified Proto-Altaic directive-case in **.u*, as against *kita*, which shows the Altaic dative in **.a*. (5) NINE: pA **gu.gu*, **gu.gu-n* '3 x 3' (Miller 1971: 236–37) :: OJ *kökö-* 'nine'.

It is particularly important to note that the operation of this specific rule was by no means restricted to the above variety of bisyllabic nouns originally incorporating two successive voiced stops. It is also to be observed in the development of the Old Japanese reflexes for larger morphs as well, and—of special significance—when a voiced consonant, e.g., *-r-* from **-l-* or **-r-* immediately preceded a voiced stop, for which see the FLOWER, ORNAMENT set cited under (3) above. In this specific etymon the simultaneous operation of the so-called "Lyman's Law" phenomenon in tandem with the rigorously demarcated split of **x-* as also set forth above can hardly be viewed as other than a unique constellation of linguistic materials, preserving particularly vivid historical evidence bearing upon the history of Japanese, not to mention the history of the relation of Japanese to the other languages entering into these same interlocking sets of comparisons.

All the above evidence, of course, deals exclusively with operations taking place on the phonological level of Japanese-Altaic comparison; but surely even there, careful consideration of the materials available shows that, when we compare Japanese with Altaic, Street is more than a little wide of the mark to complain as he does about an alleged lack of historical-linguistic formulations "like Verner's Law." Obviously, such formulations exist. If anything, they are available in our field in surprising abundance.

It would not do to leave this subject without also mentioning something about another aspect of Verner's Law, particularly in view of Street's invocation of its "strong and persuasive" powers, i.e., its simultaneous operation on the morphological as well as on the phonological level. This, to be sure, is one of the most noteworthy features of the formulation of Verner's Law. The immediately striking parallelism to be observed between its phonological statements and, e.g., the paradigmatic variation to be seen in such sets as OE *wesan* 'to be', *waes* 'was', *wǣron* 'were' or *weorθan* 'to become', *wearθ* '(he) became', *wurdon* '(we) became' is indeed an integral part of the "Law" in question.

It can hardly be denied that presently at least we lack any such impressively structured morphological implemention of the numerous phonological splits that otherwise we have been able to demonstrate as holding true for the description of the relationship between Japanese and Altaic. But the reason for this is both clear and obvious. Such morphological anomalies are all but impossible to detect in Japanese-Altaic comparisons because the variety of paradigmatic variation upon which they build (*was* vs *were*, or, in a celebrated late survival of Verner's Law in modern English, *examine* and *exert*, both with [gz], against *exit*, *exercise* with [ks]!) is itself virtually unknown to all these languages. We are not now able, and are in future also highly unlikely to become able, to locate such formulations in the morphology of the original Altaic linguistic unity for the very simple reason that such anomalies are all but unknown to the structures of the attested Altaic languages.

But to throw into question the validity of the reconstruction of that original linguistic unity, and particularly to question the referral of this or that specific attested language to that unity, solely on the grounds that such paradigmatic demonstrations of morphologically-determined distribution of phonological splits are lacking, is in actual fact not really to criticize either such reconstruction or such referral. Rather, it is merely to berate the languages in question for not possessing this or that feature of Indo-European. The split of Altaic $*r_2$ into OJ *r* and *t* does not, as it happens, generally play any specific role in the morphology either of Altaic or of Japanese. It does not participate in any paradigmatic patterns of the type illustrated by Germanic verbs such as 'to be' or 'to become'. But that is simply because there are no such verbs, and no such paradigmatic variation, anywhere in Altaic. The Altaic languages, and Japanese along with them, also lack the ablative absolute. Does this then mean that there never was a Proto-Altaic, or that Japanese is not genetically related to Mongol and Turkic and Tungus? Such is the full implication of Street's otherwise well intentioned emphasis upon the morphological aspects of Verner's Law.

At the same time, it would hardly do to overlook a few important cases in which, even within the limiting factors imposed upon our data by the nature and structure of all the Altaic languages, we are actually able to detect the functioning of certain phonological splits *vis-à-vis* the morphology of the languages in question. To be sure, none of these prove to be of the scope and order of regularity to be seen, e.g., within the German verb. Still they are of sufficient clarity and importance to be useful to the unprejudiced comparativist. Both have been adequately treated in the earlier literature, and hence need be epitomized here only in brief:

(1) One of the important functions of Proto-Altaic *r_2 was its morphological employment as a suffix for marking nouns indicating paired or symmetrical body parts, e.g., **kökür*$_2$ 'the (two) breasts', Tkc. *köküz* 'breast, chest', OJ *kököri*, later *kökörö* 'heart, mind, spirit', originally 'the breasts.' But in Japanese this suffix also regularly appears, not as *r* but as *t*, when affixed in the original formation to a morpheme with a continuant consonant rather than, as in the above example, with a stop immediately preceeding, e.g., Japanese *ago*, (dial.) *agota*, *agito*, *ageto*, 'jaws, chin', from earlier **agwir*$_2$, where the operative *-*w*- continuant is documented as late as Middle Kor. *akwi* 'mouth (vulg.).' These formations and others were fully explored in Miller 1975: 160–62. While by no means of the scope and precision of the Germanic verb paradigms, they do nevertheless demonstrate that the phonological split earlier established for the Japanese reflexes of *r_2 is by no means unrepresented on the morphological level of our materials.

(2) The same may be said of the morphological role within the Japanese verb of the split-products of original *l_2, i.e., *r* and *s*, as these phonemes may be observed to operate in the structure of a small set of verbs earlier explored in some detail (Miller 1971: 130-39), e.g., OJ *tar*- 'be sufficient', against OJ *tas*- 'fill up, make sufficient,' cf. Tkc. *tol*- against *toš*- 'id.', where the feature in question reflects a morphologically significant variation in the original language between **l* and *l_2. Menges (1975: 45-47) has rightly stressed the importance of this set of forms, along with the implications for inter-Altaic relations of its phonological-historical formulation. The point hardly needs to be further exploited here, except to point out that Street has overlooked its importance as well as its earlier documentation.

With this, we are at last in a position to answer the question posed by our title, and also to suggest why neither this question, nor the allegations that prompted it, actually point in the direction along which future work in these areas might most effectively aim to proceed.

First, the immediate answer to the question posed by our title above is surely clear by now. In the study of the relations among the Altaic languages in general, and in the consideration of the relation of Japanese to these languages in particular, there is not now, nor has there ever been for over a decade, any lack of phonological-historical statements of the order of Verner's Law. We have them, almost to excess. What has instead been lacking is careful attention to the published literature, and thoughtful exploration of the full implications of those data and formulations that are already at hand.

At the same time, even a cursory inspection of Verner's Law, and in particular the careful scrutiny of its implications for the history of Indo-European studies, makes it clear how vain it would be to continue to search for more Verner-like Laws in Altaic and Japanese. The rich four-dimensional system of specific contrasts within the original Indo-European consonantism represents a special feature of structuring that finds no parallel in Altaic, where the original consonantism operated with a mere binary contrast (either voiced and voiceless, or fortis/lenis). In a word, it is pointless to continue to search the Altaic domain looking for the vestiges of structural realignments that could only have resulted from changes within an Indo-European-type consonantal system.

Second, beyond merely correcting the misunderstandings of sets of data, it is important to issue a warning against the undue emphasis on the chimera of "proof" for hypotheses of linguistic relations. The plain fact is that "proof" is not the goal of historical-linguistic studies. That is, by the way, just as it should be, for the simple reason that no matter how much evidence may be marshalled in support of a given hypothesis of a linguistic relation, there will always be those for whom the thesis at issue is still "insufficiently proven"; let us not forget that even N. Troubetskoy to the end stubbornly resisted the entire idea of an earlier genetic relationship among the Indo-European languages.

Instead of focusing on the false hope of "proof" in such matters, we ought rather to learn from the materials now available in the literature concerning the relation of Japanese to Altaic that the ultimate test of this or that etymological suggestion or sound-law formulation is to be found, not in whether or not it "proves" anything, but instead in what may be termed its "predictive" or "explanatory" powers, i.e., how well it explains what would necessarily otherwise remain unrelated, unexplained, and hence also anomalous linguistic data. Conveniently enough, a specific case in point happens to be provided by that very split of $*r_2$ into Japanese *r* and *t* that Street found "rather uninteresting."

For several decades it has been suggested in the literature that OJ *sir-* 'to know' is somehow cognate with the Proto-Altaic $*s\ddot{a}r_2$- reflected in such forms as Mo. *sere-*, *seri-* 'to awaken, revive; recover consciousness; become sober', Ma. *sere-* 'feel, perceive, find out, experience', Ev. *serenčen* 'caution, care', Chag. *säz-* 'to feel, i.e., to perceive by the organs of sensation', and Old Tkc. *sezik* 'doubt' (Poppe 1960: 29, 82, 135, 138). This etymological suggestion was recapitulated from earlier sources but not accepted in Miller 1971: 149, where we pointed out a few of its many problems. The meanings were hardly satisfactorily uniform in the various languages; the vocalism of the reconstruction was troublesome; and above all, the attested Old Japanese *-r-* for *r_2 following the continuant *s* in morpheme-initial position in this putative etymon was totally anomalous in terms of the *t*/*r* split that even by 1977 had already by-and-large been formulated.

The real Japanese cognate of Proto-Altaic **sär*$_2$- is quite obviously not Old Japanese *sir-* 'know' but rather Old Japanese *satŏ* 'realization, enlightenment', an etymology that becomes especially clear when we recall that this noun enters into the well-known Japanese denominal verb formation *satŏ-r-*, from which derives in turn the secondary deverbal noun *satŏri* 'enlightenment, esp. Buddhist'. With this new etymology, everything now fits together. The vowels are rigorously accounted for, the split of *r_2 is regular, the meanings in all the languages show an excellent fit. The result is that in this manner we are able to "explain" a Japanese form that otherwise would have no explanation. The explanation is strong, persuasive and convincing precisely because it involves the context-sensitive split of *r_2, which appears as *-r-* in the proposed Japanese cognate as a consequence of that morpheme's *s-* initial. In other words the formulation of the *t*/*r* split for *r_2 arrived at entirely on the basis of other etymologies is also now capable of immediate application to the problem of this new etymology as well. Here there is nothing circular; the solution of one historical-phonological problem leads directly into the solution of another. The formulation of the *t*/*r* split-rules effectively "predict" that a Japanese cognate for Proto-Altaic **sär-*, should such exist, ought to have *-t-* as in *satŏ*, and not *-r-* as in the now discredited *sir-*. This prediction turns out to be accurate, indeed it is even vindicated, so to speak, by the now-regular vocal correspondence, since OJ *-a-* goes regularly with the **-ä-* of the proto-form, whereas the *-i-* of *sir-* clearly did not, not to mention the now enormously more satisfactory coincidence between all the forms at issue in the semantic sphere.

The formulation of rules such as these on the basis of data at hand, rules that subsequently reveal themselves to possess predictive or explanatory powers for new data that earlier played no part in their own prior formulation, is precisely what the comparative method is all about—not attempts to "prove" this or that linguistic relationship. Some will, no doubt, persist in finding all this "rather uninteresting." But by others, it will surely be recognized for what it is—the essence of the comparative method of the neogrammarians, and as such, the only possible intellectual validation for the enterprise of historical linguistics.

How many Verner's Laws does an Altaicist need? The answer is, none.

References

Bloomfield, Leonard. 1933. *Language*. New York: H. Holt.

Buck, Carl Darling. 1949. *A Dictionary of Selected Synonyms in the Principal Indo-European Languages*. Cambridge: University of Chicago Press.

Bynon, Theodora. 1977. Historical Linguistics. London: Cambridge University Press.

Doerfer, Gerhard. 1974. " Ist das Japanische mit den altaischen Sprachen verwandt?" *Zeitschrift der Deutschen Morganlandischen Gesellschaft* 124: 103–42.

Janhunen, Juha, and Kho Songmoo. 1982. "Is Korean related to Tungusic?" *Han'gul* 177: 179–90.

Kononov, Andrei Nikolaevič. 1977. "Terminology of the definition of cardinal points at [*sic*] the Turkic peoples." *Acta Orientalia Hung.* 31: 61–76.

Menges. Karl H. 1975. *Altajische Studien II, Japanische und Altajisch.* (Deutsche Morganlandische Gesellschaft, Abhandlungen für die Kunde des Morgenlandes, XLI, 3). Wiesbaden: F. Steiner.

Miller, Roy Andrew. 1971. *Japanese and the Other Altaic Languages.* Chicago: University of Chicago Press.

——. 1976. "Wissenschaftliche Nachrichten, A Reply to Doerfer." *Zeitschrift der Deutschen Morganlandischen Gesellschaft* 126: 2: *53*–*76*.

——. 1975. "Japanese-Altaic lexical evidence and the Proto-Turkic 'zetacism-sigmatism'." In *Researches in Altaic Languages*, ed. by L. Ligeti (Budapest: Akadémiai Kiadó), pp. 157–72.

——. 1979. "Old Korean and Altaic." *Ural-Altaische Jahrbucher* 51: 1–54.

——. 1983. "Japanese evidence for some Altaic denominal verb-stem derivational suffixes." *Acta Orientalia Hung.* 36: 391–403.

——. 1985. "Altaic connections of the Old Japanese negatives." *Central Asiatic Journal* 29: 35–84.

——. 1985b. "Externalizing internal rules: Lyman's law in Japanese and Altaic." *Diachronica* 2.2: 137–65.

——. 1985c. "Apocope and the problem of Proto-Altaic *i̯ă (I)." *Ural-Altaische Jahrbücher*, N.F., 5: 187–208 (published 1986).

——. 1986. "Apocope and the problem of Proto-Altaic *i̯ă (II)" *Ural-Altaische Jahrbücher*, N.F., 6: 184–207 (published 1987).

——. 1987. "Proto-Altaic **x*-." *Central Asiatic Journal* 31: 19–63.

——, and Nishida Tatsuo et al., translators. 1981. *Nihongo to Arutai shogo*. Tokyo: Taishukan shoten.

Poppe, N. N. 1960. *Vergleichenden Grammatik der altaischen Sprachen*. Teil 1, *Vergleichenden Lautlehre*. Wiesbaden: Harrassowitz.

Prokosch, Eduard. 1939. *A Comparative German Grammar*. Philadelphia: Linguistic Society of America.

Street, John 1972. Review of N. Poppe, *Mongolian Language Handbook*. *Language* 47: 212–14.

——. 1979. "Proto-Altaic *i̯a." *Proceedings of VIth International Symposium [of the] Korean Academy of Sciences*, pp. 51–80.

——. 1981. "Remarks on the phonological comparison of Japanese with Altaic." *Bulletin of the International Institute for Linguistic Sciences, Kyoto Sangyo University* 2.4: 293–307.

——. 1985. "Japanese reflexes of the Proto-Altaic lateral." *Journal of the American Oriental Society* 105: 637–651.

Vance, Timothy J. 1982. "On the origin of voicing alteration [*sic*] in Japanese consonants." *JAOS* 102: 333–41.

Winter, Werner. 1980. "Zum Beitrag der tocharischen Sprachen zu Problem der lautlichen Rekonstruktion des Indogermanischen." In Manfred Mayrhofer et al., ed., *Lautgeschichte und Etymologie*, (Wiesbaden), pp. 542–63.

NASALS IN OLD SOUTHERN CHINESE

JERRY NORMAN
University of Washington

The thesis of the present paper is that in the earliest dialects carried to South China there were two contrasting sets of nasals.[1] The evidence for this is found in the Chinese dialects of the Mǐn and Kèjiā groups as well as in early Chinese loan words in Vietnamese, Tai, and Yáo.

An inspection of the modern non-Hàn languages of Southern China clearly demonstrates that a two-way distinction of initial nasals is very common.[2] Both Miáo and Yáo have initial voiceless nasals (*m̥*, *n̥*, etc.) in addition to a voiced set. Máonán contrasts plain nasals with a preglottalized set (*ˀm*, *ˀn*, etc.). Shuǐ has a three-way distinction: plain voiced (*m*, *n*, *ŋ*), voiceless (*m̥*, *n̥*, *ŋ̊*), and preglottalized (*ˀm*, *ˀn*, *ˀŋ*). Wǎ distinguishes a plain voiced set from an aspirated set (*mh*, *nh*, etc.). And in addition, Mùlǎo, Pǔmǐ, Bùnǔ and Lājiā all have a distinction between voiced and voiceless nasals. In light of this widespread attestation of contrasting nasal types, it seems safe to say that this distinction is a significant areal feature of the languages of South China. It should not be too surprising, then, to find that the ancient Chinese dialects of this region also possessed a two-way contrast in their nasal initials.

A number of non-Hàn languages spoken in South China and Southeast Asia borrowed lexical material from Chinese beginning at a very early period. The earliest stratum of loan words in several of these languages exhibits a number of archaic features including evidence for more than one type of nasal.

---

[1] Research for this paper was carried out in part while in Běijīng on a fellowship from the Committee on Scholarly Communication with the People's Republic of China of the National Academy of Sciences.

[2] Data from the non-Hàn languages of South China are taken from the following sources: Miáo (Wáng 1985), Yáo (Máo, Měng and Zhèng 1982), Máonán (Liáng 1980), Shuǐ (Zhāng 1980), Wǎ (Zhōu and Yán 1984), Mùlaǒ (Wáng and Zhèng 1980), Pǔmǐ (Lù 1983), Bùnǔ and Lājiā (Máo, Měng and Zhèng 1982). Undoubtedly there are still other languages in South China which have two or more contrastive sets of initial nasals; this list is intended only as a sampling.

In Vietnamese native words show a sharp division into two tonal registers, one of which goes back to voiceless initial consonants and the other to voiced initial consonants (Haudricourt 1954a). In terms of the traditional tonal designation used in Vietnam, the tonal development was as follows:

	A	B	C	D
1. (voiceless)	*ngang*	*sắc*	*hỏi*	*sắc*
2. (voiced)	*huyền*	*nạng*	*ngã*	*nạng*

In this chart A, B, C, and D correspond respectively to the Chinese tonal categories píng, shǎng, qù and rù.[3] The numerals 1 and 2 refer respectively to original voiceless and voiced initial consonants. Haudricourt (1954b) has shown that the oldest stratum of Chinese loan words in Vietnamese corresponds exactly to this scheme. This means that if a word beginning with a nasal consonant initial has a tone from series one, it must go back to a voiceless nasal.[4] A form like *ná* 'crossbow', for example, must go back to a voiceless initial **hn*; cf. Yáo *hna*[3], Shuǐ *hna*[3], 'id.' If ancient Chinese loanwords have tones of series one, they will be considered to have had a voiceless initial at the time of borrowing.[5]

Proto-Tai is reconstructed with a two-way contrast of nasals, one voiced and the other voiceless (Li 1977). The reconstruction of voiceless nasals is made on the basis of tonal evidence; in general voiceless sonorants are posited for words with upper register tones.[6] In addition the traditional Thai (Siamese) writing system distinguishes a series of voiceless nasals

[3] In Tai comparative linguistics, tonal designations (based on the traditional Thai script) are slightly different: A corresponds to píng, B to qù, C to shǎng, and D to rù.

[4] In some cases Vietnamese nasals in upper register tones may go back to a preglottalized voiced stop. Such examples are not found in Chinese loan material however.

[5] The later systematic borrowing known as Sino-Vietnamese does not follow this scheme and shows no evidence for a two-way contrast of nasals. See Pulleyblank (1984: 159f.)

[6] Chinese linguists who work on Tai and Miáo-Yáo languages number tones with a system whereby upper register tones are given an odd number (1, 3, 5, 7) and lower register tones are given an even number (2, 4, 5, 8). The same system is used for a number of Tai-related languages (Shuǐ, Lí, Mùlǎo, Máonán, etc.) as well as for Chinese dialects. This makes the identification of upper register tones in these languages an easy matter. Thai forms in this paper are cited from Manomaivibool 1975.

written with digraphs, the first element of which is *h*. The word for 'pus' in modern Thai is *nɔ̌ɔŋ*, the tone implying an upper register nasal (Li 1977: 114). In traditional Thai spelling it has an initial *hn*. The Yáo forms cited in this paper are from the Miăn dialect, where voiceless nasals survive intact.

The evidence for two contrasting sets of nasals in Chinese dialects is chiefly tonal. In Mǐn, such tonal evidence is found in the Northeastern dialects (exemplified here by Fúān and Fúzhōu) and the far Western dialects (exemplified here by Shàowŭ and Jiānglè).[7] The following chart shows the tonal development in these dialects as it affects words with the two series of nasal initials; **m* and **mh* are used as cover symbols in this chart to represent nasals at the dental and velar points of articulation as well as the labials.[8]

	A		B		C		D	
	**m*	**mh*	**m*	**mh*	**m*	**mh*	**m*	**mh*
Fúān	2	2	3	6	6	5	8	8
Fúzhōu	2	2	3	6	6	5	8	8
Shàowŭ	2	7	3	3	6	5	6	7
Jiānglè	2	9	3/9	9	6	5	6	9

Fúān and Fúzhōu show tonal evidence for the two-way contrast in nasal initials in tonal categories B and C; in category C the evidence is perfectly regular. In category B there is a strong tendency to show the development given above, but due to the large scale importation of words from northern dialects in which all sonorant initials in the shăng (B) category become yīnshăng (3), the pattern has been disturbed to some degree. Shàowŭ preserves evidence for the two-way distinction in all categories except B where a merger has taken place. The same is actually true of Jiānglè since the split in category C appears to be random.[9]

[7] Fúzhōu forms are from my field notes and Maclay and Baldwin 1870; Fúān forms are mostly from my field notes with occasional citations from Ibañez 1941–43. Shàowŭ and Jiānglè forms are entirely cited from my field notes. Xiàmén and Jiēyáng forms are cited from Douglas 1899 and Choy 1976 respectively. Dìngān (Hăinán) forms are from material collected by William Wang and me in Taiwan in 1966.

[8] Tonal categories are designated A, B,C, D; these correspond respectively to the classical categories píng, shăng, qù, and rù.

[9] The distribution of tones 3 and 9 is in general hard to explain in

Other evidence for a second series of nasals is found in the Southern Mĭn dialects. Proto-Mĭn initials **nh* and **ŋh* become *h* in all southern Mĭn dialects before a high front vowel. There is a strong tendency for nasal articulation to be preserved in cases where denasalization would ordinarily be expected in the case of initial **mh*; the same development can be observed in the case of **nh* and **ŋh* when they occur with finals lacking a palatal medial.[10] The developments are illustrated by the following forms:

	PM	Fúān	Fúzhōu	Xiàmén	Cháozhōu	
鵝	*ŋ	ŋe²	ŋie²	gia²	go²	'goose'
蟻	*ŋh	ŋe⁶	ŋie⁶	hia⁶	hia⁴	'ant'
毋[11]	*m	mɔ²	mo²	bo²	bo²	'there is not'
毛	*mh	mɔ²	mo²	mŋ²	mõ²	'hair'

It is clear that in the case of words having the second series of nasals (**mh*, **nh*, **ŋh*) the Southern Mĭn dialects often show a very different development when compared to words beginning with the plain series.

As O'Connor (1976) has shown, it is necessary to assume a two-way contrast of nasals at the stage of Proto-Kèjiā. One series gives rise to yīn tones and the other to yáng tones as shown in the following table:

Initials	Tones A	B	C	D
*mh, *nh, *ńh, *ŋh	1	3	5	7
*m, *n, *ń, *ŋ	2	1	6	8

Kèjiā dialects, it is obvious, are excellent witnesses to the two-way distinction of nasals proposed in this paper.[12]

The remainder of this paper will be devoted to an examination of forms for which there is evidence for a voiceless nasal. The Mĭn and Kèjiā evidence will be given first, followed by supporting forms from the non-Hàn

---

the Jiānglè dialect. Suffice it to say here that I have not discovered any correlation at all between this split and the earlier two-way contrast in nasals. For further discussion of Mĭn tonal development, see Norman 1973.

[10] For a fuller discussion of this phenomenon, see Norman 1973 and especially Bodman 1985.

[11] This character is used to represent the Mĭn existential negative: 'there is not, has not'.

[12] Many Kèjiā dialects do not distinguish the upper and lower qù tones. In the case of this tonal category, only dialectal forms from dialects that possess both a yīnqù and a yángqù category will be cited.

languages of South China and Southeast Asia. The following abbreviations will be employed:

Mĭn dialects		Kèjiā dialects[13]	
Fa	Fúān	Hl	Hăilù
Fz	Fúzhōu	Mx	Méixiàn
Xm	Xiàmén		
Jy	Jiēyáng	Non-Hàn languages	
Sw	Shàowŭ	VN	Vietnamese
Jl	Jiānglè		

The names of other dialects and languages will be written out in full.

1. *ài* 艾, 'artemisia.' Fa *ŋe*^{5}, Fz *ŋie*^{5}, Xm *hiã*^{6}, Jy *hiã*^{6}, Sw *ni*^{5}, Hl *ńie*^{5}, Mx *ńe*^{5}; < **ŋh-*.
2. *é* 額, 'forehead.' Fa *ŋeʔ*^{8}, Fz *ŋieʔ*^{8}, Xm *hiaʔ*^{8}, Jy *hiaʔ*^{8}, Sw *nia*^{7}, Hl *ńiak*^{7}, Mx *ńiak*^{7}; < **ŋh-*.
3. *ĕr* 耳, 'ear.' Fa *ŋe*^{6}, Fz *ŋei*^{6}, Xm *hi*^{6}, Jy *hĩ*^{4}, Sw *nin*^{3}, Jl *ŋiŋ*^{3}, Hl *ńi*^{3}, Mx *ńi*^{3}; < **ŋh-*. Note that the vowel of the Fa word for 'ear' is irregular; *-ei* would be expected. Ibañez (1941–43: 737) has the expected regular form *ŋei*^{6} (*ngei*^{4} in the original orthography).
4. *ĕr* 餌, 'bait.' Fa *nei*^{5}, Fz *nei*^{5}, Xm *dzi*^{6}, Jy *dzi*^{6}; < **nh-*. Thai *hyɯ:a* B1. For Xiàmén and Jiēyáng an initial *h-* would be expected.
5. *má* 麻, 'hemp, sesame.' Fa *mo*^{2}, Fz *muai*^{2}, Xm *muã*^{2}, Jy *muã*^{2}, Sw *mai*^{7}, Jl *mai*^{9}; < **mh-*.
6. *mà* 罵, 'scold.' Fa *ma*^{5}, Fz *ma*^{5}, Xm *mẽ*^{6}, Jy *mẽ*^{6}, Sw *ma*^{5}, Jl *ma*^{5}, Hl *ma*^{5}; < **mh-*. These examples are in perfect agreement. The upper register tones of the Fa, Fz, Sw, Jl and Hl forms and the retained nasality of the Xm and Jy forms all point unambiguously to an earlier voiceless nasal.
7. *mài* 脈, 'vein, pulse.' Fa *maʔ*^{7}, Fz *maʔ*^{7}, Xm *mẽʔ*^{7}, Jy *meʔ*^{8}, Hl *mak*^{7}, Mx *mak*^{7}; < **mh-*. Note that Fúān, Fúzhōu and Xiàmén have exceptional upper register tones in this case.
8. *māo* 貓, 'cat.' Fa *ma*^{2}, Fz *ma*^{2}, Sw *mau*^{7}, Jl *mao*^{9}; < **mh-*.
9. *máo* 毛, 'hair, fur, feather.' Fa *mɔ*^{2}, Fz *mo*^{2}, Xm *mŋ*^{2}, Jy *mõ*^{2}, Sw *mau*^{7}, Jl *mo*^{9}, Hl *mo*^{1}, Mx *mo*^{1}; < **mh-*.
10. *máo* 茅, 'thatch.' Xm *hm*^{2}; < **mh-*. The best explanation for this peculiar Xm form is that it originally had a voiceless nasal initial. It nonetheless remains an anomaly. Cf. number 11 below.

[13] Hăilù forms are from Yáng 1957; Méixiàn forms are taken from MacIver 1926.

11. *méi* 媒, 'go-between.' Xm *hm*^{2}; < *mh-.
12. *mèi* 妹, 'younger sister.' Fa *mui*^{5}, Fz *mui*^{5}, Xm *be*^{6}, Jy *muẽ*^{6}, Sw *mei*^{5}, Jl *mø*^{5}. Hl *moi*^{5}; < *mh-.
13. *mèng* 夢, 'dream.' Fa *mœŋ*^{5}, Fz *moiŋ*^{5}, Xm *baŋ*^{6}, Jy *maŋ*^{6}, Sw *muŋ*^{5}. Hl *muŋ*^{5}; < *mh-.
14. *mí* 糜, 'rice gruel.' Fa *mui*^{2}, Xm *be*^{2}, Jy *muẽ*^{2}, Jl *mø*^{9}; < *mh-.
15. *miàn* 面, 'face.' Fa *men*^{5}, Fz *meiŋ*^{5}, Xm *bin*^{6}, Jy *meŋ*^{6}, Sw *min*^{5}, Jl *mieŋ*^{5}. Hl *mian*^{5}; < *mh-. Yáo *hmien*^{1}. The Yáo tone is anomalous.
16. *míng* 名, 'name.' Fa *miaŋ*^{2}, Fz *miaŋ*^{2}, Xm *miã*^{2}, Jy *miã*^{2}, Sw *mian*^{7}, Jl *miaŋ*^{9}; < *mh-.
17. (*mò) □, 'rotten, decayed.' Fa *mɔk*^{7}, Fz *mauk*^{7}, Mx *mut*^{7}; < *mh-.
18. *mù* 木, 'wood.' Sw *mu*^{7}. Hl *muk*^{7}, Mx *muk*^{7}; < *mh-.
19. *mù* 目, 'eye.' Fa *mœk*^{8}, Fz *møik*^{8}, Xm *bak*^{8}, Jy *mãk*^{8}, Sw *mu*^{7}, Jl *mu*^{5}, Hl *muk*^{7}, Mx *muk*^{7}; < *mh-.
20. *mù* 墓, 'grave.' Fa *mu*^{5}, Fz *muo*^{5}, Xm *baŋ*^{6}, Sw *mio*^{5}, Hl *mu*^{5}; < *mh-. VN *mả*.
21. *nián* 年, 'year.' Fa *nin*^{2}, Fz *nieŋ*^{2}, Xm *nĩ*^{2}, Jy *nĩ*^{2}, Sw *nin*^{7}, Jl *ŋieŋ*^{9}; < *nh-. In the Cháozhōu dialect of Cháoyáng (Zhāng 1982a: 61), the word for 'year' is pronounced *hĩ*^{2} in the expression *hĩ*^{2} *taŋ*^{1} 'the year's harvest'; cf. the Cháoān dialect expression *hĩ*^{2} *kẽ*^{5} 'the first three days of the new year' in which *hĩ*^{2} is the word for 'year' (Lǐ 1959: 204); the Hǎinán dialect of Dìngān has *hi*^{2} as its usual word for 'year'.
22. *nóng* 膿, 'pus.' Fa *nœŋ*^{2}, Fz *nøiŋ*^{2}, Xm *laŋ*^{2}, Jy *laŋ*^{2}, Sw *nuŋ*^{7}, Jl *luŋ*^{5}; < *nh-. Thai *hnɔ:n* A1, Wǔmíng *no:ŋ*^{1}, Lóngzhōu *no:ŋ*^{1}. Note that the Jiānglè form implies a qù tone origin; cf. Jiànyáng *noŋ*^{6}.
23. *nǔ* 弩, 'crossbow.' Xm *lɔ*^{6}, Jiànōu *noŋ*^{4} (*Jiànzhōu bāyīn*: 83b), Jiànyáng *noŋ*^{5}; < *nh-. Thai *hna:* C1, Yáo *hnaa*^{3}, Shuǐ *na*^{3}. The final *-ŋ* in the Jiànōu and Jiànyáng forms may be an indication that, as in Southern Mǐn dialects, Northwestern Mǐn dialects may once have had a strong nasalization after voiceless nasal initials even resulting ultimately in a final nasal segment in the case of words in the shǎng tonal category. Cf. the Cháoyáng form *nãu*^{4} (Zhāng 1982a: 60.)
24. *ǒu* 藕, 'lotus root.' Fa *ŋau*^{6}, Fz *ŋau*^{6}, Xm *ŋãu*^{6}, Jl *ŋẽu*^{3}, Mx *ńeu*^{3}; < *ŋh-. VN *ngó*. Thai *ŋau* B2 ~ *hŋau* C1. Cf. Cháoyáng *ŋãu*^{4} (Zhāng 1982b: 138).
25. *rán* 燃, 'burn, scorch.' Fa *niɛn*^{2} (Ibañez 1941–43: 843 'quemarse demasiado, torrarse'), Fz *niaŋ*^{2}, 'scorched, burnt', Xm *hiã*^{2} 'add fuel, warm up', Jy *hiã*^{2}, 'scorch, burn (rice)'; < *nh-.

26. *ráng* 瓤, 'pulp, flesh (of melons).' Fa nɔŋ^{2}, Fz nouŋ^{2}, Xm nŋ^{2}, Jy nŋ^{2}, Sw noŋ^{7}, Jl loŋ^{9}; < *nh-.
27. *rì* 日, 'sun, day.' Hl ńit^{7}, Mx ńit^{7}; < *nh-. Jiānglè also has ŋi^{5}, pointing to a voiceless initial.
28. *ròu* 肉, 'meat.' Fa nøk^{7}, Fz nyk^{8}, Jy nẽk^{8}, Sw ny^{7}, Jl ŋy^{5}, Hl ńiuk^{7}, Mx ńiuk^{7}; < *nh-. Douglas (1899: 124) records a Chin-chew (Jìnzhōu) form hek^{8} which occurs in a few compounds. Cf. the Hǎinán dialect of Dìngān which has hiuk^{8} for 'meat.'
29. *rùn* 潤, 'damp.' Fz nouŋ^{5}, Xm dzuŋ^{6}; < *nh-.
30. *rùo* 箬, 'leaf.' Fa niʔ^{8}, Fz nioʔ^{8}, Xm hioʔ^{8}, Jy hioʔ^{8}, Sw nio^{7}, Jl nio^{5}, Mx ńiak^{7}; < *nh-.
31. *wǎ* 瓦, 'tile.' Fa wo^{6}, Fz ua^{6}, Xm hia^{6}, Jy hia^{4}, Sw ua^{3}, Jl va^{9}. Hl ŋua^{3}, Mx ŋa^{3}; < *ŋh-.
32. *wà* 襪, 'stocking.' Xm beʔ^{8}, Jy gueʔ^{8}, Sw mei^{7}, Jl muai^{5}. Hl mat^{7}, Mx mat^{7}; < *mh-.
33. *wén* 蚊, 'mosquito.' Fa mun^{2}, Fz muoŋ^{2}, Sw mən^{7}. Hl mun^{1}, Mx mun^{1}; < *mh-.
34. *wèn* 問, 'ask.' Fa mun^{5}, Fz muoŋ^{5}, Xm mŋ^{6}, Jy mŋ^{6}, Sw mən^{5}. Hl mun^{5}; < *mh-.
35. *wǔ* 五, 'five.' Fa ŋou^{6}, Fz ŋou^{6}, Xm gɔ^{6}, Jy ŋõu^{4}, Sw ŋ^{3}, Jl ŋu^{3}. Hl ŋ^{3}, Mx ŋ^{3}; < *ŋh-. Thai *ha:* C1, Yáo hŋ^{4} (in hŋ^{4} lha^{5} 'May'), Wǔmíng ha^{3}, Lóngzhōu ha^{3}.
36. *wǔ* 舞, 'dance.' Jy mõu^{4}; < *mh-. VN *múa*.
37. *wù* 物, 'thing.' Xm mĩʔ^{8} (mĩʔ^{8} kiã^{6} 'thing'), Jiànōu mi^{4} ti^{6} 'thing'; < *mh-. The nasalized vowel of the Xm form points to an original voiceless initial.
38. *yán* 顏, 'surname.' Jy hĩa^{2}; < *ŋh-.
39. *yàn* 硯, 'inkstone.' Fa ŋin^{5}, Fz ŋieŋ^{5}, Xm hĩ^{6}; < *ŋh-.
40. *yǐ* 蟻, 'ant.' Fa ŋe^{6}, Fz ŋie^{6}, Xm hia^{6}, Jy hia^{4}, Sw nie^{3}, Jl ŋie^{9}. Hl ńie^{5}, Mx ŋe^{5}; < *ŋh-.
41. *yú* 魚, 'fish.' Fa ŋøi^{2}, Fz ŋy^{2}, Xm hi^{2}, Jy hɯ^{2}; < *ŋh-.

The following set consists of words thought to be loans from Old Southern Chinese into various non-Hàn languages of the South, and that show evidence of voiceless nasal initials in those languages. The Mǐn forms of the words do not unambiguously distinguish these as having the second series of nasal initials as against the first. Nevertheless, if they are in fact loans into Thai, Vietnamese, Yáo, etc., which languages regularly distinguish a voiced from a voiceless set of initial nasals, and these show up with the voiceless set, it follows as a likely conclusion that they had the second series of nasals in their Old Southern Chinese source.

42. *méi* 梅, 'apricot.' VN *mơ*.
43. *mǐ* 米, 'rice.' Yáo *hmei*^{3}.
44. *mò* 墨, 'ink.' Thai *hmɯk* D1.
45. *niè* 鑷, 'tweezers.' Thai *hnæ:ʔ* B1.
46. *rǎn* 染, 'dye.' VN *nhuốm*. The tones of the Mǐn forms suggest a voiced initial: Fa *nim*^{3}, Fz *nieŋ*^{3}. Xm *nĩ*^{3}, Jy *nĩ*^{3}; Méixiàn *niam*^{3}, on the other hand, points to a voiceless initial.
47. *wàn* 萬, 'ten thousand.' Thai *hmɯ:n* B1. VN *muôn*.
48. *wū* 巫, 'sorcerer, doctor.' Thai *hmɔ:* A1, VN *mo*.
49. *yàn* 雁, 'wild goose.' Thai *ha:n* B1, Wǔmíng *ha:n*^{5}, VN *ngan*.

One question remains. What was the phonetic nature of the two-way distinction of nasals in Chinese? From the evidence found in Vietnamese, Thai, Yáo and the Kèjiā dialects, it would certainly appear that the distinction was one of voicing; that is, a distinction of **m* versus **hm*, **n* versus **hn*, and **ŋ* versus **hŋ*. The Mǐn evidence is less straightforward since in a number of dialects words with what were originally voiceless initials are found in lower register tones; in the Southern Mǐn dialects this is almost always the case. It seems to me that in the case of dialects in which this happened, the original voiceless nasals shifted to a different type of phonation, most likely the breathy (or murmured) phonation found in some modern Wú dialects; that is to say, there was a shift of **hm* to **mɦ*, **hn* to **nɦ*, and **hŋ* to **ŋɦ*. In my earlier work on Proto-Mǐn initials, I symbolized this situation by writing **mh*, **nh* and **ŋh*, where the second element most likely represents a type of breathy phonation.

References

Bodman, Nicholas C. 1985. "Reflexes of initial nasals in Proto-Southern Min-Hingua. In V.Z. Acson and R.L. Leed (eds.), *For Gordon H. Fairbanks*. (*Oceanic Linguistics*, special publication no. 20). Honolulu: University of Hawaii Press.

Choy, Chun-ming. 1976. *A Dictionary of the Chao-chou Dialect.* Taibei: Sanmin Shuju.

Douglas, Carstairs. 1899. *Chinese-English Dictionary of the Vernacular or Spoken Language of Amoy.* London: Publishing Office of the Presbyterian Church of England.

Haudricourt, André G. 1954a. "De l'origine des tons en vietnamien." *Journal asiatique* 242: 69-82.

——. 1954b. "Comment reconstruire le chinoise archaïque." *Word* 10: 351–364.

Ibañez, Ignatio, O.P. 1941-43. *Diccionario español-chino, dialecto de Fu-an (houc an)*. Shanghai: Imprimerie Commerciale—"Don Bosco."

Jiànzhōu bāyīn 建州八音. 1795. Jiànzhōu.

Li, Fang Kuei. 1977. *A Handbook of Comparative Tai.* Honolulu: University Press of Hawaii.

Lĭ Yŏngmíng 李永明. 1959. *Cháozhōu fāngyán* 潮州方言. Peking: Zhonghua.

Liáng Mĭn 梁敏. 1980. *Máonányŭ jiănzhì* 毛难语简志. Peking: Minzu.

Lù Shàozūn 陆少尊. 1983. *Pŭmĭyŭ jiănzhì* 普米语简志. Peking: Minzu.

MacIver, D. 1926. *A Chinese-English Dictionary: Hakka Dialect as Spoken in Kwang-tung Province.* Shanghai: Presbyterian Mission Press.

Maclay, R. S., and C. C. Baldwin. 1870. *An Alphabetic Dictionary of the Chinese Language in the Foochow Dialect.* Foochow: Methodist Episcopal Mission Press.

Manomaivibool, Prapin. 1975. "A study of Sino-Thai lexical correspondences." Unpublished Ph.D dissertation, University of Washington, Seattle.

Máo Zōngwŭ 毛宗武, Mĕng Cháojí 梦朝吉, and Zhèng Zōngzé 郑宗泽. 1982. *Yáozú yŭyán jiănzhì* 瑶族语言简志. Peking: Minzu.

Norman, Jerry. 1973. "Tonal development in Min." *Journal of Chinese Linguistics* 1: 222–238.

O'Connor, Kevin. 1976. "Proto-Hakka." *Journal of Asian and African Studies* 11: 1–64.

Pulleyblank, Edwin G. 1984. *Middle Chinese: a Study in Historical Phonology*. Vancouver: University of British Columbia Press.

Wáng Fǔshì 王辅世. 1985. *Miáoyǔ jiǎnzhì* 苗语简志. Peking: Minzu.

Wáng Jūn 王均, and Zhèng Guóqiáo 郑国桥. 1980. *Mùlǎoyǔ jiǎnzhì* 仫佬语简志. Peking: Minzu.

Wěi Qìngwěn 韦庆稳, and Tán Guóshēng 覃国生. 1980. *Zhuàngyǔ jiǎnzhì* 壮语简志. Peking: Minzu.

Yáng Shíh-fēng 楊時逢. 1957. *Táiwān Táoyuán kèjiā fāngyán* 台灣桃源客家方言. (Academia Sinica, Institute of History and Philology monograph, series A, no. 22.) Taipei.

Yù Cuìróng 喻翠容. 1980. *Bùyīyǔ jiǎnzhì* 布依语简志. Peking: Minzu.

Zhāng Jūnrú 張均如. 1980. *Shuǐyǔ jiǎnzhì* 水語簡志. Peking: Minzu.

Zhāng Shèngyù 張盛裕. 1982a. "Cháoyáng shēngmǔ yǔ 'Guǎngyùn' shēngmǔ de bǐjiào (1)." 潮陽聲母與廣韻聲母的比較 *Fāngyán* 1: 52–65.

——. l982b. "Cháoyáng shēngmǔ yǔ 'Guǎngyùn' shēngmǔ de bǐjiào (2)." *Fāngyán* 2: 129–145.

Zhōu Zhízhì 周植志 and Yán Qíxiāng 颜其香. 1984. *Wǎyǔ jiǎnzhì* 佤语简志. Peking: Minzu.

PROTO-KOREAN AND THE ORIGIN OF KOREAN ACCENT

S. ROBERT RAMSEY
The University of Maryland

The earliest systematic records of the Korean language are the alphabetic materials of the fifteenth and sixteenth centuries.* The variety of the

---

* Research for this paper was supported, in part, by a grant from the Social Science Research Council and by a grant from the Graduate Research Board of the University of Maryland.

Linguistic forms are transliterated from the Korean alphabet according to the following conventions:

Consonants	ㄱ	ㄷ	ㅂ	ㅈ	ㅅ	ㆆ
	k	t	p	c	s	ʔ
	ㅋ	ㅌ	ㅍ	ㅊ		ㅎ
	k^h	t^h	p^h	c^h		h
	ㄲ	ㄸ	ㅃ	ㅉ	ㅆ	ㆅ
	kk	tt	pp	cc	ss	hh
	ㆁ	ㄴ	ㅁ		ㅿ	ㅇ
	ŋ	n	m		z	'
		ㄹ	ㅸ			ㆀ
		l	β			''

Vowels	ㅏ	ㅑ	ㅓ	ㅕ	ㅗ	ㅛ	ㅜ	ㅠ	ㅡ	ㅣ	ㆍ	ㆎ	ㅐ	ㅔ	ㅚ	ㅟ	ㅢ
Middle Korean:	a	ya	e	ye	o	yo	u	yu	ɨ	i	ʌ	ʌy	ay	ey	oy	uy	ɨy
Modern Korean (Seoul Dialect):	a	ya	ə	yə	o	yo	u	yu	ɨ	i			ɛ	e		wi	ɨy

Accent

Middle Korean: no dots (low pitch): grave accent over vowel (`)
one dot (high pitch): acute accent over vowel (´)
two dots (rising pitch): both accents together (ˇ)

For the modern accenting dialect of South Hamgyŏng, the accented syllable will be indicated with an acute accent mark over the vowel.

language reflected in these materials is usually known as Middle Korean.[1]

Within the Middle Korean phonological system there were a number of irregularities. By applying the method of internal reconstruction to these irregularities, and by supplementing and corroborating the results with comparative and structural evidence from the modern dialects, it is possible to recover a stage of the language significantly earlier than Middle Korean. This reconstructed stage of the language will be referred to here as Proto-Korean.

The role of accent in the reconstruction

Accent provides an important key to the reconstruction of Proto-Korean. Pitch was distinctive in the phonological system of Middle Korean, and it is still used distinctively in a number of modern dialects.

Dialect accent. Although lexical pitch distinctions disappeared centuries ago in the Seoul dialect, systems of pitch accent are still found in Kyŏngsang in the Southeast and in Hamgyŏng in the Northeast[2]. The dialect spoken in Pukch'ŏng, South Hamgyŏng Province, is typical of the latter group.[3] In this dialect, just as in the familiar Tokyo-type dialects of Japanese, distinctive pitch shapes can be accounted for by an accent marking the location of the last high-pitched syllable in the phrase. As can be seen

[1] In their phonological and morphological detail, the Korean alphabetic materials of the fifteenth and sixteenth centuries are equal to, if not superior to, any other pre-modern body of works in the world. The records of the Korean language that predate the invention of the alphabet, on the other hand, are poor and scanty. Chinese characters were occasionally employed as phonograms to transcribe native words and grammatical elements. Few of these pre-alphabetic transcriptions survive, and those that do are fragmentary, difficult to interpret, and in the best of cases little more than hints as to what words might have sounded like before Middle Korean. What is called Old Korean consists of a few linguistic forms reconstructed from such pre-alphabetic transcriptions.

[2] A few varieties of Korean dialect accent have yet to be reported upon. In particular, little is known about pitch distinctions in some Chŏlla dialects in the Southwest, and the prosodic features of dialects in the extreme northeastern corner of the peninsula have, to the best of my knowledge, never been described in any published source.

[3] The accenting dialects of Kyŏngsang attest to the same accentual distinctions, but the pitch patterns in those dialects have been complicated by historical changes: see Ramsey 1978a: 78–81.

from the examples given in Table I, the locus can occur on any, or no, syllable of the stem. Oxytonic nouns are distinguished from atonic nouns morphophonemically, by the pitch of an enclitic particle.

Middle Korean accent. The Middle Korean pitch system is quite well documented. In texts of the period, each syllable was consistently marked as low, high, or rising in pitch.[4] No vowel length was transcribed as such, but from philological sources we know that syllables with rising pitch were pronounced long. Morphophonemic evidence indicates that these rising-pitched syllables were composed of one low-pitched mora plus one high-pitched mora.[5] Table II provides examples of all possible pitch contrasts for nouns one, two, and three syllables long. Forms with variable pitch are given both in isolation and followed by a particle.

The pitches in these forms are often referred to in the literature as tones, but the system was clearly accentual. The locus of the accent was the first high-pitched syllable, or mora, in the word. After that point pitch differences were variable and non-distinctive. Rising-pitched syllables (which were composed of a low-pitched mora plus a high-pitched mora) were accented on the second mora.

Reconstructing earlier accentual distinctions. When the Middle Korean accent classes are compared to those of the modern dialects, certain problems become apparent. The most troublesome problem is with accents that fall on the first syllable of a word. Although the correspondences for Middle Korean atonic (òò) and oxytonic (òó) nouns are almost exceptionless, the correspondences for protonic (óo) nouns are extremely poor. More than 30% of the reflexes of Middle Korean protonic dissyllabic nouns have a different type of accent (either atonic or oxytonic) in the accenting dialects of Hamgyŏng and Kyŏngsang. The correspondences are even worse for

[4] In the transliterations of Middle Korean given here low pitch is represented with a grave accent, a high pitch with an acute accent mark, and a rising pitch with both accent marks placed together (ˇ) over the vowel. The same conventions will be used to represent Proto-Korean pitches even though it is claimed these pitches were not distinctive. When stems with variable pitch are cited in isolation, accent marks are omitted. Also, in complex lists of Middle Korean verb forms, only the pitch of the distinctive accent locus is marked (cf. fn. 17).

[5] Kōno Rokurō (1944) was the first to show that the "rising tone" was a complex phonological unit, but a number of Korean scholars have also helped document the evidence. See Ramsey 1978a: 113–30 for details.

mal 'horse'	*mál* 'measure'; 'speech'		
mal I	*MAL i*		
poli 'barley'	*móki* 'mosquito'	*məlí* 'hair'	
poLI KA	*MOki ka*	*məLI ka*	
kalakci 'ring'	*múcikɛ* 'rainbow'	*kalmɛ́ki* 'seagull'	*kkamakwí* 'raven'
kaLAKCI KA	*MUcikɛ ka*	*kalMƐki ka*	*kkaMAKWI ka*

Table I. Accent Distinctions in a Northeastern Korean Dialect
NOTE: Pitch shapes are given with an enclitic particle.

mʌ̀l 'horse'	*mál* 'measure'	*mǎl* 'speech, language'	
pòlì 'barley'	*émí* 'mother'	*mèlí* 'hair'	*sǎlʌ́m* 'human being'
	émì nɨ́n		*sǎlʌ̀m ʌ́n*
sònskàlàk 'finger'	*tóskàpí* 'devil'	*kʌ̀lmyékí* 'seagull'	*kàmàkóy* 'raven'
		kʌ̀lmyékì nɨ́n	
			sǎmàkóy 'mole'

Table II. Pitch Distinctions in Middle Korean

protonic trisyllabic nouns (óoo), where about half of the dialect reflexes fall into a different accent class. Moreover, there is little agreement between the modern dialects as to which words are exceptional. There is obviously something aberrant about the historical development of accent on an initial syllable. Unless it can be shown how and why protonic classes decayed, it will be very difficult to find a non-arbitrary way to reconstruct this kind of accent into the lexicon of earlier Korean.

An even more pervasive problem with Korean accent is the overall lexical distribution among the various classes. The following chart is a display of the statistics for 398 Middle Korean nouns:[6]

The Accentual Distribution of 398 Middle Korean Nouns

				Totals
Accent class:	1.0	1.1		
Example:	*mʌ̀l* 'horse'	*mál* 'measure'		
Class size:	35 (22%)	127 (78%)		162
Accent class:	2.0	2.1	2.2	
Example:	*pòlì* 'barley'	*mókʌy* 'mosquito'	*mèlí* 'hair'	
Class size:	46 (19%)	30 (13%)	160* (68%)	236
				398

* A total of 39 rising-pitched nouns are included in this number. (Cf. fn 6.)

As can be seen from this chart, the classes in which the accent falls on the last syllable of the morpheme—that is, oxytonic—nouns are far larger than the other classes. In the case of monosyllables, there are more than three times as many (oxy)tonic nouns as atonic nouns; for dissyllables, there are more than twice as many oxytonic nouns as atonic and protonic nouns combined.

I believe that this faulty distribution was caused by the fact that Proto-Korean did not have pitch distinctions, and that the oxytonic classes—1.1 and 2.2—represent the pitch pattern originally carried by all Korean morphemes. In other words, I believe that proto-Korean was characterized by a non-distinctive prosodic system in which the last (or only) syllable of a morpheme was automatically given prominence. If this hypothesis is correct, pitch shapes different from the canonical, oxytonic pattern must have been the result of phonological change, compounding, and borrowing.

[6] In this display nouns longer than two syllables are omitted since almost all were morphemically complex. Middle Korean rising pitches are treated as dissyllables.

Much of the atonic vocabulary looks as if pitch may have been phonologically conditioned. For example, few Middle Korean nouns end in *-ng*, but those that do are normally characterized by a low-pitched final syllable; e.g., *skwèng* 'pheasant', *stòng* 'dung', *tìng* 'back', *k*^{h}*òng* 'soybeans', *kòlàng* 'furrow'. In almost 30% of the dissyllabic, atonic nouns, the vocalism of both syllables is of a peculiar[7] type, the minimal vowel *ʌ*/*ɨ*; e.g., *kʌ̀zʌ̀l* 'autumn', *kɨ̀tɨ̀y* 'thou', *mʌ̀tʌ̀y* 'joint', *mʌ̀zʌ̀m* 'heart', *pʌ̀lʌ̀m* 'wind'. Even more suggestive is the fact that almost half of the atonic dissyllables have the shape CVC_1VC_2,[8] where C_1 and C_2 are voiced consonants; examples (besides those given above that fit this description) include **kùmɨ̀ɣ* 'hole', **nàmʌ̀ɣ* 'wood', **nòlʌ̀ɣ* '(a kind of) deer', **mùzɨ̀ɣ* 'daikon', **sìlɨ̀ɣ* 'steamer', **àzʌ̀ɣ* 'younger brother', **yèzɨ̀ɣ* 'fox', **cyàlʌ̀ɣ* 'sack', **kʌ̀lʌ̀l* 'powder', and many more. In time, as our understanding of Korea's linguistic prehistory grows, the phonological processes through which these forms were created will surely be brought to light.

Many protonic nouns are morphemically complex. For example, *yémso* 'goat' is said to have the etymological meaning 'bearded ox' (Martin, et al. 1967: 1183); *úl.ey* 'thunder' is a nominalization of the verb 'to cry, roar'; *áki* 'baby', *émi* 'mother', and *p*^{h}*ʌ́li* 'fly' contain the suffix *-í* (*p*^{h}*ʌ́l* is attested).

Other nouns in aberrant pitch classes are loans, usually from Chinese. Such atonic forms include *pyèng* 'bottle', *pì* 'monument, stele', *c*^{h}*àng* 'window', *c*^{h}*àng* 'spear', *c*^{h}*ò* 'vinegar', *kàcì* 'eggplant', *kòc*^{h}*yò* 'pepper', *tòcʌ̀k* 'thief', *lòktù* 'green peas', *syàkòng* 'boatman', *cyèksàm* 'jacket',[9] *cyùngsʌ̀yng* 'animal', *p*^{h}*yèngp*^{h}*ùng* 'folding screen', and many, many more. An equally large number of atonic nouns may be borrowings of some kind,

[7] Peculiar because it is the minimal vowel that, in Middle Korean at least, appeared most commonly in non-initial syllables. The choice of *ʌ* or *ɨ* was one of vowel harmony and depended upon the identity of the vowel in the first syllable of the word.

[8] A significant (though lesser) number of nouns with this segmental shape have the otherwise expected oxytonic accent. I have found twelve such examples: *kɨ̀lɨ́m* 'oil', *kyèzɨ́l* 'winter', *nyèlɨ́m* 'summer', *màzʌ́n* 'forty', *pànʌ́l* 'needle', *pàlʌ́l (~ pàtáh)* 'sea', *pìnɨ́l* '(fish) scale', *èlɨ́m* 'ice', *yèlɨ́m* 'fruit', *ònʌ́l* 'today', *ùmɨ́l* 'well', *hèmɨ́l* 'misdeed'. Many of these nouns are morphemically complex: 'forty', 'today', and 'well' are compounds; 'ice', 'fruit', and possibly 'summer' as well, are nominalizations derived from verb stems. 'Oil', 'winter', 'needle', 'scale', and 'misdeed' are more difficult to explain.

[9] The morpheme *cyèk* is problematic, but *sàm* is clearly from Chinese.

but definite sources have not yet been identified. These words include such culture-bound terms as *tàk* 'paper mulberry', *tòt^h* 'swine', *mʌ̀l* 'horse',[10] *pʌ̀y* 'pear', *pàt^h* 'field', *òs* 'lacquer', *pòlì* 'barley', *pɨ̀t^hye* 'Buddha',[11] *pìnhyè* 'hairpin', *sòkòm* 'salt', and *sòòm* 'cotton'. (Could words like *sòn* 'guest', *nòh* 'cord', *tòk* 'crock', *pɨ̀t* 'debt', *sòt^h* 'kettle', *hwàl* 'bow', *pòsyèn* '(Korean) socks', and *stàpò* 'weederplow' be added to this list?) There remain many cases where it is extremely difficult to separate loanwords from the etymologies of native Korean nouns.

Verbs. Accounting for accentual distinctions in the Korean verbs is a more straightforward task. It is here that internal reconstruction yields the clearest results. As Martin has noted (1966: 197), the Korean inflectional system is almost completely resistant to borrowing. Verb forms are composed entirely of native elements, and the method of internal reconstruction can be applied to them with confidence. The same does not hold true for nouns, where, as we have seen, it is often difficult to separate loans from native vocabulary.

The stem of a Korean verb cannot occur in isolation. In every environment it is followed by an inflectional ending.[12] By phonological (including accentual) behavior, these endings fall generally into two groups: those that begin with the minimal vowel *ɨ* (or, in Middle Korean, *ʌ*) and those that do not. The difference is illustrated by the following forms of the Middle Korean verb 'to be bent':

(a)		(b)	
kùptá 'it's bent'		*kùpɨ́ní* 'since it's bent,'	
kùpkó 'it's bent, and...'		*kùpɨ́myén* 'if it's bent,'	
kùpkéy 'so that it's bent'		*kùpɨ́lìlá* 'it will be bent'	
kùptí (*mót...*) 'it's (not) bent'		*kùpɨ́n* 'the bent (one)'	
kùpsólá 'what with being bent'		*kùpɨ́lq* 'the (one) that will be bent'	

Notice that the minimal vowel consistently appears before sonorants (i.e., *l*, *m*, and *n*)[13] and is not generally found before endings that begin

---

[10] The languages in which variant forms of this word appear are of course legion.

[11] The first syllable is almost surely from some variety of Chinese, but the rest of the word is not so easy to explain. The Korean form was in any case the most probable source of the Japanese word for 'Buddha', *hotoké*.

[12] In modern Korean, the total number of paradigmatic endings is well over 400 (Martin 1974: 354); and in Middle Korean the number was almost certainly comparable.

[13] There are a small number of exceptions—most notably before the

with an obstruent.[14] This difference figures prominently in my reconstruction of earlier verb forms.

Korean verbs fall into inflecting classes by segmental and accentual behavior. A comparison of Middle Korean and the modern accenting dialects shows that verbs whose stems are sometimes, or always, one syllable long, can be divided into eight classes.[15] Here are Middle Korean examples, together with the reflexes found in Seoul and in an accenting dialect of South Hamgyŏng:

Verb Classes in Middle Korean

	Class 1 'eat'	Class 2 'use'
Middle Korean	*mèktá*, *mèkɨ́ní*	*psɨ́tá*, *psɨ́ní*
South Hamgyŏng	*məktá*, *məkɨ́ni*	*ssɨ́ta*, *ssɨ́ni*
Seoul	*məkta*, *məkɨni*	*ssɨta*, *ssɨni*

	Class 3 'see'	Class 4 'stand'
MK	*pòkó*, *pòmyén*, *pókèná*, *póá*	*syèkó*, *syèmyén*, *syèkèná*, *syéá*
SH	*pokú*, *pomún*, *pókəna*, *páa*	*səkú*, *səmún*, *səkə́na*, *sə́ə́*
Seoul	*poko*, *pomyən*, *pokəna*, *pwa*	*səko*, *səmyən*, *səkəna*, *səə*

	Class 5 'be many'	Class 6 'be hot'
MK	*tyŏt*^{h}*a*, *tyŏhʌ̀nyé*	*tĕpta*, *tèβɨ́myén*, *tèβé*
SH	*cót*^{h}*a*, *cóɨni*	*tə́pta*, *təpúmyən*, *təpə*
Seoul	*cot*^{h}*a*, *coɨni*	*təpta*, *təumyən*, *təwə*

	Class 7 'lie down'	Class 8 'flow'
MK	*nùpkócyé*, *nùβɨ̀myé*, *nùβé*	*hɨ̀lɨ̀kéy*, *hɨ̀llé*
SH	*nupkú*, *nupumyə́*, *nupə́*	*hɨlɨké*, *hɨllə́*
Seoul	*nupko*, *nuumyə*, *nuwə*	*hɨlɨke*, *hɨllə*

The largest verb class is Class 1.

---

processive marker -*nʌ̀*-, which appears directly after a stem-final obstruent; e.g., *mèknʌ̀tá* '(he) is eating'. I believe that this marker may be derived from an independent verb stem.

[14] The minimal vowel is also not found before vowels; e.g., *kùpé* 'it's bent, and so...', *kùpéstá* 'it was bent'.

[15] Longer stems, far fewer in number and in general morphemically complex, will not be discussed here.

Class 1 verbs. The stem of a Middle Korean Class 1 verb is always one low-pitched syllable, and the syllable is always closed by a consonant or consonant cluster or the semivowel *y*. Both the accent and the last segment of the stem are different from those of the other classes.

Table III shows the distribution of 472 verbal stems according to the last segment of the stem. (For the sake of comparison, the morphophonemic, second-syllable vowel in classes 6, 7, and 8 is omitted.)

The complementarity is almost perfect: Class 1 stems are closed by voiceless obstruents; the stems of the other classes are not.

The only significant exceptions to this rule are the stems that end in *-y* or *-l*. The *l*-stem forms will be set aside; they present special problems that will not be discussed here. (But see Ramsey 1978: 224 ff.) The *y*-stem forms are exceptional in a more demonstrable way. Many are morphemically complex; among them, for example, are stems that incorporate the causative/passive morpheme *-.í-*. Here are a few examples:[16]

psʌ́- 'wrap'	+ *-.í-* →	*psʌ̀y-* 'be wrapped'
ptɨ́- 'float'	+ *-.í-* →	*ptɨ̀y-* 'make float'
c^h*ɨ́-* 'remove'	+ *-.í-* →	c^h*ɨ̀y-* 'have (someone) get rid of'

Other *y*-stems seem to be contractions of longer stems; e.g., the Middle Korean Class 1 stem *ùy-* 'poke, scrape' has as its modern Seoul dialect reflex the form *upi-* 'id.'. The accent of still other Class 1 stems, such as *pʌ̀y-* 'soak into', is suspect because the modern reflexes have vowel length, a suprasegmental that normally corresponds to rising pitch in Middle Korean. The *y*-stems will also be excluded from the discussion.

The remaining Class 1 stems have a shape comparable to Class 6 stems. The verbs in these two classes contrast in the following way:[17]

---

[16] It should be noted, however, that the accent rules involved in derivations are problematic, as can be seen from the following examples:

p^h*ʌ́-* 'dig'	+ *-í-* →	p^h*ʌ́y-* 'be dug'
sye- 'stand'	+ *-.í-* →	*syěy-* 'stand (something) up'

[17] Accent marks, except those marking the distinctive locus, are omitted in order to simplify the display. The rising tones that appear in Class 6 forms such as *kǔptá* are transcribed here as dissyllables; e.g., *kuúpta*.

Stem-final segment(s)	Class	1	2	3	4	5	6	7	8
-p		10							
-t		16	1			1			
-s		7							
-c		15	2						
-k		17				1			
-sk		12							
-st		1							
-ps						1			
-p^h		7							
-t^h		10							
-c^h		9							
-l		17	16			2	38		
-lh		7	1						
-lk		10				1			
-lβ						1	8		
-lm							5		
-h						1		14	
-β			1			2	7	3	
-t/l							10	2	
-z							15	3	
-m			8			1	9		
-n			1				3	1	
-nc								2	
-nh						1			
-l.									21
-z.									5
-m.									1
-ll									8
-y		14	16			26	1		
-V			50	15	13	1			
Totals:		152	96	15	13	40	96	25	35

Table III. Distribution of verbal stems according to last segment of stem.

	Verb Class 1			Verb Class 6	
a.	*kuptá*	'it's bent'	a.	*kuúpta*	'(I) bake it'
	kupkó	'it's bent, and...'		*kuúpko*	'(I) bake it, and...'
	kupkéy	'so that it's bent'		*kuúpkey*	'so that (I) bake it'
b.	*kupíni*	'since it's bent'	b.	*kuβíni*	'since (I) bake it'
	kupímyen	'if it's bent'		*kuβímyen*	'if (I) bake it'
	kupílila	'it will be bent'		*kuβílila*	'(I) will bake it'

Here are examples of stem shapes found in these two classes:

	Class 1			Class 6	
	a	b		a	b
'carry on back'	*eptá*	*epíni*	'be hot'	*teépta*	*teβíni*
'be bent'	*kuptá*	*kupíni*	'bake'	*kuúpta*	*kuβíni*
'be narrow'	*coptá*	*copʌ́ni*	'help'	*toópta*	*toβʌ́ni*
'gather'	*kettá*	*ketíni*	'walk'	*keétta*	*kelíni*
'believe'	*mittá*	*mitíni*	'pump'	*kiítta*	*kilíni*
'receive'	*pattá*	*patʌ́ni*			
'take off'	*pestá*	*pesíni*	'laugh'	*uústa*	*uzíni*
'comb'	*pistá*	*pisíni*	'pick up'	*cuústa*	*cuzíni*
'spurt out'	*sostá*	*sosʌ́ni*	'peck'	*coósta*	*cozʌ́ni*
'be wet'	*cestá*	*cecíni*	'exceed'	*neémta*	*nemíni*
'meet'	*mastá*	*macʌ́ni*	'wind'	*kaámta*	*kamʌ́ni*
'die'	*cuktá*	*cukíni*	'wear (shoes)'	*siínta*	*siníni*
'eat'	*mektá*	*mekíni*	'embrace'	*aánta*	*anʌ́ni*
'stop'	*maktá*	*makʌ́ni*			
'rejoice'	*kistá*	*kiskíni*			
'be deep'	*kiptá*	*kip*^{h}*íni*			
'be, grow old'	*nɨlktá*	*nɨlkíni*			
'be worn out'	*nʌlktá*	*nʌlkʌ́ni*			

The last consonant in Class 6 stems is *β, t/l, z, m, n,* (*l*, or the semivowel *y*). I believe that these consonants reflect original contrasts with the voiceless obstruents of Class 1. If this original contrast was one of voicing, it follows naturally that the nasals *m* and *n* would pattern with the voiced consonants.[18] Here are some proposed reconstructions:

---

[18] In 1975 I suggested that the stems of Class 1 had always been monosyllabic and closed by a consonant since I could find no direct evidence (such as historical attestations) to prove otherwise. From this assumption I then argued that the voiced consonants in the Class 6 stems had originally been identical to the unvoiced phonemes found in Class 1, and that they had lenited because of their intervocalic position. That is to say, the consonants in Class 6 stems weakened because they were followed by a vowel, *V*p*V > V*β*V; *V*s*V > V*z*V; and so on. This solution implies that all the Middle Korean voiced obstruents were historically derived from unvoiced consonants, and that the only obstruents in the earlier reconstructable stage of Korean were all unvoiced. The hypothesis had several problems. One is that it gave no way to explain why Class 1 stems never end in *m* (or *n*), while there are so many occurrences of the nasal *m* in Class 6 stems. This distribution is peculiar. If Class 1 stems could be closed by other consonants that existed at the Proto-Korean stage, why not by *m* (or *n*)? The nasals must surely be reconstructed for Proto-Korean: they cannot be explained as the products of lenition—after all, there are no unvoiced nasals or any other consonants from which they could have lenited. An even more troublesome aspect of lenition is the phonological condition necessary for the application of the rule. Under the lenition hypothesis, the **p* in **kùpímyén* meaning 'if I bake' (< **kùpɨ́-* + ending) would have had to lenite, while the identical **p* in **kùpímyén* meaning 'if it's bent' (< **kùp-* + ending) could not have. Rules can of course be written so that lenition occurred sometime in the derivation before arriving at these surface forms, but what such rules boil down to is a claim that speakers of earlier Korean could somehow tell the difference between a stem-final vowel and an ending-initial vowel. In the kinds of Korean we know from first-hand experience, native speakers are not very adept at this kind of segmentation. Since a verb stem never occurs in isolation, speakers of the language are only dimly, if at all, aware of this part of the verb as a separate entity. Another derivational problem is the concatenation of minimal vowels. For example, the vowel /ɨ/ appears twice in **kùpɨ́-* + *-ímyén*, an underlying form that is suspicious since no more than one vowel ever appears on the surface, in any environment. In the case of Middle Korean Class 7 stems, such as *nùβɨ̀-* 'lie down', the concatenation requires the following derivation: *nùβɨ̀-* + *-ímyén* → *nùβɨ̀myén*, with elision of the second, high-pitched occurrence of the minimal vowel. This derivation is *ad hoc*. It runs counter to the following morhophonemic rule of Middle Korean: v̀ + v́ → v̌. In other words, the high-pitched mora,

Middle Korean	Proto-Korean
β	**b*
t/l	**d*
z	**z*
(.)	**g*
m	**m*
n	**n*

In the framework proposed here, Class 6 stems were originally distinguished from Class 1 stems only by this voicing contrast. Both classes were two syllables long in Proto-Korean and belonged to a single class of inflecting stems with the shape (C)VCV-.

**kùpɨ́-* 'be bent' **kùbɨ́-* 'bake'

Then, sometime after the Proto-Korean stage, stem-final vowels elided under certain conditions. The change can be roughly formulated as follows (it will be emended later): *ʌ,ɨ i* > ∅ C_1__C_2, where C_1 and C_2 are voiceless obstruents. That is, the minimal vowels *ʌ* and *ɨ* were lost by syncope between voiceless obstruents. Here are examples:

**kùpɨ́tá* > *kùptá* 'it's bent'
**sòsʌ́kó* > *sòskó* 'it spurts out, and ...'
**pàtʌ́kéy* > *pàtkéy* 'so that (he) receives (it)'

The stems that underwent this change formed Class 1. Notice that if C_2 was any consonant besides a voiceless obstruent, syncope did not occur; for example: **kùpɨ́myén* 'if it's bent'; **kùbɨ́myén* 'if (I) bake (it)'.

If C_1 was voiced, the final vowel of the stem was also subject to syncope. But, in this case, syncope left a trace of the elided vowel in compensatory lengthening of the vowel in the preceding syllable. The accent, or high pitch, of the elided vowel also moved across the voiced consonant. Now the first syllable had a long vowel with a high pitch on its second mora. Voiced obstruents were then devoiced in the presence of the voiceless obstruent that followed.

**kubɨ́ta* > **kuúbta* → *kuúpta*[20] '(I) bake it'

---

the carrier of the accent locus in Middle Korean, should be preserved in the surface form. Why should we believe that the high-pitched mora was ever there in the first place?

Problems such as these, I believe, represent fatal weaknesses of the lenition hypothesis.

19 This consonant does not appear in Class 6 stems.

20 The long-vowel forms are of course transcribed in Middle Korean as

**kedíko* > **keédko* → *keétko* '(I) walk, and...'
**cozʌ́key* > **coózkey* → *coóskey* 'so that (it) pecks'
**kamʌ́key* > *kaámkey* 'so that (it) winds'

The stems where this change occurred formed Class 6. After syncope had taken place, certain intervocalic consonants lenited, a process by which **b* and **d* weakened into *β* and *l* ([r])[21]; other stem consonants remained unchanged. Here are examples:

**kùbɨ́ní* > *kùβɨ́ní* 'since it's bent,'
**kèdɨ́myén* > *kèlɨ́myén* [kərɨmyən] 'if (I) walk'

Table IV presents a summary of the processes proposed to explain the development of Class 1 and Class 6 stems.

Class 2 verbs. The second class of verbs with a stable stem shape is Class 2. In Middle Korean, these stems are always high pitched. They are subdivided into two subclasses by segmental structure:

Class 2a: The syllable of these stems is closed by a sonorant, *l* or *m*, or by *y*:[22] e.g., *kʌ́l-* 'grind', *súm-* 'hide'.

The majority of the stems in this subclass seem to have been closed by a sonorant ever since the Proto-Korean stage.[23]

---

kŭptá, *kĕtkó*, *cŏskéy*, and *kămkéy*. (See the brief description of Class 5 stems, above.)

[21] It should be remembered that /l/ is a phonemic transcription; the symbol *r* would of course serve equally well.

[22] There are five exceptions with obstruent finals: *ptʰɨ́t-* 'pluck', *sɨ́s-* ~ *sɨ́c-* 'wash' (these two forms are apparently variants of *sis-* 'id.', a Class 1 stem with the expected low pitch), *cʰʌ́c-* 'search for', *pcɨ́c-* 'tear', *kʌ́tʰ-* 'be alike'. This last exceptional stem meaning 'be alike' has a variant form *kʌ́thʌ̀-* 'id.' which is equally well attested; the variant shows that the stem is derived from the noun *kʌ́t-* '-like' (attested only in compounds) + the verb *hʌ-* 'do, be'. There are also *ólh-* 'be correct < **ól* + *hʌ-* 'be, do'; *cóh-* 'be clean' < **có* + *hʌ-* 'be, do'; and *sɨ́lh-* (*sɨ́lhʌ-*) 'dislike' < **sɨ́l* + *hʌ-* 'be, do' (the accentual behavior shows that these three stems have the structure Noun + *hʌ-*). Finally, the common stem *cʰíp-* ~ *cʰíβ* - '(the weather) feels cold' is derived from **cʰi-*, which is probably a variant of *cʰʌ́-* 'be cold (to the touch)', + *-βɨ̀-*, a postverb used to derive adjectivals (cf. Ramsey 1978a: 223–23).

[23] But note that I would derive stems with complex initials, such as *pʰʌ́l-* 'sell' and *cʰʌ́m-* 'endure', from dissyllabic stems: e.g., **pʌ̀Hʌ́l-* and **cʌ̀Hʌ́m-*.

Proto-Korean	Syncope	Devoicing	Lenition	Middle Korean	
**kùpɨ́-* 'be bent'					Class 1
**kùpɨ́tá* >	*kùptá*			*kùptá*	
**kùpɨ́ní*				*kùpɨ́ní*	
**pàtʌ́-* 'receive'					
**pàtʌ́tá* >	*pàttá*			*pàttá*	
**pàtʌ́ní*				*pàtʌ́ní*	
**pèsɨ́-* 'take off'					
**pèsɨ́tá* >	*pèstá*			*pèstá*	
**pèsɨ́ní*				*pèsɨ́ní*	
**mèkɨ́-* 'eat'					
**mèkɨ́tá* >	*mèktá*			*mèktá*	
**mèkɨ́ní*				*mèkɨ́ní*	
**kùbɨ́-* 'bake'					Class 6
**kùbɨ́tá* >	**kùúbtá* >	*kùúptá*		*kŭptá*	
**kùbɨ́ní* >			*kùβɨ́ní*	*kùβɨ́ní*	
**kèdɨ́-* 'walk'					
**kèdɨ́tá* >	**kèédtá* >	*kèéttá*		*kěttá*	
**kèdɨ́ní* >			*kèlɨ́ní*	*kèlɨ́ní*	
**nàzʌ́-* 'improve'					
**nàzʌ́tá* >	**nàáztá* >	*nàástá*		*nàstá*	
**nàzʌ́ní*				*nàzʌ́ní*	
**kàmʌ́-* 'wind'					
**kàmʌ́tá* >	*kàámtá*			*kàmtá*	
**kàmʌ́ní*				*kàmʌ́ní*	

Table IV. Summary of development of Class 1 and Class 6 verb stems.

Class 2b: Open-syllable stems. Here are a few examples:

	a	b
'scoop'	*stɨ́ta*	*stɨ́ni*
'write'	*ssɨ́ta*	*ssɨ́ni*
'open (eyes)'	*ptɨ́ta*	*ptɨ́ni*
'use'	*psɨ́ta*	*psɨ́ni*
'squeeze'	*pcʌ́ta*	*pcʌ́ni*
'spread'	p^h*ɨ́ta*	p^h*ɨ́ni*
'burn'	t^h*ʌ́ta*	t^h*ʌ́ni*
'kick'	c^h*ʌ́ta*	c^h*ʌ́ni*
'be big'	k^h*ɨ́ta*	k^h*ɨ́ni*
'steam'	*ptɨ́ta*	*ptɨ́ni*
'hit, strike'	t^h*ɨ́ta*	t^h*ɨ́ni*

These stems were originally two syllables long, as is indicated by their unique canonical shape in Middle Korean. They have four characteristics:

(1) the pitch is high;

(2) the syllable is open;

(3) the initial consonant is a cluster or an aspirate;

(4) the vowel is a minimal vowel, *ʌ* or *ɨ*, or *i*.

In Proto-Korean, the consonants in the initial clusters were separated by a vowel. This vowel, which can be reconstructed as one of the minimal vowels, **ʌ* or **ɨ*, was lost by syncope. Here are the proposed reconstructions for some of the examples given above:

**sɨ̀tɨ́tá*	>	*stɨ́tá*	'scoop'
**sɨ̀sɨ́tá*	>	*ssɨ́tá*	'write'
**pɨ̀tɨ́tá*	>	*ptɨ́tá*	'open (eyes)'
**pɨ̀sɨ́tá*	>	*psɨ́tá*	'use'
**pʌ̀cʌ́tá*	>	*pcʌ́tá*	'squeeze'

In a morphophonemic sense, the aspirates can be considered clusters of C + *h*, in the modern Korean dialects as well as in Middle Korean, and an intervening minimal vowel can thus be postulated for the proto forms. A voiceless fricative **h* may not be reconstructable for Proto-Korean.[24] Nevertheless, it seems clear that the source of aspiration in these clusters

---

[24] The origin of Middle Korean *h* has often been a subject of question. There are suspiciously few morpheme-initial occurrences of this consonant; at the end of Middle Korean nouns, there seem to be too many. Comparativists such as Ramstedt and Poppe would derive it from Altaic **s*. In

had to have been some sort of voiceless velar obstruent.[25] For this reason, the identity of the consonant will be left an open question and the Proto-Korean obstruent written with the symbol **H*. Here are the reconstructions for the above examples with initial aspirates:

**pìHítá*	>	p^h*ítá*	'spread'
**tʌ̀Hʌ́tá*	>	t^h*ʌ́tá*	'burn'
**cʌ̀Hʌ́tá*	>	c^h*ʌ́tá*	'kick'
**kìHítá*	>	k^h*ítá*	'be big'

The minimal vowel at the end of Class 2b stems was not subject to syncope. Thus, for example, the following change did not take place: *psítá* (< **pìsítá*) > ˣ*pstá*. Since the Syncope Rule proposed for Class 1 stems should apply here, the rule will have to be emended by adding the condition that the vowel not be the only vowel of the stem. Presumably, at least one vowel in the morpheme needed to be preserved for stem identity.

Under this hypothesis, the phonological difference between Class 2 stems and Class 1 stems at the Proto-Korean stage would have been, instead of accent, the quality of the vowel in the first syllable; compare:

Class 1	Class 2
**pèsí-* 'take off'	**pìsí-* 'use'

Vowel syncope would have had to apply in the following way:

Proto-Korean		Middle Korean	
**pèsítá* 'take off'	>	*pèstá*	(Class 1)
**pìsítá* 'use'	>	*psítá*	(Class 2)

The application of this rule would explain why there are so few occurrences of the minimal vowel *ʌ/i* in Class 1 verb stems. But there are

addition, there are (non-initial) reflexes in many modern dialects with a *k* corresponding to *h* in Middle Korean (or in modern Seoul dialect). Cf. Ramsey 1977.

[25] I believe that this Proto-Korean consonant may well have been the simple velar stop *k*, but there is not yet sufficient evidence for a convincing reconstruction. Some distributional evidence can be derived from the fact that no clusters with *k* exist in Middle Korean except *sk* and *psk*—recall that there is no aspirated *s* (ˣs^h) in Middle Korean! Thus *k*-clusters and aspiration are in complementary distribution. Comparative evidence for a **k* as the source of aspiration is presented in Ramsey 1977.

exceptions. Here are ten Class 1 stems that I have found with this kind of vocalism:[26]

Class 1 stems with exceptional vocalism

nʌ̀c-	'be low'
nɨ̀c-	'be late'
kʌ̀c-	'be endowed with'
cʌ̀c-	'be frequent'
cɨ̀c-	'bark'
kʌ̀sk-	'make efforts' Probably derived from *kʌ̀c-* 'endowed with'
pɨ̀tʰ-	'stick; depend'
pɨ̀tʰ-	'start a fire'
kɨ̀cʰ-	'end' Probably related to the noun *kɨ́tʰ* 'end'
mʌ̀cʰ-	'stop'

Notice that these stems all end in *c* or complex dental obstruents. Perhaps, for whatever reason, syncope did not occur before /c/. If this was the case, the fact might also be used to explain why there is no **sc* cluster in the Middle Korean obstruent series *sp*, *st*, *ss*, *sk*.

In any event, there are approximately fifty Class 1 verb stems ending in /p, t, s, k/, and none of them has *ʌ* or *ɨ* as its vocalism.

Classes 3 and 4: Monosyllabic Stems. Class 3 and Class 4 comprise a small number of basic verbs with extremely irregular accent. The stems appear to have always been monosyllabic.

There are thirteen stems in Class 3: *ca-* 'sleep', *ca-* '(the wind) dies down',[27] *cu-* 'give', *hʌ-* 'do', *ha-* 'be big, many', *ka-* 'go', *na-* 'grow; emerge; become; etc.', *nu-* 'evacuate (urine, feces)', *nu-* 'maintain',[28] *o-* 'come', *po-* 'see', *sa-* 'buy', *tu-* 'put'.

There are thirteen stems in Class 4: *ci-* 'fatten', *ci-* 'carry on the back', *hye-* ~ *hhye-* 'pull', *hye-* ~ *hhye-* 'kindle',[29] *i-* 'carry on the head',[30]

[26] There were also a significant number of *y*-stems with this vocalism; these will not be discussed here.

[27] This stem is not well attested; it probably represents metaphoric use of Another Class 3 stem, *ca-* 'sleep'.

[28] A late hapax.

[29] This stem is perhaps to be identified etymologically with the previous stem meaning 'pull'. Modern dialect forms are *kʰi-* and *kʰyə-*.

[30] Also attested as *ni-*, but the initial *n* is probably not etymologically genuine.

(*-ni-* 'continue',[31]) *nye-* 'go about',[32] p^h*ye-* 'spread out',[33] *si-* 'exist',[34] *sye-* 'stand', *ti-* 'lose; fall; turn upside down; die', *ti-* 'be cheap'[35] (*-ti-* 'form, become'[36]).

The division of these verbs into two classes is based principally upon accentual behavior in the modern accenting dialects. In Middle Korean there is little evidence for an accentual contrast between the two. Here are Middle Korean examples of these verbs:

Class 3			Class 4		
	po- 'to see'			*sye-* 'to stand'	
pokó	*pónonka*	*poóyesinʌl*	*syetá*	*syézʌβʌmye*	*syeélq*
pol	*pósikoza*	*poómila*	*syekó*	*syée*	*syeemi*
polóta	*pózʌβʌlila*		*syemyén*	*syéa*	
pomyé	*pókena*		*syekená*	*syésya*	
	pósya				
	hʌ- 'to do'			*ti-* 'fall; lose; die'	
hʌníngita	*hʌ́sini*	*hʌ́yyʌlila*	*tiníngita*	*tínʌta*	*tiío*
hʌtá	*hʌ́sya*			*tíkenʌl*	
hʌtós	*hʌ́zʌβʌni*				
hʌkéy	*hʌ́ya*				
hʌkó	*hʌ́teni*				
hʌní	*hʌ́nʌn*				
hʌlílato					
hʌmyé					
hʌn					
hʌl					

---

[31] This stem apparently only occurs before the retrospective marker *-kè-*.

[32] Probably related, at least etymologically, with the previous stem *ni-*, which also seems to be used in the sense of 'go'.

[33] The stem is related to, or derived from, p^h*ɨ́-* 'spread, bloom' (a Class 2 stem).

[34] This stem may not belong in this class; it is derived by apocope from the much better attested form *ìsì-*, which has the same meaning and function.

[35] There are only sixteenth-century attestations; the form is probably a semantic variant of the preceding stem.

[36] A postverb.

In the modern dialects, Class 3 and Class 4 are quite distinct accentually. In Hamgyŏng, for example, Class 4 stems are almost always atonic, becoming tonic only before a handful of endings, most notably the infinitive ending *-á/ə́*: *syə́ə* 'stand and then ...' In Middle Korean, however, the irregularities in the two classes were the same. A few marginal contrasts can be found; for example, *syèkèná* 'stand, or ...' is recorded in *Sokpo sangcel* 9:5 with a low-pitched first syllable, alongside Class 3 *pókèná* 'see, or ...' (*Sokpo sangcel* 9:24). This contrast is curious. In most Middle Korean texts Class 4 stems are attested as high before the retrospective marker *-kè-*; e.g., *tíkènʌ́l*, *nyékètín* (*nye-* 'to go').

The most important fact about Class 3 and Class 4 stems is that they were in complete complementary distribution by vocalism. The vowel of a Class 3 stem was *a*, *o*, *u*, or *ʌ*, while the vocalism of a Class 4 stem was *ye* or *i*. Otherwise, the two classes had the same segmental shape: one open syllable with a simple (C)V- structure.

Because the complementarity was so perfect, the two classes must have formed a single class of monosyllabic stems in Proto-Korean.

In Middle Korean, the accentual behavior of Class 3 and Class 4 stems was extremely complex. Before some inflectional endings, the pitch was high; before other endings, it was low.[37]

Although it is not clear how these irregularities in pitch arose historically, the stems appear to have been uniformly high pitched at the Proto-Korean stage of the language. Evidence for this surmise comes from compounding phenomena.

The only place in Middle Korean the stem of an inflecting form appeared bare of its inflectional endings—and thus of the accentual influence of those endings—was in compounds. Compounds made up of Class 3 stems behaved accentually as follows:

na- 'emerge' + *ka-* 'go' → *náka-* 'go out'

The compound was always accented on the first syllable. In compounds made up of monosyllabic nouns, such a protonic accent indicated that the constituent morphemes were both tonic:

---

[37] Kim Wanjin (1973: 58) divides the Middle Korean inflectional endings into two classes according to how they affect the accent of Class 4 verb stems. As far as I know, no one has proposed an explanation for how the variation arose historically. In any case, we are not dealing with an artifact of Middle Korean texts; the variation is substantiated in detail by the accentual behavior of the stems in the modern dialects (cf. Ramsey 1978a: 192ff.)

kóh 'nose' + *mɨ́l* 'water' → *kósmɨl* 'snivel'

If either member of the noun compound was atonic, the first syllable of the compound was not accented (cf Kim Wanjin 1973: 73–74):

kòc 'flower'	+	*níp*^{h} 'leaf'	→	*kòsníp*^{h} 'flower petal'
kúy 'ear'	+	*mìt*^{h} 'bottom'	→	*kùmìt*^{h} 'base of the ear'
són 'hand'	+	*t*^{h}*òp* 'unguis'	→	*sònt*^{h}*òp* 'fingernail'

The compounding rules in the modern accenting dialects of South Hamgyŏng are the same in these cases (cf. Ramsey 1978b: 133ff.).

Let us assume that the compounding rules for verbs parallel the compounding rules for nouns. If this assumption is correct, it follows that the monosyllabic verb stems were—in a morphophonemic sense at least—accented in Middle Korean. The stems, then, must have been high pitched in Proto-Korean.

To summarize, here are examples of the proposed reconstructions for forms in each of the Middle Korean stem classes discussed above:

Proto-Korean		Middle Korean		
*pó-		po-	'see'	(Class 3)
*cí-		ci-	'shoulder'	(Class 4)
*kʌ́l-		kʌ́l-	'grind'	(Class 2a)
*kùpí-	*kùpítá > kùptá *kùpíní > kùpíní	kùp-	'be bent'	(Class 1)
*pìsí-	*pìsítá > psítá *pìsíní > psíní	psí-	'use'	(Class 2b)
*kùbí-	*kùbítá > kùúptá *kùbíní > kùβíní	kŭp- ~ kùβ-	'bake'	(Class 6)

The three remaining verb stem classes were all two syllables (or moras) long in Middle Korean. The first of these is Class 5, a small class of stems with a long, rising pitch. An example of a Class 5 verb is *hŏ-* 'to sew', the stem of which was also written *hòó-*, underscoring the fact that it was indeed composed of two moras.

Class 7. This was a small class of some 25 verbs. The stems of these verbs had a morphophonemic second-syllable vowel, and the accent contrasted with that of Class 6 stems (which were discussed above together with Class 1 stems) as follows:

	Class 7			Class 6	
	a	b		a	b
'be hateful'	*miyptá*	*miyβiní*	'bake'	*kuúpta*	*kuβíni*
'bear (young)'	*nat^há*	*nahʌní*			
'hear'	*tittá*	*tiliní*	'walk'	*keétta*	*kelíni*
'pour'	*pistá*	*piziní*	'laugh'	*uústa*	*uzíni*

Most Class 7 stems were demonstrably composed of more than one morpheme. More than half ended in *h* plus the morphophonemic vowel, and this *-hì/hʌ̀-* was a postverbal variant of the ubiquitous Middle Korean verb *hʌ-* 'to do'. The verb *nàh(ʌ̀)-* 'bear (young)', for example, was derived in this way from *na-* 'to be realized; come out'; *cìh(ì)-* 'give (a name)' was from *ci-* 'support; carry on the back' (Lee Ki-Moon 1972: 149). *Mìyp- ~ mìyβì-* 'be hateful' was composed of *mìy-* 'hate' plus the postverb *-βʌ̀/βì-*, a morpheme used to derive descriptive verbs from action verbs. The Class 7 verbs that cannot be explained along similar lines were very small in number.

Class 8. This irregular class of some 35 verbs had a peculiar morphology. Here are examples of three of its members:

'turn (something)'	*tolʌtá*	*tolʌnósta*	*tol.íta*	*tol.á*
'pull'	*kizitá*	*kizinʌnkó*	*kiz.úm*	*kiz.é*
'flow'	*hilitá*	*hilikéy*		*hillé*

Many, perhaps most, of these verbs were morphemically complex, particularly those with the final segments *-lʌ̀- -l.-*; for example, *tòlʌ̀tá* 'turn (something)' was a causative form of the Class 6 verb *tòól- ~ tòl-* 'turn'. The "*l*-doubling" verbs in this class, such as *hilì- ~ hìll-* 'flow' were different. They appear to have been derived from earlier dissyllabic shapes such as **hilil-*. How and why the pitch of the second syllable came to be low is a problem related to the complexities of the *l*-stem verbs. These will be discussed in a later paper. (But see Ramsey 1978a: 224ff.)

Conclusions. Proto-Korean, as reconstructed along lines outlined above, differed in a number of ways from later, attested varieties of the language. Some of the most important differences are as follows:

1. Proto-Korean had no pitch, length, or stress distinctions. Instead, pitch patterns were determined by the length of a word since the last syllable of a stem (or morpheme) was automatically given prominence.[38] The complex pitch distinctions found at the Middle Korean stage of the language and in many of the modern dialects resulted from changes that took place in the segmentals.

2. The most important of these segmental changes were vowel syncope and apocope, phonological processes which altered the syllable structure of Korean. Apocope[39] produced closed syllables for many morphemes, and syncope gave rise to obstruent clusters that had previously not existed.

3. The clusters produced by syncope were eventually reduced to unit phonemes, the aspirated consonants and the reinforced (*toen-sori*) consonants found in modern Korean.

(a) The clusters that became reinforced (or "tense" or "glottalized") phonemes began with the labial *p* or the dental *s*. These are the clusters attested in texts of the Middle Korean period. Their historical development into reinforced consonants has in large part already been documented (cf. Lee Ki-Moon 1977, Ho Ung 1965, Ramsey 1978b).

(b) Aspirates developed from clusters containing a velar obstruent.

4. Proto-Korean had a consonant system in which obstruents, including stops, were distinguished by voice.

This paper summarizes some of the reasons for these deductions. Omitted from discussion are issues related to vocalism and the vowel system, including that of the vowel shift believed to have taken place a century or so before the beginning of the Middle Korean period (cf. Lee Ki-Moon 1977: 101–117). The vowel harmony system to be reconstructed into Proto-Korean is another important issue. Finally, and most directly related to the hypotheses described in this paper, are questions about the origins of the "minimal vowels" *ʌ* and *ɨ*. These minimal vowels occur in non-initial position in Middle Korean verb stems almost to the complete exclusion of the other vowels (except /i/, which is the neutral vowel in the vowel harmony system). I have proposed reconstructing them in other positions as

[38] The non-distinctive prosody that I would reconstruct into proto-Korean—that is, a system in which the last syllable is automatically given a high pitch—is the kind of system found in Mongolian and many Tungus languages (cf. Poppe 1960: 144). Note, however, that this fact has not entered into the arguments summarized here; the reconstructions described in this paper are all based upon internal evidence.

[39] Arguments for the occurrence of apocope are not presented here.

well. The question that arises is, to what extent do these minimal vowels represent the neutralization of a fuller set of vocalic distinctions? Or, on the other hand, could some occurrences of these minimal vowels have been epenthetic? The study of Korean etymology has yet to produce easy answers to these questions.

References

Hŏ Ung. 1965. *Kugŏ ŭmun-hak*. Seoul: Chŏngŭm-sa.

Kim Wanjin. 1973. *Chungse Kugŏ sŏngjo ŭi yŏn'gu*. Seoul: Han'guk munhwa yŏn'gu-so.

Kōno Rokurō. 1944. Chōsen hōgengaku sikō. Keijō (=Seoul).

Lee Ki-Moon. 1972. *Kugŏ-sa kaesŏl*. Revision of 1961 first edition. Seoul: Tower Press.

——. 1977. *Kugŏ ŭmun-sa yŏn'gu*. Seoul: Tower Press.

Martin, Samuel E. 1966. "Lexical evidence relating Korean to Japanese." *Language* 42.2: 185–251.

——. 1974. *Korean Reference Grammar*. Unpublished manuscript.

——, Yang Ha Lee, and Sung-Un Chang. 1967. *A Korean-English Dictionary*. New Haven: Yale University Press.

Poppe, N. N. 1960. *Vergleichende Grammatik der altaischen Sprachen. Teil I. Vergleichende Lautlehre*. Wiesbaden: Otto Harrassowitz.

Ramsey, S. Robert. 1975. "Middle Korean *W*, *z*, and *t/l* verb stems." *Language Research* 11.1: 59–67.

——. 1977. "Velar lenition in Korean." In *Festschrift Commemorating the Seventieth Birthday of Doctor Lee Sung Nyong* (Seoul: Uryu Press), pp. 125–32.

——. 1978a. *Accent and Morphology in Korean Dialects*. Seoul: Tower Press.

——. 1978b. "*S*-clusters and reinforced consonants." In Chin-W.Kim, ed., *Papers in Korean Linguistics* (Columbia, South Carolina: Hornbeam), pp. 59-66.

INDEX OF LANGUAGES

Ahom, 54n, 55, 59–60, 62–3, 65
Altaic, 35–49, 77, 81, 92, 176–202, 230
  Proto-, 177–79, 179n, 180, 186–87, 191–97, 198, 200–02
Altay, 76
  Standard, 77
Amharic, 61
Arabic, 38, 39n, 61, 70n, 71n, 82, 88, 92
Armenian, 104, 153
Assamese, 160n, 163–64
Aśokan, see Prakrit, Aśokan
Austronesian, Proto, 177
Avestan, 127–28, 145, 149, 153, 160n, 163
Avadhi, see Hindi, Avadhi
Azerbaijan, see Azerbaijani
Azerbaijani, 45, 71n, 73, 75, 91
  Tabrizi Soviet Standard, 91
Bantu, 197
Baoan, 42–43, 45, 46n
Barguzin, see Buriat, Barguzin
Bashqir, 77
Bengali, 160n, 163–64
Bhojpuri, 160n, 163
Brahui, 160n, 168
Bunu, 205
Buriat, 44
  Alar, 44
  Barguzin, 46
  Kachug, 46
  Literary, 46
Celtic, 184
Chaghatay, see Uzbek, Old
Chakhar, 44
Cheremis, 47n
  Eastern, 43
Chinese, 1–30, 53–65, 70n, 82, 181, 205–12, 216n, 220, 221n
  Ancient, see Chinese, Middle
  Early Middle, 54n, 55–56, 60–62, 64–65
  Foochow, see Min, Fuzhou
  Hakka, see Kejia
  Kejia, see Kejia
  Middle, 1–30, 53–65
  Min, see Min
  Old, 1–30, 53–65
  Old Southern, 205–12
Chulym Turki, see Turki, Chulym
Churari, see Romani
Chuvash, 43, 46, 47, 177, 180
Dagur, 44, 48
Danish, 196
Dioi, 54n, 58
Dravidian, 153n, 160, 162, 164–73
  Central, 160n, 166–69
  North, 160n, 166–67
  Proto-, 160n, 162, 164–66, 168–69, 172–73, 177
  South-Central, 160n, 166–67, 169
Dunghsiang, 42–43, 45, 46n
English, 48, 104, 137n, 198
  Middle, 171
  Modern, see English, New

New, 171, 190, 196
Old, 151, 171, 196, 199
Erli, see Romani
Estonian, 37
Evenki, 41, 196–97, 201
Farsi, see Persian
Finnic, 43, 47n, 77
Proto-, 42
Finnish, 35, 36n, 37n, 38, 39, 42, 47n
Finno-Ugric, Proto, 42n
French, 38, 39, 70n
Gadba, 160n, 165, 167, 169
Gagauz, 73, 75
German, 48, 199
Middle Low, 196
New High, 196
Germanic, 184, 190, 199
Proto-, 184, 189
Gondi, 160n, 165–69
Gothic, 151, 178
Greek, 104, 154, 178, 184, 197
Byzantine, 104
Gujarati, 160n, 163–64
Halič, 43
Hebrew, 61
Hindi, 140n, 153, 163, 164, 173
Avadhi, 163
Hindi-Urdu, 124
Hittite, 66
Hungarian, 35, 36n, 37n, 38, 39, 41, 42n, 43, 47n, 48n, 106
Ili Turki, see Turki, Ili
Indic, see Indo-Aryan
Early Old, see Indo-Aryan, Early Old
Indo-Aryan, 104, 119–54, 160–66, 169–73
Early, 119–54
Early Middle, 172
Early Modern, see Indo-Aryan, Early New
Early, New, 139n
Early Old, 163, 173
Eastern ('Magadhan'), 120, 123, 136
Literary Old, 162
Middle, 120, 138, 139, 140–48, 149–51, 160n, 161–62, 169–70, 173
Modern, see Indo-Aryan, New
New, 120, 122, 129, 140n, 160n, 161–62, 173
New, East, 172
New, South, 172
New, West, 172
Old, 119–54, 160n, 161–62, 172
Pre-, 134
Proto-, 145
Indo-European, 66, 119, 134, 136, 184–86, 189–91, 197, 201
Proto-, 134, 138, 178
Indo-Iranian, 136, 138
Proto-, 144–45, 149
Iranian, 37, 83
Early, 136
Italian, 39, 130, 169
Italic, 170, 184
Japanese, 176–202, 216, 221n
Middle, 196
New, 180, 196
Old, 176–202

Pre-, 192–93
Pre-Old, 194
Proto-, 180
Ryukyu, 196
Kachug, see Buriat, Kachug
Kalderash, see Romani
Kalmuck, 44, 45, 47, 48–49
Dörbet, 44, 47
Ölöt, 47
Kamassian, 47n
Kannada, 160n, 165–69
Pre-, 170
Karachay-Balkar, 75
Karaim, 73, 75
Lutsk, 43
Troki (Lithuanian), 80
Karakirghiz, 47n
Soyon, 47n
Kashmiri, 160n, 162–63, 172
Kazakh, 43, 71n, 74–75, 92
Literary, 86
Xinjiang, 74n
Western, 45
Written, 75
Kejia, 205, 208
Hailu, 209–11
Meixian, 209–12
Proto-, 208
Khalka, 38, 40, 41, 44, 45
Khotan, see Uyghur, Khotan
Kirghiz, 44, 73, 74n, 76, 78, 81, 89
Koḍaga, 160n, 165–66, 168
Kolami, 160n, 166–67, 169
Konḍa, 165, 167–69
Konja Giese Osman, see Osman, Konja Giese
Konkani, 160n, 163–64, 166, 168
Korean, 178, 181, 186, 191, 196, 215–38
Chŏlla, 216n
Hamgyŏng, 216–17, 234
Hamgyŏng, South, 216, 222, 235
Kyŏngsang, 216–17
Middle, 182–83, 191, 197, 200, 215–38
New, 181–83, 196
Old, 181–83, 186–87, 191–92
Proto-, 180, 215–38
Pukch'ŏng, 216
Seoul, 222
Kota, 160n, 167
Kui, 165, 167–69
Kumauni, 160n, 163
Kumyk, 75
Kurukh, 160n, 165, 168
Kuvi, 165, 167–69
Lahnda, 160n, 162–63, 172
Lajia, 205
Lamut, 41, 197
Lao, 53
Lapp, 37
Lule, 43
Latin, 137n, 178, 190
Li, 206n
Lithuanian, 137n, 154
Lopnari, see Uyghur, Lopnari
Lovari, see Romani
Lü, 54n, 55–56, 58–59, 62
Lule Lapp, see Lapp, Lule
Lutsk Karaim, see Karaim, Lutsk
Mačvano, see Romani

Magadhi, see Prakrit, Magadhi
Maithili, 160n, 163
Malayalam, 160n, 166–71
Malto, 165, 167–68
Manchu, 37n, 41, 42, 44
Manda, 165, 167
Manush, see Romani
Maonan, 205, 206n
Marathi, 140n, 160n, 163–64, 173
Marwari, 160n, 163
Miao, 205, 207
Min, 205–15
  Chaozhou, 208
  Chaozhou, Chaoan, 210
  Chaozhou, Chaoyang, 210
  Dingan, 207n, 210–11
  Fuan, 207–12
  Fuzhou, 63, 207–12
  Jiangle, 207, 208n, 210–11
  Jianou, 210–11
  Jianyang, 210
  Jieyang, 209–12
  Jinzhou, 211
  Northwestern, 210
  Proto-, 208, 212
  Shaowu, 207, 209–11
  Southern, 210, 212
  Xiamen, 207n, 208–12
Moghol, 41, 44n, 45n, 83
Moghul, see Moghol
Mongolian, 35, 36n, 38, 39, 41, 42, 43, 44, 46, 48, 92, 177–78, 180, 195, 199, 201, 237n
  Classical, 41, 42–43, 44, 45, 46n, 48
  Middle, 41, 45, 198
  Written, 79, 196–97
Mongolic, 71n, 77
  Post-medieval, 83
Monguor, 37n, 42–43, 44n, 45, 46n
Mordvin, 43, 47n
Mulao, 205, 206n
Naiki of Chanda, 160n, 167, 169
Naikṛi, 160, 166, 168–69
Nanaj, 196, 197
Negidal, 196
Nepali, 160n, 164
Oghuz, see Turkic, Western
Olca, 196–97
Ollari, 160n, 165, 167
Ölöt, See Kalmuck, Ölöt
Ordos, 44
Oriya, 160n, 163–64
Orochi, 197
Oroki, 196–97
Osman, Konya Giese, 43, 47n
Osmanli, 196
Ossetic, 153
Ostyak, 43, 47n
Ottoman, see Turkish, Ottoman
Pahari, West, 160n, 163–64, 172
Pali, 139, 141, 148–49, 151, 160n, 162–64, 167, 170, 173
Panjabi, 160n, 163–64, 172
  Western, 162
Parji, 160n, 165, 169
Pengo, 165, 167–68
Persian, 71n, 82, 104, 163
  New, 153
Portuguese, Iberian, 82

Prakrit, 104, 119–20, 122, 129, 131, 133, 138, 139, 142–48, 149–52, 160n, 163–64, 173
  Aśokan, 139, 142, 146, 151, 162
  Aśokan, East, 141
  Aśokan, Northwestern, 140, 141
  Early, 162
  Magadhi, 136, 152
  Middle, 162
  Niya, 140
Pumi, 205
Punjabi, see Panjabi
Pu-yi, 54n, 55–56, 58–59, 61, 63
Qaraqalpaq, 74
Qazaq, see Kazakh
Qypchaq, 75
Qirghiz, see Kirghiz
Romani, 102–15
  Romani, Common, 102–15
Rumanian, 104, 106, 108
  Standard, 105–06
Russian, 38, 70n, 71n, 87n, 88, 103
  Standard, 82
Ryukyu, see Japanese, Ryukyu
Saek, 53–65
Salar, 83
Samoyed, Tavgi, 43
Samoyedic, 77
San-chuan, 42
Sanskrit, 104, 119–54, 160n, 163, 169, 178, 184, 190
  Classical, 143, 152–53
  Early, 143–44
  Later, 149
  Modern, 140
  Post-Rig-Vedic, 147, 148n
  Pre-, 134, 163
  Pre-Vedic, 145, 163
  Rig-Vedic, 136–37, 147–48, 149, 151, 160n, 163
  Vedic, 123–27, 132–35, 138, 142–44, 146–48, 149–50, 152–43
Shor, 77, 94n
Shui, 205, 206, 210
Siamese, 206, 207, 210–12
  Standard, 53, 57
Sibe, 37n, 44, 45
Sindhi, 160n, 162–64, 172
Sinhala, 160n, 162, 163–64
Sino-Vietnamese, 206n
Sinti, see Romani
Slavic, 37
  Southern, 104
Spanish, 131
Swedish, 39
Syriac, 61
Tai, 53–65, 205, 206n
  Central, 53n
  Longzhou, 211
  Northern, 53n, 60
  Proto-, 53n, 56–57, 206
  Southwest, 53n
  Wuming, 211, 212
Tajik, 83
Tamil, 160n, 162, 164–66, 168–71
Taranchi, see Uyghur, Taranchi
Tatar, 77
Telugu, 160n, 165–69
  Early, 168
  Pre-, 170
Thai, see Siamese

Tibetan, 39
Tocharian, 190–91
A, 190
B, 190–91
Toda, 160n, 166–69
Troki Karaim, see Karaim, Troki
Tuḷu, 160n, 165–66, 168–69
Tungusic, 37n, 41, 46, 77, 177–78, 182–83, 194, 199, 237n
Proto-, 41n. 192–97
Turki,
Chulym, 75
East, see Uyghur
Ili, 74n
Taranchi East, see Uyghur, Taranchi
Turkic, 43, 44, 47n, 68–95, 177–80, 182, 183n, 186, 192, 194–95, 197–20
Chaghatay, see Uzbek, Old
Common, 71n, 77
Early, 91
Early Written, 72, 80, 88, 90
Eastern, 41, 75, 82
Kök, 72, 88
Middle, 197
Oghuz, see Turkic, Western
Old, 194, 197, 201
Runic, 72
South-western, 73
Western, 73, 83, 85
Turkish, 35, 38, 39, 40, 43, 46, 73–74, 75–76, 78–81, 89–94
Ottoman, 75
(Modern) Standard, 68, 70n, 75, 86, 90, 92
Old Ottoman, 90
Western, 73
Turkmen, 43, 75, 89, 197
Standard, 77
Ugric, 77
Ural-Altaic, 37, 77
Uralic, 35–49, 77, 83
Uyghur, 41, 43, 68–95, 197
Khotan, 93
Lopnari, 76
(Modern) Standard, 43, 68–95
Old, 72, 74n, 87–88, 92
Taranchi, 43, 44
Western, 80
Uzbek, 43, 72, 86, 89
Modern, 81, 90
Old, 83, 196, 201
Standard, 81, 83
Written Iranized Dialect, 37, 81
Vedic, see Sanskrit, Vedic
Vietnamese, 59–60, 62–63, 65, 205–06, 209–12
Hanoi Standard, 60
Vlax, see Romani
Vogul, 43, 47n
Votyak, 43, 47n
Wa, 205
Yakut, 77, 89, 196–97
Yao, 205–07, 210–12
Mian, 207
Yay, 54n, 55–62, 65
Yiddish, 48
Ziryene, 43, 47n

INDEX OF NAMES

Abduraxmânov, G., 72, 75
Ackerley, F., 105, 107
Acton, T., 106
Ajdarov, G., 72
Allen, W. S., 123n, 127
Ammer, K., 135
Amirpur-Ahrandjani, M., 71n, 73
Anderson, S. R., 35, 36n, 43, 77
Aoki, H., 36n, 40
Ard, J., 44
Arnold, E. V., 137
Arun, V. Bh., 163
Axmatov, T. K., 76
Azimov, P., 75
Bailey, H. W., 153-54
Baldwin, C. C., 207n
Barannikov, A. P., 105
Barnard, N., 1n
Barthélémy, Y., 111
Bartholomae, C., 137, 150-51
Baskakov, N. A., 77
Baxter, W. H., 3, 4, 7, 25
Beames, J., 163, 169
Benfey, T., 144
Berger, H., 141
Bischoff, F., 105
Bloch, J., 135, 140, 142, 144, 147, 149, 163, 170
Bloomfield, L., 184, 185, 189
Bodman, N. C., 3, 4n, 6, 7n, 15n, 208n
von Bradke, P., 147
Buck, C. D., 197
Burrow, T., 150, 153-54, 165
Bynon, T., 189
Caldwell, R., 169
Calotă, I., 106
Calvet, G., 105
Campbell, L., 36n, 39, 42
Cardona, G., 127
Cazacu, B., 106
Chatterji, S. K., 119, 121-22, 142, 170
Chen Zongzhen, 77, 80
Chomsky, N., 10, 15
Chou Fa-kao, 9n
Choy Chun-ming, 207n
Cibula, J., 110
Clements, G. N., 77, 90
Coblin, W. S., 12-13, 28, 30
Collinder, B., 42n, 43, 47n
Collinge, N. E., 151n
Crothers, J., 36n, 75, 78, 80
Debrunner, A., 147, 149
Deshpande, M. M., 120, 134, 142, 143
Dilçin, C., 90
Ding Bangxin, 27
Ding Fubao, 11
Doerfer, G., 75, 177-78
Dong, Tonghe, 1, 6, 9, 25-26
Douglas, C., 207n, 211
Downer, G. B., 6n
Duan, Yucai, 27
Dul'zon, A. P., 75
Eckmann, J., 83

Edgerton, F., 119, 138, 147, 148n
Egerod, S., 65
Emeneau, M. B., 119, 132, 147, 153, 160, 162, 165
Erimer, K., 72
Ferguson, C. A., 146
Fortunatov, Ph., 119, 137, 150-52
von Gabain, A., 37, 72, 79n, 80, 83, 87, 92
Gadžieva, N. Z., 73, 75, 91
Gamillscheg, E., 106
Gao Ming, 14n, 23, 26n
Gao You, 12
Ğappariwa, A., 75, 76n
Gedney, W. J., 53, 54n, 56, 65-66
Geng Shimin, 71n, 74-75
Gjerdman, O., 105, 107-8
Greenberg, J., 36n-37n
Grimm, J., 189
Hahn, R. F., 35n, 68n, 69n, 70, 74n, 75, 76n, 82, 83n, 90n, 92n, 94
Hakulainen, L., 37n, 42
Halle, M., 10, 15, 171
Hamp, E. P., 140n, 150
Hancock, I., 102, 103, 104, 105
Hanser, O., 75, 77
Hašim, 69n, 74n
Hasler, J. A., 106
Hatiboğlu, V., 79
Haudricourt, A. G., 6n, 53n, 65, 206
Hebert, R. J., 76
Ho Ung, 237
Hock, H. H., 119, 121, 123, 126, 128-34, 138, 139n, 140n, 143, 144n, 148-49, 150, 172
Hoffman, K., 152n
Householder, F. W., 91
Hu Zhenhua, 76, 79
Huang Kan, 4n
Hyman, L. M., 163
Ibañez, I., 207n, 209
Ibrahim, Ablahat, 68n
Ikeda, Suetoshi, 14n
Ilčen, 77
Janhunen, J., 183n
Jarring, G., 75
Jaxontov, S. E., 3, 6-7, 12, 14n
Jensen, J., 41
Johnson, C. D., 44, 68, 76-77, 79
Juldašev, A. A., 77
Junasaliev, B. M., 76
Jung, C., 105
Kaisse, E. M., 90, 91n
Kajdarov, A.-A. T., 81
Kálmán, B., 37n, 42n
Kałużyński, S., 44
Kaminski, I.-M., 106
Karaševa, N. B., 74
Kardestuncer, A. B., 75, 80n, 89, 90
Karlgren, B., 2, 4, 5, 6n, 7, 9, 10n, 12, 13n, 16, 19, 20n, 21n, 22n, 24-26, 29n, 59
Kaufman, T., 103-4
Kenesbaev, S., 74
Kenrick, D., 110
Kho Songmoo, 183n
Kim Wanjin, 234n
Kiparsky, P., 78, 171
Krueger, J. R., 46

Kochanowski, V., 105, 109-10
Kong Yingda, 21n
Kōno Rokurō, 217n
Kononov, A. N., 198
Kounavin, M., 102
Krishnamurti, Bh., 164
Kumaraswami Raja, N., 168
Lee Ki-Moon, 236-37
Lees, R. B., 75
Lei Xuanchong, 80
Lessing, F. D., 38
Lewis, G. L., 38, 39, 70n, 79, 80, 90, 92
Li, F. K., see Li Fang-kuei
Li Fang-kuei, 4, 5n, 6, 7n, 9, 12, 25, 26n, 28, 29, 53, 54n, 56, 58, 59, 60, 61, 62, 63, 64, 65, 75-76, 206-7
Li Xiaoding, 14
Li Yongming, 210
Li Zongxuan, 71n, 74
Liang Min, 205n
Lightner, T. M., 36n, 41
Lindblad, V. M., 68n, 70n, 82, 85, 94
Ljungberg, E., 107-8
Lotfi, M., 91
Lu Shaozun, 205n
Luo Changpei, 16, 24
Luo Fuyi, 11
Luo Zhenyu, 14, 24
Lyman, B. S., 197
MacIver, D., 209n
Maclay, R. S., 207n
Magomedov, A. G., 75
Malov, S. E., 72
Manomaivibool, P., 206n
Mansion, J., 119, 143, 148n
Mao Zongwu, 205n
Martin, S. E., 220-21
Maximoff, M., 103, 107
Mayrhofer, M., 129, 133n, 139, 144, 149
Mehendale, M. A., 132, 162
Meillet, A., 147. 150-51
Meng Chaoji, 205n
Meng Dageng, 70
Menges, K. H., 74n, 76, 81, 200
Menzies, J. M., 14
Meyer, I. R., 72
Miklosich, F., 104-5
Miller, R. A., 61, 176-80, 181, 183, 186-88, 192-94, 195n, 196, 197, 198, 200-1
Miranda, R. V., 139n
Mishra, V., 123n, 127
Mixri, 69n, 75, 76n
Mohanan, K., 171
Murayama Shichirō, 194n, 195n
Murray, R. W., 129-30
Musaev, K. M., 73, 75, 80
Nasilov, V. M., 72
Nishida Tatsuo, 176n, 195n
Norman, J., 35n, 45, 53n, 208
O'Connor, K., 208
Odden, D., 41
Osmanop, M., 75, 76n
Pandharipande, R., 121, 123, 132, 138, 143, 144n, 148, 150
Pāṇini, 126, 128, 134
Papp, G., 106
Pierce, J. E., 75

Pischel, R., 133n, 149
Pobożniak, T., 105
Pokrovskaja, L. A., 73, 75
Polat, A., 69n
Polomé, E., 144n
Pop, S., 106
Poppe, N. N., 35n, 41-45, 46n, 71n, 75-77, 79n, 83, 87, 179, 194, 196, 197, 198, 201, 230n, 237n
Pott, A. F., 144
Pritsak, O., 73, 75, 76n, 77
Prokosch, E., 185n
Pulleyblank, E. G., 6-8, 15n-16n, 53n, 54n, 56, 60, 61, 62, 63, 64, 65, 206n
Puşcariu, S. I., 106
Puxon, G., 110
Ramachandra Rao, B., 168
Ramsey, S. R., 216, 217n, 223, 228n, 231n, 234n, 235, 236-7
Ramstedt, G. J., 44, 47-49, 179, 230n
Räsänen, M., 37, 43, 44,4 47, 80, 90, 92
Rassadin, V. I., 46
Renou, L., 119-20, 135, 143, 148n
Ringen, C. O., 38-39, 41
Roleine, R., 103
Sadvakasov, G., 75
Sampson, J., 105
Ščerbak. A. M., 83
Schiffman, H. F., 35n
Schmid, W. P., 144n
Schwarzschild, L. A., 140
Sevortjan, E. V., 40
Sezer, E., 75, 77, 90
Shao Rongfen, 24
Shapiro, M. C., 35n
Shibatani, M., 36n, 75, 78-80
Shima Kunio, 14n
Sjoberg, A. F., 81
Stampe, D., 171
Steinitz, W., 42n
Strecker, D., 53n
Street, J. C., 39-41, 46, 176-78, 179n, 184-89, 192, 195n, 198- 201
Subrahmanyam, P. S., 164, 166
Tedesco, P., 144-45
Tenišev, E. R., 43, 45, 75, 76n
Thieme, P., 135, 152
Todaeva, B. Kh., 43, 45, 46n
Tohti, Litip, 68n
Troubetskoy, N., 201
Turner, R. L., 162-63
Uhlik, R., 104, 107
Vago, R., 35, 37n, 39-43, 77
Valtonen, P., 105
Vance, T. J., 197
Varma, S., 123n, 124n, 126-30
Vekerdi, J., 105
Vergnaud, J. R., 171
Verner, K., 184, 185n, 186, 189
Wackernagel, J., 132, 135, 137, 144-45, 148n, 149-52
Wang Fushi, 205n
Wang Jun, 205n
Wang, W. S.-Y., 207n
Weber, A., 144
Whitney, W. D., 123n, 127, 133
Winstedt, E. O., 103
Winter, W., 191
Wulff, K., 58, 59

Wurm, S., 37, 44
Xabičev, M. A., 75
Xu Shen, 12, 28
Xu Zhongshu, 14n, 23, 26n
Yan Qixiang, 205n
Yang Shih-feng, 209n
Yavaş, M., 70n
Zakiev, M. Z., 77
Zhang Junru, 205n
Zhang Shengyu, 210
Zhang Hongyi, 70
Zhao Xiangru, 68n, 74n, 76n, 83, 92
Zheng Guoqiao, 205n
Zheng Xuan, 21, 22n
Zheng Zongze, 205n
Zhou Fagao, see Chou, Fa-kao
Zhou Zhizhi, 205n
Zhou Zumo, 4n, 16, 24
Zhu Junsheng, 11
Zhu Zhining, 76n, 83
Zimmer, H., 119, 136
Zimmer, K. E., 75
Zvelebil, K., 164

In the CURRENT ISSUES IN LINGUISTIC THEORY (CILT) series (Series Editor: E.F. Konrad Koerner) the following volumes have been published thus far, and will be published during 1991:

1. KOERNER, E.F. Konrad (ed.): *The Transformational-Generative Paradigm and Modern Linguistic Theory*. Amsterdam, 1975.
2. WEIDERT, Alfons: *Componential Analysis of Lushai Phonology*. Amsterdam, 1975.
3. MAHER, J. Peter: *Papers on Language Theory and History I: Creation and Tradition in Language*. Foreword by Raimo Anttila. Amsterdam, 1977.
4. HOPPER, Paul J. (ed.): *Studies in Descriptive and Historical Linguistics: Festschrift for Winfred P. Lehmann*. Amsterdam, 1977. Out of print.
5. ITKONEN, Esa: *Grammatical Theory and Metascience: A critical investigation into the methodological and philosophical foundations of 'autonomous' linguistics*. Amsterdam, 1978.
6. ANTTILA, Raimo: *Historical and Comparative Linguistics*. Amsterdam/Philadelphia, 1989.
7. MEISEL, Jürgen M. & Martin D. PAM (eds): *Linear Order and Generative Theory*. Amsterdam, 1979.
8. WILBUR, Terence H.: *Prolegomena to a Grammar of Basque*. Amsterdam, 1979.
9. HOLLIEN, Harry & Patricia (eds): *Current Issues in the Phonetic Sciences, Proceedings of the IPS-77 Congress, Miami Beach, Fla., 17-19 December 1977*. Amsterdam, 1979. 2 vols.
10. PRIDEAUX, Gary (ed.): *Perspectives in Experimental Linguistics. Papers from the University of Alberta Conference on Experimental Linguistics, Edmonton, 13-14 Oct. 1978*. Amsterdam, 1979.
11. BROGYANYI, Bela (ed.): *Studies in Diachronic, Synchronic, and Typological Linguistics: Festschrift for Oswald Szemerényi on the Occasion of his 65th Birthday*. Amsterdam, 1980.
12. FISIAK, Jacek (ed.): *Theoretical Issues in Contrastive Linguistics*. Amsterdam, 1980.
13. MAHER, J. Peter with coll. of Allan R. Bomhard & E.F. Konrad Koerner (ed.): *Papers from the Third International Conference on Historical Linguistics, Hamburg, August 22-26, 1977*. Amsterdam, 1982.
14. TRAUGOTT, Elizabeth C., Rebecca LaBRUM, Susan SHEPHERD (eds): *Papers from the Fourth International Conference on Historical Linguistics, Stanford, March 26-30, 1980*. Amsterdam, 1980.
15. ANDERSON, John (ed.): *Language Form and Linguistic Variation. Papers dedicated to Angus McIntosh*. Amsterdam, 1982.
16. ARBEITMAN, Yoël & Allan R. BOMHARD (eds): *Bono Homini Donum: Essays in Historical Linguistics, in Memory of J. Alexander Kerns*. Amsterdam, 1981.
17. LIEB, Hans-Heinrich: *Integrational Linguistics*. 6 volumes. Amsterdam, 1984-1986. Vol. I available; Vol. 2-6 n.y.p.
18. IZZO, Herbert J. (ed.): *Italic and Romance. Linguistic Studies in Honor of Ernst Pulgram*. Amsterdam, 1980.
19. RAMAT, Paolo et al. (eds): *Linguistic Reconstruction and Indo-European Syntax. Proceedings of the Coll. of the 'Indogermanische Gesellschaft' Univ. of Pavia, 6-7 Sept. 1979*. Amsterdam, 1980.
20. NORRICK, Neal R.: *Semiotic Principles in Semantic Theory*. Amsterdam, 1981.
21. AHLQVIST, Anders (ed.): *Papers from the Fifth International Conference on Historical Linguistics, Galway, April 6-10, 1981*. Amsterdam, 1982.

22. UNTERMANN, Jürgen & Bela BROGYANYI (eds): *Das Germanische und die Rekonstruktion der Indogermanische Grundsprache.* Akten, Proceedings from the Colloquium of the Indogermanische Gesellschaft, Freiburg, 26-27 February 1981. Amsterdam, 1984.
23. DANIELSEN, Niels: *Papers in Theoretical Linguistics.* Amsterdam, n.y.p.
24. LEHMANN, Winfred P. & Yakov MALKIEL (eds): *Perspectives on Historical Linguistics. Papers from a conference held at the meeting of the Language Theory Division, Modern Language Ass., San Francisco, 27-30 December 1979.* Amsterdam, 1982.
25. ANDERSEN, Paul Kent: *Word Order Typology and Comparative Constructions.* Amsterdam, 1983.
26. BALDI, Philip (ed.) *Papers from the XIIth Linguistic Symposium on Romance Languages, University Park, April 1-3, 1982.* Amsterdam, 1984.
27. BOMHARD, Alan: *Toward Proto-Nostratic.* Amsterdam, 1984.
28. BYNON, James: *Current Progress in Afroasiatic Linguistics: Papers of the Third International Hamito-Semitic Congress, London, 1978.* Amsterdam, 1984.
29. PAPROTTÉ, Wolf & René DIRVEN (eds): *The Ubiquity of Metaphor: Metaphor in Language and Thought.* Amsterdam, 1985.
30. HALL, Robert A., Jr.: *Proto-Romance Morphology*. Amsterdam, 1984.
31. GUILLAUME, Gustave: *Foundations for a Science of Language*. Translated and with an introd. by Walter Hirtle and John Hewson. Amsterdam, 1984.
32. COPELAND, James E. (ed.): *New Directions in Linguistics and Semiotics*. Houston/Amsterdam, 1984. No rights for US/Can. *Customers from USA and Canada: please order from Rice University*.
33. VERSTEEGH, Kees: *Pidginization and Creolization: The Case of Arabic.* Amsterdam, 1984.
34. FISIAK, Jacek (ed.): *Papers from the VIth International Conference on Historical Linguistics, Poznan, 22-26 August 1983.* Amsterdam, 1985.
35. COLLINGE, N.E.: *The Laws of Indo-European*. Amsterdam, 1985.
36. KING, Larry D. & Catherine A. MALEY (eds): *Selected Papers from the XIIIth Linguistics Symposium on Romance Languages.* Amsterdam, 1985.
37. GRIFFEN, T.D.: *Aspects of Dynamic Phonology*. Amsterdam, 1985.
38. BROGYANYI, Bela & Thomas KRÖMMELBEIN (eds): *Germanic Dialects: Linguistic and Philological Investigations.* Amsterdam, 1986.
39. BENSON, James D., Michael J. CUMMINGS & William S. GREAVES (eds): *Linguistics in a Systemic Perspective.* Amsterdam, 1988.
40. FRIES, Peter Howard and Nancy (eds): *Toward an Understanding of Language: Charles C. Fries in Perspective.* Amsterdam, 1985.
41. EATON, Roger, et al. (eds): *Papers from the 4th International Conference on English Historical Linguistics.* Amsterdam, 1985.
42. MAKKAI, Adam & Alan K. MELBY (eds): *Linguistics and Philosophy. Essays in honor of Rulon S. Wells.* Amsterdam, 1985.
43. AKAMATSU, Tsutomu: *The Theory of Neutralization and the Archiphoneme in Functional Phonology*. Amsterdam, 1988.
44. JUNGRAITHMAYR, Herrmann & Walter W. MUELLER (eds): *Proceedings of the 4th International Hamito-Semitic Congress*. Amsterdam, 1987.
45. KOOPMAN, W.F., F.C. VAN DER LEEK, O. FISCHER & R. EATON (eds): *Explanation and Linguistic Change*. Amsterdam, 1987.

46. PRIDEAUX, Gary D., and William J. BAKER: *Strategies and Structures: The Processing of Relative Clauses*. Amsterdam, 1986.
47. LEHMANN, Winfred P.: *Language Typology 1985. Papers from the Linguistic Typology Symposium, Moscow, 9-13 Dec. 1985*. Amsterdam, 1986.
48. RAMAT, Anna Giacalone (ed.): *Proceedings of the VII International Conference on Historical Linguistics, Pavia 9-13 September 1985*. Amsterdam, 1987.
49. WAUGH, Linda R. & Stephen RUDY (eds): *New Vistas in Grammar: Invariance and Variation*. Amsterdam/Philadelphia, n.y.p.
50. RUDZKA-OSTYN, Brygida (ed.): *Topics in Cognitive Linguistics*. Amsterdam/Philadelphia, 1988.
51. CHATTERJEE, Ranjit: *Aspect and Meaning in Slavic and Indic*. Amsterdam/Philadelphia, 1988.
52. FASOLD, Ralph & Deborah SCHIFFRIN (eds): *Language Change and Variation*. Amsterdam/Philadelphia, 1989.
53. SANKOFF, David (ed.): *Diversity and Diachrony*. Amsterdam, 1986.
54. WEIDERT, Alfons: *Tibeto-Burman Tonology. A Comparative Analysis*. Amsterdam, 1987.
55. HALL, Robert A. Jr.: *Linguistics and Pseudo-Linguistics*. Amsterdam, 1987.
56. HOCKETT, Charles F.: *Refurbishing our Foundations. Elementary Linguistics from an Advanced Point of View*. Amsterdam, 1987.
57. BUBENIK, Vít: *Hellenistic and Roman Greece as a Sociolinguistic Area*. Amsterdam/Philadelphia, 1989.
58. ARBEITMAN, Yoël L.: *FUCUS. A Semitic/Afrasian Gathering in Remembrance of Albert Ehrman*. Amsterdam/Philadelphia, 1988.
59. VOORST, Jan van: *Event Structure*. Amsterdam/Philadelphia, 1988.
60. KIRSCHNER, Carl and Janet DECESARIS (eds): *Studies in Romance Linguistics*. Amsterdam/Philadelphia, 1989.
61. CORRIGAN, Roberta, Fred ECKMAN and Michael NOONAN (eds): *Linguistic Categorization*. Amsterdam/Philadelphia, 1989.
62. FRAJZYNGIER, Zygmunt (ed.): *Current Progress in Chadic Linguistics*. Amsterdam/Philadelphia, 1989.
63. EID, Mushira (ed.): *Perspectives on Arabic Linguistics I. Papers from the First Annual Symposium on Arabic Linguistics*. Amsterdam/Philadelphia, 1990.
64. BROGYANYI, Bela (ed.): *Essays in Linguistics. Offered in honor of Oswald Szemerényi on the occasion of his 75th birthday*. Amsterdam/Philadelphia, n.y.p.
65. ADAMSON, Sylvia, Vivien A. LAW, Nigel VINCENT and Susan WRIGHT (eds): *Papers from the 5th International Conference of English Historical Linguistics*. Amsterdam/Philadelphia, 1990.
66. ANDERSEN, Henning and Konrad KOERNER (eds): *Historical Linguistics 1987. Papers from the 8th International Conference on Historical Linguistics, Lille, August 30-September 4, 1987*. Amsterdam/Philadelphia, 1990.
67. LEHMANN, Winfred (ed.): *Language Typology 1987. Systematic Balance in Language. Papers from the Linguistic Typology Symposium, Berkeley, 1-3 December 1987*. Amsterdam/Philadelphia, 1990.
68. BALL, Martin, James FIFE, Erich POPPE and Jenny ROWLAND (eds): *Celtic Linguistics / Ieithyddiaeth Geltaidd. Readings in the Brythonic Languages. Festschrift for T. Arwyn Watkins*. Amsterdam/Philadelphia, 1990.

69. WANNER, Dieter and Douglas A. KIBBEE (eds): *New Analyses in Romance Linguistics. Papers from the XVIII Linguistic Symposium on Romance Languages, Urbana-Champaign, April 7-9, 1988*. Amsterdam/Philadelphia, 1991.
70. JENSEN, John T.: *Morphology. Word Structure in Generative Grammar*. Amsterdam/Philadelphia, 1990.
71. O'GRADY, WILLIAM: *Categories and Case. The sentence structure of Korean*. Amsterdam/Philadelphia, 1991.
72. EID, Mushira and John McCARTHY (eds): *Perspectives on Arabic Linguistics II Papers from the Second Annual Symposium on Arabic Linguistics*. Amsterdam/Philadelphia, 1990.
73. STAMENOV, Maxim (ed.): *Current Advances in Semantic Theory*. Amsterdam/Philadelphia, n.y.p.
74. LAEUFER, Christiane and Terrell A. MORGAN (eds): *Theoretical Analyses in Romance Linguistics*. Amsterdam/Philadelphia, n.y.p.
75. DROSTE, Flip G. and John E. JOSEPH (eds): *Linguistic Theory and Grammatical Description*. Amsterdam/Philadelphia, n.y.p.
76. WICKENS, Mark A.: *Grammatical Number in English Nouns*. Amsterdam/Philadelphia, 1991.
77. BOLTZ, William G. and Michael C. SHAPIRO (eds): *Studies in the Historical Phonology of Asian Languages*. Amsterdam/Philadelphia, 1991.
78. KAC, Michael: *Grammars and Grammaticality*. Amsterdam/Philadelphia, 1991. n.y.p.
79. ANTONSEN, Elmer H. and Hans Henrich HOCK (eds): *STÆFCRÆFT: Studies in Germanic Linguistics*. Amsterdam/Philadelphia, 1991.
80. COMRIE, Bernard and Mushira EID (eds): *Perspectives on Arabic Linguistics III*. Amsterdam/Philadelphia, 1991.
81. LEHMANN, Winfred P. & H.J. HEWITT (eds): *Language Typology 1988. Typological Models in Reconstruction*. Amsterdam/Philadelphia, 1991.
82. VAN VALIN, Robert D. (ed.): *Advances in Role and Reference Grammar*. Amsterdam/Philadelphia, n.y.p.
83. FIFE, James & Erich POPPE (eds): *Studies in Brythonic Word Order*. Amsterdam/Philadelphia, n.y.p.
84. DAVIS, Garry W. & Gregory K. IVERSON (eds): *Explanation in Historical Linguistics*. Amsterdam/Philadelphia, n.y.p.
85. BROSELOW, Ellen, Mushira EID & John McCARTHY (eds): *Perspectives on Arabic Linguistics IV*. Amsterdam/Philadelphia, 1991. n.y.p.